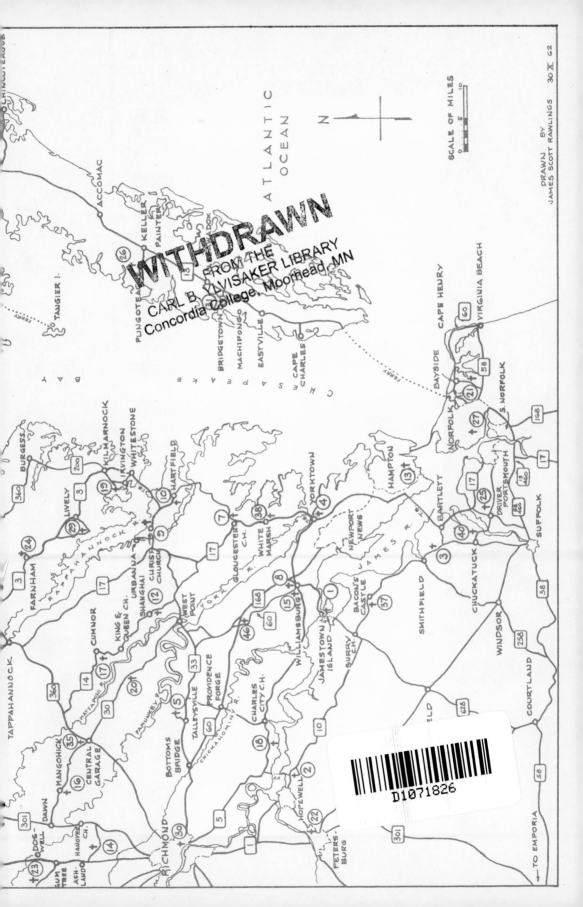

ATLANTIC OCEAN

ATLANTIC OCEAN

N

SCALE OF MILES
0   5   10

DRAWN BY
JAMES SCOTT RAWLINGS

30 X G2

CHINCOTEAGUE

ACCOMAC

KELLER

PAINTER

FOX

PUNGOTEAGUE

BRIDGETOWN

MACHIPONGO

EASTVILLE

CAPE CHARLES

TANGIER I.

FERRY

CHESAPEAKE BAY

BAY

FERRY

CAPE HENRY

VIRGINIA BEACH

BAYSIDE

NORFOLK

S. NORFOLK

PORTSMOUTH

DRIVER

SUFFOLK

WINDSOR

COURTLAND

BURGESS

FARNHAM

TAPPAHANNOCK

LIVELY

KILMARNOCK

IRVINGTON

WHITESTONE

HARTFIELD

RAPPAHANNOCK R.

CHRIST CHURCH

URBANNA

SHANGHAI

KING & QUEEN CH.

CUMNOR

MATTAPONI R.

PAMUNKEY R.

MANGOHICK

CENTRAL GARAGE

DOS WELL

HANOVER C.H.

ASHLAND

GUM TREE

DAWN

RICHMOND

BOTTOMS BRIDGE

TALLEYSVILLE

PROVIDENCE FORGE

CHICKAHOMINY R.

CHARLES CITY C.H.

WEST POINT

YORK R.

GLOUCESTER C.H.

WHITE MARSH

YORKTOWN

NEWPORT NEWS

HAMPTON

JAMES R.

WILLIAMSBURG

JAMESTOWN ISLAND

SURRY C.H.

BACON'S CASTLE

SMITHFIELD

CHUCKATUCK

BARTLETT

HOPEWELL

PETERSBURG

TO EMPORIA

DRAWN BY
JAMES SCOTT RAWLINGS

D1071826

Nieuwenhuis

The Author

James Scott Rawlings is the senior
member of the architectural firm of Rawlings and Wilson in Richmond. He is a
graduate of the University of Virginia
and Princeton University and has for
several years been visiting lecturer in the
School of Architecture of the University
of Virginia. He is a member of the architectural commission of the Diocese of Virginia and the commission of architectural
review of the City of Richmond. He also
serves his Church from time to time as
both lay-reader and chorister. Mr Rawlings's book is the result of a number of
years spent in recording, photographing,
and studying the colonial churches of the
Old Dominion.

Virginia's Colonial Churches:
An Architectural Guide

MERCHANT'S HOPE

VIRGINIA'S COLONIAL CHURCHES:

An Architectural Guide

together with
their
Surviving Books, Silver, & Furnishings

BY

JAMES SCOTT RAWLINGS

GARRETT & MASSIE • RICHMOND

1963

Acknowledgements

The author's great gratitude for countless favors goes to:

Colonel Basil A. Wood of Alexandria

Mrs Henry Eagle of Aylett

Professor William Bainter O'Neal AIA of Charlottesville

Mrs Floyd Paul Davis of Courtland

The Rev'd Mr Francis W. Hayes jr of Hampton

Miss Marjorie Stewart Eastwick of Lively

Miss L. Gertrude Williams of Petersburg

Mr John Melville Jennings, Senator G. Edmond Massie jr, Mrs Chauncy-Williams Meyer, Miss Virginia Moncure, Mrs William Edgar Seaton, and Mrs Parham F. Tuck of Richmond

Miss Anne E. Moncure of Stafford Courthouse

Mr Lucien Dade Winston III of Winston

Mr Charles E. Hatch jr of Yorktown

and to

Mr John E. Wilson AIA	Mrs Garland Benton
Mr John Tabb Heyward jr AIA	Mrs Arnold Ellis

of the firm of

Rawlings and Wilson, Architects, of Richmond

The author also wishes to express his gratitude to a number of persons who have so courteously assisted him, particularly in the case of individual churches:

Accomac Courthouse—The Rev'd Mr Thomas Bowers and the Rev'd Mr Samuel F. Gouldthorpe jr; Alexandria—The Rt Rev'd Samuel B. Chilton, Mr Dan C. Dwelle, and the Rev'd Mr Holt Mallalieu Jenkins; Amelia Courthouse—The Hon. Valentine W. Southall; Appomattox Courthouse—The Rev'd Dr W. Twyman Williams; Ashland—The Rev'd Mr William F. Abernathey and the Rev'd Mr Robert B. Johnson; Bayside—Mrs Rufus Parks and the Rev'd Mr Beverley D. Tucker jr; Blacksburg—Professor Duncan Lyle Kinnear; Bowling Green—The Rev'd Mr Macon B. Walton; Boydton—The Hon. Sterling C. Hutcheson; Chance—Mrs J. Sale Shaw; Charles City Courthouse—The Rev'd Mr Mortimer Tuttle Bowman and Mrs Walter O. Major; Charlottesville—Professor Joseph Norwood Bosserman and Miss Annie Rives Goodloe; Chatham—The Rev'd Mr D. C. Loving; Christchurch—The Rev'd Mr and Mrs Charles Van Orden Covell; Chuckatuck—Mr George Denno, Lt Governor Mills E. Godwin jr, and Mr J. Russell Kirk.

Courtland—Mr Handy Moore and Mr John William Rollison jr; Culpeper—Miss Mary Stevens Jones; Doswell—The Rev'd Mr J. Philip H. Mason; Driver—The Rev'd Mr William Edward Thomsen jr; Earlysville—The Rev'd Mr James H. Cunningham; Eastville—The Rev'd Mr Wilson M. Stitt; Emporia—The Rev'd Mr A. Hume Cox; Falls Church—The Rev'd Mr J. Hodge Alves and Mr Harold J. Spelman; Falmouth—Mrs Wallace Harrison; Farnham—Mrs H. Norman Edwards and Mr Norman L. Edwards; Fort Defiance—The Rev'd Mr Richard E. Hildebrandt; Gloucester Courthouse—The Rev'd Mr Reginald W. Eastman; Gum Springs—The Rev'd Mr Eugene J. Boelte, Mrs Stephen F. Hart, and Mr R. V. Lancaster jr; Hague—Mr W. T. Griffith, the Rev'd Mr Lawrence W. Mason, Senator Blake T. Newton, and Mr Charles M. Sanford.

Hampton—Mrs John Allen Charles jr; Hardyville—The Rev'd Mr Benjamin H. Watkins; Hartfield—The Rev'd Mr M. N. DeHaven; Hopewell—Mr Waverly Cox AIA and Mr A. Robbins jr; Ino—Mr Walter Harper; Kenbridge—Mrs

Cralle F. Blackwell and Mr Scott Irby; King George Courthouse—The Rev'd Mr Morton Townsend; Lexington—The Rev'd Professor Brewster Sherwood Ford; Lorton—The Rev'd Mr Ralph E. Fall and the Rev'd Mr Albert N. Jones; Lunenburg Courthouse—Mr W. E. Neblett; Lynchburg—The Rev'd Mr James G. Thompson; Madison Courthouse—The Rev'd Pastor Glenn A. Shackelford and the Rev'd Pastor C. Bernard Troutman; Manassas—The Rev'd Mr Blake B. Hammond; Millwood—The Rev'd Mr Frank Q. Cayce; Mount Solon—The Rev'd Dr Howard M. Wilson; Norfolk—Mr W. W. Pearce, Mrs Alice H. Spivey, and Mr Herbert Weissberger; Nuttsville—Mrs Chichester T. Peirce; Orange—The Rev'd Mr William D. Boyd, Mrs Gray Dunnington, and Mrs Frank S. Walker; Petersburg—Mr Edward A. Wyatt IV; Prince George Courthouse—Mrs Fenner Barnard and Mrs Samuel B. Nickels; Quinton—Mr L. T. Southall; Remo—Mr Charles E. Tomlin jr.

Richmond—The Rev'd Dr James Edwin Bethea, the Rev'd Dr George MacLaren Brydon, Mr Bachman Doar jr, the Rev'd Mr Edward Meeks Gregory, the Rev'd Mr Joseph T. Heistand, Mr J. Ambler Johnston AIA, Mr Bruce Keith, Mr Robert J. Leary AIA, Mr John H. Loving, the Rev'd Mr Albert C. Muller, Mr Kemp Norman, Mr H. W. O'Grady, Mrs E. F. Robinson, Mr A. V. Spott, Miss Nancy Byrd Turner, Mrs Charles S. Valentine, and the Rev'd Mr Frederick J. Warnecke jr; Saluda—Mrs George Anderton; Shanghai—Mr J. W. Brown; Stafford Courthouse—Mr John Moncure; Staunton—The Rev'd Mr William H. Ramkey and Mrs James L. Stilley; Suffolk—Mr William Wellington Jones and the Rev'd Mr H. Walter Whichard jr.

Tappahannock—The Rev'd Mr Joseph S. Ewing and Mr Harden deVoe Pratt; Timber Ridge—Mr John D. Sterrett sr; Toano—Mrs William B. Piggott and Mr D. W. Ware; Topping—Mr C. D. Marchant; Tunstall—The Rev'd Mr Edward W. Eanes, Mrs Richard C. Richardson, and Mr William J. Wallace jr; Urbanna—Mr Carroll C. Chowning jr and Mr Barton Palmer; Warsaw—Miss Eliza Bland Lamb and the Rev'd Mr T. Dabney Wellford; West Point—Dr Malcolm H. Harris and the Rev'd Mr William H. Jones; White Marsh—The Rev'd Mr Howard McC. Mueller; White Stone—Mrs James Ackerman and Miss Laura Virginia Francis; Williamsburg—Mr Paul Buchanan, Mr James Glenn Driver, Mrs. Rutherfoord Goodwin, Mr J. P. James jr, Mr A. Edwin Kendrew FAIA, the Rev'd Dr Cotesworth Pinckney Lewis, and the Rev'd Dr Arthur Pierce Middleton.

St Luke's Day 1962.

Foreword

History is a curious amalgam of fact and legend, the fact serving as the skeleton and the legend (or, perhaps, to put it more politely, the inferences derived from fact by the historian) becoming the flesh on the skeleton. It is, of course, the historian's major task to reconstruct as robust a skeleton as possible so that the fleshing out of this solid basis of fact deviates no more than humanly necessary from the original.

Virginia is so rich in both fact and legend that the task of the historian is peculiarly difficult when dealing with the Commonwealth. This truth certainly applies to Virginia's architecture, and especially so to its colonial churches. Even the word "colonial" is sadly misunderstood to-day by a large number of those whose interest in history is stronger than their submission to a compulsory study of it during the course of their school years.

It would seem to be a simple task to define colonial building in Virginia, for it is surely that building which occurred while the area was still a colony, that is, up until 1776. But to-day one finds the term most loosely used, both in printed matter and by word of mouth, to describe much later buildings, even sometimes for those erected just before the War between the States.

Virginia's Colonial Churches most skillfully avoids the embonpoint of legend and the inaccuracy of stretching the meaning of colonial. The search for fact, both documentary and architectural, has been unending while the fleshing out of legend has been clearly indicated, and, in addition, kept spare and lean.

At last it is possible to have an accurate guide to Virginia's forty-eight surviving pre-1776 churches. They in themselves are so marvelous a legacy that they need few embellishments of legend overlaying their firm foundation of fact to return them to their proper places not only in the architectural history of Virginia but also in that of the nation.

William B. O'Neal

University of Virginia,
St James's Day 1962.

CONTENTS

Acknowledgements   v

Foreword by William B. O'Neal   vii

Our Architectural and Liturgical Heritage   1

1. Jamestown Church . . . . (1647)   18
2. Merchant's Hope Church . . . . (1657)   27
3. Newport Parish Church (St Luke's) . . . . (1682)   31
4. York-Hampton Parish Church (Grace) . . . . (1697)   38
5. St Peter's Parish Church . . . . (1701-03)   41
6. Yeocomico Church . . . . (1706)   50
7. Ware Parish Church . . . . (1710-15)   58
8. Bruton Parish Church . . . . (1711-15)   62
9. Christ Church, Middlesex . . . . (1714)   80
10. Lower Chapel, Middlesex . . . . (1717)   86
11. Vawter's Church . . . . (1719)   89
12. Upper Church, Stratton Major, King and Queen . . . . (1724-29)   96
13. Elizabeth City Parish Church (St John's) . . . . (1728)   99
14. Upper Church, St Paul's (Slash) . . . . (1729-30)   103
15. Chapel of the College of William and Mary . . . . (1729-32)   105
16. Mangohick Church . . . . (1730-32)   111
17. Lower Church, St Stephen's (Mattaponi) . . . . (1730-34)   113
18. Westover Parish Church . . . . (1731)   116
19. Christ Church, Lancaster . . . . (1732)   120
20. St John's Church, King William . . . . (1734)   127
21. Old Donation Church (Lynnhaven Parish Church) . . . . . . (1736)   133
22. Blandford Church (Bristol Parish Church) . . . . (1736-37)   138
23. Fork Church . . . . (1736-40)   142
24. Farnham Church . . . . (1737)   145
25. Glebe Church (Bennett's Creek) . . . . (1737-38)   148
26. Pungoteague Church (St George's) . . . . (1738)   151
27. Borough Church, Norfolk (St Paul's) . . . . (1739)   153

28. Hebron Church ....(1740)   158

29. St Mary's Whitechapel ....(1740-41)   162

30. Henrico Parish Church, Richmond (St John's) ....(1741)   165

31. Hungars Parish Church ....(1742-51)   171

32. Buck Mountain Church ....(1747)   174

33. Providence Church ....(1747)   177

34. Augusta Stone Church ....(1747-49)   180

35. Cattail Church ....(1751)   183

36. Aquia Church ....(1751-57)   184

37. Lower Church, Southwark ....(1754)   196

38. Abingdon Parish Church ....(1755)   199

39. Timber Ridge Church ....(1755-56)   205

40. Chuckatuck Church (St John's) ....(1756)   208

41. St Paul's Parish Church, King George ....(1766-67)   211

42. The Falls Church ....(1767-69)   216

43. Christ Church, Alexandria ....(1767-73)   219

44. Lamb's Creek Church ....(1769-70)   225

45. Pohick Church ....(1769-74)   228

46. Hickory Neck Church (Lower Church, Blisland) ....(1773-74)   232

47. The Meeting House, Alexandria ....(1774)   235

48. Little Fork Church ....(1774-76)   239

Appendix I: Hours of Divine Service and Access to the Churches'
    Interiors at Other Times   244

Appendix II: Vestry Books and Registers   248

Glossary   253

Partial Bibliography   271

Index   275

ILLUSTRATIONS

Photographs (in color)

Merchant's Hope Church (1657) ....frontispiece

Yeocomico Church (1706)

St Peter's Parish Church (1701-03)

Aquia Church (1751-57)   between pages 204 and 205

Abingdon Parish Church (1755)

Glossary Drawings

		Page
Fig. I:	Semi-circular Arch	264
Fig. II:	Segmental, Relieving, and Gothic Arches	264
Fig. III:	Bricks	265
Fig. IV:	Bonds	265
Fig. V:	Cruciform Church	266
Fig. VI:	Pediment	266
Fig. VII:	Roman Doric Order	267
Fig. VIII:	Certain Mouldings	268
Fig. IX:	Roofs	268
Fig. X:	Roof Structure	268
Fig. XI:	Window with Flat Arch in Masonry Wall	269
Fig. XII:	Stone Quoins	270
Fig. XIII:	Gables	270
Fig. XIV:	Framework	270

VIRGINIA'S COLONIAL CHURCHES:

An Architectural Guide

OUR ARCHITECTURAL AND LITURGICAL HERITAGE

Of all Virginia's historic treasures, none can surpass in value her approximately fifty surviving colonial churches and shrines. Not only did these buildings in colonial times serve the purposes of divine worship (chiefly though not exclusively in the Anglican faith of the Established Church)—and have, on the whole, continued to do so—but they were also intimately related to the Old Dominion's political and social life throughout the colonial era.

No other state—not even Maryland—can approach Virginia as to the number of such churches and no other state of English origin has ever claimed a church building so old as our several oldest churches. It would also be impossible to find an American church, colonial or modern, more admired for its beauty and elegance than, for example, Abingdon Church (Gloucester County) or Christ Church (Lancaster County), or one quainter than Yeocomico Church (Westmoreland County), or more famous than the parish churches of Bruton (Williamsburg) or Henrico (St John's in Richmond).

Despite their many similarities, the churches of colonial Virginia embrace a great deal of variety. Although most of them are of brick (usually laid in Flemish bond), several—Slash Church (Hanover County), Henrico Parish Church, Providence Presbyterian Church (Louisa County), Hebron Lutheran Church (Madison County), and Buck Mountain Church (Albemarle County)—are of wooden construction, two (the Presbyterian churches at Ft Defiance in Augusta County and Timber Ridge in Rockbridge County) are of stone, and one (at Yorktown) is built of marl. The only brick churches that are laid principally or in great part in English bond are the Tower at Jamestown, St Peter's Church (New Kent County), Yeocomico Church, and Lower Chapel in Middlesex County.

It may be useful to state here that the bricks for our colonial churches were made from our own kilns rather than brought over from England (as error and legend have so long had it) as ballast for ships. Probably the best evidence for local manufacture lies in the kilns that still may be detected adjacent to Jamestown, Yeocomico, St Peter's, Aquia, and yet other churches.

Many of our churches are rectangular, whereas others are cruciform—in either Greek or Latin manner. Some retain the T-shapes to which they were altered in colonial times. Examples also exist of rectangular churches that were cruciform in colonial times—and likewise the other way round. Some are, indeed, but fragments of their colonial selves. Few porches and bell towers exist and they more often than not represent later albeit colonial additions. Many—even early—churches have

1

no colonial graveyards, for the faithful were often buried near their homes. Although some of these buildings have always served settlements of some size, most of them still stand by waysides or at quiet crossroads. Most of them comprise but a single storey, although the Potomac region includes several churches of two storeys. None of these buildings are large, but they usually present a more vertical than horizontal appearance.

Styles of Architecture

Inigo Jones's Banqueting Hall (1622) for Whitehall Palace is usually cited by architectural historians as the first well-known, significant monument of the mature Renaissance in England, although the Renaissance itself is said to have begun with the accession of Elizabeth I in 1585. However, as in all shifts of tastes and manners, evidences of the Classical style in England antedate not only Jones's celebrated edifice but even the Elizabethan reign; and, similarly, many buildings continued to be erected in the mediæval style long after 1622, particularly in folk architecture.

With due allowance for the inevitable lag in time between England and Virginia and for the conservative views of all vestries towards music and architecture, it can be said that the Gothic form of the Mediæval style dominated seventeenth-century architecture in Virginia, both ecclesiastical and domestic, whereas the Georgian manner of the Renaissance completely characterized Virginia's eighteenth-century churches, with the notable exceptions of one or two churches of ambivalent style erected shortly after 1700.

Owing to the fewness of the surviving churches in Virginia that are probably seventeenth-century in origin and also owing to their simplicity in comparison with their English counterparts, the subdivisions of the Mediæval Gothic and Renaissance styles that are customarily made need not concern most visitors to the Old Dominion's early churches. One may encounter occasional references to a Decorated (or Early Fourteenth-Century) traceried window or to Flemish crow-stepped gables; one may also hear of such Jacobean (1600-25) ornaments as brick quoins and curvilinear gables on otherwise mediæval churches. However, aside from a few such references, it is quite satisfactory for ordinary purposes to speak simply of Gothic for the surviving seventeenth-century churches of Virginia, and of Georgian for those churches that were built during the remainder of the colonial period.

Just as the mediæval influence is still to be noted in Virginia's Georgian churches in, for example, their general plan, three-decker pulpits, and Flemish-bond brickwork, so the classical pediment in embryonic form is to be found on at least one of our churches built in mediæval style. The plain, unadorned west doorways of the Jamestown Tower and Merchant's Hope Church (Prince George County) are significant in this respect, for we thus have a Gothic church (in Isle of Wight County) with an embryonic Renaissance pediment and two Renaissance churches with no pediments at all. All this is particularly significant when one considers that they represent our three great seventeenth-century churches and that there is a great deal of conflicting data concerning their several dates of construction.

As one can see from the foregoing few remarks, it is, indeed, hazardous to judge the date of a building entirely by its style, for there will be found active at almost any given time both retrospective and experimental architects.

The following brief comparison of certain characteristics of the Gothic and Georgian styles, as they apply principally to our surviving Virginia churches, may prove of some help to visitors and worshippers:

MEDIÆVAL: GOTHIC	RENAISSANCE: GEORGIAN
1) steep A-roofs with plain (or crow-stepped or curvilinear) gables; up-turns at eaves	1) A-roofs, but usually not so steep, with plain gable-ends or with hipped gables or with clipped gables
2) thatch (earliest), wood shingles, clay tiles, or slate	2) shingles or slate
3) windows either segmental-arched or pointed (sometimes with brick mullions forming tracery)	3) windows with flat arches or with semi-circular or segmental arches; circular windows in gable-ends
4) wrought-iron or wooden casements with diamond panes (quarrels) held in by lead calmes (cames)	4) vertical-sliding sashes (without weights and, therefore, called "guillotine") with rectangular panes of glass set in wooden muntins
5) doorways plain and undecorated, usually with semi-circular or segmental arches, sometimes of rubbed and gauged brick; sometimes also with embryonic pediments	5) doorways with flat-headed or semi-circular arches, usually of rubbed brick, with classical pilasters and pediments
6) battened doors, moulded or plain, often with wicket doors and a variety of hinges such as strap and H-L	6) raised wooden panels for doors, frequently with H-L hinges
7) English and Flemish bond brick-work or a combination of the two bonds; glazed headers; sometimes brick quoins; diapering; water tables of moulded brick; belt or string courses	7) usually Flemish bond; glazed headers; usually rubbed brick or stone quoins at corners; water tables of moulded brick; belt or string courses
8) wood (crucks with rushes, palisades, puncheons with wattle and daub interstices, or timber (frame) with clapboard, tile, or slate siding) or brick	8) brick or frame (clapboards)

3

9) interior walls plastered and white-washed; and possibly wainscoting, with vertical battens
10) floors of earth (in earliest buildings), pegged planks, and often brick-tiles or stones for aisles and chancel
11) beamed ceilings, with plaster
12) plain cornices
13) benches (in earliest churches) and box-pews
14) one storey

15) board shutters

16) rectangular (and, perhaps, also cruciform)
17) no chimneys
18) no provision for lights except, perhaps, occasional wall sconces for tapers
19) three-decker and two-decker pulpits
20) porches; buttresses; towers (with bells), often battlemented; rood or chancel screens; galleries

9) interior walls plastered and white-washed; sometimes wainscoting
10) stone aisles with raised wooden or brick floors in chancel and beneath pews
11) generally, plastered ceilings
12) cornices with dentils and modillions
13) box-pews (with raised panels) and slip-pews
14) one storey or, in northern Virginia, two storeys
15) raised-panel, slatted, board, or no shutters
16) rectangular, cruciform (Greek or Latin), and T-shaped
17) no chimneys
18) no provision for lights except occasional sconces and chandeliers
19) three-decker and two-decker pulpits
20) rare porch; no buttresses; a few towers with bells; no screens; often several galleries, sometimes with separate outside staircases

Assignment of Dates to Colonial Churches

It is seldom if ever possible to give an exact date for the erection of any of our colonial churches. This is sometimes owing to incomplete records, sometimes owing to vagueness in terminology—one cannot always be certain, for example, as to just what was meant in vestry minutes by the verb, to repair—and at other times owing to the fact that the actual building of a church may have continued over a period of years. The assignment of a specific year of construction is, perhaps, most hazardous in regard to three of our earliest and most significant houses of worship: the last church on Jamestown Island; Merchant's Hope Church in Prince George County; and the former Newport Parish Church in Isle of Wight County (which is also known as Old Brick Church and more recently as St Luke's Church).

Captain John Smith's awning or old sail tied to three or four trees—with rails of wood for walls, unhewn trees (or, later, planks) for seats, and a bar of wood nailed to two neighboring trees for a pulpit—can hardly be considered a building; nor can the "old rotten tent" that the founders of 1607 used "in foul weather". However, the services that were held under the awning and the tent are still commemorated on the Island to-day by the Robert Hunt Shrine.

The first true building of 1607 was described by Captain Smith as a "homely thing like a barne, set upon cratchets, covered with raftes [rafters], sedge, and earth", in which the Rev'd Mr Hunt celebrated the morning and evening Offices daily with two sermons every Sunday and the Holy Communion every three months. One opinion has it that by "cratchets" (crotchets or crotches) Captain Smith meant not merely forked poles, but rather a later, fourteenth-century form known as "crucks": pairs of tree-trunks bent or curved like Gothic arches. This church of 1607 was burnt in the fire of January, 1608, but a second church was promptly built by the mariners of Captain Newport, who had arrived with the first supply ship only three days before the fire. The 1608 church was probably also fashioned of crucks.

When Lord de la Warr reached Jamestown in June of 1610, he found a church, which was probably Captain Newport's structure, "ruined and unfrequented". He thereupon ordered it to be "repaired", which in this instance has frequently been taken to mean that he had an entirely new church built. This building was 60′ long and 24′ wide, had its chancel, pulpit, windows, and pews built of cedar, its Communion table of black walnut, and a font hewn hollow like a canoe. It also had two bells at the west end and windows that could be opened and closed (as opposed to merely barred openings). It is believed that Lord de la Warr's church was built of sawn or hewn timbers and was, therefore, probably the first church on the Island that can be correctly described as a building with pretensions to architecture.

It is possible that the chancel of cedar in the 1610 church may indicate a chancel (or rood) screen of cedar rather than a cedar floor or cedar panels within the chancel. At any rate, Lord de la Warr's church, which he is said to have kept fragrant with flowers (rather than incense), was the scene of the wedding of the Indian princess and convert to Christianity, Pocahontas, and Mr John Rolfe in 1614.

Although this building of 1610 was badly in need of repairs even in 1611, the year of Sir Thomas Dale's arrival, the next church to be built on the Island seems to have been the one that Captain Samuel Argall erected when he arrived as governor in 1617 and found the colonists worshipping in the storehouse. Argall's church was only 50′ x 20′ and was probably also built of timber. In it occurred one of the great events of American history when the first General Assembly of Virginia met in its quire on July 30, 1619, as the first representative parliament in the New World. It is also worth noting that its deliberations were not allowed to begin until the Rev'd Master Buck, who had also officiated at the Rolfe wedding, had delivered a prayer.

This church of 1617 was in great need of repairs in 1619, and it may have been the same building that is said to have possessed a latticed gallery for women and visitors in 1623 and to have been in need of repairs in 1624.

The number of churches—if any—that were built between Argall's church of 1617 and the celebrated brick church is conjectural owing to want of reliable records. There is, however, a reference to a "new" church of 1636, and it has been suggested that the remains of a brick foundation and cobblestone footing within the present reconstructed brick church may belong to a wooden church of 1636 or to another wooden church rather than to the 1617 church and also that, at the rate at which these early churches had to be rebuilt on Jamestown Island, it is entirely possible that two or more wooden churches were built between 1617 and 1639-44. However, in another view, the "500 waight" of tobacco in the mention of 1636 that was bequeathed to "a new church at James Cittie in Virginia" more than likely went towards the erection of the brick church. In any case, the present footings of cobbles and bricks are generally taken as representing the 1617 church, despite the slightly larger measurements that are indicated by the existing remnants.

Authorities also disagree as to the year of the construction of the brick church at Jamestown. Those who support the years 1639-44 base their view principally upon a letter of January 1638/39 from the Governor and Council of Virginia to the Privy Council in London in which they acknowledge that certain shipmasters and planters as well as themselves had "largely contributed to the building of a brick church". The year 1647 is put forth by others as the date of erection of the famous church because a statement in a decree of 1647 that set up Southwark Parish (across the James in Surry County) required those in the new parish to pay "toward the finishing and repairement of the church at Ja. Citty". However, it seems wise to accept, for the present, the late Mr Mason's view that the brick church was in all probability under construction in the years 1639-44.

Although the tower was certainly built separately from the body of the church and seems to have been connected only at the sides and top of the doorway that runs between the two, the fact that the foundations were shown in the excavations of 1901 to be continuous has led some students to the belief that both tower and nave were built at the same time. The greater simplicity of the design of the tower in comparison with that of the Newport Parish Church (Isle of Wight County) has also been adduced as evidence in favor of an early date for the construction of the celebrated tower on the Island. The late date of 1699 has, however, also been suggested as the year of the tower's building because of a reference from that year to the building of a steeple, although this steeple may easily have been merely a wooden spire that was added on top of the tower.

It has been pointed out that the east wall of the tower is completely devoid of raked mortar joints and that this is probably due to the fact that the masons were unable to get themselves between the west wall of the church and the east wall of the tower to perform the usual raking. Despite the fact that this indicates that the tower was completed after the church, the lapse of time between the completion of the church and that of the tower may easily have been only a few months rather than necessarily a number of years. Therefore, 1699 seems far less likely than a year in the late 1640's. Indeed, the aforementioned enactment of 1647 might well refer to the addition of the tower to the church of 1639-44 rather than to the completion of the church itself.

1657 is the only date that is usually assigned for the completion of Merchant's Hope Church in Prince George County. This date is cut into one of the large beams of the building; and the church seems to have been erected as the first parish church of Jordan's Parish, which was created in 1655 or a bit earlier and was again merged with Westover Parish in 1688. A court record of 1655 refers to a burial being held in the parish church of "Jerdons parish". In this connection, it will be remembered that in colonial times burials as well as other services were frequently held while a church was still under construction. Yet other references to Jordan's Parish Church appear in records of Charles City County (of which Jordan's Parish was then still a part) in both 1665 and 1675.

Although some authorities have considered 1657 as too early a date for the erection of so simple a church, other scholarly investigators have, in defense of the early date, called our attention to the almost unique, unadorned, circular-headed western doorway, to the similarity of the brickwork to demonstrably seventeenth-century examples on the Eastern Shore, and to the Tudor swag (or slight, graceful flattening of the roof) at the eaves.

Therefore, until proof to the contrary is brought forth, it would seem to be the part of wisdom to accept 1657 as the probable date of erection for Merchant's Hope Church.

Various years have been ascribed to the famous building in Isle of Wight County that long served as the Newport Parish Church but is better known to-day as the Old Brick Church or, more recently, as St Luke's Church. The earliest date that has been brought forth is 1632 and the latest date is 1682. Always strongly in support of the earlier year has been county tradition, which itself received even greater support from two events of recent times. The first was a windstorm in 1887 that collapsed the roof and part of the east gable. In the course of subsequent repairs, two bricks were uncovered with incised numbers. The numbers on one of them, which now rests above the altar, are read by many persons as 1632. On fragments of the other brick may be seen a 1 and a 2. The second event in support of 1632 resulted from the recovery of two early vestry books a century and a half after they had been buried (in 1781) by a woman of the county to prevent their harm at the hands of the British troops under Colonel Tarleton. At their exhumation, reliable persons assert that, before the books became utter dust, they clearly saw 1632 given in the first book as the date of the old church's construction.

In opposition to this early date, a great deal of evidence and opinion has been marshalled. Some persons have read the dated brick as 1682. It has also been maintained that the shapes of the numerals incised on that brick are unlike any other known examples from the first part of the seventeenth century, and that the brick probably represents a forgery perpetrated, by a workman during the restoration of the 1890's, to please an enthusiastic Smithfield lawyer. The suggestion has likewise been put forth that the incised bricks may easily have derived from a previous church, for they seem to have been used in the walls' interior. The 1632 noted in the vestry books may, in the opinion of some scholars, also refer to an earlier church on the same site.

Certain seventeenth-century parishes had their church sites deeded to them only after fifty or more years' use of the land and apparently only when a new building replaced an old one. It has, therefore, been suggested that this may also be true of Newport Parish Church, for its deed seems to have been obtained half a century after the putative date of the church's construction.

The reduction in the parish's numbers, from Indian massacre and disease, in the decade before 1632 has been cited as evidence against the erection of such a building at that time, but still weightier evidence against the acceptance of 1632 derives from the fact that people in the county seem always to have thought that the church was built by a certain Colonel Joseph Bridger, who, in still another tradition, was assisted by members of the Driver family. Unfortunately, Colonel Bridger's tombstone (now in the chancel) records that he was born in 1628 and no Bridger or Driver has been proved as being in the county before the year 1657. The workmanship of Drivers on the building seems to be assured, however, by the initials "C.D." and "T.D.", which are carved in the brickwork of the third storey of the church's tower. These initials are taken to stand for Charles and Thomas Driver, who are known to have reached adulthood only in the last quarter of the seventeenth century.

One of the weightiest arguments for the year 1682 was produced by the late Mr Waterman when he pointed out the remarkable similarities in size and design between the Newport Parish Church and the second Bruton Parish Church of 1683.

Needless to say, little can, in most instances, be proved about the age of a building from the tombs that lie in its yard, for they may easily belong to an earlier church on the same site or they may have been moved from neighboring plantations (or from even farther away), as has happened in so many cases in recent decades. Also, as with Merchant's Hope Church, very little can be proved from the architectural style of the Newport Parish Church, for evidences of both Mediæval and Renaissance manners are abundantly present.

As a result of the most recent restoration (1950's) of Newport Parish Church, a somewhat new theory as to its age has been advanced that attempts to reconcile these various and conflicting data. In this opinion, the church was begun in 1632, was worked on for a number of years, and sometime after 1657 had a third storey (with the initials) added to its tower and the Jacobean quoins added to the two lower storeys, and was otherwise "finished" by Colonel Bridger and the Messrs Driver.

Although this theory is as latitudinous as conjecture could allow—and too much so for some observers—another conjecture seems to provide us with the most likely answer until and unless other, more precise information is available. This more probable conjecture points to the years 1662-65 or later for the erection of the building (including the tower, which, unlike that at Jamestown, is an integral part of the structure) and is based in great degree upon the fact that an act of the General Assembly in March 1662 required "that there be a church decently built in each parish of this country".

Pungoteague Church on the Eastern Shore was for long believed to have been built as early as 1660 or even 1652, but in recent decades it has been universally agreed that the original building (of which only the transepts remain) was most probably erected in 1738. The only other surviving church with a claim to seventeenth-century construction is York Church (now Grace Church) at Yorktown, which is generally thought to have been built (of marl) in 1697 or 1698.

Although the dates of our surviving eighteenth-century churches are not so controversial or doubtful as are those of the Jamestown, Merchant's Hope, and Newport Parish Churches, none of them are entirely devoid of some vagueness. This is partly owing to the fact that colonial vestries seldom if ever acknowledged in their books either the beginning or the ending of actual construction, although they were somewhat more likely to mention the date of an order for construction.

Sites

The Jamestown Churches of 1607, 1608, and 1610 were built in the midst of the triangular, palisaded James Fort. Until this century no one doubted that the James Fort was located anywhere except in the western part of the Island, 100 to 200 yards from the present church ruins. However, the theory was propounded several decades ago that the James Fort of 1607 was actually built below Orchard Run, or about half a mile downstream (east), on what is known as the Elay-Swan tract. The archæological tests of 1937 and 1955 have now proved "that no seventeenth-century occupational evidence exists in this area near Orchard Run, either structural or artifact" (page 17 of John L. Cotter's *Archæological Excavations at Jamestown* (1958)). On the other hand, seventeenth-century artifacts were, indeed, found in 1955 both underneath the Confederate Fort and in the James River within 200 yards of the seawall at the Confederate Fort, although these artifacts are not considered by all authorities to be of great significance. More important is the early seventeenth-century cemetery on the "Third Ridge", which was also discovered in 1955 and would seem to support the traditional site for the James Fort, as would the indefinitely southward extension of the graveyard of the present church ruins. Therefore, although the last archæological word has yet to be said at Jamestown and although no direct trace of James Fort has ever been found, it seems best to assume until further evidence appears that the James Fort and its churches of 1607, 1608, and 1610 (as well as the barn that served as a temporary chapel) were all located on ground that has since been washed into the James at a spot, not far off shore, to the southwest of the Robert Hunt Shrine and the Confederate earthwork.

Any churches that may have been built after these early wooden structures and before the frame building of the extant cobblestone and brick footings would also in all probability have been erected near the present site, although no definite traces of any of Jamestown's churches have ever been detected beyond the foundations of the two churches (believed to be of 1617 and 1639-44) now lying within the reconstructed church and the surviving brick tower.

The early churches at Jamestown are by no means the only ones the sites for which are still uncertain or unknown. For example, the locations of the Fishing Point Churches (c. 1624 and c. 1639) on the Eastern Shore and the first Lower Church (by 1685 or earlier) of St Peter's Parish in New Kent County are but three of the many seventeenth-century (as well as eighteenth-century) church sites that have never been satisfactorily established.

Names of Colonial Churches

Most of the surviving colonial churches still bear geographical designations, some of which derive from their parish titles and others of which derive from their own distinctions. Some are named for early settlements (James City, Elizabeth City, Henrico, and Blandford), plantations (Merchant's Hope, Westover, and Hickory Neck), or for English places (Lower Southwark, Bruton, and St Mary's Whitechapel); some for rivers (York, Ware, Yeocomico, Eastern Shore [of Lynnhaven River] Chapel, and Mattaponi as well as Fork and Little Fork) or even a swamp (Cattail) or falls (The Falls Church); and many for creeks (Hungars, Pungoteague, Aquia, Pohick, Farnham, Bennett's Creek, Chuckatuck, Mangohick, and Lamb's Creek). Other names, such as Borough and Vawter's, are completely distinctive.

Although they are indirectly derived, of course, Indian names are numerous among these church-names: Mattaponi, Mangohick, Hungars, Pungoteague, Yeocomico, Chuckatuck, and others.

Some churches were always known simply as the Parish Church or the Church, without further description. Many of them were upper or lower chapels (Lower Chapel in Middlesex County is a surviving example)—or even upper or lower churches.

Saints' names were also used in colonial times to designate some parishes and churches: Christ Church (Middlesex and Lancaster Counties), St Peter's (New Kent County), St John's (King William County), St Mary's Whitechapel (Lancaster County), St Paul's (King George County—formerly Stafford County), and St George's (Accomack County). On the other hand, it was only around 1820-40 that many of our colonial edifices were renamed in honor of saints: Elizabeth City Parish Church at Hampton into St John's (1827), Newport Parish Church (Isle of Wight County) into St Luke's (1828), Chuckatuck Church (Nansemond County) into St John's (1828), Henrico Parish Church at Richmond into St John's (1832), and York Church into Grace Church (probably 1848). An attempt was also made to rename Bruton Parish Church (Williamsburg) as St David's Church. The failure of this attempt has left Bruton the only church consistently to retain the word, parish, in common use.

Hebron Lutheran Church near Madison Courthouse is the only extant colonial building with a name derived from the Old Testament, although the use of Old Testament names has remained popular with many non-Anglican Churches.

It is interesting to note that, although our early counties and parishes were often coeval and coterminous, each parish (with a few

11

exceptions like James City and Elizabeth City) was given a name quite distinct from that bestowed upon the county.

A few churches have given their names to villages that still exist (Christchurch in Middlesex County; Farnham in Richmond County; and Falls Church in Fairfax County); and countless streams are still known as Church Run or Church Creek.

Several churches have received their presently unique designations since the Revolution: Glebe Church (Nansemond County), Old Donation Church (Princess Anne County), and Slash Church (Hanover County).

Much confusion has been caused by the continued use in some localities of such general terms as the Old Church, the Brick Church, or the Stone Church. Indeed, all of our colonial buildings are, of course, old and most of them are built of brick. The term, the Brick Church, is used of at least two of our famous buildings. It would, therefore, seem wiser to speak of the Isle of Wight brick church as the Newport Parish Church (as one writer has already done) if one prefers to avoid the recent name of St Luke's. A similar confusion exists with the stone churches at Timber Ridge (Rockbridge County) and Fort Defiance (Augusta County). Although there were many meeting houses of the Quakers, Presbyterians, and Baptists in colonial times, only one building (a Presbyterian Church at Alexandria) that uses the term has survived, so that we are spared confusion in the case of that designation.

Those buildings that were lost to the Anglican Church in the early nineteenth century and were subsequently taken over by Methodists, Baptists, or Disciples have usually had their names changed or altered in some way.

After so long a time, it is now to be hoped that the surviving churches will be allowed to retain their colonial designations.

The most significant change in name or status that was ever suggested for one of our colonial churches was never effected. A charter was drafted in the reign (1660-85) of Charles II that said in part: "Cum itaque inter omnia nostra Territoria regis. . .plantatio Virginia sit prima et antiquissima quasi Alma mater, unde reliquae plantationes originem duxerunt. . .eandem Civitatem Jacobi et Ecclesiam ejusdem, Sedem Episcopalem et Ecclesiam Cathedralem realiter et ad plenum Creamus, Erigimus fundamus ordinamus facimus Constituimus & Stabilimus perpetuis futuris temporibus duriter". The charter, however, for some reason was never signed and, therefore, although among all the "royal territories, the plantation of Virginia is the first and most ancient, as it were, fostering mother, whence the rest of the plantations took their origins", Jamestown never became the see city for America nor its church a cathedral.

Colonial Liturgical and Ecclesiastical Customs

In colonial times a lower parish or church represented an earlier or more populous community, whereas the word, upper, referred to a later or frontier settlement. The two terms, therefore, had no geographical or directional significance. Usually only one church held the rank of the parish church, and it was frequently known simply as The Church. A parish usually also included one or more chapels of ease, which were served not only by the rector upon certain Sundays of the month, but also regularly for the offices of Mattins and Evensong (as well as certain occasional rites) by a clerk or lay reader. They were called chapels of ease because they were built for the ease and convenience of those who lived in the remote parts of the parish.

Virginia's churches were all, by canon law, oriented: their altars were always in the east. Inasmuch as the singers in our early churches sat informally either in a regular pew near the altar or pulpit or else in a gallery (generally in the west), the word, quire, whenever it is encountered, refers to what we more frequently call the chancel. The rest of the church consists of the nave and, in cruciform churches, the transepts. The famous three-decker pulpits consist of the pulpit itself at the top (with a sounding board overhead) where the sermon was delivered (from a cushion), a reading desk (in the middle) for the minister's use during the Service, and a stand (at the bottom) from which the clerk led the singing and the responses.

Records exist proving that organs were used in certain of our colonial churches (the third Petsworth Parish Church of 1737 in Gloucester County; Hungars Church, around 1751; Suffolk Church, 1753; Bruton Parish Church, 1755; and Stratton Major Parish Church of King and Queen County, around 1767). Organs are also known to have occupied galleries or lofts, but this certainly must not have been invariably true. It will also be noted that all these purchases occurred late in the colonial era. Throughout the period the instrument of greatest liturgical importance was the tuning-fork or pitch-pipe, for one of these was used by the clerk of every church, in the colonies no less than in England and Scotland, for "lining out" the metrical psalms and a few hymns. There is no reason to believe, however, that certain wind or string instruments were not occasionally (or even regularly) used in some parishes, for they continued to be used regularly in many churches in England even into the nineteenth century. Also, we have indications that opposition to the introduction of organs into parish churches seems to have been just as strong in Virginia as in England (though, of course, considerably less so than in Presbyterian Scotland).

Until 1751, New Year's Day in England and America fell on

March the 25th (Annunciation). It is for this reason that events between January the 1st and March the 25th in most of the colonial period are usually marked in double fashion, as in "February 3, 1710/11". In 1752 was also adopted the new style of calendar by which it was. ordained that September the 2nd of that year should be followed immediately by September the 14th, for the Old and New Styles were eleven days apart in the eighteenth century (and ten days apart in the seventeenth century, twelve days in the nineteenth, and thirteen days now).

Damages to the Buildings through the Years

In accounts of our old churches, mention is regularly made of the ravages of time and wars (Bacon's Rebellion, the Revolution, the War of 1812, and the War between the States) as well as of the unfortunate lapses in taste that have occurred—principally in the late nineteenth century, but also, alas! in very recent years. However, all these alterations taken together—and few churches have been spared abuse by Federal troops and "restorers"—do not equal the damages and losses sustained by the buildings of the Church of Virginia from acts of the General Assembly that were passed in 1779, 1784, and 1802. The first of these acts remitted all parish levies for the support of the churches and their clergymen; the second act provided the final disestablishment of the Church of Virginia with the allowance of marriages by any minister of the Gospel, the appointment of overseers to care for the poor in place of the vestrymen of the Established Church, the general release of the Church and its clergy from civil restraints, and the incorporation of the Episcopal Church as a self-governing body. The most serious damage to the fabric of the buildings, however, resulted from the seizure and sale in 1802 of all the Church's glebe lands, silver plate, bells, and endowments, with very few exceptions. This extraordinary action was. unique in America and in such marked contrast to the loyalty of Anglican Virginia to its faith in the years of Puritan rule under Cromwell. The present distinguished historiographer of the diocese of Virginia has attributed the Church's "devastation and spoliation" to "a school of deistic and infidel thought" that "had developed before the Revolution and spread by the year 1800 throughout the greater part of the state, eventually gaining control of the Virginia legislature", and to "an intense hatred of the Anglican Church" that had developed "in the two Calvinistic Churches, the Baptist and the Presbyterian", and the concomitant "determination to destroy that Church [Anglican] by taking away all property of every kind" (cp. pages 30-31 of *A History of Abingdon Parish, 1655-1955* (1955) and, for further details, Volume II, chapters XVIII-XXIV of Dr Brydon's *Virginia's Mother Church* (1952)).

It is owing to this sequestration of the Church's property rather

14

than to military damage that one has to write of so many of Virginia's churches: "abandoned after the Revolution". Needless to say, many more colonial churches went permanently to ruin than were ever revived and restored to service.

Churches That Have No Right to be Considered Colonial

A number of buildings from time to time have been included on lists of colonial churches for which claims can no longer be substantiated or which have been erroneously listed as colonial buildings.

It was for a long time believed that the north wall and both end foundations of the Portsmouth Parish Church of 1762 were retained when the church was repaired in 1829. This has recently been found to be untrue, so that the present Trinity Church (which received that name around 1825-29) no longer has any claim to colonial origin.

The Eastern Shore Chapel (formerly of Lynnhaven Parish and now the parish church of East Lynnhaven Parish) in Princess Anne County, which was built in 1755, was demolished in 1953 so that the Naval Air Station at Oceana might have its land. It was replaced, not too far away, by an entirely new building, for the old bricks were found to be unusable.

Hermitage Baptist Church near Church View in Middlesex County, which was built in 1773 as the Upper Chapel of Christ Church Parish, was completely destroyed by fire in 1948.

Saponey (Sapony or Sapponey) Chapel of Bristol Parish (and later of Bath Parish) in Dinwiddie County was built in 1726 but collapsed in 1870 and lay in ruins for two years. Although it was rebuilt in 1872 with some of the timber and furnishings of the old church, the present structure cannot be considered a colonial edifice. The same is true of Wood's Church in Dale Parish of Chesterfield County. It was built in 1756 and, when it was replaced in 1890, some of the timber of the old structure was used in the new building.

Around 1913 a building that had been erected about 1710 at Urbanna (Middlesex County) as the county courthouse was bought and converted into Epiphany Chapel of Christ Church Parish, but is now used as a library and a woman's club. Situated across the street from the local cinema, this colonial building should never be included among our colonial churches.

Prior to the creation of Mecklenburg County in 1764, the Lunenburg County courthouse stood about a mile west of the present Chase City (on the west side of Church Creek). A church is believed to have been erected on Otter Creek (or River) not far west of Chase City as early as 1751 and a church known as Bluestone Church (from one of the

15

three creeks bearing that name in some form) is believed to have been erected not too far south of Chase City by 1754. This latter church soon came to be known as the Court House Church; or else, a new and larger church bearing that designation soon replaced both the Otter River and the Bluestone Churches. In 1766 David Christopher gave the parish trustees the lot of land upon which the Court House Church was then standing. In 1764 the old courthouse was replaced by two new courthouses, the one for Mecklenburg County at Boydton and the courthouse for the reduced Lunenburg County ultimately at the present Lunenburg Courthouse. St James's Parish (Mecklenburg County) seems to have bought the old Lunenburg courthouse some time after its aban-donment, for use as a church (perhaps in place of repairing the Court House Church). This purchase and its subsequent removal to a spot within the limits of modern Chase City may have taken place in the period 1785-95. At a later date, perhaps after the War between the States, the church was moved to its present site. Therefore, it is believed that the existing church at Chase City (which was probably named St John's in the 1830's) consists in part of timbers deriving from the old Lunenburg courthouse, which itself was probably built not too long after the county's creation in 1746 from Brunswick County.

Flat Rock or Bethel Church in Cumberland Parish, Lunenburg County, was ordered in 1757, but was replaced sometime in the nine-teenth century by the existing structure, which stands at the junction of routes 612 and 613. The site of the church (now called St John's Woodend) may be reached from Kenbridge by going south on route 637 for about 7 miles and turning left on route 613 for 1.7 miles. From South Hill this junction of routes 637 and 613 is a distance of about 12 miles. The only portions of the present building that are probably colonial are six of the eight columns under the west gallery (the six that have wooden pegs) and some of the diagonal bracing and upright studs on the northern part of the exterior chancel wall, which may best be seen, with their Roman numerals, through the window in the modern vestry. The church is still oriented, but measures approximately 34'-4" x 26'-5" against the colonial orders of 48' x 24'. Some of the stone foundations, the wainscoting, and clapboards, and the two barkeepers on the west doorway may possibly be of colonial origin. All else (including the western porch and its two small rooms) is clearly from one of at least two nineteenth-century renewals. Some of the rough gravestones in the woods that now all but surround the little church in its forlorn state may also possibly be of colonial origin.

Several other churches have been cited as colonial but only through egregious errors: the Grub Hill Church in Amelia County was completed in 1852; the Tinkling Springs Presbyterian Church near Fishersville

16

in Augusta County was dedicated in 1850; and the walls of the South River Meeting House near Lynchburg (which first supported a Quaker Meeting House and then around 1900 a Presbyterian Church and is now an historical shrine) were first erected in 1798. Claims for a Mauck Meeting House near Luray to a 1738-40 origin have yet to be proved.

Visiting Colonial Churches

The attitude of many present-day Americans upon visiting churches of historical or architectural as well as spiritual interest is too often similar to that of most Russian tourists towards the great Orthodox Churches such as St Basil's Cathedral in Moscow, for in both instances the churches are treated as museums rather than religious edifices. To visit a church for Divine Service should, however, certainly remain the desired norm, for not only are the spiritual benefits of worship to be derived, but it is only when a building is used for its true purpose that one is, indeed, able rightly to assess its real architectural value. It is for these reasons that the hours of Service have been given in this guide in most instances.

It is not always convenient, however, to attend a Service in one of our churches. For one thing, several of our colonial churches hold services only once a year—or even less frequently—and one or two others are all but museums. Therefore, it has seemed helpful to list means of access to the churches at times outside the hours of Divine Worship.

It would be a good thing for all concerned if our colonial churches would provide boxes in their yards for any visitors who might care to contribute towards the preservation of the fabric of these venerable fanes.

It is somewhat surprising but true that the churches that have been the most difficult to chronicle are the several that have been restored in the last two or three decades. Indeed, the information of earlier years is usually more accessible—and, one might add, clearer—than are the records of the recent renewals.

Inasmuch as the colonial vestry books (and also, in some cases, the parish registers) offer a mine of information (which, to be sure, has at times to be handled with great circumspection), there has been appended a list of all the extant manuscripts of which the author has at present any knowledge. The terminal dates are in some instances a bit vague. Vestry books and registers that have been published are also listed insofar as the author knows of them.

That which follows is intended as a brief guide rather than a catalogue or photographic survey, for it is hoped that interested persons will not be content merely with reading about these colonial churches

17

or with looking at photographs of them, but will instead seek them out and support both their fabric and their continued mission. To be a church, a building must have life.

Inasmuch as so much in the colonial churches as they exist to-day is of legendary ascription rather than of authentic date, it is also hoped that any errors that may exist in these various descriptions will be called to the attention of the author (c/o Rawlings and Wilson, Architects, 1000 North Thompson Street, Richmond 30, Virginia), for he is only too eager to ascertain the true facts in every possible instance and to hold them in readiness for possible revision of the present manuscript.

1. JAMESTOWN CHURCH

Jamestown is not only Virginia's foremost shrine: it is also America's, for here is the birthplace of the nation. Its church still dominates Jamestown in the twentieth century as fully as it did seventeenth-century James City. Furthermore, the beauty of the Island and the James River is of such constant appeal to us Virginians as well as other Americans that it cannot be surpassed—or truly described: rather must it be felt. It is, therefore, a joy to be able to report that not only the church but the entire island and the adjacent mainland have been preserved by the Association for the Preservation of Virginia Antiquities and by the National Park Service with a taste and an elegance that are all too seldom equalled.

The Island (which in its great period was a peninsula) is rich in religious shrines, for, in addition to the tower and ruins of two churches —one of which in the seventeenth century almost became the first of our American cathedrals because of a king's gratitude for the Old Dominion's loyalty—there are: the Robert Hunt Shrine; the Memorial Cross dedicated to those buried (possibly 1609-10) on the "Third Ridge"; countless other graves; various religious objects discovered near the church and now exhibited in the Visitor Center; and the wattle-and-daub church in the reconstructed James Fort at the Festival Park on the mainland.

The sole seventeenth-century structure still standing above ground on the Island is the tower of the 1639-44 church. This tower is believed to have been built in 1647 or later. It is a separate structure, as most such towers of Virginia's colonial period are. The underground portions of the walls of the church's original doorway are said to have extended under the tower when the latter was built. The rear wall of the tower was apparently joined to the church only at the sides and top of the connecting doorway. The west wall of the church is only 11″ from the east wall of the tower. This rear wall of the tower is the only one of the four tower walls on which the mortar joints are not tooled with an incised line, probably because of the narrow space. There is also evidence of repair work on this wall at the entrance from tower to church.

The original height of the structure is estimated at 46′ at the peak of the pointed roof, although it is now only 36′ high. The bricks are broken at the present summit, which is highest on the south side and progressively lower on the west, north, and east sides. The interior is also now covered with cement. The tower is laid in English bond except for the two courses in the projecting belt (at the level of the second storey), which have Flemish bond with glazed headers. Random glazed headers also mark the entire structure, although some of the glazing is peeling off. There is no rubbed brick. There are four set-backs in all on the interior walls including the water table and those at the first and second storeys and the belfry. The walls are three feet thick at the base, diminishing to 17″ at the top. The water table is in the form of an ovolo.

The tower is 18′-3″ square on the outside. There were originally doorways in both east and west. Above the west doorway there was a window and above the doorway of the east wall was another doorway that led to the west gallery of the church. All these four arches were semi-circular and their simplicity is paralleled among surviving examples from early times only by those at Merchant's Hope Church in Prince George County. The arches of the lower storey have fallen in, so that now two enormous openings almost 20′ high exist at front and back instead of the original four. From the remaining two (upper) arches and from the fragments at the spring of the other two (lower) arches, it can be seen that the arches were one brick-length deep and alternated a full brick with a pair of headers, with the outer headers all glazed. The arches of the front and back doorways have brick imposts, as are also to be noted at the Isle of Wight Church.

In the third storey are also six small slotted openings or ports (two each on the south, west, and north) with splayed sides. They may or may not have been used for defense against the Indians because there was a general pacification of the Indians after the Indian War of

19

1644 (if not before), but these openings surely served the usual purposes of tintinnabulation and, perhaps, also of ornamentation. From the charred remains that have been found in the beam holes, it is believed that a wooden spire or belfry once surmounted the tower, which may also have been crenellated at one time.

Archæological Findings

In 1901, 1902, and 1906 certain excavations were made under the ægis of the Association for the Preservation of Virginia Antiquities. These explorations uncovered foundations of two churches on the present site that are generally taken to represent those of the 1617 church and the first brick church. Footings of both these foundations are still to be seen close to the side walls of the present reconstructed church. The earlier examples, which lie within the later foundations on these side walls, are cobblestones (1' wide) beneath one to two courses of bricks (which are both longer and broader than those of the brick church). Each course of the earlier foundations is the width of one brick-length. The mortar of both sets of foundations has been found to contain oyster shell. The cobbles and bricks of the earlier footings extend only approximately 25' on the south and still less on the north. There is a right-angle turn at the west end of the south wall. Inasmuch as one of the graves of the 1617 chancel was discovered under the east wall of the brick church, the 1617 church seems to have extended at least somewhat farther east than the brick church. Furthermore, it was said in the reports of the church's excavation that the north footing ran under the west wall of the brick church (although at present it is difficult to be positive about this). Although these two evidences seem to indicate a somewhat longer length for the 1617 church than the 50' cited in a 1624 publication, these foundations are still generally accepted as deriving from 1617, partly because the figures in the 1624 description may have been round ones rather than specific measurements. The width of these footings is 21', whereas the 1624 document spoke of 20'.

The foundations of the brick church measure 55' in outside length and almost 51' in inside length. The width inside is 22'-8" and outside 28'. Its walls are from 2' to 3' thick. The four buttresses on each of the side walls—there are none along the end walls—extend 3'-1", are 2'-6" wide, and are about 14' apart. The westernmost bay is the shortest. The westernmost buttresses are in line with the wall, but the easternmost ones are 3' west of the east wall.

Actually there seems to be a discrepancy between the seventeenth-century church and its twentieth-century reconstruction in the matter of the westernmost buttresses on each side. In both churches, the westernmost pair of buttresses projects somewhat west of the western wall of the church, but (according to a plan prepared in 1901 for the Association for the Preservation of Virginia Antiquities) the buttresses at the western corners extend north and south only about a third as far as do the other three pairs (which extend about 3 feet) (cp. p. 20 of Cotter's *Archæological Excavations at Jamestown* (1958)).

Two patches of brick (some integral and others fragmentary) now lie just north of the crossing and just east of the west entrance to the nave, both patches being bordered by bricks set on edge. These bricks are presumably remnants of the brick aisles that are believed to have been laid after Bacon's Rebellion. The present south door in the reconstructed church is also said to lie slightly west of the south door in the 1639-44 church. Fragments of plaster that have been found indicate that the brick church was plastered on the inside. Fragments of lead cames and clear, thin glass that have also been found indicate the use of casement windows, with diamond-shaped panes.

Also uncovered in the first decade of this century were two chancel pavements of square brick tiles of differing sizes, laid in beds of mortar and separated by a layer of earth mixed with débris as from a burned building. The lower chancel is generally taken as belonging to the 1617 building. It extended about 10′ west from the east wall of the brick church, whereas the upper chancel was found to extend 5½′ and had a low wall at its western edge. The lower chancel also extended farther east, as indicated by the aforementioned grave lying under the brick church's eastern wall. Although only the central portion of this lower chancel was found intact, its width was determined, from tile impressions that were discovered, as 21′. One authority has suggested that this chancel served not only the 1617 church but also the first brick church and cites in support of this opinion the fact that the frame building of 1617 might have been continued in use for Divine Service while the first brick church was still under construction. He also points out that such a continued use might be indicated by the fact that the walls of the brick church lie outside the foundations of the earlier church. If this use of the lower chancel for the two churches is held to be true, then the upper chancel is taken to derive from the rebuilding of the church following the fire in Bacon's Rebellion of 1676. However, the more widely accepted view has it that the upper chancel represents only the first brick church. The charred remnants beneath it would, therefore, seem to indicate an earlier fire, probably of the frame building. The only parts of these chancels that are currently visible are a few bricks and two markers just east of the rail of the restored church, although both of the chancel pavements are still in place beneath the wooden floor that was constructed for the 1957 celebration when an Anglican parson was once again in daily residence.

Reconstruction of 1907

The reconstructed church of 1907 seems to rest on the 1639-44 foundations, but is in fact carried by a system of steel beams and concrete piers. The reconstruction was carried out under the architect, Ralph Adams Cram. It derives the details of the ramps of its buttresses, its windows (three on the north, two on the south, and a great window in the east), and its crow-step gables from the former Newport Parish Church in Isle of Wight County; its exterior brickwork comes from that of its own tower. The pointed arches of its exposed wooden trusses derive from the lancets of the windows. There are now neither aisles nor pews. Instead, the entire nave is paved with bricks. It would, perhaps, have been wiser to delineate the T-shape of the aisles in some way. The south doorway has a plain semi-circular arch.

On the walls of the 1907 church are numerous plaques in commemoration of various seventeenth-century figures, including Captain John Smith, the Princess Pocahontas, Chanco (the young Indian who saved the colonists in the 1622 massacre), John Rolfe, Lord de la Warr, Captain Edwin Maria Wingfield, William Claiborne (treasurer of the colony), John Pott (a physician), and the first poet in America, George Sandys. Although Sandys is better known for his Psalm-paraphrases, his translation of Ovid's "Metamorphoses" is considered the first such work accomplished on our soil, as the Latin inscription placed on the north wall by the Classical Society of Virginia indicates. The introduction of common law is also memorialized on one of the plaques.

The restored furnishings of the chancel include a communion table with a blue velvet covering (extending to the floor), a credence table, a priedieu, three chairs, a lectern, and a pair of silver candlesticks. All of these pieces are of seventeenth-century design, although no specific models were used. On the east wall are two tablets containing the Decalogue; on the west wall above the entrance are the royal arms.

Besides the footings, the most interesting features of the church are two markers that were uncovered in 1901 lying in the bricks of the transverse aisle on the Epistle side. The one found nearer to the south door and lying north and south is known as the Knight's Tomb and is believed to mark the grave of an early governor, Sir George Yeardley (†1627). It is the only memorial of its kind and time in America. It was formerly inlaid with brass tablets that have long been stolen. Represented on this tomb are a shield, a scroll, a knight in armor, and a plate on which there was undoubtedly an inscription. Lying east and west against the north side of the knight's tomb was found another tomb with this inscription: "Here lyeth interred the body of John Clough, minister, who departed this life the 11th day of January, 16 ." The missing year is thought to be 1687.

Burials

Also discovered in the first decade of this century were two tiers of burials, presumably a tier beneath each of the two chancels and each tier presumably containing ten graves. Several other graves were found under the chancel or partly under it, and a large but indefinite number of other unidentified graves were discovered in the nave on both sides of the center aisle. At present, 21 square white stones are to be seen in the nave, although some of these numbered stones represent two or more burials each rather than but a single one.

Two seventeenth-century cemeteries are now known at Jamestown. The first is that at and around the church, the limits of which are believed to be the "greate road" on the east and north, the low ground to the west, and toward the seventeenth-century shore line on the south. These graves are, of course, principally unidentified and unmarked. The fragmentary marker to Lady Berkeley in the southwest part of the present enclosure as well as several stones within the brick walls are the exceptions. Two graves east of the present cemetery wall were discovered only in 1955; and graves are said to have been disturbed when the Confederate Fort on the west was built in 1861.

The second cemetery that, like the churchyard, contains graves from the early part (probably from the first quarter) of the seventeenth century was discovered only by accident in 1955. It lies on the "Third Ridge" under the Ludwell-Statehouse foundations west of the modern Yeardley House and apparently once extended from the site of that dwelling westward to the seventeenth-century shore line of the James River. As many as three hundred persons are believed to lie there, most of them without coffins. A large, wooden cross has recently been raised in their memory.

There are still other known burials on the Island, for many people adhered to the early practice of burying their dead near their own houses. Some burials have also been uncovered in ditches, including several Indian remains. The Travis graveyard of at least sixty-two burials lies one and one-half miles from the church on the returning Island Loop Road and derives its name from an early family on the peninsula. The only four markers in this plot range from 1700 to 1761.

The eighteenth-century graves and markers of the Rev'd Commis-

Virginia's Colonial Churches

sary James Blair (†1743) and others as well as the several stones and numerous graves from the preceding century lie immediately southeast of the present church within the existing brick wall. Dr Blair was the Bishop of London's Commissary for fifty-four years; he was also at one time or another president of the College of William and Mary, rector of the James City and Bruton Parish Churches, president of the Council, and governor of the Colony. His grave and those of his wife's family have formed the basis of a delightful discourse inimitably delivered for countless visitors for many years by the Negro sexton, Sam Robinson. The gnarled sycamore that has become the Mother-in-law tree of his narration is, however, not destined to live many more years if one may judge from its present mutilated condition—although split tombs it certainly has!

The present graveyard wall was erected around 1800—some reports say 1793, others 1803 or later—by a Mr John Ambler of Jamestown (who also had the benefit of a bequest for this purpose from a Mr William Ludwell Lee of "Green Spring") to protect the graves of their families. The west wall (1½' thick) was, indeed, built across the old church itself, entering the church's south wall 16.8' from the east and its north wall 13.1' from the east. This angle was apparently assumed to include the priest's and knight's tombs. The graveyard wall was built of bricks derived from the 1639-44 church itself. About two thousand of the church's bricks were also used to renew the old Newport Parish Church in 1890-94. How many of the church's bricks were taken as souvenirs by tourists and vandals in the nineteenth century—and even in the twentieth century, despite the remarkable work of the APVA—will never be known! The portion of the graveyard wall that crossed the church is now, of course, removed, but the end portions of the west wall and the other three sides still stand.

The 1639-44 church was burned in Bacon's Rebellion of 1676, but was rebuilt and the brick aisles that were *in situ* in the early 1900's are believed to have been laid in this rebuilding (about 1680). The capital was moved to Williamsburg in 1700, but the church seems to have continued in use until around 1758. Contrary to rumor, the Island was never abandoned despite its lack of salubrious qualities, for even as late as 1781 there were no fewer than twenty houses still in use. By 1807 the church was a ruin, however. It remained for its foundations and the surviving portions of its tower to be saved from ineluctable loss by the gallant efforts of the APVA just after the turn of the century. The APVA still owns it and administers it jointly with the National Park Service.

James City Parish and County

James City Parish (which, except for the first decade if that long, never included all of James City County within its bounds) lost Lawne's Creek Parish in 1640 and Southwark Parish in 1647, both on the south side of the James River; and Harrop Parish (below Jamestown) was cut off in 1646. Harrop Parish later formed part of Middletown Parish and ultimately (1674) of Bruton Parish. In 1720 the eastern part of Wallingford (originally Chickahominy) Parish was annexed to James City Parish, and in 1725 the lower part of Wilmington Parish was also added. About 1750 a new parish church was erected on the mainland, two miles north of the last church on the Island, and this church stood until the 1850's. Although the parish no longer has an active congregation, it cannot, because of the Tower Church and the Robert Hunt Shrine, be considered exactly dormant.

James City County was one of the four boroughs of 1618 and one of the eight shires of 1634. The area west of the Chickahominy River that lay in Chickahominy (later Wallingford) Parish at that parish's creation (by 1639) was apparently added to James City County between 1634 and 1639, but in 1720 this territory was returned to Charles City County. The area of James City County was reduced in 1652 by the formation of Surry County on the south side of the river. In 1766 James City County exchanged its long upper end for New Kent County's lower end. In 1880 the York County portion of Williamsburg was annexed by James City County and four years later the old capital became an independent city.

Most of the Jamestown communion silver—chalice and paten-cover (c. 1660); alms bason (1739-40); and footed paten (1691-92)—is now at Bruton Parish Church in Williamsburg, although a baptismal bowl (1733-34) from the Jamestown parish church is at Monumental Church in Richmond. What is believed to be the seventeenth-century font of the James City Church is also at Bruton Parish Church. Included in the superb collection at the National Park Service Visitor Center are coffin handles, tacks, book hinges, lead cames, fragments of glass, iron frames, and pieces of charred timber that were all uncovered in or near the site of the present church by the APVA in 1900-02. Also on display are a New Testament (1609, Geneva Bible) and a Bible (King James version) combined with the Prayer-Book that derives from 1622, although neither of these particular copies is known to have been used at Jamestown.

The Robert Hunt Shrine

In the old Confederate earthwork of 1861 stands the Robert Hunt Shrine, which was built in 1922 as a memorial to the first clergyman at Jamestown. The titular rector for James City in 1607 was the Rev'd Richard Hakluyt, a prebendary of Westminster Abbey and a noted geographer, but Parson Hunt was his vicar and it was he who sailed with the Founders and conducted the first worship at Cape Henry and Jamestown Island. It is sometimes forgotten—even by Episcopalians—that it was from the first little church in James Fort of 1607 that Anglicanism in America developed. The Robert Hunt Shrine and the Tower Church are still within the ecclesiastical jurisdiction of the Bishop of Southern Virginia. The shrine is really an outdoor chancel of brick and stone, for, in addition to the stone altar, there are protecting side walls and a canopy of brick construction, a reredos with a bronze bas-relief (commemorating Parson Hunt's celebration of the Holy Communion under a sail stretched between trees), and a chancel rail for communicants. The shrine was moved a short distance in 1960 in order that celebrants and congregations might worship without the early morning sun shining in their faces, although the present location lacks the appeal of the original site on an eminence almost at the river's edge.

The chief Service at the shrine is now held on the Third Sunday after Trinity, for that day in the Church's kalendar marks the first recorded celebration of the Sacrament at Jamestown. However, the Founders landed at Jamestown on May 13, 1607, which in that year was Rogation Wednesday or Ascension Eve. Ascension Day, therefore, followed immediately, and Whitsunday fell on May the 24th. The Third Sunday after Trinity did not occur until June the 21st. It was certainly the duty and privilege of Parson Hunt to celebrate the Holy Communion on Whitsunday, one of the three greatest feasts of the Church, and he may very well also have done so on Ascension Day and the Sunday following (May the 17th). Furthermore, there would be no reason for anyone at Jamestown to record that he had celebrated at such a time as Whitsunday; on the contrary, had Parson Hunt not been able to celebrate on such an occasion, this would have been more likely to be noted as a thing out of the ordinary. Thus, a celebration of the Holy Communion on Ascension Day or Whitsunday would be a more logical and appropriate commemoration than the present custom. Evensong on the Eve of Ascension, as representing the first Office that Parson Hunt's vows required him to conduct on Jamestown Island, should also not be forgotten.

A fitting summary of the Christian significance of Jamestown is found in remarks penned for a hymn-festival in the tercentennial year of 1957 by the distinguished historiographer of the diocese of Virginia, the Rev'd Dr George MacLaren Brydon:

The First Day at Jamestown: Ascensiontide

May 13, 1607—the day upon which the Settlers landed at Jamestown as their permanent settlement—was, in Anglican worship, Rogation Wednesday; and the next day (Thursday the 14th) was the Feast of the Ascension of Our Lord and Saviour Jesus Christ.

As Robert Hunt, priest and prophet of God, read Morning Prayer on that Day of Taking Possession, he read that most significant Psalm LXVIII, which is appointed in the Psalter to be read on the morning of the 13th day of the month. He read these words of verse 18:

"Thou art gone up on high, thou hast led captivity captive,
and received gifts for men: yea, even for thine enemies, that
the Lord God might dwell among them."

On that day of the first "setting of the watch", he prayed for the first time on Virginian soil the petition of the Founders' own prayer: "And seeing, Lord, the highest end of our plantation here is to set up the standard and display the banner of Jesus Christ, even here where Satan's throne is, Lord, let our labour be blessed in labouring for the conversion of the heathen."

So the Day of Occupation passed through the sunset to "the evening and the morning" of the Day that is the age-long affirmation of the Christian Faith, the Day on which man's salvation from sin has been won, and the Day that Christ in His glorious Ascension received the gifts of salvation for all mankind.

It is a momentous fact that this first religious observance of Christian settlers in a new land was the great shout of Faith in God as the Father of all mankind, and in Jesus Christ as the Saviour of all.

2. MERCHANT'S HOPE CHURCH

Venerable Merchant's Hope Church lies on the north side of route 641 in Prince George County, .5 mile west of that road's intersection with route 10, which in turn is 6.5 miles east of Hopewell. The church derives its name from a plantation of the same title. A seventeenth-century ship called "Merchant's Hope" is also thought to have been named for the plantation. The "Merchant" in the title is believed to have been originally Martin, as in Martin's Brandon plantation and parish. The confusion seems to have arisen from the fact that words like Merchant and Merbecke were in earlier times pronounced as Marchant and Marbeck, just as clerk is still pronounced in many lands as clark.

The traditional date of the building's erection, 1657 (cp. page 7), is cut into one of the beams of the roof trusses. The church was built to serve as the parish church of Jordan's Parish, but became a chapel of ease of Westover Parish in 1688 and the upper chapel of Martin's Brandon Parish in 1720. Jordan's Parish was created by 1655 out of the western portion of Westover Parish that lay south of the James River. All of the parishes of Prince George County (except Bristol Parish) were united with Martin's Brandon Parish in 1720. Martin's Brandon Parish was a plantation parish in 1618 and its final establishment as a separate parish occurred in 1655.

The building, which measures about 60' x 25' on the inside, is of brick laid in Flemish bond with glazed headers above the bevelled water table and in English bond below the water table. Both gables are marked by a line of glazed headers along the barge board. The walls (22½" thick) are remarkably well preserved. In fact, the walls of no colonial church in Virginia, regardless of its age, are in better shape than Merchant's Hope's walls. Among the few repairs are: 1) repointing above and below the north window and above the south window as well as a crack on each side of the chancel wall; 2) heavy repointing all along the top and around the joint at the outer edge of the window arches as well as some repointing in the lower portions of the north wall; 3) cracks above and to the right of the small window, a long crack down the right side, and several small spots of repointing on the west wall; and 4) repointing all along the top and on each side of the doorway (along the lower portion) as well as cracks below each window on the south wall. New patches also occur near the eave lines on both sides of each of the gables. A brick is also missing in the water table on the south wall near the southeast corner.

The use of queen closers is unusually regular, for they are to be seen on both jambs of all openings and at all corners.

Semi-circular arches mark the ten windows—four on the north, three on the south, two on the east, and a smaller one in the west gable—as well as the west doorway; and rubbed brick marks the jambs and arches of the windows and the south and the west doorways as well as the four corners of the building. The south doorway, near the chancel, has a flat arch, with a rowlock course (including alternate glazed headers) immediately above the arch proper. The voussoirs of the arches of the two doorways alternate header over stretcher with stretcher over header, whereas the voussoirs of the window arches alternate a stretcher with a pair of headers, except for the small window, which contains only stretchers. Neither doorway has pilasters.

Repairs to the windows include: 1) five new bricks in the arch of the westernmost window and three or four new bricks in the arch of the middle window on the south wall; 2) two or three new bricks in the arch of the south window and four new bricks in the arch of the north window of the chancel wall; 3) one or two new bricks in each of the arches of the four windows on the north wall; and 4) four or five new bricks in the arch of the small window in the west gable. Repairs have been made in the masonry at the sides of the brick arch over the south doorway, and fifteen to twenty new bricks mark the top of the arch of the west doorway.

The nine large windows have bevelled brick sills immediately below the wooden sills. The small ventilation slots below the water table have been bricked up within the past decade.

The wood doors and trim are very old, but there exists some difference of opinion as to whether they are original or, perhaps, from a later colonial date. Double doors (all with H-L hinges) exist in both the west and the south, and the former have a wooden lunette at the top. Evidence of the insertion of a stove pipe still exists in this lunette. Both pairs of doors have a small horizontal panel over two larger vertical panels. The wood trim of the doorways consists of three planes separated by cyma reversas. Wooden pegs abound in both doorways and windows. The west doors are secured by a wooden bar, whereas the south doors have been altered to allow for a modern lock and latch.

The window sash and frames are also very old, and surely colonial, although their exact age is indeterminate. They have twenty-four over sixteen lights, many of which are likewise old. The frames comprise two planes (one much wider than the other) divided by a cyma reversa. The muntins are approximately 1″ in width. The lower sash of the second window from the east on the north wall seems to be the only modern replacement. All the sash are true guillotines: they have no weights.

The original tiles (18″ square) of Portland stone still remain in the aisles (6′ wide), although the shape of the aisles has at some time for some reason been changed from a liturgical T to an L. Also believed to be original are the stairway to the west gallery and the handrail across the front of that gallery.

A problem exists in regard to the level of the bottom rail of the doors and the level of the stone aisles. If the original level of the aisles was as low as their recent setting, then the doors (if original) have either been shortened at the bottom, or they have been replaced. If the doors are original and unaltered, then the aisles are presently too low. The existence of a stile in the beginning is highly unlikely.

Most of the wooden beams and trusses of the roof are original, although the slate shingles, dentil cornice, plastering, and interior furnishings are obviously post-colonial. The most interesting feature of the roof is the change in the slope at the eaves (sometimes known as a kick). The pulpit is believed to have originally stood in the middle of the south wall, according to recently uncovered evidence.

The church was abandoned after the Disestablishment and is said to have been used as a picket station in the War between the States. Any extensive use in a war would, however, have hardly left the doors and windows in such good condition. The building was restored for use in Divine Service in 1870.

The Church owns a Bible (a folio edition of 1639) that was left to Martin's Brandon Parish in a will executed in 1658. The Bible is now kept in the Bank of Southside Virginia at Prince George Courthouse. Bishop Andrewes's sermons, which were also left to the Church in the same will, have long been lost. The communion silver (chalice and paten-cover) that was bought according to this legacy is in the possession of the present Brandon Church at Burrowsville, as is a baptismal bowl that was given to the parish in 1731. All three pieces are inscribed to the parish. The chalice derives from London in 1659-60, whereas the paten-cover is unmarked. The baptismal bowl was made by Thomas Farrer of London in 1731-32. Such bowls were preferred to fonts during Cromwell's rule.

There are no churchyard walls around Merchant's Hope Church and there was no cemetery nearby in colonial times.

Perhaps, the chief evidence in favor of a seventeenth-century origin for this remarkable building is the utter simplicity of its west doorway, a simplicity that is matched among surviving structures only at Jamestown (and even at Jamestown the arch is ornamented by imposts). Merchant's Hope is probably our oldest church, and it is without a doubt our most enigmatic church. Because of its excellent state of preservation and the details of its masonry, its exterior, which is so devoid of unnecessary adornment, represents the supremely classical example of ecclesiastical architecture in colonial Virginia.

3. Newport Parish Church (St Luke's)

One of the best-known churches in Virginia may be seen in Isle of Wight County, four miles southeast of Smithfield on route 10. The building is situated just northwest of the junction of route 10 and the highway that leads to Newport News over the James River Bridge.

Confusion exists concerning both the title and year of construction of this church. In colonial times it was the Newport Parish Church, but from 1828 it became known as St Luke's Church, although the saint's name was never legally adopted. The use of "Newport Parish Church" is complicated to-day by the fact that the building ceased to be the parish church in the nineteenth century. Vestry records in the last century referred to it also as "The Isle of Wight Church" and "The Brick Church". This last appellation has been much used despite the fact that it is hardly distinctive in Virginia where we have around forty other colonial churches constructed of brick. The existing evidence and the resultant conjectures concerning the origins of the present structure have already been presented (on pages 7-9). Suffice it to say here that it seems hazardous to claim any date before 1665 and wiser to accept 1682 as the most likely year for its erection, as probably a second church on the same site.

Warrosquyoake County was one of the original shires of 1634. The name was derived from the then resident tribe of Indians, but it was replaced by 1637 with Isle of Wight, after the earliest settlement in the area. Isle of Wight County was reduced in area at the formation of Brunswick County in 1733 and Southampton County in 1749.

The plantation parish of Warrosquyoake is first recorded in 1629. In 1643 the parish was subdivided into Upper (later Warrosquyoake) and Lower (later Newport) Parishes. In 1734 the lower sections of these two parishes were formed into Newport Parish and the upper sections into Nottoway Parish (which became coterminous with Southampton County fifteen years later).

The first Newport Parish Church was probably erected around 1632. It is believed (but not positively known) that the parish (like the city of Newport News) was named for Captain Christopher Newport, commander of the Jamestown expedition of 1607 (and pilot of the *Susan Constant*).

The existing brick church and its brick tower (which is engaged rather than independent) are laid in rough Flemish bond (without the glazed headers so usual in Virginia) both above and below the double water table. Both water tables are bevelled. The upper one is located just below the moulded brick sills of the principal windows. The church measures about 60½' x 24'-3", inside the upper walls, and the tower 18′ east and west by 20′ north and south on the outside at the ground level. Around two thousand bricks from the Jamestown Church were used in the repairs of the 1890's, but the compliment was returned when the church on Jamestown Island was rebuilt by the Colonial Dames in 1907 and several of the Newport Parish Church's features were used in that restoration. The walls of the Isle of Wight Church are 26″ thick and rest on foundations 3′ thick; the walls of the tower are nearly 2½′ thick.

Three buttresses support both the north and south sides of the church, and each buttress is marked by three ramps. The roof and part of the east gable came down in a storm in 1887, but were rebuilt by 1894. The repairs on the east wall occupy almost the entire upper portion. The eight crow-steps and haunches of the east gable have all been faithfully replaced. The gable projects at the cornice. The original west gable still consists of the haunches and the first and part of the second crow-steps on each side. Each of the haunches has a moulded brick decoration at the point where the step that it replaces would begin. Other places on the building that have been repaired or heavily repointed include: the windows on the south and the areas immediately above those openings; the windows on the north and the areas above and below those openings; the three windows of the second storey in the tower; and the east side of the tower along the rake. The two elliptical windows in the tower porch and some of the sills of the principal windows may also have been repointed.

The northwest and southwest corners of the tower are rusticated through the use of Jacobean brick quoins on the first two storeys. These quoins also exist at the other two corners of the tower on the upper third of the second storey, but stop short of the juncture of the roof and crow-steps, so that there remains a short unadorned stretch in each case. In the third storey of the tower, these quoins are replaced by simple brick pilaster strips. Every other quoin is marked by a V-cut down its middle. The quoins follow the projections of both water tables. The three belt courses of the tower are of moulded brick. Above the highest of these are three courses of heavily repaired brick in mixed bond. It is in the brickwork of the third storey that the initials, "CD" and "TD", are deeply carved (near the southwest corner, on the front). The height of the tower at the top of the third storey is approximately 60 feet.

Above the third storey there is now a wood cornice and a shingled, hipped roof of recent construction. It is believed by some authorities that the tower may have originally consisted of but two storeys, surmounted by a crenellated parapet, and that the third storey was added only after 1675. If true, this would account for the initials of persons active only after 1675, but this opinion is by no means universally held. A classical cornice is said to have been added to the third storey in the eighteenth century and removed in the next century. The change in style between the second and third storeys is as interesting as it is perplexing. In any case, the tower certainly resembles a Norman keep, as others have pointed out. The first storey seems always to have served as a porch, as it still does.

The eaves of the body of the church are plain and the pitch is steep. The restored shingled roof of the church now has a very plain, wooden cornice.

Lancet Windows

There are four windows on both the north and south sides of the church; a great window in the east; one window each on the north, west, and south sides of the second storey of the tower; one each on all four sides of the third storey; an elliptical window on both sides of the porch; and a small circular window high up in the east gable. The eight windows on the sides of the nave are lancets and each of these lancet windows consists of a pair of lancets surmounted by a triangular remnant, all of which are divided by brick mullions. The mullions as well as the jambs, sills, and arches of these windows, of those of the second storey in the tower, and of the large east window all consist of moulded and rubbed brick in a single course in the form of an ovolo and a fillet. This constitutes one of the church's principal Gothic charms.

The easternmost windows on the sides of the church are out of line with each other. The two elliptical windows also have rims of a single ovolo-and-fillet brick. The arches of the windows of the tower's third storey are of flattened, semi-circular shape and now contain wooden louvers. A rowlock course marks the arches, and headers are used at the sills in the third storey.

The east window is a great lancet consisting of two tiers of four circular-headed windows each, beneath a group of three progressively smaller tiers: four lancets at the bottom, three quasi-diamonds, and two elongated triangles in almost horizontal position at the top. The whole is joined by the same brick tracery as in the other lancet windows. Two brick spandrels separate the three principal tiers.

All the windows originally had clear glass with leaded diamond panes, but since the 1890's have contained stained glass.

The usual entrances exist in the west and the south. Over the west entrance to the tower is a large, slightly flattened, semi-circular arch (alternating full bricks with pairs of halves) with brick imposts. Rubbed brick may possibly have once marked the jambs of this entrance.

33

Above the entrance is also a primitive triangular pediment of moulded brick, the horizontal member of which extends beyond the slanting members. Both the raked and horizontal cornices consist of a fascia on the upper course and the usual fillet and ovolo on the lower course. The tympanum seems to have been at one time a panel of white cement. Later a marble tablet was inserted, but it is now filled with a wash of mortar. The south entrance, which is just east of the eastern-most buttress, is new, although its location is original. Its arch is flat and is marked by the prevailing ovolo brick, but has no relieving arch. The doorway that leads from the room in the second storey of the tower to the west gallery has a semi-circular relieving arch and two wooden lintels, which are separated by corbelled bricks.

The only woodwork that remains from the seventeenth century are a part of the classical architrave over the door leading from the tower porch into the church, a single turned baluster (second from left end) in the altar rail, and the sounding board over the pulpit. The original portions of the mouldings of the remarkable, primitive architrave include the fascia and cyma reversa (across the top), a wide fascia (partly across the top), and small sections of a small cyma reversa, a fascia, and an ovolo (at the extremities of the top). Restored are the bottom fascia (with the chamfer and lamb's tongue mouldings), the sides of the doorway, and the missing portions at the top. The mouldings are hewn from a single oak beam rather than applied. The wicket door itself is a copy of the famous example at Yeocomico Church. The five-paneled door on the south is also a replacement, as are the various strap hinges and latches.

The new tie-beam timber roof structure of the church is based, according to Mr James Grote Van Derpool, on a design that was found, complete with mouldings, outlined on the west wall when work on the restoration of the 1950's was undertaken. It is from these mouldings that the chamfer and lamb's tongue in use elsewhere in the building derive. Gothic mouldings also mark the present window frames and trim, some of which seem to be at least as old as the early or middle nineteenth century. A sample of what is believed to be the original plastering is now preserved under glass above the doorway leading from the gallery to the tower. A horizontal ceiling of plaster is now applied between the collar beams, after what is considered to be the original fashion.

The wooden sills under the three windows in the second-storey room of the tower seem to be quite old, if not colonial. A step-back in the walls may also be seen in this room. The interior of the tower porch is marked by mortar wash on the walls and exposed beams. Traces of the original west gallery are said to have been found recently. This gallery is also said to have had oak balusters. It has now been beautifully replaced, with stairs.

The only recorded mention of the church's interior occurs in 1746 and has to do with the assignment of a corner pew of the chancel for wives of justices and vestrymen and their former pew for the young women of the parish. In the present interior there are many replacements and restorations. Among them are two box or "family" pews (with turned balusters around the top) just west of the chancel screen, seventeen slip pews in the nave, and a square pew on each side of the altar; T-shaped aisles of square bricks (based on remnants from the original floor that was recently uncovered beneath two later floors); a wooden floor under the pews; a chancel or rood screen with turned balusters; a kneeling rail (including the single original baluster); and a three-decker pulpit. One of the mediæval emphases of the recent work is the bench attached on the east of the chancel screen. This allows communicants to move here for the Communion in much the same way as they move from nave to choir in English and Continental cathedrals.

Some of the pews derive in part from older ones in use in the building in the last century. A trace of the footings of a rood screen is said to have been uncovered in the recent restoration. A sounding board and pulpit were found in 1894 in a barn at a nearby plantation, "Macclesfield", and restored to use then, but only the former has now been considered to be of seventeenth-century origin, so that a new octagonal, panelled pulpit is presently in use. The clerk's desk and space are almost non-existent. One is, therefore, led to think that, perhaps, a two-decker pulpit marked the seventeenth-century church instead of the present three levels.

The balusters of the rood screen, box pews, west gallery, and the columns under the gallery all seem to have been derived as to character from the unique relic in the altar rail.

A splendid array of ecclesiastical furnishings from various places has been assembled for exhibition. Among them are pieces from both America and England. The American antiques include: 1) a white walnut communion table from c. 1640; 2) a chair (mid-seventeenth) with an arched-wainscot back from the Bolles collection; 3) a chair by Thomas Dennis (mid-seventeenth), the earliest of identified American cabinetmakers; 4) a credence table (seventeenth); 5) iron torcheres on the west wall (seventeenth); and 6) a table, now near the west entrance (early seventeenth). From England have come: 1) an organ (c. 1665) signed by the well-known Bernard Smith; 2) a silver-gilt chalice (early seventeenth); 3) a brass alms box (now at the rear of the church on an antique table), which has fighting cocks and an Oriental touch or two; 4) two 1629 books containing both the Bible and the Book of Common Prayer; 5) a pair of brass alms basons (early seventeenth); and 6) embroidered lectern hangings (early eighteenth).

The altar cloth, eight pricket candlesticks (now with small electric candles!), and cut-velvet furnishings (including two chair pads, a cushion, and a table cover (at the rear of the church)) are also English pieces from the seventeenth century. Very interesting is the presence of the tasselled cushion, for the sermon was regularly placed on such a cushion in colonial Virginia. There is no display of royal or other arms, or of the devotional tablets usually found in colonial churches, but there are Oriental rugs in the "family" pews. The kneeling pads at the altar are of hand-loomed dark red wool.

The furnishings also include a pair of alms basons, a credence shelf, and a stand for the Service-books that were made in Norfolk, England, by Mr John Golden from the remnants of an old oaken bell tower of the seventeenth century that had been demolished. They were presented to the church by Mr Golden in 1957.

A font and its cover have been "hewen hollow like a canoa" [hewn hollow like a canoe] out of a single tree-trunk after the fashion of one described for the 1610 church at Jamestown Island. In it is now another American antique, a silver bason ascribed to a certain Jacob Boelen (1654-1729).

Use of single tree-trunks, fillet-and-ovolo, chamfer, and lamb's tongue mouldings, and balusters turned after the single relic seems to have set the tone for a great deal of the recent restoration.

On display above the altar is one of the two dating bricks that were found in the débris of the storm of 1887. The figures on this brick seem to have been cut more deeply in recent times. In the crossing are two grave markers. The one on the left commemorates Joseph Bridger (†1686), whose name is prominently associated with the construction of this church. His remains and tomb were removed from "Whitemarsh" and re-interred here in 1894. The other marker derives from 1696. The only other colonial marker seems to be from 1767 and lies in the yard a short distance east of the chancel.

The yard is a large and beautiful park with trees, shrubs, graves, and a charming pond. The ground level around the porch had to be lowered several inches in the recent restoration in order that the original floor level of the church might be resumed.

Colonel Tarleton's troops were active in the area in the Revolution and are said to have encamped in the churchyard, but the building suffered no damage therefrom. After the Disestablishment, services were only occasionally held and the church fell into disrepair. Around 1820 services were resumed and some repairs were made, but Divine

Worship was again discontinued in 1836 and the church was in ruins by 1843 or earlier. One of the chief factors behind all this seeming neglect was the construction of Christ Church at Smithfield in 1832. Among the major restorations are those of 1894 and 1957. In 1953 the church and land were transferred by deed to a "non-denominational organization chartered by the Virginia State Corporation Commission" as "Historic St Luke's Restoration".

The vestry book (1724-72) of Newport Parish is on deposit at the State Library in Richmond. From 1724 to 1734 the minutes of this manuscript concern only Upper Parish, Isle of Wight County.

Although so much has been done for the church by so many—and a great deal of it undeniably admirable in both intention and execution—it must reluctantly be acknowledged that several false steps have been taken, and it is to be hoped that our other colonial churches of great significance will not err in the same ways in the future. For one thing, the approach to the church and its sward is marred by the presence of a none too gainly gate house that serves as a gift shop. Worse still is the fact that all visitors must pass through this gift shop upon both entering and leaving. The commercial and un-Virginian atmosphere that is engendered by this is deepened by the fact that no photography is allowed at any time within the building. Although all sensitive persons resent cameras in Divine Worship, permission should be—and elsewhere is nearly always—granted to serious students of the Church, its history, and its architecture at some time (at least upon formal request or advance notice) to make their own sketches or take their own photographs. The policy at the Isle of Wight Church, insofar as the author knows, is unique in Virginia or its neighboring states.

The large assemblage of antiques and replacements of antiques has created more of a museum that is occasionally used for Divine Service than a venerable chapel. One feels that one is visiting at Colonial Williamsburg or at the Sainte Chapelle in Paris rather than in an edifice of Anglican consecration. The emphasis on the museum is also felt through the fluorescent cove lighting high on the side walls and the aforementioned electric candles in the nave. Furthermore, this brilliant display of ecclesiastical plate and furnishings is a highly unlikely representation of the belongings of a 1682 church in Isle of Wight County in Virginia, much less of a 1632 edifice. For example, such an organ as that presently in use is completely inappropriate both economically and liturgically!

Also, in the writings and advertisements released in behalf of the church since the latest restoration, there has existed an unnecessary note of belligerency, particularly as to the date of its construction. One of the most unfortunate albeit minor tones from this last restoration

37

is, however, struck by the present electronic tintinnabulation in the tower, when a simple country church bell would be both authentic and less expensive as well as more appealing.

Despite all this, the old Newport Parish Church remains a monument of great beauty that combines in ever interesting manner features of both Gothic and Classical architecture.

4. YORK-HAMPTON PARISH CHURCH (GRACE)

The parish church of York-Hampton Parish stands on the bluff of the York River in historic Yorktown on the east side of a dead-end lane named for itself, Church Street.

The colonial antecedents of the present parish are manifold. A Chiskiack parish (which gradually came to be pronounced "Cheesecake") in York County had its own clergyman as early as 1635 and, when it was officially established five years later, it also included the plantation (Middle Plantation) that was to become Williamsburg (although Middle Plantation Parish became independent before 1658). In 1643 Chiskiack Parish's name became Hampton. York Parish was a plantation parish with its own parson by at least 1638. York and Hampton Parishes were joined together in 1706, and six years later Martin's Hundred Parish in James City County became a part of York-Hampton Parish.

Charles River County, which lay on both sides of that river, was one of the eight original shires of 1634, but was reduced on the north by the formation of Northumberland County in 1645 and Lancaster and Gloucester Counties around 1651 and on the west by the formation of New Kent County in 1654. Charles River and Charles River County were both renamed York in 1643.

The site of the first York Church of around 1642 is believed to be the same as that of the second church (around 1667), which is located at the old York settlement, now within the Coast Guard Reserve Training Center about two miles below Yorktown. Also at this spot may be seen the second oldest (1655) legible tombstone in Virginia.

The present building is, therefore, believed to be the third parish church of York Parish and the only parish church in the long history of York-Hampton Parish, for neither of the two Cheesecake Churches (around 1640-45 and 1710, respectively) seems ever to have served this purpose. The existing structure is also believed to have been built as early as 1697. This year has been arrived at by historians because Governor Francis Nicholson is recorded in the county order book (on October 26, 1696) as having pledged twenty pounds sterling towards a "brick church". The church was constructed, however, not of brick but rather of marl slabs that were cut out of the cliffs of the York River. In Mr Charles E. Hatch's definition, the marl of Yorktown is derived from "deposits of shells of various types mixed with muck and clay of the once ocean bottom" and it is the lime in these "decomposing shells in composition with the clay" that has produced the "dense rocky substance known as marl". Although the slabs of marl were originally cut in a soft state, exposure to air soon hardened them almost to stone.

The church at Yorktown was originally built as a rectangle and the (former) north wing represents a later addition. The body of the church measures 55'-9" x 28'-8" on the outside. The north wing had the same width as the main part of the church and projected 29'. The foundation walls are 27" thick.

The church lost its windows and pews in the Revolution when it became a magazine for Lord Cornwallis. It was burned in 1814 along with much of Yorktown, although this was a fire caused by accident rather than by the British, who from all indications did not even enter Yorktown in that year. The church was not rebuilt and restored to service until 1848, and the north wing has never been rebuilt. The foundations of this wing are still exposed (where not covered by vines). It was in 1848 that the building was heavily stuccoed (as it still is) and also that the name of Grace Church was first used. During the War between the States, a signal tower was erected for the Federal forces on the church's roof, the building itself greatly damaged through use as a hospital, and its colonial churchyard wall demolished. It is thought that the church was restored for worship soon after the War, possibly around 1870.

The cornice seems to have been extended over the west gable sometime before 1871. In 1926 the present, vaguely classical belfry, western doorway, and circular window were added and these help to give the church a distinctly post-colonial and non-Virginian appearance. In 1931 the churchyard wall was restored and the interior modernized. Perhaps, the most prominent aspect of the modern interior is the use here (as well as in the modern interior of Hickory Neck Church in neighboring

James City County) of the somewhat mediæval chandelier known as a corona lucis. This corona lucis seems to have been made by a craftsman from Hampton and installed around 1930. It was at first equipped with candles.

The church at Yorktown now has three unusually wide windows on each side. Evidences of the original south door can still be detected. Although a parish house was annexed to the east wall around 1951, sections of the original marl have been exposed to view in recent years on the other three walls. While these walls of marl cannot be said to possess great beauty, they are, together with their age, certainly the building's most interesting feature. The structure also possesses a second exterior offset, rather high above the usual water table.

The bell that is still in use is inscribed "County of York, Virginia, 1725". This may or may not indicate that the bell was originally hung in some other building in the village (probably the courthouse) rather than in the church, but in any case it seems to have rung from the church's belfry in colonial times. It is also uncertain whether the bell fell and broke in the 1814 fire or during the War between the States, but all are agreed that the fragments were carried off during that War, in all probability by Federal soldiers. The pieces were found in Philadelphia in 1882 and identified through the inscription. The bell was then recast and restored to service at Yorktown in 1889.

Likewise still in constant use at the church is the second oldest set of communion silver in Virginia. It consists of a chalice and a flagon of 1649-50 and both are inscribed to Hampton Parish in York County. The latter is probably the earliest English silver flagon in an American church. It has a flat top (instead of the domed top of later periods), and its simple design may be owing to the Puritan period of its manufacture. A silver paten (1698-99) that was apparently given to Martin's Hundred Parish before it joined York-Hampton Parish in 1712 is now at St John's Church in Hampton.

There are a few tombs from the seventeenth and eighteenth centuries (including the handsome Nelson tombs) in the south portion of the churchyard. The tombs from 1674 and 1696 were originally placed in a graveyard elsewhere in the village. They were found when repairs were being made on the roads and were moved to the churchyard in 1931.

In addition to the uniqueness of its marl walls, the smallness of the structure and the irregular alignment of the church walls and yard contribute much to the somewhat quaint appearance and village atmosphere of the church at Yorktown.

The first confirmation service ever held in Virginia is believed to have been conducted in 1791 at old York Church.

40

The parish register (1648-1789) of another colonial York County parish, Charles (originally New Poquoson) Parish, has been published and the original manuscript is on loan at the State Library in Richmond from the vestry of Grace Church, Yorktown.

5. ST PETER'S PARISH CHURCH, NEW KENT

St Peter's Parish Church in New Kent County stands in a magnificent setting, almost completely surrounded by forests. It may be reached from route 33 (between West Point and Richmond) by going about a mile north of Talleysville on route 609 and about .5 mile farther on route 642. The immediate approach to the church through the woods is as beautiful as the church and its large yard.

St Peter's Parish was created out of Blisland Parish in 1679. In 1704 St Paul's Parish, which became Hanover County in 1720, was cut off and before that, in 1691, that part of St Peter's lying north of the Pamunkey River was annexed to St John's Parish. In 1725 St Peter's Parish received part of Wilmington Parish. As a result, St Peter's Parish included part of James City County as well as a great deal of (modern) New Kent County until 1767 when an exchange of territory between New Kent and James City Counties (that did not, however, affect the parish's boundaries) once again left all of the parish in New Kent County. At present, St Peter's Parish includes all of New Kent County except the easternmost portion, which is still officially listed by the diocese of Virginia as a dormant parish (Blissland [sic]), although the only church in modern Blisland Parish stands in James City County and the diocese of Southern Virginia.

The first Lower Church of the parish has been called the "Broken-Back'd" Church because of its structural weakness and was, perhaps, erected as early as 1685. Its location is not known. One authority has placed it near the present route 33 not too far east of the junction of that highway with route 608 (leading to Providence Forge), but it is more generally believed to have stood southeast of Black Creek, not far east of Tunstall Station and near "Mt Prospect". This church seems to have been used, at least occasionally, for an indefinite period after

41

the erection of its successor (1701-03) and the creation of St Paul's Parish. Two churches were in existence in St Peter's Parish in 1685, but the second Upper Church (1690) as well as a frame chapel (1702-1704), also in the upper area, were cut off with St Paul's Parish.

The body of the existing second Lower Church was started in 1701 and was in use by 1703. Its dimensions are approximately 64'-4" x 28'-4". Its bricks are laid in English bond (without glazed headers save a few on the west gable), except for Flemish bond at the water table and—on the south wall—for three courses above the water table from the south doorway to the western end. At the eastern end of the wall these three courses are partly Flemish and partly English. In a vestry minute of 1700, a certain William Hughes is cited as the builder.

Sometime between 1758 and the Revolution, a wing (24' square and 10' off center towards the east) was added to the church on the north, but this addition was removed sometime between 1843 and 1862, probably in the 1850's. A brick wall was added (probably in the 1820's) between the wing and the church so that the former could be used as a schoolroom. The effects of these alterations on the north are visible to-day in the repaired brickwork (extending from the right jamb of the westernmost window to a point midway between the two remaining windows), in the obvious change in the water table, and in the style of the two westernmost windows. The north wall (at its juncture with the former wing) was rebuilt with original or colonial bricks and bats and occasional bricks from other times. A number of random bricks have also been replaced elsewhere on the north wall in later times and a small doorway has been inserted near the eastern end.

The masonry on the west wall of the church seems to be in good shape, although the condition of that portion covered by the porch is somewhat indeterminate, owing to the present white coating.

On the east wall, the great semi-circular arched window (about 9' wide and 12' high) is now completely bricked up, although the repaired brickwork indicates that two smaller windows were inserted in the original patching and have themselves been bricked up at a later date. The reveal of this great window still exists in the church's interior.

The restored Flemish gables or strapwork were derived from several indications discovered in the fabric of the building in the 1940's. The central pediment of such a gable was revealed by a brick projection (above the western end of the ridge pole) that had long been cemented over. The pediment is also said to have been seen in the 1951-52 work when necessary replacements were made in the tower's east wall. Still other evidence for Flemish gables was seen at the church's eastern end (where the strapwork may have lasted until the nineteenth century) and on the east wall of the tower (where a curving line of cement flashing was easily traced a few feet above the roof). The only portions of the present Flemish gables that are not of recent restoration are sections of the horizontal bands that lie high up in the east and west gables, and the corbelled projections of the walls at the height of the cornice. The parapet of the gable outside the tower was modelled upon that at Pine End Cottage, one of "two or three ancient brick-and-stone cottages" embellished with Dutch gables that still stand on what once formed part of an ancient churchyard near St Peter's Church, St Peter's village (not far from Sandwich) on the Isle of Thanet in Kent, England. These English models are believed to have been built around 1690. Some persons have thought that these cottages might have been erected as chapels, although the grounds for this supposition are not clear. However, the recent restorers were struck by the similarities in names, dates, and architectural manners between the English and Virginian examples. Others have, on the other hand, felt that Dutch gables would not be so uncommon in England at that time as to cause great surprise and also that the gables in Virginia might have been simpler than the restored examples.

The original south doorway seems to have been bricked up around 1820-25, for the upper portion of this brick fill was formerly marked by the same size of brick (9⅜" x 3⅞" x 4⅜") that is used on the greater portion of the fill-in at the chancel window and these portions were all once painted, like most of the church's walls. The original bricks for the church were ordered to be 9¾" x 4¾" x 4¼", but as burnt they are slightly different. The bricks of the two small, filled-in windows still evident in the east and formerly evident in the lower part of the bricked-in south doorway measure 8" x 2" x 4", were not painted like the others, and were possibly inserted in the 1850's. At the same time, the middle window on the south wall seems to have been moved eastward by 3'-8½".

The south wall, the hue of which is still a much brighter red than that found elsewhere on the building, was reworked in 1953. The south doorway has been restored, a new bull's eye window inserted above the doorway, and the entire wall treated with a bleaching preparation, weather-proofed, and heavily repaired and repointed, particularly west of the middle window and below the water table. It will be noted that the restored south doorway does not at present afford an entrance into the church. The modern chimney derives from sometime after the War between the States.

The three windows on the south, the easternmost window on the north, and the original west doorway have segmental arches, whereas the two replaced windows on the north wall and the new south doorway (between the two easternmost windows) are marked by flat arches. All the locations of these eight openings are undoubtedly original except for the middle window on the south wall, which seems never to have been moved back (west) to its original location.

No one seems able to vouch for it, but the present immaculate condition of the arches of the six windows on the side walls makes one feel certain that all six of these arches have been put in their present state of excellence in 1872 or later. A line of mortar immediately above the segmental arches would also seem to indicate this. They are marked by buttered or thin mortar joints. Below the four segmental arches are brick lunettes, which are also believed to be colonial albeit heavily renewed. The voussoirs of these arches alternate full bricks with pairs of half-bricks. A soldier course serves as the arch of the south doorway. Rubbed brick is used only on the five original (or partly original) window arches and jambs of the church, the modern bull's eye, and the arches of the three windows in the second storey of the tower. Because of the white coating, one cannot tell the details of the western portal.

The present, six casement windows on the church and the glass used in them and in the bull's eye window were installed along with their hardware and frames in 1953. Their use was based on lead cames and glass quarrels found under several of the windows. Inasmuch as sash (guillotine) windows were known in England as far back as 1630 and were specified for the Capitol at Williamsburg in 1699, the "Glass for Sash Windoes" ordered from England in 1701 might have been for either casements or sash. However, because of the recently found artifacts and the 1704 order for "Glass Lead Sodder and Casements for the Chappell" of St Peter's Parish, it seems more than likely that St Peter's Parish Church also had casement windows in the original instance.

Queen closers are found on the church at all the window jambs except for those on the rebuilt portion of the north wall (which includes the left jamb of the westernmost window and both jambs of the middle window) and an irregular use on the right jamb of the relocated, middle window on the south wall. Queen closers are also found at all four corners of the church and on both jambs of the replaced south doorway.

The water table of both church and tower includes cavetto and ovolo mouldings. On the church the water table is considerably higher than it is on the tower, where it occurs only at the base of the four pilasters. In the replaced portion of the north wall of the church and on the inside of the porch, the mouldings of the water table give way to simple fascias (although both moulded bricks and fascias are somewhat irregularly found under the end windows on the north wall).

The large ventilation holes (three on each of the side walls and a single one on the east) must be later additions, for the height of the original floor as indicated by brick remains seems too low (18″ lower than at present) for these apertures to fulfill their function.

The initials that may be seen on the walls seem to have been carved at various periods and include some from the 1860's.

Tower

Although a wooden belfry was built (probably above the western end of the church) in 1722, the present imposing tower (approximately 18′ square) on the west seems to have been in existence by 1740 or shortly before. It apparently was originally built as an arched porch (and payment was made on this portion) and then augmented by a vestry room and steeple above the porch. The tower, with its three large semi-circular openings, is certainly one of the most remarkable features of St Peter's Parish Church.

The brickwork of the tower varies from section to section. The lower piers are essentially laid in English bond, whereas the spandrels and the sides of the arches as well as the second-storey walls are laid in Flemish bond (with glazed headers). The masonry of the upper piers is quite interesting. On the outer piers, courses with queen closers (embracing a pair of stretchers) alternate with courses in which a stretcher on each end embraces three headers. The piers next to the church, which are somewhat wider, have a header separating the pairs of stretchers in the courses with queen closers. Perhaps, the most striking aspect of the upper piers is the glazing of the outer two of each group of three headers. Glazing is to be noted chiefly in the upper sections of the lower storey and in the upper storey.

At the spring line on each side of the arches are these mouldings: fascia, ovolo, and fascia. They do not, however, carry across the pilasters. The belt course at the floor line of the second storey does, on the other hand, carry across the pilasters as well as the tower walls, and breaks out at the former. It includes: ovolo, cavetto, fascia (two courses high), ovolo, fascia, and cavetto. The mouldings of the termination of the brick portion continue around the tower and break out over the pilasters. They are as follows: fascia, cavetto, ovolo, fascia, ovolo, cavetto, and fascia. The fascias were painted white in 1951-52. The four square piers are carried above these mouldings and each of them is surmounted by two fascias and an urn-like ornament. The northwest urn actually serves as a chimney for a corner fireplace in the second-storey room of the tower and this fireplace is original as to location. These urns are composed of stuccoed brick (as can be seen from the present state of the northwest urn) and are probably original.

The windows on the three exposed sides of the tower's second storey have flat arches of rubbed brick. The voussoirs alternate a full brick over a half-brick with a half-brick over a full brick. The voussoirs of the arches of the porch alternate stretchers with pairs of headers, and a number of the latter are glazed. The extensive repairs to the tower's masonry in 1951-52 include: 1) the replacements of bricks here and there (some of which may mark scaffolding holes); 2) replacement of the brickwork at the top of the northeast corner; 3) considerable re-pointing; and 4) the painting of the three fascias to imitate "the white cement finish" seen in early photographs (although much of the paint has already worn off). Beneath each of the three windows is a recessed panel of bricks that are mitered at the corners and have at some time probably been stuccoed. These panels are not unlike the three circles above the entrance to the porch at Yeocomico Church in Westmoreland County.

The east wall of the tower is distinct from the west wall of the church only from a point above the door that leads from the second storey down to the west gallery, as may be seen by the brick relieving arch that is partly visible from the room in the tower.

On the tower, queen closers mark: 1) the right jambs of the north and south windows and the left jamb of the west window; 2) the piers (even below the water table); and 3) the left jambs of the north and west arches. The four, louvered dormer windows of the pyramidal, wooden steeple are of recent restoration (albeit "antiqued"), but framing for these openings was discovered in 1950. These windows are not shown on the Brady photograph (taken during the War between the States) or on more recent representations, but are shown on a "primitive sketch of the church on the survey plat of 'Marl Hill'", which served as the model for the present windows; and "dormant" windows were ordered by the vestry on June 3 and September 29 of 1742. In any case, the existence of louvers that would admit rain helps to explain the presence of the greatly weathered, oaken drain spouts that project on both the south and north sides, just above the second-storey windows. Indeed, these spouts are among the church's objects of greatest curiosity, and it is believed that an inverted roof within the tower in the original instance carried water to a valley running south and north and terminating in these spouts. Remains of tar flashing as recently found indicated plainly the shape of the original inverted roof.

Another use for the dormers may have been the emission of sound from the bell, which was originally given in 1719 (and probably continued in use—first in the wooden belfry and then in the tower—until it was sold in 1841). The existing bell represents a gift in 1952 from

46

the late Judge Richard C. Richardson, although the bell had seen prior use elsewhere.

The tower roof is of slate (from around 1900) and has a change of slope at the eave line. It is believed that the wood framing of the tower is original (although repaired). Mr William Walker was ordered on November 22, 1758 to be paid 130 pounds for building a steeple "according to the first agreement" (and the bill seems to have been dated 1741). The wooden replacements in the tower in 1951-52 were numerous and included new beams and plastered ceiling above the vestry room, new beams and floor below this room, and "appropriate Jacobean woodwork" within the room itself, such as the over-mantel and the panelled door and latch. A new ceiling for the porch was also installed. Lockers for vestments were added in the vestry room and placed, in one case, above the previous stairwell. Decayed woodwork at the top of the northeast corner of the tower was likewise replaced, although the inverted roof above the vestry room was not restored.

The original opening for the fireplace in the northwest corner of the vestry room was discovered behind a smaller aperture that is believed to derive only from the third decade of the nineteenth century when a Presbyterian parson-schoolmaster lived in the room.

Also restored were the tapering copper spire (6′ in height) and a copper weathercock. The former is derived from early photographs and the latter from the early sketch on the survey plat of "Marl Hill". The crossed keys and compass points are believed to be original. The pavement of the porch was relaid with old brick and the inside walls of the porch were whitewashed.

The former existence of an outside stairway leading up across the north archway of the tower is marked by indications that were reputedly found on the porch walls and the framing of the floor of the vestry room as well as by a photograph taken during the War between the States. In the vestry room there was found hewn wood except for the fill-in over the former stairwell where there was timber derived from a sawmill. This stairwell was closed up sometime after the War between the States (probably in 1872). It is believed by some authorities that the doorway leading from the west gallery up into the vestry room was probably not cut through until 1872 (when the present gallery was erected). This entrance was probably accomplished by enlarging a window in the original west gable of the church. Until then (1872), therefore, the room in the tower's second storey was for the sole use of the vestry, who entered through the outside stairway. However, owing to the large relieving arch in the tower room on the tower's east wall and the large wooden lintel below it, it is entirely possible that a doorway was opened from the original west gallery to the vestry room when

the second storey of the tower was built. In this case, the outside stairway was possibly added when the vestry room became the habitation
of the aforementioned schoolmaster in the early 1800's and was removed
after the War between the States.

The three casement windows (with leaded glass in diamond panes)
and their frames that have been restored in the second storey of the
tower and the new Jacobean woodwork in the vestry room may not be
after the original examples, for this portion of the tower is so much
later than the church, with its Jacobean touches.

Some of the present roof structure of the church probably derives
from 1872, as also probably does the primitive wooden cornice. Several
original beams and trusses are believed to have survived, although new
trusses were installed in the early 1930's. The present slates of the church
were put on around 1900.

It has often been pointed out that St Peter's Church and Yeocomico
Church eminently represent the transition in Virginia's ecclesiastical
buildings from late Gothic to Classical. This claim for St Peter's may
be noted principally by the restored strapwork and the double casement
windows on the one hand and by the original chancel window and the
differences in the two storeys of the tower on the other hand.

The most interesting features of the existing interior are the two
marble wall plaques that can now be seen only in the modern vesting
rooms on each side of the chancel. The plaque on the north wall, which
is no longer legible, honors the Rev'd David Mossom (1690-1767),
who was rector for four decades and officiated at the marriage of George
Washington and Martha Dandridge Custis in 1759. The Latin inscription (a translation of which may be read in the yard near the south
wall of the church) indicates that Parson Mossom may be buried beneath the chancel. The plaque on the Epistle side dates from 1737 and
was carved by M. Sidnell of Bristol (England). It is surmounted by
a full entablature (with cushion frieze). It is a pity that such a handsome monument should be all but out of sight.

On the inside of the church, the six windows are slightly splayed
at the jambs but more so at the arches, all of which are segmental on
the interior. The plastering of both walls and ceiling are modern and the
plastering has been much altered. The shape of the present ceiling is also
not original. The two rooms off the chancel were probably installed in
1872. The floor of the central aisle and also that leading to the south doorway was apparently paved in the original instance with brick, while the
raised floor under the chancel and pews consisted of pine on oak sleepers.
Wainscoting was ordered for the chancel in 1732. The present floor
is modern; its supports were renewed in 1948. Underneath the chancel
was in recent times discovered a pile of bricks, which could represent

a central wall support for the wooden floor joists or possibly remnants of a brick floor itself. The modern gallery does not match the specifications given in the colonial vestry book. Electricity was first installed in the church around 1947.

The church was abandoned after the Disestablishment and used by the Presbyterians from around 1810-20 to 1843, and from 1843 to 1856 by the Episcopalians and the Presbyterians on alternate Sundays. During the War between the States the building was desecrated through use as a stable by Federal troops. Major repairs have been made on the church in 1810-20 and 1872 and the recent restorations have included at various times the talents and labors of two architects, J. Ambler Johnston and Harden deVoe Pratt, and two ecclesiastical historians, the Rev'd Dr Brydon and George Carrington Mason (1885-1955), the last of whom lies buried not far from the present gates.

In the yard there are, in addition to the many handsome trees (including walnuts, cedars, and oaks), a number of colonial tombs, principally lying near the east and south walls of the church. The curious, pointed posts to the north of the tower are remnants of grave markers. The location of the "handsome", 100'-square brick churchyard wall that was ordered in 1719 can still be traced in the earth on the east, north, and west sides. What may have been a kiln is also to be detected in the west. Although payment for "a large palisado gate" is ordered on the next to last page of the colonial vestry book, no such gate adorns the present yard. Ferns abound along the lower portion of the church's north wall.

St Peter's vestry book (1684-1758) and register (1685-1786) have been published twice, in the latest instance (1937) in a single volume. The originals are on loan at the State Library in Richmond.

Authorities differ as to whether the marriage of our first president and first first-lady was solemnized in St Peter's Church or at a nearby house called "The White House", but the church is becoming widely known as "The First Church of the First First-Lady".

6. Yeocomico Church

If there is a unique church anywhere, it is Yeocomico Church in Westmoreland County. It lies at the top of a wooded slope about .4 mile west of Tucker Hill post office and may most easily be reached from the hamlet of Lyells, the junction of routes 3 and 203 that is itself three miles north of Warsaw. One goes east from Lyells on route 203 for 6.6 miles and turns left on route 604. One then crosses route 202 in 1.3 miles and continues 2.3 miles farther on route 604 until the junction of routes 604 and 606 is reached. The church lies 1.3 miles north (on the left) of this last junction.

The present building is the only surviving colonial church in Westmoreland County or Cople Parish. This county and Nominy Parish were both created in 1653. The upper part of Nominy Parish became Appomattox Parish around 1661 and the upper part of Appomattox Parish became Potomac Parish in 1662. In this latter year, Westmoreland County was divided into three parishes, although the middle parish seems never to have been organized. The lower parish apparently went unnamed at first, but was soon called Nominy and before 1668 became known as Cople Parish, after an English parish of that name (whence one of the early settlers presumably derived).

The first church on the present site was put up around 1655 "of oak timbers, sheathed with clapboards" and originally was a chapel of ease for Chicacone Parish in Northumberland County. It became a part of Nominy Parish and Westmoreland County in 1664 when the county and parish's limits were extended eastward. The name of Yeocomico for the river and church is derived from that of an Indian tribe. The Yeocomico River or Bay is but two miles southeast of the church.

The existing, second Yeocomico Church was built in 1706 as the second Lower Church of Cople Parish and is constructed of bricks made in a nearby kiln. Its dimensions are of unusual interest. The chief portion (east to west) is 51'-3" long, but the widths of the chancel and west walls differ from each other. The former is 26'-3" wide, whereas the latter is 27'-4" wide. The fact that these widths vary by over a foot and the further fact that the two sections of the north wall are said to be out of line with each other have led some authorities to believe that Yeocomico Church is that rarity, a church originally built as a T. The overall dimensions of the church (exclusive of the south porch) are 50'-8" south to north and 51'-4" east to west. The north wall of the north wing is 26'-7" wide, whereas the east and west walls of the north wing are 24'-4" and 23'-11" respectively. The porch is 13'-1" wide (on the south), 12'-9" long on the west, and 12'-11" long on the east.

50

The north wing and the south porch are both off center to the west, but are not in line with each other, for the porch is farther west than the north wing. The walls of the church are approximately 19″ thick.

The bonds of the masonry are also delightfully varied. Flemish bond marks the porch and all of the south wall of the principal part of the church except the upper right-hand portion (above the height of 5′-8″). The east and west gables and the two sections of the north wall of the nave and chancel as well as the aforementioned upper, eastern portion of the south wall of the nave are laid in English bond, whereas the three walls of the north wing are a combination of Flemish and irregular bonds. English bond is used below the ovolo water table, which is now very low to the ground and changes height at the south-east corner of the church.

The repairs to Yeocomico's interesting walls are numerous. Indeed, it is impossible to assess the reworkings with any great degree of accuracy. The lower portions of the south wall of the porch are heavily repaired; there is much repointing under the sill of the east opening of the porch and also some repointing on the west wall of the porch. On the south wall of the church, most of the upper right-hand portion has been extensively reworked (and surely more than once), as have the areas above the window and at the lower left corner. A vertical line may be detected between the window and the eastern doorway on this wall. The courses immediately below the water table are also interchanged at this point. The chancel wall on the east gives evidence of an even more extensive series of repairs. The gabled section is the most recently repaired. The water table has also been repointed on this wall.

On the north wall of the chancel, repairs are to be noted around the small window. Part of this wall and part of the east wall of the wing are now invisible because of the addition of a modern chimney and basement hatchway. On this east wall of the wing as well as on the west wall opposite it, the most recent reworking occurs above the window-head. The apex of the north gable is the product of repairs and there is repointing below the two courses that make up the belt course. There is likewise repointing on the lower left of the west wall of the wing and on the upper left of the western section of the north wall of the nave. On the west wall of the nave, the gable and some of the lower right portion have also been repointed.

All the corbelled bricks at the six corners of the church and at the two corners of the porch are replacements. These corbels were probably originally composed of ovolo and cavetto bricks. The two courses of brick that constitute the belt course on the north wall of the wing do not quite extend to the ends. This belt course has led some persons to the belief that stepped gables might possibly have marked the original church, or at least the earliest form of the north wing.

There is no rubbed brick on the building, but queen closers mark all the salient corners of the building, the chancel window, the right jamb and part of the left jamb of the west window in the wing, and the window in the north gable. On the porch there are queen closers on the right side of the east opening, on both sides of the west opening, and on the left jamb of the south opening. Glazed headers are to be seen throughout the building, but most prominently on the south, next most prominently on the east and west gables, and least prominently on the walls of the wing. There are no ventilation holes in evidence.

The brickwork is marked by a number of ornaments. Inset above the main opening of the porch is "SGM" with a Scottish thistle below it. Above this is a rare example of brick diapering, which consists of a diamond, tilted and off center (to the right). (An "S" and traces of a "G" are also said once to have existed in the upper part of the porch gable, but they are no longer to be seen.) Glazed headers also follow the line of the upper portions of the barge board of the porch. Immediately above the south opening of the porch are three superimposed semi-circles, the arches of which consist of headers. At present, parts of all three of these arches are recessed (and, therefore, are apparently replaced). One glazed header remains of the three original, embryonic keystones, and the pair of headers connecting the two lower semi-circles is also glazed. Above the arch of the southeast doorway is now a brick carved "R.L." High in the south wall (near the southeast corner) is "1706 IGI" and, below the "G", an "English rose". These markings probably originally were located over the nearby doorway. On the chancel wall (below the circular window) are the initials of eight vestrymen or workmen: "IB-IS-WL-IS-IC-IT-AD-TB". (The names John or Joseph or both seem to have been held in high favor in Cople Parish around 1706.) Between the "I" and the "B" and between the "I" and the "S", there is some sort of a star. Above the circular window, vestrymen and workmen of 1928 have also memorialized themselves in similar manner. The bottom row of the brick surround of these ornaments forms an ovolo sill. The initials on the porch are incised, whereas those elsewhere are in bas-relief.

A recently published statement that the initials near the two south doorways relate to marriages of certain of the royal George's can only be described as fanciful, owing to the historical inaccuracies of the suppositions involved.

The shallow segmental arch of the eastern doorway of the south wall has been rebuilt or repaired. This doorway seems originally to

52

have possessed some sort of a pediment. On each side of this doorway are, however, still to be seen curious pilasters marked by three moulded projections: an ovolo at the top, a torus in the middle, and an ovolo at the juncture of shaft and pedestal. The uppermost portions of these pilasters seem to have been repaired and, indeed, they fall above the line marking the change of bond that delimits the area of prominent repairs. There is at present a plastered area between the flat wooden lintel and the segmental brick arch. The present arch of the north doorway is a replacement.

Wicket Door

There are, therefore, three entrances: the principal one from the porch on the south, the secondary one on the south (that formerly opened into the chancel), and the north doorway in the wing. The main doorway on the south is an extraordinary monument of our colonial heritage. It is an enormous Tudor battened door that also includes the only wicket door known in colonial America. By wicket is meant a separate door (with its own hinges) that is set in the main door. The advantage of such a door is that only the wicket need be opened in times of inclemency. On the outside of this great door, the battens create five vertical panels over five much longer but also vertical panels, and the wicket door occupies the middle three of the lower row of these panels. Cyma reversa mouldings around the edge of the battens frame the various panels. Over this doorway is a segmental arch, but nothing can be told of its details at present, for the entire interior of the porch is currently stuccoed. A screen door now mars the appearance of the wicket. The original wood trim of the doorway is marked by lamb's tongue and ovolo mouldings. Also on the outside (on the wood trim at the extreme left) is a large wooden peg that prevents the upper hinge from pulling out of the frame.

The celebrated door is 6′ wide and 8′ high and consists of two thicknesses. On the inside are a very large board at the top, then two small boards, and (at the bottom) four medium-sized boards, all of which are horizontal. At the top and bottom are enormous hand-wrought strap hinges that are hung on "stout pintles", and on the left of this door are two deadbolts. The wicket door, which occupies the central portion of the two smaller and four of the medium-sized boards, also has two strap hinges, of similar but smaller design, and a single deadbolt. There is now a new strip applied at the bottom of the main door. There is no lock, latch, or knob. The entire doorway is recessed. Some persons have claimed that this battened door derives from the 1655 church, but this seems difficult to prove, unlikely to be true, and unnecessary with a church itself so old.

The north door, which is also original and battened, but much smaller, includes three rails (top, middle, and bottom), four vertical panels, and two strap hinges and a deadbolt, all similar to those of the porch door. A new latch has been added. The wood trim of this door is a replacement, but the lintel may possibly be old, if not colonial. This doorway was probably once also characterized by a segmental arch.

The south doorway has been somewhat altered and is the only one of the three to have a lock and key. The present (new) lintel is shorter than in the original instance and the pair of narrow doors seems also to have been shortened. These doors and most of the wood trim are certainly old if not original. The small area above the present lintel and below the original arch is now electrically lit, apparently so that whoever is charged with locking the church can have a last glimmer as he wends his way in the otherwise dark building.

In addition to the entrance on the south, each of the side walls (east and west) of the porch has a long horizontal opening that extends from slightly above bench level almost to the cornice. The entrance has a flat arch beneath the Gothic semi-circle. All three sides of the original wood trim have a fascia and an ovolo moulding and are put together with wooden pegs. They are but three pieces of a tree-trunk and are temporarily resting on various pieces of rubble. There are now new concrete sills and wooden lintels for the side openings (and comfortable benches below them). The present ceiling is a stuccoed barrel vault. The interlocked pavement of coping bricks was laid around 1820.

For some time large double windows have adorned the lower chancel wall, the south wall (between the doorways), and the west and north gables. The east window is no less than 9' wide and 8'-2" high and the south window 7'-2" wide and 8' high. Smaller double windows mark each side of the north wing (south of the gallery). A single window lights the north chancel wall. The largest windows have 16 over 16 lights and the others but 12 over 12. That the locations of these windows are original is entirely probable, but their exact sizes, shapes, styles, and wood trim mostly represent later workings, probably in great part from the nineteenth century. Some authorities feel that the present fenestration is all out of keeping with a church of so great age and that this is particularly true of the circular window in the east gable. It has also been suggested that leaded sashes existed in the original instance. Some of the large windows still have wooden shutters, but these are not colonial. There are at present no masonry arches for any of the windows or for the north doorway. None of the glass panes are old. All the windows have ovolo brick sills except the double window on the north wall of the wing, although the ovolo sill on the chancel wall has almost been obliterated.

One of our most careful historians has stated that a millstone was formerly inserted in the circular window of the east gable and was one of the church's unique adornments. However, the present parishioners maintain that the present window (installed in 1930) replaced plaster-work and rubble that were removed in 1928. In a photograph taken in the early part of the century, this aperture could have contained either a millstone or plaster and rubble, although a streak leading from its center down to the lower rim might easily indicate the central opening of a millstone whence rain ran down.

The interior of Yeocomico is also somewhat out of the ordinary. The chancel is still located, with liturgical correctness, in the east, but the pulpit, which is said to have once stood at the northeast corner between chancel and north wing, is now in the middle of the south wall. The north wing has, therefore, become the nave, for its pews face the pulpit. With the choir stalls facing north and most of the congregational pews facing south, the worshipper gets a choirwise effect for the whole church, particularly at the Creed, doxologies, and other times in Divine Worship when the assemblage turns east. There were originally shallow galleries in both west and north, but only the latter survives (although the western one still stood in 1814). The present gallery and possibly the balusters are old if not original; all else was restored in 1959. The reading desk, with inside raised panels and wooden pegs, may possibly be a remnant of an old octagonal pulpit or even of the original pulpit. The niche near the bottom of the west wall is believed to have originally held a font, but it is not certain just how it might have contained the original octagonal marble font (with leaf motif) that the parish still uses with great pride. The painted stone base of the font is not original, but is possibly colonial.

Famous Holy Table

Another of Yeocomico's glories is the original walnut Holy Table (65" x 30"), the lower parts of which are unfortunately now painted white. The top of the Table, which is said to have been used as a chopping block by American soldiers in the War of 1812, has been redone, so that no traces of such abuse survive. The legs are similar to turned balusters, and there is a bottom rail around all four sides. A cyma reversa marks the bottom edge of the four sides of the upper rail (just below the top of the Table).

The present chancel panelling (with high, panelled rails along the east-to-west sides and with large tablets on each side of the altar) derives from the 1906 renovation of Archdeacon Tyler (later Bishop of North Dakota) and is not at all consonant with the church's age or architectural style. The brick aisles are perforce irregular: two short ones from the south doorways, a long one from the north entrance to the pulpit, and a fourth one from the chancel west as far as the porch-doorway walk. These aisles are believed to have been laid in 1814, although they may derive from 1873, and they have been repaired many times. The present pews probably derive from 1873. The original pews were of box rather than slip style. The pulpit and stairs (by the south window) derive from 1928. The wooden floors were replaced in 1928 and redone in 1959.

The original hand-rived oak ceiling that is said to have been laid directly on the exposed rafters and collar-beams was removed in 1928 and the present clapboard ceiling (following the original trapezoidal shape) installed in 1939. Of the present exposed tie-beams, only those with chamfer and lamb's tongue mouldings would seem to be original. The northernmost beam in the north wing is also marked "iiii". The southernmost beam in the wing is a rough, later insertion. The roof trusses probably date from the 1820's, although those of the porch may be colonial or original. The present roof shingles were put on in 1954. Electricity was first installed in 1947 and a heating system in 1949.

The church probably had a modillion cornice in the beginning, but the present cornice is a renewal, as are the slates. The pronounced splay at the eaves of the roof is also present on the porch. In the repairs of 1928 a plate is said to have been found imbedded in the brickwork with marks indicating the windows and the main doorway as they are presently disposed. It is also said that a corner post of wood was found, at the same time, imbedded in the southeast corner of the east gable. A section of a cornice beam with a painted modillion that was removed in these repairs was later investigated and found to have originally belonged to a building of frame construction. Mr Harden deVoe Pratt of Tappahannock has, therefore, come to the conclusion that Yeocomico was originally a wooden building (erected on the same site or nearer the river), that later on its walls were bricked over, and that with the possible exception of the eastern extension these walls are *in situ* yet. Although these conclusions cannot now easily be proved or disproved, it may possibly be true "that the original studs are enclosed within the brick walls", but it may also possibly—or even more likely—be true that certain wooden portions of an earlier building were simply re-used in the brick building wherever suitable.

A silver-plated chalice that is owned by the church has probably been reworked from an old piece.

A remarkable sun-dial in the yard still gives true time, although it was given (or possibly made) by Philip Smith in 1717. Also in the large yard are five colonial markers, three of which are now illegible. Two of them are table-tombs and were moved here from "Wilmington" (in Westmoreland County) about ten years ago. These two and two of the others occupy a small mound east of the chancel. Other colonial graves without markers are also said to lie among the oak, walnut, hickory, and cedar trees within the brick wall. This wall is the product of several reworkings, and ferns are now growing in the oldest sections, which are undoubtedly very old. A frame vestry that once stood outside the west wall went to ruin by 1820. The present iron gates may derive from 1820, for iron gates are shown in an early painting.

The church is said to have been used as a barracks in the American Revolution and the yard as an abattoir. After the Disestablishment, the building was deserted and ready to fall down by 1812, when it was used by an American patrol. These American soldiers are said to have profaned the font as a drinking bowl, but they are also said to have instituted repairs of some nature. The Methodists later disputed the Episcopalians' possession of their own church, but were defeated in 1844. The Confederate Home Guard used the old fane in the War between the States. Repairs and renovations have been made in 1773, c. 1820, 1906, 1928, and 1958-59.

Many distinguished Virginian families have been represented among the communicants of Yeocomico Church over the centuries.

A single wall of Nomini Church, the third Upper Church (1757) of Cople Parish, at Mount Holly (about five miles northwest of Hague) is said to have been retained in the present (1852) building on that site. However, this cannot now be easily proved, for the whole structure is covered by a coat of stucco and has its long axis south to north. Ventilation holes seem to exist only on the east.

The parish's colonial glebe house still exists, though long in private hands, and is located (near Erica and a tributary of Lower Machodoc Creek) about ten miles from Hague.

When it is said that Yeocomico Church is fascinating, quaint, and artless beyond compare, it must also be said that it is equally perplexing, particularly as to its original shape and masonry. In view of the obvious reworkings of the east wall and the eastern, upper portion of the south wall and the change in bonds at various points, one is tempted to think that the Flemish portions possibly antedate the English portions of the church. It is also possible that the south wall as the principal wall (with the chancel and porch entrances) was originally laid in Flemish bond for beauty and the other three walls of the church laid in English bond for strength, as was often said to be the case when it came to the achievement of beauty or strength on these old walls. The difference in bond would also seem to indicate a somewhat later date of construction for the north wing. All this, however, would be difficult to prove one way or another.

As to architectural style, Yeocomico Church is often rightly cited as a transitional example—between Gothic and Classical. Indeed, it would be hard to find any colonial church with a greater number of Gothic features than are to be found at Yeocomico: the tracery motif of the semi-circles; the diapering; the chamfer and lamb's tongue mouldings; the battened doors; the wicket; the belt course; the brick ornaments (initials, emblems, and millstone); possibly the kick at the eaves; and the corbels and stepped gables (if original). While the greater part of the church, of course, owes a great deal to both the late Gothic and the early Classical manners of building, much of it also derives from the naïve and primitive skills and ways of its early artificers, who built and ornamented their church in much the same natural and God-fearing way as did many of their mediæval ancestors in the motherland; and, after all, even to-day Yeocomico is still a relatively remote spot that is blessedly not too much overcome by latter-day sophistication.

7. WARE PARISH CHURCH

The second Ware Parish Church stands in a beautiful grove of many and various trees (including cedars as well as flowering genera) on the south side of routes 3 and 14, about one and one-half miles east of Gloucester Courthouse. The parish is named for the Ware River. The date of the present building's construction has never been definitely established. For a long time the year, 1693, was given and this date is still to be seen on the historical marker near the county seat. However, more recent authorities are inclined towards the years, 1710-15, and base their conjecture on architectural evidence in the absence of documentary proof. The one certainty that exists is the fact that it was built during the rectorship (1679-1723) of the Rev'd James Clack.

The first Ware Church was built on the opposite side of the river, near the road leading into Ware Neck, and was probably standing by 1660.

Gloucester County was formed from York County around 1651 and has been reduced in area only at the formation of Mathews County in 1791. The four parishes of the county (Abingdon, Kingston, Petsworth, and Ware) were formed around 1656, apparently out of territory belonging to York Parish, which had been one of the early plantation parishes. None of these four parishes of Gloucester County were ever in colonial times reduced in area. Kingston Parish became coterminous with Mathews County at the latter's creation. Petsworth Parish ceased to exist in 1797, but it is still listed in records as a dormant parish.

Like its neighbor (Abingdon), Ware Church exhibits Flemish bond masonry of the highest elegance and most remarkable preservation. The same bond (with glazed headers) also carries below the water table. One of the interesting features of the brickwork is the ovolo water table, which, on the pedestals of the doorway jambs, turns into an upside down cyma reversa.

The dimensions of this fine rectangular church are no less than 80'-9" by 40'-9" outside the upper walls. The walls are 26' high to the cornice, and the roof has a 20' pitch. The walls are remarkably thick—four brick-lengths or over 3', above the water table—and may be compared in this respect only with those of the later (probably 1728) Christ Church in Lancaster County, where the walls are 35" thick. The foundations of Ware Church are 3'-9" thick above ground and the footings below are 5' thick.

The walls exhibit as great a variety of color in the bricks as they have fewness of repairs. On the north wall some repointing has taken place under the two easternmost windows, and a stove pipe has at one time been inserted. The apex has been replaced on both gables. On the west wall there are scaffolding or putlock holes and a crack down the middle. There are no obvious repairs on the south, although there are new foundation vents and a bad crack over the easternmost window. All the bevelled brick sills of the windows have been repointed.

Another distinctive feature of Ware Church is the fact that it is the only surviving rectangular colonial church that retains its original three entrances. Hungars Church on the Eastern Shore also once had doorways on both south and north as well as east, but its side doors were removed in the last century. It is probably the doorways, particularly the principal one on the west, that form Ware's greatest attraction. The west doorway has a semi-circular arch and, above this, a unique albeit somewhat primitive archivolt or projecting cornice. The archivolt consists of a cyma recta and a cyma reversa separated by a fascia. The arch itself contains voussoirs that alternate a whole brick over a half with a half brick over a whole. The pilasters alternate a pair of stretchers with five small bricks gauged in two sizes, and sit on pedestals.

59

The south and north doorways have triangular pediments. The top moulding of the raked cornice is now missing in each instance, but was originally a cyma recta. On the north pediment the next moulding is also gone, but the cyma reversa remains on the south. The other two mouldings are a fascia and a cyma reversa, and on the north these may be replacements. The horizontal cornice also has a missing upper course; the fascias and cyma reversa, however, remain, although at least one of the fascias may likewise be a replacement. The tympanum has been replaced on both pediments and many of the voussoirs on the south are new. Both entrances have flat arches. The voussoirs of the arches and the pilasters are arranged as on the west. The pilasters rest on pedestals.

Rubbed brick is used at the jambs and arches of all openings as well as at the four corners of the building.

There are two windows of double width in the east and five windows on each side of the church. The side doors are located west of the easternmost window in each instance. The circular window over the west doorway is a later addition. The voussoirs of the semi-circular arches of the windows are arranged as in the arches of the entrances. The use of queen closers at the jambs of the windows is as capricious here at Ware as at Bruton Parish Church in Williamsburg. On the south wall queen closers are found only on the left jambs of the four windows west of the south doorway and only at the bottom of the left jamb of the easternmost window. On the east wall, queen closers are used only on the right jamb of the left window, although seven are present on the left jamb of this window and two on the left jamb of the other great window. On the north wall they mark only the right jamb of the easternmost window and the left jambs of the three westernmost windows. Queen closers are also to be noted at the four corners of the building.

The wood doors and frames and the wood window sills and trim are replacements, although some of them may be old. The H-L and strap hinges and barkeepers on the west and south doors are colonial, however, as are many of the sash (of 16 over 16 lights with 6 in each fanlight) and many random panes of crown glass. The windows have enormously inclined sills. Guillotine windows still mark the chancel. The cornice and roof are modern, although the roof trusses are said still to be in good shape.

Although the interior has been greatly changed through the years, a few original fragments have remained. Among these is some of the colonial panelling (probably of wainscoting but possibly of pews) that now surrounds the upper part of the stairway to the west gallery and some that is also used on the soffit and door of the vesting room beneath these stairs. The columnar supports of the gallery may be old if not colonial. Three flagstones from the original aisles may still be trod on at the north entrance, and there are sixteen at the western entrance. In the original design, the church not only had two longitudinal aisles but also two cross aisles (the one between the side entrances and the other under the west gallery).

American infantrymen camped at the church in the Revolution. After the Disestablishment, the parish was inactive and the building somewhat abandoned until the church was repaired for worship again in 1827. The Methodists also used the building from time to time during this period. Ware Church was "modernized" in 1854, and this involved the extension of a wooden floor over the entire church, the removal of the flagstones and the box-pews, the addition of a new pulpit in a new location, and the re-arrangement of the seating plan. Federal troops also camped in the yard in the War between the States, and this required another set of repairs, which were, however, not undertaken until 1878. In 1902 a new slate roof and a plastered ceiling were installed; and in the 1930's considerable redecoration took place. A single devotional tablet is now located on the reredos and is said to have come from an old Baltimore church in 1878, but this tablet is not likely to be of colonial origin. The parish also owns other tablets of this set. To many persons, the present rather severe chandeliers are particularly jarring.

A row of tombstones lies under the present cross aisle. Represented among them are the graves of at least two colonial rectors (†1735 and †1758) and the wife (†1725) of one of these. The tomb of Parson Clack lies four feet east of the chancel wall.

The oldest part (about 160' square) of the churchyard is enclosed by a brick wall (with a semi-circular coping and a bevelled water table) that is undoubtedly of colonial origin, although the several gates are replacements. The yard is now enlarged by several almost sylvan acres on the south and west. In the northwest portion there are now a number of tombstones that have recently (1924, 1927, 1939) been removed from various plantations in the county by the Association for the Preservation of Virginia Antiquities. Among them are markers from 1703-69.

The parish owns two silver chalices and two patens of colonial manufacture. They were inherited by Ware Parish from the long defunct Petsworth Parish in the same county and bear the year markings for London plate of 1675-76. Their maker's mark—an I superimposed upon an S—represents an otherwise anonymous goldsmith who was registered as early as 1674-75. The name, John Sutton, has been suggested by one authority.

The vestry books of Petsworth (originally Petsoe) Parish for 1677-1793 and Kingston Parish for 1679-1796 have both been published. The original of the former book is kept at the clerk's office in Gloucester Courthouse and the original of the latter is on deposit at the State

Library in Richmond, as is the register (1749-1827) of Kingston Parish.

Although the charms of Ware Parish Church are not always so immediately apparent at first acquaintance as with some of our other churches, these charms are undeniable; and such interesting features as the "extra" doorway on the north, the great windows in the east, the enormous thickness of its walls, the unique archivolt on the west, and the considerable variation in color as well as the remarkable preservation of its masonry (after two and a half centuries) are not to be missed.

8. Bruton Parish Church

Bruton Parish Church is one of the celebrated churches of Virginia—and all America. Indeed, it undoubtedly welcomes more visitors than any other church in the Old Dominion, more even than Christ Church in Alexandria. It occupies the northwestern corner of the Duke of Gloucester Street and the Palace Green in Williamsburg. In colonial times—and in fact until 1880—Bruton Parish Church was located on the York County side of the line (which ran down the middle of the Duke of Gloucester Street at that point). From 1880 to 1884 all of Williamsburg was included in James City County. In the latter year, the town became an independent city. Williamsburg was known as Middle Plantation (midway between the James and York Rivers) until 1700, when it succeeded Jamestown as our capital and was renamed in honor of William III (of William and Mary).

The antecedents of Bruton Parish are also a bit involved. Middle Plantation Parish was independent for several years before 1658, but was originally a part of Chiskiack Parish. Both of these were York County parishes. In 1658 the Middle Plantation Parish was united with Harrop Parish of James City County to become Middletown Parish. In 1674 Middletown Parish and Marston Parish (a York County parish) joined together and became Bruton. The name of Bruton seems to have been derived from Bruton in Somerset, England, whence the Governor, Sir William Berkeley (†1677), and the Secretary of Virginia, Thomas Ludwell (†1678), came to Virginia.

Around 1660 a church (probably wooden) was built for Middletown Parish and in 1674 this building became the first Bruton Parish Church. It is possible that it was built upon the site of the present church, for traces of an earlier foundation were detected in 1905. The second Bruton Parish Church of 1683 was a Gothic brick structure with buttresses, the foundations of which were excavated in 1939, in the center of the present churchyard to the northwest of the existing building. This 1683 church was probably modelled upon the Jamestown Church and is remarkably similar in design and time to the Isle of Wight Church. It also seems to have had a lych gate and was repaired several times during its brief existence.

The original portion of the present (third) Bruton Parish Church was completed in 1715 under the rectorship of the Rev'd Dr James Blair, who was for many years not only the Bishop of London's commissary for Virginia, but also the president of the College of William and Mary. The original draught or design of the church was made in 1711 by Lt Governor Alexander Spotswood, who was also responsible in large part for the plan of Williamsburg, for the completion of the Palace, the gardens, and other buildings, and to some extent for the second form of the Wren Building of the College of William and Mary. James Morris was the builder of the church and John Tyler the overseer for the transepts. The building was paid for in part by the general assembly because the church had become the Court Church of Virginia in 1699 and, therefore, had to accommodate not only its own parishioners but the governor, the council of state, and the house of burgesses as well as the faculty and scholars of the College of William and Mary. The colonial custom of segregation by sex seems to have obtained at Bruton as elsewhere: the men on the north and the women on the south.

The church was originally 75' long on the inside from east to west and reached its present inside length of approximately 100' and outside length of 103'-9" only in 1752. (The outside length of church and tower (1769) is 123'-10½".) The transepts were in the first instance designed to be 19' long on the inside, but were ordered to be shortened to 14½' in 1712 (although the present exterior measurement is only a little longer than this latter figure). This shortening was owing to the fact that the lieutenant governor thought that the house of burgesses would be content with the smaller size—and probably also with the smaller cost, for the transepts were the responsibility of the general assembly. Governor Spotswood also promised in 1711 to take care of 22' of the church's length.

The transepts are 26'-1" wide east to west on the outside (and 22' wide on the inside) and the nave arm is 38'-10" long on the outside. The church's outside north to south dimension is approximately 62'. The chancel arm was originally only 14' long, but is now approximately the same length as the nave arm (actually a little over an inch shorter). The nave and chancel are 32'-10" wide on the outside (and 28' inside). The side walls of Bruton Church are 23' high and are 2'-8⅝" thick below the bevelled water table and 2'-5" thick above it.

The dimensions of Bruton Parish Church, the Wren Building, and other great edifices at Williamsburg were not casually determined, but instead were chosen according to a strict system of geometrical proportions involving such highly fancied Renaissance formulas as the Golden Section. An interesting analysis of Bruton's proportions has been made by Mr Marcus Whiffen in his *The Public Buildings of Williamsburg* (pages 80-82).

The present Bruton Parish Church is the oldest surviving cruciform church in Virginia, although this shape was not at all unusual later on in eighteenth-century Virginia. The last Elizabeth City Parish Church (1728) at Hampton, the Borough Church (1739) at Norfolk, and Mattaponi Church (probably 1730-34) in King and Queen County seem to have been modelled upon Bruton Church.

The brickwork of Bruton is laid in handsome Flemish bond (with glazed headers) above and below the water table. The pattern of glazed headers is more regular in the east, and on the east gable it is more regular in the lower portion than in the gable proper. The church seems once to have had brick ornaments, on the gable ends, but these were removed in 1742. One of the greatest tributes to the high skill of those responsible for the recent restorations of the church lies in the fact that no casual visitor is likely to notice the extensive repairs that have been made to the walls. Large cracks on both church and tower were remedied and iron braces installed in certain places before 1907, and around 1939 a great deal of the exterior brickwork was repointed or repaired where necessary. The mortar used in the most recent work was composed of cement, lime, sand, and bits of oyster shell to match the original mortar in color and texture.

In the chancel, the arches of the middle and west windows and the area below the east window on the south wall have been repaired, as have the large central area (replacing a door or doors) in the east gable (including a few bricks in the rim of the large wheel window) and the areas of the north wall of the chancel above the middle and west windows and below the middle window. The bottom four courses of the south wall of the chancel are also new. On the north wing, numerous spots of repairs and heavy repointing may be seen on the side walls. The arches of the large circular windows and the arches over the doors of both transepts seem to be replacements. Also repaired on the north wall of the north wing is a spot on the upper portion near the cornice on the west, and possibly another one where a small window would be expected to match that on the south (and east). On the north wall of the nave, the arches are heavily repaired; and on the south wall of the nave, there is some repointing. A few new bricks have also been inserted at the summits of the arches of these side walls of the nave.

On the visible portions of the west wall of the nave, there are repairs along the rake as well as some repointing elsewhere. On the south transept walls, there are repairs above the great wheel window and at both sides of the doorway arch as well as various areas of repointing. On the east wall of this wing, two new bricks mark the southeast corner, repointing occurs around the sill of the window, and a crack or two are evident, whereas, on the west, heavy repointing occurs in the lower right-hand portion.

Nine scaffolding or putlock holes on the south wall of the chancel and ten on the east wall are now used as birds' nests and shelters.

The tower has fewer patches of repair than has the church. On the south and north walls of the tower may be seen a very few bricks that have been replaced, and on the west a few obvious repairs include the bevelled bricks of the water table, which are mostly new. There appear to be no repairs on the small exposed portion of the tower's east wall. A new base-of-wall brick gutter has been added around the tower and church, for convenience' sake rather than after colonial precedent, although much evidence exists for such gutters elsewhere in Williamsburg.

If the casual visitor is not struck by the numerous altered spots in Bruton Parish Church's masonry because of the superb craftsmanship of recent work, the more assiduous visitor may for the same reason not easily detect all such renewed brickwork.

One of the most interesting and curious features of the building concerns the seemingly capricious use of queen closers in the jambs of the windows and doorways. There are none: 1) on the south chancel wall, on the right jamb of the west window or at the bottom of the right jamb of the east window; 2) on the north wall of the chancel, on the right jamb of the middle window; 3) on the north transept's east wall, on the right jamb; 4) on the left jambs of the middle and west windows in the north wall of the nave (save for three at the bottom of the left jamb of the middle window); 5) on the right jamb of the west window, on either jamb of the middle window, or on the left jamb of the east window in the south wall of the nave; or 6) on the left jambs of the windows in the east and west walls of the south transept. There are only a few queen closers at the bottom of the right jamb of the window in the west wall of the south transept. The queen closers on the left jambs of the middle window in the south wall of the chancel and the solitary window in the west wall of the north transept occur, as in several instances at Old Donation Church in Princess Anne County, at the ends

65

of the stretchers. This more or less cancels any ornamental effect that the queen closers may have. There are, of course, no closers at the circular windows. They do, however, mark all the windows of the tower, all three doorways (of church and tower), and the salient corners of both church and tower. They may likewise be seen on the inside jambs of the four openings of the tower (first storey) as well as below the water table.

A similar irregularity in the use of queen closers also characterizes the walls of Ware Parish Church, Gloucester County, and still other colonial churches in Virginia.

Rubbed brick marks all the arches and jambs of openings as well as the salient corners of the building. A recent, necessary chimney now exists on the exterior in the northeast corner of the crossing and obliterates brickwork at the two window jambs. This chimney seems to derive from the 1880's, but was rebuilt in 1938 despite certain architectural protests. The barge board has been cut back at all the gables. The modern heating system is of the forced warm-air type.

The west gallery is believed to have been built in 1715 and was in part occupied from 1718 on by collegians from William and Mary, many of whose initials were found carved on the handrail and turned balusters when layers of paint were removed in 1905 (and these initials are still to be seen). The stairs of this gallery were provided with a door, lock, and key; and the key was kept by the sexton. This apparently had less to do with the demeanor of the students than with that of the parishioners, who were wont to crowd the collegians unduly when the rest of the church was filled.

Series of Additions

Soon after the church's erection, there began a series of additions and enlargements. A gallery was built in the south transept by 1720, and in 1721 a gallery was added on the south side of the nave for the small boys of the parish. This latter gallery was extended in 1744. Major improvements and repairs were undertaken in 1742 and 1744, and these included new shingles and pews, relocation of the pulpit, raising of the floor, and whitewashing and painting of the interior. In 1752, 25' were added to the length of the chancel at the expense of the government, so that the chancel and nave arms became of equal length. The original length of the eastern end of the church was formerly marked by a boundary stone in the chancel, but this slab was moved (probably in 1938-40) to the choir's vestry in the crypt (where its east side is, according to its inscription, still 21' from the 1752 east wall). The original eastern foundations were uncovered shortly after the turn of this century.

The present handsome wall (with a coping of half-round bricks set on sloping bricks standing on end) was erected around the church-

66

yard by Samuel Spurr in 1754. The foundations of this wall were renewed and repairs instituted in or around 1937, although this was by no means the first instance of repairs to the wall, which is laid generally in Flemish bond. New steps and wooden gates have also been introduced in the most recent redoing, after the known examples at St Peter's Church in New Kent County as well as after common English practice.

At some unknown time, a gallery was provided in the north transept for colored servants, who entered through an outside covered stairway on the west wall of this wing. In 1755 an organ was bought and installed in a loft, the location of which has been a matter of some disagreement in modern times. A loft in the east, however, does appear to have been built for some purpose—also at some unknown time during the colonial era—and likewise to have had an outside covered stairway, which led up from the northeast corner of the chancel to a doorway in the east gable.

The 1755 organ was paid for by the colonial government, and Mr Peter Pelham was "unanimously appointed and chosen organist" by the vestry. Mr Pelham also served the community as jailer.

In 1769-71 the present tower was erected by Benjamin Powell to replace an already existing small bell-tower. It was erected as a separate structure, for the church's west wall has tooled mortar joints that could not have been raked after the building of the tower. Furthermore, the bricks of the tower are markedly different in color from those of the church and are of later manufacture: the church's bricks are, perhaps, more like peaches and plums, whereas those of the tower are more like apples. The theory that the Bruton tower may have been a "stump" tower (like that at St Peter's) does not seem to stand up, despite the step up as one goes from tower into church.

Still in use is the bell that was presented and inscribed as "The gift of Joseph Tarpley to Bruton Parish—1761". This seems to have replaced one given by Governor Spotswood in 1711 that had originally come off a wrecked ship. In a vestry note of 1685 a "steeple and a ring of bells" were proposed, but unfortunately the ring of bells was never secured and thus the first sounds of change-ringing on our shores were considerably delayed. In a letter of 1769 we learn that the church's organist had to practice his Felton, Handel, and "Vivally" [Vivaldi] with the doors open during the building of the tower, much to the pleasure of the church's neighbors.

In sum, the colonial building of Bruton was the result of a series of additions and enlargements that lasted from 1715 to 1769. Indeed, the vestry records would seem to "indicate an almost continuous state of roof and wall deterioration" throughout the eighteenth (as well as the nineteenth) century despite an equally "untiring agitation on the part of parishioners to keep the building in a state of good repair".

Remarkably enough, both the church and the Church survived the Revolution and the Disestablishment and continued in Anglican service. Repairs were made in 1827 and the pews were cut down in 1829. In 1838-40 a drastic re-arrangement of the church's interior took place when, in order to create a Sunday-school room out of the nave west of the easternmost pair of windows, the altar was placed against the east side of the partition between the new Sunday-school room and the crossing, a new door was cut into the east end, the west doorway was closed, and the tower room on the ground level was used for storing coal. At this time the pulpit, pews, and flagstones of the chancel and the aisles were also removed and the church was redone in the then modern style from funds raised by a church fair! Sometime before that date, the governor's pew had been removed.

The church served as a hospital during part of the War between the States and the rector held services in the rectory for a time rather than recite the prayer for the President of the United States as he was ordered to do while the town was in Federal hands. The building does not seem to have suffered unduly, however, although repairs were again made around 1886 when the walls were plastered and calcimined, the side lamps were replaced by chandeliers, and the pulpit gave way to a new pulpit, reading desk, and Table.

In 1905-07 the Rev'd Dr William Archer Rutherfoord Goodwin, who is so largely responsible for the initial efforts towards the restoration of all of colonial Williamsburg, conducted the first of the old capital's renovations at his own church. The foundations and roof-timbers were reinforced where necessary; the roof was shingled anew; and a reinforced concrete floor was laid. In addition to many graves, two large cannon balls and numerous unused army cartridges were found. The woodwork of the tower was also braced and its exterior panel-work put over the tin that was already on the tower before 1905. The dial-plate of a clock that is believed to have originally been used in the House of Burgesses and was placed in the steeple in 1840 was retained when a new clock was bought in 1905. The works of this new clock (made by Seth Thomas and dated December 5, 1905) were stored in 1938-40 in the lower wooden storey of the tower (where they still may be seen) and the plate removed to an undisclosed place.

The restoration of 1938-39 was also begun by Dr Goodwin (during his second period as rector of the church), but was completed by Colonial Williamsburg, Inc. Still further modifications, however, were made in 1940-42.

There are three large windows in each side of the nave and the chancel, and one in each side of each transept; and all these windows have semi-circular arches. Only one pair of windows marked the sides of the original chancel. The semi-circular arches alternate stretchers with pairs of headers, the outermost of each pair of headers being glazed. These windows have splayed sills. In the first of Dr Goodwin's renewals, "a door or window" (near the southeast corner of the chancel) is said to have been found and to have been bricked up at some previous date. A large Catherine wheel window is set in each of the three gables (chancel and transepts), ornamented by rubbed brick. Above the large window in the south transept and that in the chancel is a small circular window, consisting of a rubbed rowlock course, but none exists in the north transept, and no one seems to know why. None existed in 1886, according to a representation of the church in *Leslie's Illustrated* of September 29th in that year. The arches of the three large circular windows consist of stretchers alternating with pairs of headers. The arches of the four doorways—two in the tower and one in each of the transepts—are the same as those of the sixteen principal windows.

The modillion cornice of the church was believed in 1938-40 to be "largely original", although it had been variously patched through the ages. It was also extensively repaired in 1938-40, probably mostly in respect to the crown moulding. The cornice end-boards are replacements in the latest restoration and were modelled upon those at a tavern near Gloucester Courthouse. The roof of the church was covered in 1938-39 with cement-asbestos shingles that are similar in appearance to the original shingles of split cypress or cedar. The original trusses, purlins, and rafters of the church roof are largely intact, although structural reinforcements have been instituted at various times in the church's history, including both restorations.

Tower

The tower is 20'-1½" square on the outside and is approximately 100' high. Above the water table, the brickwork is laid in Flemish bond with random glazed headers, and below there is English bond (without glazed headers). The walls are 2½' thick above the water table and 2'-9½" thick below the water table. The brick portion of the tower consists of three storeys. At each storey on all sides except the east there is a window, although at the ground level there are entrances on the east and west. The arches of all these openings are the same as those of the doorways and semi-circular windows of the church. The room at the base of the tower is particularly interesting because it is one of the few instances with these towers or porches in which the details of the four arches of the openings can still be seen on the interior.

The octagonal, wooden superstructure of the tower consists of two progressively smaller storeys and a spire. A glazed window is set in each of the four principal sides of the lower storey, and an opening with wooden louvers in the same positions in the upper storey. A panel of applied moulding has been placed above each opening. All these openings have simple, flat heads. The small, concave roofs that separate the brick portion of the tower from its superstructure and also the two storeys of the superstructure from each other are once again shingled (with cypress), as is the conical spire (which terminates in a kick at the eaves).

The general contour of the steeple was considered at the most recent restoration to be authentic and its preservation may have been aided by the fact that it was sheathed in metal for some time until the metal was removed in 1938-40. Of the original woodwork in the superstructure, a number of fragments of corner boards, bolection mouldings (around the rectangular panels), panels, and vertical boarding were, indeed, authenticated, but an almost entire replacement of the exterior woodwork of the steeple was found to be expedient. Louvered openings were retained in the upper storey of the superstructure owing to evidence for them that was discovered in the old framing. The new louvered openings of this upper wooden storey were inserted in accordance with the existing indications in the framing members of that storey. Only one window frame of the superstructure is old (and probably original): that on the south side of the lower wooden storey. The others on that storey are modelled upon the single remnant.

Below the cornice, the tower appears to have had louvered openings for a hundred years or more, but windows were considered to be the more likely in colonial times. The windows in the brick portion of the tower are slightly smaller in scale than those in the church and have nine over nine lights (with four in each transom). The glazed windows in the lower storey of the superstructure are still smaller and have six over six lights.

The frames of the windows in the brick portion of the tower are original, but have been repaired. The sash and sills of all the tower windows are new.

The tower cornice is also all new and modelled chiefly upon the church's cornice, although the former has a more abbreviated crown moulding than that on the church and the tower fascia is wider (apparently because it serves as a base for the rising spire). This same cornice (albeit somewhat smaller and without the modillions) is also used at the shingled edges of the middle and upper roofs. If one stands beneath the tower on the west, one can see that the middle cornice is racked. Each of the wooden storeys also has sloping sides.

The framing of the tower was strengthened at the topmost roof of the superstructure, but basically the framing is intact albeit repaired wherever necessary because of decay or termites. The entire super-structure is now covered with shiplap siding. The spire is crowned with a weather vane and a finial. The weather vane is considered to be of 1769 and was repaired and painted in the recent work. Its compass points are, however, lost. The wooden finial, which is also believed to be old (possibly even colonial), was likewise recently repaired and painted.

Of the interior woodwork of the church, a great deal of the windows and window frames, the western doorway (leading from the church to the tower), and the railing, turned balusters, and framing of the west gallery are original, although some of the windows may contain colonial rather than original parts. Of the sixteen arched windows in the church, all have new sills, all have old frames that have been patched and repaired or pieced out, all have new stop beads and new interior trim, and all have new brick mouldings, although the other mouldings have in every case been repaired and patched. Of the transoms, ten are old but considerably repaired. In the case of the sash, the only completely new window is the middle window on the north side of the chancel. Every other sash, upper or lower, has been greatly repaired. The transom and sash that were formerly on the middle window of the north side of the chancel were moved in the most recent changes to the eastern window on the south side of the chancel. The upper sash in the windows of the north transept and the north wall of the nave are colonial and possibly original; the other sash (except for the single new window) may be colonial (or even in some instances original). These windows have twenty-one over sixteen lights.

The three great round windows have old, repaired frames. The sash of the east window was modelled upon the original window, which was removed in 1905 and still exists (though in too great a degree of deterioration for further service). The sash in the large circular windows of the transepts are believed to be colonial or original, although they have been repaired. Certain differences are to be noted between the east window and the transept windows. The former, which is somewhat larger, has an extra-wide muntin at the center that extends vertically and horizontally, whereas the latter two windows are marked by two heavy vertical mullions. The central part of each of the side windows has sash that operates, and the subdivisions of the windows are largely rectangular and approximately of the size of the panes of glass in the arched windows. The eastern window, on the other hand, is a wheel window composed of four concentric circles of small panes. Some old panes of glass have been re-used and all of the replacements are of English crown glass.

The brick openings of the small round windows on the south and east were extant in 1938-40, but the sash and frames are new. The window on the south had nineteenth-century louvers before the recent changes.

The doorways in the transepts and the outer doorway in the tower are modelled upon the colonial and probably original doorway that leads from the church to the tower. This inner doorway (on the west) has raised panels on both sides of the double doors. The panels on each door are: (from the top) horizontal, long vertical, horizontal, and horizontal. In the transom are two quarter-circle raised panels separated by a bead. The panelling in each instance involves: quarter-round, splay, quarter-round, and field. The church-side trim (of this inner doorway), which is old and probably colonial, includes (beginning at the wall) a fillet, a cyma reversa, a fascia, and a bead, whereas the trim on the tower-side (which appears to be recent) includes: fillet, cyma reversa, fascia, cyma reversa, fascia, and bead.

Among the original hardware still in existence are the strap hinges on the doors leading from the tower to the church and from the west gallery to the second storey of the tower as well as bar-hooks and catches on the former doors and two wrought-iron braces supporting the west gallery railing. An iron key that may have opened the door from the nave to the west gallery also remains, but is no longer in use.

A doorway that existed in the east as an entrance to a vestry behind the reredos for over a hundred years was removed at the most recent restoration. The large door from the west gallery to the upper portions of the tower may be very old, as also may be a part of the stairwell (from the gallery to the turn) that leads from nave to gallery.

The floors of the pews are largely old (although probably not colonial), whereas those in the balconies and sanctuary are new. The granolithic floor behind the reredos is of uncertain though relatively recent date and was retained by the restorers. The crypt was dug in 1905.

Of the various colonial galleries (other than the partly original example that remains in the west), only those in the chancel and transepts have been replaced. The latter were installed in 1905 (and replaced in 1938-39), but the eastern gallery derives only from the last renewal. The transept galleries were modelled upon the west gallery and, like it, are sloping. The fluted Tuscan (or Roman Doric) columnar supports are modelled upon the original examples in St John's Church, King William County, although at Bruton the bases of the fluted shafts occur above the height of the pew-rails and rest upon square posts.

The moulded plaster cornice is of recent installation and is not considered authentic by authorities on colonial architecture. Athough fragments of the old Purbeck flagstones exist, new stones were obtained from an old quarry off the coast of England in 1938-40 to replace the marble installed in the aisles at the earlier restoration. The paint in current use has been duplicated from granules of old paint that were found at the church.

Except for its liturgical disposition, much of the interior arrangement of Bruton Parish Church derives from the latest improvements and, particularly in the case of the chancel and the pews, represents somewhat of a compromise between colonial manners on the one hand and modern exigencies and inventions on the other hand.

When the plaster was removed in 1905, various wood nailing blocks built into the masonry walls were found, thus enabling the size and elevation of the colonial pews (as well as the locations of the sounding board, the supports for the canopy in the governor's pew, and the principal galleries) to be determined. The current pews are of pine, painted stone color with brown trim, in box style and are new. The moulded cap that surrounds the pew-enclosures derives from that at Christ Church, Lancaster County. In each of the large box-style pews of the nave, another bench has been inserted, so that, except for the second pair of box-pews from the crossing and except for the rear pew on the Gospel-side (which have but a single slip-pew each), the restored, panelled pews (fourteen in number) of the nave give the effect of a series of slip-pews, with every other bench (the front one of each pair) slightly shortened in length and with a door only for each pair. The sloping backs of the pews in the west gallery, which are old albeit not colonial, served as models for the intermediate pews and the other balcony pews. In each of the transepts there are four real box-pews (with seats on three sides) and a single slip-pew. The names of those honored with commemorative pews in 1907 were put on bronze plates outside the pew-doors; in 1939 these names were painted on the inside of the pew-doors.

The two progressively smaller pairs of choirwise pews to the east of the pulpit and the governor's pew were once used by parish officials, but are now assigned to the choristers and the organist. The rector's pew (with pulpit) on the southeast of the crossing still faces the governor's pew across the choir aisle as in the 1905 disposition, but the contents of these two great pews stem from the late 1930's. A new pulpit and reading desk have replaced the former three-decker pulpit of 1905, for the clerk's desk is—like the clerk himself—but a memory. The pulpit proper has been redesigned, with those of Christ Church in Lancaster County and certain English churches as well as examples in eighteenth-century books of design as models.

In the earlier (1905-07) arrangement of the governor's pew, an enormous silk canopy (with "Alexander Spotswood" lettered in gilt) hung over the governor's chair. A somewhat more chaste gold canopy now surmounts the governor's throne chair, which is covered with red cut-velvet on white satin. The governor's pew is distinguished by a brass rail (placed about 2′ above the top of the pew) with twisted iron standards and brass finials. From this rail is hung a curtain of pleated linen damask in "sacramental scarlet". A similar curtain hung on a brass rail also protects the organist in his pew just east of the pulpit and likewise adorns the east gallery. The cushions in the governor's pew (which is modelled upon a pew at Christ Church in Lancaster County) are also of scarlet damask; those in the nave and transepts are of rep—all of the same hue, as are the velvet seats in the cane chairs and kneelers of the chancel, reading desk, and pulpit. The kneeling pad at the altar rail is of the same scarlet, but is made of rep. Red tassels now hang from pulpit, reading desk, and governor's throne chair, and a red fringe hangs below the wood rail of the governor's pew.

Restored Chancel

The present chancel bears even less resemblance to that of 1905 than does the present body of the church to its counterpart in the earlier renewal, for the chancel at the most recent reworking presented to the authorities in charge well nigh insuperable problems, posed chiefly by the musical demands of the Service.

The 1905 arrangement of the church included a recessed chancel (with a circular window and a vaulted ceiling with coffers) east of a partitioning wall that extended from ceiling to floor on the sides of the chancel (except for a small door on the north and a similar opening with organ pipes on the south).

Although references to an organ gallery in the west in colonial times do exist and although this was certainly the more usual thing to expect, incontrovertible evidence seemed lacking and, indeed, to some persons seemed unlikely in the case of a large organ (such as was apparently bought by the parish) in so steep and shallow gallery as the original west balcony. On the other hand, architectural and documentary evidence points to the existence of the aforementioned northeast gallery, and traditional as well as pictorial information does exist concerning its outside stairway (later replaced—according to plaster marks found in the 1930's—by an interior stair). These arguments bolstered the decision to build an organ gallery in the east, although the universal sanction of the architectural authorities seems not to have been forthcoming.

Despite the fact that no vested choir sang in any of our colonial churches (whether near the chancel or in a gallery), Bruton Parish Church was not prepared at the recent renovation to surrender the leadership or beauty of its trained choristers. Furthermore, it was decided

74

that the choir at Divine Service was to enter its pews (east of the governor's pew) in procession from the direction of the chancel rather than through the nave or transepts. This required a spot for the formation of choir and clergy into a procession for the formal entrance. In addition, it was felt that the glare from the wheel window, which it was suggested may also have been annoying to some worshippers in olden as well as modern times, might possibly have been avoided somewhat in colonial times by the top of the reredos. With all of this in mind, the authorities decreed that the choir's vestry in the crypt be enlarged, the stair from the crypt to the chancel be retained, and the colonial reredos be reproduced, not against the east wall as in the general tradition of colonial churches, but against a partition 5'-9" west of the east wall. On each side of the sanctuary is a door for the use of choir and clergy. The space between the partition-reredos and the east wall is, therefore, a minuscule retro-choir for the formation of the procession. There is only a ladder for access to the gallery that has been built over this retro-choir as well as to the northeast and southeast galleries. These latter galleries are but spurs to the main, central gallery in the east.

Evidence indicating a gallery on the southeast as well as on the northeast seems also to have existed. An organ (1785) by Samuel Green of London has been purchased and placed in the middle of the east gallery. This, too, helps to eliminate the glare that seems to be more disconcerting at Jamestown and Williamsburg than elsewhere in Virginia. The decorative possibilities of the antique organ's case and pipes seem also to have been a determinant both for its location within the church and for the concomitant erection of an unprecedented central gallery in the east. The eastern galleries are marked by a panelled front with a light balustrade and railing and are in great part modelled upon the 1740-41 example that is still to be seen on the eastern side of the (original) south transept of St Mary's Whitechapel in Lancaster County.

Although the solution for the chancel at Bruton Parish Church has been beautifully executed, it is at best an elegantly executed compromise. Indeed, because of the arrangement of its chancel and pews, Bruton Parish Church is hardly the most representative of our colonial churches. Something more representative of a late colonial style might have been retained if only the spur galleries had been constructed in the east (with an antique organ on the northeast and choir stalls or chairs in the southeast), if the choir had been granted access from the crypt to its seats via one of the transepts rather than through the chancel, and if the reredos had been placed against the east wall and below the Catherine wheel. Beneath the side galleries of the chancel might have been built stairs as well as vesting rooms for the clergy.

The present reredos includes a segmental arch over the center panel

75

and six Ionic pilasters with fluted shafts and has been reconstructed from two carved oak Ionic capitals and part of a pilaster shaft (with fluting) that have been preserved from the original reredos as well as from a photograph of the old reredos that is extant. Certain parts of the reredos are also said to have been modelled upon a reredos in a northern Virginia church (though exactly which one seems not to be clear) and other parts upon old representations. In the three panels (the middle one of which is divided) are the Law, the Creed, and the Lord's Prayer, which have been painted in gold upon portrait canvas with colonial lettering. The wording of the tablets follows that of the Prayer-Book of the early eighteenth century.

The reconstructed Table is modelled upon the celebrated example at Yeocomico Church in Westmoreland County. The American Institute of Architects gave the church a high, caned, and carved arm chair of the period of James I for use as a bishop's chair (on the Epistle side); a second, identical one was later made and these now flank the Table. The other reconstructions include two credence tables in Jacobean manner as well as two litany-desks. The original chair is wholly or partly of black walnut, whereas the work of recent construction in the chancel is entirely of black walnut. In addition to the throne chair and gold canopy, the governor's pew is also adorned with an Oriental rug.

Owing to the fact that evening services were almost never held in our colonial churches and also to the fact that few of our modern churches can do without electricity, the lighting of any old church is never easy to arrange. In the late 1930's Bruton Parish Church seems to have been illuminated in part through holes pierced in the ceiling, but, at present, light for Evensong is provided only by candle sconces (with hurricane shades) fixed on the walls between the windows and by three chandeliers (one large and two small) in the chancel, although, of course, the parson and the choirmaster-organist are granted extra light for the reverent execution of their duties.

The Green organ is connected to the principal organ, which is an Æolian-Skinner that was rebuilt in 1955. The pipes are installed in the attic and their sound is introduced in grills over the chancel. The console is placed in the pew just east of the pulpit.

One of the most attractive features of Bruton Parish Church to-day has to do with its use of the seasonal colors, for almost alone among our churches it follows English tradition and freedom rather than the modern Roman scheme. The sequence of colors for Bruton Parish Church includes blue for penitential times such as Advent and Lent, red for more ordinary times like Epiphanytide and Trinitytide, and white or gold for festivals such as Christmas, Easter, Ascension, Whitsunday, and Trinity Sunday as well as for weddings, confirmations, and ordinations. The parish's first use of gold is said to derive from a gift of some sort made in the seventeenth century by Mrs John Page, the wife of the donor of the land for the church. The choir at Bruton also to-day wears blue cassocks.

Because it has fallen heir to two sets of communion silver in addition to its own, Bruton Parish is richer in colonial plate than any other of our churches except Augusta Stone Presbyterian Church. From the Jamestown Church have come to Bruton Parish Church an undated chalice and paten-cover (which were given to Jamestown in 1661); an alms bason that was made in London in 1739-40 (possibly by Thomas Farren); and a footed paten that was made in London in 1691-92 (probably by Benjamin Pyne) and was given to Jamestown by Governor Sir Edmund Andros. Like much else, this last piece was sold at the Disestablishment, but was returned from Mobile in 1856. These Jamestown vessels came to Williamsburg in 1758. Also in the possession of the parish is what is believed to be the seventeenth-century stone baptismal font from the church at Jamestown. From the Chapel of the College of William and Mary have come two fine silver-gilt pieces. Bruton Parish became the guardian of the William and Mary silver when the old college was transferred in 1906 from the Episcopal Church to the Commonwealth of Virginia.

Bruton Parish's own silver service was given by George III while Francis Fauquier was governor (1758-68) and consists of a chalice (1764-65), a cylindrical flagon (1766-67), and an alms bason (probably around 1765). Each piece is engraved with the royal arms ("G III R") and the "Honi soit qui mal y pense" of the Order of the Garter. The chalice and flagon were made in London by Thomas Heming and the bason is also probably of English manufacture.

The lectern in the north aisle was given in 1907 by President Theodore Roosevelt, and the Bible on it by King Edward VII. Also in the parish's possession are a Prayer-Book of 1729 (which is stamped "Bruton Parish, 1752" and contains certain Revolutionary glosses) as well as a Bible of 1753. The colonial parish register is likewise kept. A number of its pages have, however, apparently been torn from the book, for the baptisms extend from 1739 to 1797, whereas the deaths run from 1662 to 1761. (The records before 1674 belong to Marston Parish.) The Church also owns a Bible given by President Wilson and a Prayer-Book in which the Prayer for the President of the United States was emended on April 17, 1861, to be read for the Governor of the Commonwealth of Virginia.

Tombs and Graves

On the south side of the Tower interior are now four marble tombstones. One (from 1692) has been moved there from the churchyard; the others (from the first half of the eighteenth century) were moved to the Tower in 1906 from a plantation on the York River. There are, however, six persons represented by these stones in the Tower, in addition to Nathaniel Bacon sr (the councillor rather than the leader of the rebellion) (†1692), whose stone was moved to the north side from another York River plantation in 1938-40.

In the nave are four graves, two of which are of unknown persons and are unmarked, one of which derives from 1742, and the fourth of which is marked only by "P. G. Æ. 61". In the north aisle is Governor Francis Fauquier (†1768); and just north of this grave lies that of the patriot, Edmund Pendleton (†1803), whose remains and stone (as well as the remains of his two wives and a child) were moved to this spot from Caroline County around 1906. The only original colonial slab in the aisles of the nave or transepts is that of Henry Hacker (†1742). Under or near the choir aisle are Dr William Cocke (†1720) and Governor Edmund Jenings (†1727) as well as six others (only one (†1694) of whom is known and marked). The Rev'd Dr Goodwin was also buried in the chancel aisle in front of the pulpit in 1939.

Deeper in the chancel are four stones and eight burials ranging from 1719 to 1744, all of which except one ("R. P. 1730 Æ. 32") are known. These stones were undoubtedly put there while their graves were yet in the churchyard (before the church was extended and included them in 1752), for they lie east of the boundary stone of the 1715 church. The widow of one of the parish's early rectors was moved to the chancel from New Kent County in 1905. Also east of the boundary stone lie twelve graves of unknown persons as well as the stone of the Rev'd Mr Rowland Jones (†1688) on the north and the grave and stone of the Rev'd Mr Wilmer (†1827) on the south. Mr Jones's stone with its Latin inscription was moved into the chancel in 1905 from the yard. Those graves found by Dr Goodwin under the chancel were re-interred under the floor of the then new crypt. The only colonial stones in the chancel that are still in their original locations are those of Orlando Jones (†1719), the Blair children, and Mrs Monro (with two other Blair children). Old mural tablets include those for Daniel Parke (†1679) and Dr Cocke.

Within the church there are, therefore, no fewer than thirty-five burials that still lie in or close to their original locations (although nine or more of these were originally made in the churchyard east of the 1715 chancel). These are in addition to the five that have been moved to Bruton Church in this century from elsewhere in Virginia. The court and urban functions of Bruton Parish Church in colonial times are in no way more vividly evidenced than through these many graves and markers, scattered throughout the church and yard.

In the large churchyard are at least eight seventeenth-century graves and at least thirty-one eighteenth-century graves that are both identified and marked, as well as countless others from the colonial period that lie unknown or unmarked or both (and four colonial graves that have been removed from other places and reburied in this yard).

Among the tombs of the greatest sculptural interest are those of Governor Edward Nott (†1706), David Bray (†1731) and his wife (†1734), and Edward Barradall (†1743). The first two of these monuments are in the center of the yard (at the site of the 1683 church) and the last is to be found in the southeast corner. The elaborate, gadrooned chest-tomb of Governor Nott was set up in 1720 and is marked by trophies on the ends and curtains (above a skull) that are held back by cherubim on the sides. The marble Bray marker has an obelisk (supported by eagles' feet) above a base adorned with the Bray arms. The baroque Barradall tomb includes an enormous scroll splayed from each corner. Like all the other early tombs, these stones derive from England. The tomb of Colonel Page (†1692), who gave the present site to the parish, is now (as was mentioned above) to be seen in the tower and a recent tomb marks his grave in the yard, northwest of the tower and near the center of the yard.

Despite the large number of identified colonial graves in the yard, probably four times as many known burials date from 1776 to recent times, including those of Confederate soldiers (along with a Confederate monument). The yard has built up noticeably along the north wall of the nave. Concrete bases were built under all the tombstones in the yard and the markers themselves thoroughly repaired in the 1938-39 renewal. A few people have been buried in the Bruton yard in recent decades, even as late as 1956 (ashes have been interred as late as 1962), and a few other people apparently still have burial rights there. A sundial has been erected between the south wall and the tower: the shaft by Thomas T. Waterman in 1932 and the present gnomon by Colonial Williamsburg in 1962.

The George Wythe House served as the parish house from 1926 to 1938, when a new parish house was put into use.

The late historian, Douglas Southall Freeman, wrote in an introduction (1953) to a book on Virginia's old houses and gardens that "not a few of the historic gardens probably are lovelier to-day than ever they were in the eighteenth century". Others have said much the same thing of several of our restored churches, among them Bruton Parish Church, but it must be remembered that Bruton Church was the Royal Church and grew in stature as the Old Dominion grew. Thus, a bit of flamboyance is certainly not out of keeping here or in certain other colonial fanes (as witness such former, elaborate edifices as Petsworth Church in Gloucester County and Stratton Major Church in King and Queen County). Furthermore, the recent renewals at Williamsburg have been concerned with the later or High Colonial stages of Bruton Parish Church rather than with its earlier decades.

As a shrine, the church is as much honored for the early American patriots who were associated with it as for the fact that it is the oldest Episcopal church in the country in continuous use for Divine Worship.

9. Christ Church, Middlesex

The second parish church of Christ Church Parish in Middlesex County stands at the village named for it (Christchurch), about 2½ miles east of Saluda and the same distance southeast of Urbanna. The church and Christchurch School lie on the north side of route 33, not far south of the Rappahannock River.

The first parish church of 1666-67 also stood on this site. Christ Church Parish was formed in 1666 by the union of Lancaster (upper) and Peanckatanck (lower) Parishes. The united parish became coterminous with the county when the latter was established in 1669. The two earlier parishes had themselves been parts of still older parishes before their separate establishment.

The date of the existing building's erection (or at least the completion of its walls) is 1714. This date is to be seen on three bricks now placed in the tympanum of the modern vestibule on the west. On one of these bricks, "IH" (probably standing for John Hipkins, who did the carpentry, "plumbing", and glazing) is associated with the numerals; on another there is added "EC"; and on the third H or H. A fourth brick has "W. Johnson" on it. Mr. Hipkins's plumbing may have involved such lead fixtures as gutters and drainspouts and even "lead putty" for the windows. Alexander Graves, who did the masonry, seems not to be memorialized in his own handiwork.

The rectangular building (60' x 33½' on the outside) is laid in

Flemish bond. However, all four walls have been repaired from eight courses below the present cornice up to the top in each instance. On the south and west walls there is fine Flemish bond with glazed headers in the original portions, whereas on the other two walls the masonry possesses very few glazed headers. Indeed, these latter walls are reminiscent of those at the Lower Chapel of this parish in regard to their ruggedness. The walls at the Mother Church were ordered to be 2½ bricks thick above the water table, 3 below it, and 1½ in the gables. The ovolo water table has been variously repointed, notably on the south wall. Rubbed brick marks the corners of the building and probably once also marked the original jambs of the openings. Queen closers are to be seen at the corners and the window jambs, although on the south wall queen closers are in evidence only on the original eastern window (now second from the east). There are indications that the jambs of the south wall may have all been replaced or repointed.

There might possibly have been four windows on the north wall in the original instance, although none of the specifications for the three churches built within the same decade call for more than three on either side and the general recollection of the parish is that only three openings existed on the north wall prior to 1931. At any rate, there are now only three on the north, for a doorway exists where the fourth window (near the east end) would have been. Three windows were also ordered for the south wall, but now there are four, for the south doorway (leading into the chancel) has been converted into a window.

The side windows were probably originally 5' x 10' and were probably 10 to 11 courses higher at the top and 3 courses higher at the bottom, and in support of this are the several queen closers that are still to be seen above the ends of the present arches. In these replaced arches the extrados projects. The sides of the windows are splayed. The original arches were probably semi-circular, like the similar openings ordered and still in existence at the Lower Chapel.

The rows of queen closers still visible on each side of the present chancel window indicate the width (10') of the original great window. Inasmuch as the head of the arch of the original chancel window extended above the topmost course of the surviving original brickwork, no one can be absolutely certain of its shape. However, it is surely not likely that it was a Palladian window, as one authority avers, for this sophisticated adornment is a late manifestation in Virginia's colonial architecture. The end window in each of the sets of specifications for Christ Church Parish in Middlesex was ordered "to be from the arch within six foot of the sill, ten foot wide". This does not, as another authority has it, mean that the spring line of the arch was only 6' above the sill—a most unlikely dimension for a 10' width—but rather that the window was to be 10' wide and the height of the window was to extend from the bottom of the arch down to within 6' of the sill of the wooden floor. However, this, too, gives no clue as to the full height of the window. Perhaps, the best clues lie in the semi-circular arch still in existence at St Peter's Church (1701-03) in New Kent County and a similar one (for which there is still evidence of a semi-circular shape) at the Lower Chapel, both of which arches are also 10' wide and both of which are approximately 10' from the spring line of the arch down to the window sill (which is approximately 6' from the sill that supported the floor joists). It is also entirely possible that a double window, on the order of the example at Yeocomico Church (1706) in Westmoreland County or the pair of examples at Ware Church (probably 1710-15) in Glouces-ter County, also existed in the Christ Church chancel. This great window in the Christ Church chancel has, however, long been supplanted by a much smaller one.

If we are allowed to judge from indications at the Lower Chapel, the western doorway at the Mother Church was probably segmental. Despite certain plaster markings, the height of this opening is now in-determinate, although it was ordered in 1712 to be 8½' high. Its width (as ordered at that time) is still 5½'.

Although the south doorway was ordered to be 6'-4" x 3', this open-ing is now 4' wide, and it seems that a masonry opening 6'-10" x 4' would be required to take the usual trim and a door 6'-4" x 3'. The width (4') of the colonial opening is verified by the queen closers that mark it below the water table. A lower height for the south doorway in relation to the height of the side windows is still to be noted between the arch of the window that has replaced the original south doorway on the one hand and the arches of the other openings on that wall.

Inasmuch as a gallery does not seem to have been built in the west end of the nave in colonial times, one can only speculate as to whether or not a small window (like the present circular one or a bull's-eye as at the Lower Chapel) existed in the eighteenth century. According to the vestry orders, the building originally possessed clipped gables like those still to be seen at the Lower Chapel. The interior of the second Christ Church Parish Church and its contemporaneous Upper and Lower Chapels as well as one (and possibly two) of these churches' predecessors was distinguished by a rood screen, undoubtedly wooden, with balusters or tracery above the lower panels. Removal of a certain amount of plaster some years ago is said to have revealed a large square hole in the north wall about 12' from the east wall, which might have formed the seat for the large beam of the rood screen. The use of a rood screen seems to have been inherited by the 1666-67 churches of Christ Church Parish from the 1660 church at Middle Plantation (later Williamsburg), which served as their model. As a mark of Christ Church Parish's churchmanship, the fact has been pointed out that at the church and the two chapels of 1712-17 the chancel was ordered to be raised 6″ above the nave floor and the Communion Table raised 1′ above the chancel.

In the case of the parish church, it is impossible to state positively where the pulpit was and exactly how the pews (particularly those of greatest prominence) were arranged. The vestry orders of December 6, 1714 and an undated order immediately following that date called for the pulpit and two desks to be placed "in the alley . . . between the double pews" ("below the screen") at both the Mother Church and the Lower Chapel. However, the other requirements of that order could not in every respect have been followed at the Mother Church. For example, the two single pews "of three foot and an halfe wide each one of each side of the Communion Table" in all probability could not have been executed at the Parish Church because the south doorway of that building entered the chancel. Also, if the screen was only 12′ from the east end, as is believed to be true according to the recent, aforementioned findings, this would represent still another difference, for the changes of December 6, 1714 included a depth of 16′ between the rood screen and the east wall. Furthermore, these changes were never followed at the Lower Chapel, but were rescinded on the 3rd of January, 1715, less than a month later, and this change may have easily also affected the design of the Mother Church. Therefore, the pulpit is more than likely to have been located on the north side rather than in the central alley. In support of the northside view is the fact that, in the other specifications of the parish, the pulpits were all ordered to be on the north side "below the high pews" (except for the January 1715 order, which also placed the pulpit on the north side but "opposite to the south door"). This northern location at the parish church would seem to lie between the present second and third windows from the west rather than just west of the screen. The parish's vestry book is likewise confusing as to the ultimate arrangement of the pews, notably those close to the screen and altar. (However, the "two upper pews" that were ordered to be altered in April 15, 1762 may have been the same as the four "raised" pews of June 7, 1714 or the "two double pews" of December 6, 1714 and January 3, 1715.) This confusion and the fact that vestry books tend to mention orders issued rather than those executed or unexecuted make it impossible to offer categorical solutions, although a joint architectural-archæological survey made by skilled persons might easily turn up new evidence.

An interesting exception in regard to vestry books lies in a note of August 5, 1717, which is a complaint by the vestry "that the builders of the Lower Chapel are putting up inconvenient pews contrary to agreement and former orders of vestry"; this is followed by the vestry's further order that "the undertakers of the said building . . . pursue the orders of vestry relating to the pews in the said chapel".

All of the church's interesting interior (as well as the upper walls, gables, and roof) was, however, long gone when the church was reconstructed in 1843. The building was abandoned after the Disestablishment and by 1843 trees and earth had taken such possession that it must have looked then much as the ruins of the Lower Church of Southwark Parish in Surry County do to-day. Gone also by 1843 were the cupola or bellcote (first ordered in 1718), the stone aisles (1731), and the churchyard wall (1733). The pews had been re-arranged in 1762; these, of course, had also vanished. In 1843 the chancel was made into a vestry, the large chancel window was reduced, and the vestibule added on the west. The chancel has since been recovered. Further remodelling was undertaken in 1900 and again in the 1930's. About 1931 the sacristy was added on the northeast, a doorway was inserted in the eastern end of the north wall, the doorway on the south converted into a window (with the frame of the former north window), and the chancel newly floored. At some time chimneys have been added (but only on the top of the building). The present flagstones (down the central aisle only) derive from the former Upper Church (1773) of the parish at Churchview and were bought in 1931 for $265.00. Recent restorations include a chandelier, a Holy Table in Queen Anne style, and chairs for the chancel. The handsome walls around the spacious and beautiful churchyard, with its many trees and shrubs and sylvan background, were erected by the Garden Club of Virginia in 1942. The colonial churchyard walls embraced a much smaller area.

The story of the colonial silver of Christ Church Parish is of absorbing and even poignant interest. During the trying days of the early part of the last century when the parish was dormant, the silver of its Lower Chapel was kept by one of the parish's communicants until she moved from the county and lent it to a church in Richmond. When Christ Church Parish was revived in the early 1840's, the Lower Chapel silver was duly returned to the parish according to the stipulations of the loan. However, the vestry then sold the Lower Chapel silver to St Paul's Church in Richmond in 1846 because the parish still had the five pieces of the Mother Church's set (which is thought to have been given in 1687). This latter set had been in a vault of a Fredericksburg bank for over three decades after the Disestablishment. Following its return to Middlesex County, it was damaged by fire. S. Kirk and Son of Baltimore "remoulded" three pieces—chalice, paten, and alms bason—and it is assumed that these three pieces were fashioned anew out of the old silver.

The Lower Chapel silver, which is still regularly used at St Paul's Church in Richmond, includes a flagon and a paten-cover made in

1718-19 by John Backe of London and an alms bason made in London in 1721-22 (with the maker's mark now indistinct). The inscriptions vary between the earlier pieces and the bason, for on the former two there is "A Gift to the Lower Chappell in Christ Church Parish", whereas the bason is inscribed as "A Gift to ye Lower Chappel in Christ Church Parish 1722". The purchase of these three pieces by the vestry of St Paul's is also inscribed on each of the vessels, as it likewise is upon one of two chalices owned by St Paul's Church. This last is an enigmatic piece of silver, for it bears in somewhat irregular fashion both eighteenth-century English and 1805 New York marks. Some part of this chalice is probably colonial, but it is difficult to say just what part derives from Christ Church Parish. The second chalice, which is also inscribed "Christ-Church", is a copy (of the earlier chalice) that was made in Richmond by Charles Lumsden and Sons, a firm that was in business from around 1890 to around 1930.

Likewise of unusual interest is the fact that the colonial parish's vestry book is the only extant one that antedates Bacon's Rebellion of 1676: it begins with 1663 as the record of Lancaster (upper) Parish and continues as the book of the united Christ Church Parish from 1666 to 1767, although the seventeenth-century records were copied into a new book in 1701. The old documents are now on deposit in the State Library at Richmond, but, through the benefaction of Mrs Charles Beatty Moore, are available in published form from the rector at Christchurch. The Parish Register of 1653-1812 with certain recent additions may also be seen in the State Library.

A fragment of the colonial marble font is now the possession of Mr Carroll C. Chowning of Urbanna.

On the south and east sides of the church is a superb array of large tombs, most of which are colonial, although several derive from the early decades of the republic. Six of them are very large, indeed. Three have enormous scrolls splayed at the corners. Several others are equally elaborated with fluting or ellipses, fans, and leaves. This Rappahannock area is rich in striking tombs, for across the river from Christchurch several noble examples exist at both of the colonial churches of Lancaster County. Unfortunately, these monumental sculptures in Middlesex are in wretched condition: most of them are undecipherable, several are broken or cracked, and others lie in utter fragments, particularly among the tombs of the east. A series of fragments also lies, almost in a heap, on the south side of the church among several of the great chest-tombs. It is sad to note that as long ago as 1913 Mr Chowning, in a published lament about the condition of these tombs, reported that "part of the splendidly carved tombs have been removed to make boundary markers for land in the community".

In view of the fact that so little of Christ Church's original self remains and so little has been restored, it is a bit hard to explain the undeniable appeal that the old building still possesses; the fact remains, however, that in few of the many other colonial churches of Virginia is the longing for "the snows of yesteryear" so appropriate as with this delightful and venerable house of God.

10. LOWER CHAPEL, MIDDLESEX

One of the most interesting of our less well-known colonial churches is the former second Lower Chapel of Christ Church Parish in Middlesex County, which the Methodists have for some time called Lower Church. The building lies just south of routes 3 and 33, 2.8 miles east of the junction of those routes and only a fraction of a mile east of the present post office of Hartfield.

The existing church occupies the same site as the first Lower Chapel (c. 1665-1666) of the parish. The first chapel also possibly served as the Peanckatanck Parish Church until that parish united with the upper parish of Middlesex County (named, confusingly enough, Lancaster Parish) in 1666. The Methodists have recently adopted the name of Piankatank Parish for their circuit of churches served by the minister of the present Lower Church. The spelling of this Indian name, given to a river as well as to a church, occurs in over a dozen forms in the colonial vestry book.

The date of the church's completion is 1717. A dating brick on the left of the west doorway (about 7' from the ground) is marked "17A15" (although the "5" is poorly outlined) and this is taken to indicate the completion of the walls to that height by 1715. The "A" possibly represents a Mr Armistead, the builder. Another brick, on the opposite side of this doorway, is marked "I:W" (possibly for James Walker, an overseer for the vestry), although the first part of this inscription is not clear. Mortar remains in part of these carvings, which are similar in style to those at the Mother Church at Christchurch. Other initials at the Chapel include a "B" on the east and "IG" and "TG" on the north.

The brickwork is laid in English bond above and below the water

86

table. This is one of the building's distinctive features, for on our colonial churches the only other English bond to be seen is at the Jamestown Tower, St Peter's Church in New Kent County, and part of Yeocomico Church in Westmoreland County. There are random glazed headers at Lower Chapel, and even some glazed stretchers, although there seems never to have been any rubbed brick. The bricks are large and the walls are nearly 27" thick. A setback is clearly evident on the wall above the west gallery. These walls, with their great variation in color, give an impression of ruggedness rather than beauty. The dimensions of the edifice are 56' x 34' on the outside.

The ruggedness of the masonry has undoubtedly contributed to its continued soundness. There is, however, recent (and rather poor) repointing below the bevelled water table on all four sides. On the west may be seen concrete spots at the corners, and also two scaffolding holes; and on the south a modern chimney and basement window. Repairs have been made on the east above the water table. On the north wall, large modern ventilation holes have been added to the colonial (vertical) ones, which also may be seen elsewhere on the building.

Of the original doorways (west and south), very little can be seen. The details of the south doorway were covered by plaster when the annex was added. On the west, only small portions of the arch can be seen above the existing later porch. The arch seems, from a ground view, to have been segmental.

There are now three large windows on each side (the south door opening between the eastern and middle windows). Each of these has a semi-circular arch, alternating a full brick with two halves. These arches are in good condition, although a single brick has been replaced in the east arch on the north side. Queen closers mark the jambs of these six windows (as well as the west doorway and the corners of the building). From these queen closers one can infer that the windows have probably been lengthened by one or two courses. They are, therefore, now 5' x 11', but originally were probably 5' x 10', as ordered in 1714. There is also an elliptical (or bull's-eye) window high up in the west gable, with a rowlock course for its arch (in which there is still evidence of glazing). The large window ("from the arch within six foot of the sill, ten foot wide") in the original chancel is now gone and its place has been taken by a frame chancel recess, which can hardly be said to add to the church's beauty. However, evidence of the original window's semi-circular arch still exists on each side of this frame recess. One can easily detect both the spring-line of the arch and the queen closers of the jambs. The sill of the original window occurred about 6' above the probable level of the wood sills upon which the floor construction rested. From the probable sill of the window to the spring-line is approximately 10'.

Another of Lower Chapel's distinctive features lies in its clipped gables, which are still seen under the modern roof of sheet metal. Besides this example, only the solitary one at Augusta Stone Church in the Valley survives in Virginia, although Westover Parish Church in Charles City County and Chuckatuck Church in Nansemond County are among those churches that once possessed clipped gables. Lower Chapel also has the kick at the eaves that one recalls from Merchant's Hope Church in Prince George County as well as from later churches.

Although Lower Chapel, like the Mother Church and the Upper Chapel, also had a rood screen, this and all the other distinctly Anglican details of the interior have long been gone. In fact, all of the interior and the furnishings (except for one remarkable example) vanished in the nineteenth century, as did the churchyard walls of 1733 and the flagstones of 1731. An interesting feature of the modern interior is presented by the window seats, for they would seem to indicate that all of the wall below each window has been removed except the outermost courses. The present gallery seems to be a replacement for the gallery that was added around 1750, but the date of the replacement is unknown.

The Chapel seems not to have survived the Disestablishment as a place of active worship, although it is said to have been used by Baptists and Methodists as well as for a school during part of the early 1800's. The building is also reported to have been bought by a Methodist in 1857 and presented by him to his co-religionists, who have worshipped there ever since. The various repairs and additions of recent times have included the west porch (in the late 1920's), the annex on the south (1946), the chancel recess (1912), the partition under the gallery, the new gallery itself, and other interior woodwork as well as a modern ceiling and a succession of new floors. The roof trusses are said still to be sound.

When one of the new floors was installed in this century, a 1687 tomb from the aisle of the first Lower Chapel was discovered. This marker now lies flush with the floor near the south door. Two other colonial tombs of 1726 and 1727 may also be seen in the yard just east of the chancel recess. Although their inscriptions are no longer legible, they probably represent more than one burial in each instance. A number of other but unidentified colonial graves also lie in the churchyard.

The Lower Chapel colonial silver has been owned by St Paul's Church in Richmond since 1846.

The solitary remnant of the Chapel's colonial furnishings is a splendid chest for the communion plate and linen, which has been dated through both documents and style as around 1677 in origin. About 5' long, 2' wide, and 2½' high, it is constructed of solid oak, with side and back panels and bottom of poplar. The raised and moulded panels on the front and the rails and corner posts are entirely carved with primitive

88

designs. A gadroon motive marks the upper rail, and interlocked lunettes and leaf-figures mark the bottom rail. The four vertical panels are identically carved—and with considerable elaboration. The three stiles and corner posts contain two columns of opposed crescents separated by a column of "buttons". The lid is held by two hand-wrought iron strap hinges; only a part of the hasp of the lock that was provided in 1762 remains. The chest is at present, probably unwisely, being used as an altar.

11. VAWTER'S CHURCH

Vawter's Church stands in Essex County on the north side of route 17, .5 mile west of the hamlet of Loretto and about 12.5 miles southeast of the junction of routes 17 and 301 near Port Royal. Vawter's Church is the second Upper Church of St Anne's Parish, which was created in 1704 out of Sittingbourne Parish. This latter parish and Farnham Parish were formed in 1661 and, like Old Rappahannock County (which was coterminous with their combined boundaries), each of them included territory on both sides of the Rappahannock River. Out of the western portion (also lying on both sides of the river) of Sittingbourne Parish was created, around 1677, St Mary's Parish. The name of Sittingbourne Parish was retained in 1704 by the portion of the parish remaining on the north side, but in 1732 it ceased to exist when its upper part was combined with Hanover Parish in King George County and its lower section became part of the new Lunenburg Parish in Richmond County. Rappahannock County also ceased to exist when it was divided into Essex and Richmond in 1692.

The first Upper Church of St Anne's Parish was probably in existence sometime between 1704 and 1711 and was undoubtedly of frame construction. There were two Lower Churches in the parish in colonial times. A frame church that was standing on Occupacia Creek as early as 1664 or 1665 became the first of these Lower Churches of St Anne's in 1704, and was replaced sometime between 1721 and 1739 by the second Lower Church. This latter church was known as Sale's Church because the land represented a donation from Cornelius Sale.

The original portion of the church near Loretto is believed to have been built around 1719 and the south wing was added in 1731, as a brick above and to the right of the south doorway attests. Other supporting evidence in regard to the addition of the south wing lies in the fact that the windows of the nave and the wing are so close to each other at the corners that the shutters overlap, and also in the slivers of flagstones that have been used at the junction of the T. The name, Vawter, is derived from that of a family whose land adjoined the site of the church when it was built, but just when this name was first used with the church seems to be uncertain.

The outside dimensions of the original rectangle are 56'-6" x 30'-2". The wing is also 30'-2" wide and projects 16'. The (former) nave extends 16' (on the south side) from the southwest corner to the wing, and the chancel arm extends about 10'-3" (on the south side) from the southeast corner to the wing. The walls are 2' thick. The brickwork of the church is laid in Flemish bond above the bevelled water table and in English bond below it. Glazed headers abound on all of these superbly laid walls, and a few glazed headers are also to be seen below the water table.

The excellence of Vawter's masonry is equalled by its splendid state of preservation. On the west wall of the nave there are some small repairs below the water table and just above and to the left of the pediment, in addition to repointing at the apex of the lofty gable. On the north wall of the church there is a bit of repointing along the water table and the several courses above it. Two cracks above the westernmost window and two spots that once held stove pipes have been mended. Cracks above and below each of the windows on the (former) chancel or east end have also been mended. Repointing and repairs (mostly on the right side) mark the apex of the east gable; both corners of this wall have also been repaired below the water table. A spot of repaired masonry exists in the center of this east wall, and there is repointing in the sill of the left window. On the short, south wall of the chancel there is repointing above and below the window as well as repaired work at the corner below the water table. On the (original) nave portion of the south wall, repointing is to be noted above the window as well as below the water table, and two or three headers have also been replaced.

On the south wall of the south wing there are repairs for a bad crack above the doorway and another crack above the left window. Repointing on the east wall of the wing is to be seen above and below the window and near the corner; on the west wall of the wing there is repointing above the window, and one or two headers have been replaced.

These replacements are all, however, minor in comparison with those on most of our colonial walls. Among the striking features of this masonry are the rows of glazed headers along the barge boards of the three gables and the glazed headers in every other course next to the pilasters of the south doorway. These latter headers also produce a vertical series of slightly staggered stretchers on the left of this doorway.

Rubbed brick marks both doorways, the salient corners above the water table, and the jambs of all the windows. Queen closers are used on: 1) the inside jambs of the two small windows; 2) both jambs of the south wall of the (original) chancel; 3) the upper half of the left jamb and all of the right jamb of the south window of the east end; 4) the upper half of both jambs of the north window of the east gable; 5) both jambs of the easternmost window and the right jamb of the next to the easternmost window on the north wall; 6) the salient corners (even below the water table); and 7) the sides of the pilasters of the west doorway. Queen closers are also to be seen at some of the ventilation holes, and a single one marks the north wall's westernmost window. The bottoms of the ventilation holes are still to be seen two courses above the ground.

The western doorway is surmounted by a segmental-arched pediment. The raked cornice includes cyma recta, cyma reversa, fascia, and cyma reversa mouldings. The horizontal cornice omits only the cyma recta. The tympanum is laid in Flemish bond with glazed headers. The horizontal cornice breaks out over the pilasters to form an embryonic abacus, and the capitals are formed by the cyma reversa mouldings of this cornice. The pilasters are made of the usual three sizes of rubbed brick. The bases of the pilasters consist of the bevelled brick course and the projection at the water table. The bevelled water table turns and runs downwards to within three courses of the ground. The rudimentary pedestals also stop within three courses of the ground.

The arch of the western doorway is semi-circular and consists of full bricks and pairs of half-bricks, which are also used down both jambs. The lower jambs are marked by glazed headers and very small queen closers. Ten bricks in the center of the arch are replacements, as are five bricks in the lower cyma reversa moulding of the horizontal cornice. These latter bricks may possibly have replaced a keystone.

The south doorway has a triangular pediment. The uppermost moulding of its raked cornice was a cyma recta, but it is now missing. The existing mouldings on both the raked and horizontal cornices are two cyma reversas separated by a fascia. The tympanum is exactly like that on the west. In the flat arch of the doorway, each voussoir has rubbed brick of three sizes, and at least three of the voussoirs have been replaced. The jambs, likewise with three sizes of brick, are rudimentary pilasters in that they project. They do not, however, have capitals, although they do possess bases.

Both doorways very probably in the original instance possessed stone or brick stoops, and in support of this is the fact that in both cases the projections stop several courses above ground. The stoop on the west was possibly semi-circular.

There are four large windows on the north side, two on the east wall, and one on each side of the wing and in each section of the original church's south wall. In addition, there are two small windows on the south wall of the wing at the gallery level. The arches of the large windows are semi-circular and are marked by full bricks alternating with pairs of half-bricks. Bricks replaced in the arches include: 1) one in the east window of the wing; 2) three in the west window of the wing; 3) one in the south window of the chancel (east) wall and five or six in the north window of the same wall; 4) one or two in the south window of the chancel's south wall; and 5) one in the easternmost window and two in the westernmost window of the long north wall.

All the large windows are splayed at both the sides and the top. All the windows have sloping brick sills. It is not known just when chimneys were inserted on each side of the wing, but they are of late date. The two small windows in the south gallery have arches that consist only of a rowlock course, and they may possibly have been repaired. They are shallow segmental arches with flattened ends. These windows are splayed only at the sides.

The modillion cornice may possibly be original. The steep roof has a slight upturn at the eaves and is unfortunately now sheathed in metal. The original roof trusses are believed to be largely intact.

Original Doors and Frames

Both sets of door frames and the western doors are apparently original, and the south doors probably are colonial (although the moulding around the raised panels of the south doors appears nineteenth-century in character). On the western doorway, the top of the semi-circular wood trim may not be so old as the rest of that remarkable doorway's wood-work, but it, too, is very old and very probably colonial. The mouldings on the trim include: cyma reversa, fascia, possibly another cyma reversa (now obscured), fascia, and bead. The whole architrave is put together with wooden pegs, but no pegs mark the doors themselves. Each of the doors on the west has four raised panels: (from the top) small horizontal, long vertical, small horizontal, and long vertical. The fixed panel above the doors allows the doors to be square-topped, and the fixed panel itself has two quarter-circle raised panels. The overlapping bead along the edge of the left door is carried up the center of the fixed panel. The moulding on the panelling includes an ovolo and the raised field. On the inside of the doors are a bar and its supports as well as large H-L

92

hinges, all undoubtedly original. Nails rather than pegs are used on the doors. The sides and tops of the plaster reveal are splayed.

The mouldings of the door frame on the south include a large bullnose, a bead, a deep and flat reveal, a cyma reversa, and a flat door stop. The four panels of each of the south doors are: (from the top) small horizontal, medium-sized vertical, small horizontal, and long vertical. There is no fixed panel above. However, the panels are raised only on the inside and this leads one to the conclusion that these doors have at some time been reversed, for the raised panels were probably intended for the outside in the original instance. The fact that the raised panels seem never to have been exposed to weather probably indicates that the doors were reversed in the initial installation. An overlapping astragal exists here, as do large H-L hinges on the inside. There is a new rim lock. The panel moulding on the south doors is actually more characteristic of the nineteenth century than of earlier times and is similar to the mouldings on the flat panels of the clerk's desk. This fact, along with the aforementioned reversing of these doors, makes one less certain of their antiquity. The sides of the doorway on the interior are splayed.

The wood trim of the windows is possibly original. The windows themselves with their muntins and most of the lights are certainly old and undoubtedly colonial. The wood sills may also be original except for three new ones: 1) on both windows in the south wall of the original church; and 2) on the north window in the chancel (east) end. The lights in the large windows are nine over nine, with four in each fanlight. The little windows have six over six lights, and the top sash in each instance is segmental-arched. On the interior these windows are slightly recessed at the lintels and splayed at the sides. The shutters of board and batten for the church's various windows have H-L hinges and are in all probability colonial.

Much of the interior of Vawter's Church is also of colonial origin, although some of it derives from 1827. The flagstones of the nave and wing aisles are probably original. The chancel was moved from its original position in the east, in all probability, at the time of the revisions of 1827. The bricks of the chancel floor were replaced by flagstones in the easternmost section of the aisle only in 1925. The aisle under the west gallery is likewise not of colonial origin. Remnants of a brick floor are said to lie under the present wooden floors of the pews. The current slip-pews with doors are composed of original benches and sides, but were cut down in 1827. Irregular re-use of the raised panels when the pews were lowered may be seen in a number of instances, notably in the east end. The portions of the pews that may be seen under the benches were derived from the old pew-sides, too. The caps of the present rails are probably original and the original H-hinges are still in use.

The pulpit may always have stood against the north wall between the pairs of windows as it does now, but the old three-decker pulpit was removed and a Table put beneath its replacement in 1827 (under the influence of Bishop Hobart of New York, who is known to have visited in the neighborhood as a young man). Portions of the present pulpit— such as the primitive reeding around the front of the pulpit itself and the front and back (with crude raised panels) of the clerk's desk—may come from the colonial pulpit. The pulpit is now reached by a stair from the west; access to the reading desk (on a landing) is from the east. The furnishings are not old, although a part of what is believed to be the colonial (after 1724) font is now used as a door stop.

The flat ceiling is presently sagging in spots. The walls are plastered. The west gallery, with its floor on three levels, seems to be original, although the rails and pickets on both galleries appear to be from the nineteenth century, as does the chancel rail. Both sets of stairs are apparently old, but the partition beneath the west gallery probably derives from 1827. The raised panelling along the south stairwell and gallery-siding is probably original, but it was installed in this manner when the pews were cut down. The south gallery floor is probably more recent in origin than is that of the west. The fronts of both galleries with their series of simple mouldings may easily be colonial if not original. The west gallery is said to have been used by slaves and the south gallery by singers because the slaves did not need to read the metrical psalms and, therefore, did not need the extra light in the south gallery.

Vawter's Church owns a silver communion service made in 1724-25 by William Pearson of London. All of it except one chalice was stolen, apparently during the War between the States. However, two pieces—a paten and another chalice—were returned to the parish in 1909 through the keen eye of the then chatelaine of a nearby plantation, "Elmwood", who spotted them in a collection in the North. Each of the pieces is inscribed "St Ann's Parish Essex County". The flagon has never been found. The parish also owns a Bible that was published at Oxford in 1739 and is presently kept in the South Side Bank at Tappahannock.

The yard is most notable for two colonial gravestones (1761 and 1764) in the east, an unidentified slab and fragment in the northeast, a number of cedar and walnut trees, a parish house (1961), and a bay-berry hedge (also 1961) along the main highway.

After the Disestablishment, the church seems to have been unused until around 1814. Vawter's was one of the few churches to be somewhat saved from the generally severe sequestration imposed in Virginia after the Revolution. This was owing to claims made by the Garnett family that the church stood on land that the family had bought. Regular services at Vawter's Church seem not to have been resumed, however, until 1822. The interior was redone five years later. The church apparently did not suffer physical damage during the Revolution, the War of 1812, or the War between the States. The colonial glebe house of St Anne's Parish still stands about six miles from the site of the church on Occupacia Creek and is nearest to Chance Post Office. The property was seized and sold in 1803.

The resemblance of St Anne's Parish Church to St John's Parish Church in King William County—particularly as to the doorways—has been noted. Although neither of these churches is by any means so well known as are a number of our other colonial fanes, the splendid doorways of Vawter's and its apparently original wood doors and frames—there are, after all, only a very few original doors left in all of Virginia's colonial churches—as well as the superb masonry and state of preservation of its walls and the large amount of original or colonial work on the interior give this somewhat unpretentious building an undeniable authenticity that few other such churches can equal.

Mount Church Organ

In 1713 the name of St Mary's was retained by the southside parish when the parish was divided at the river and the northside parish became known as Hanover Parish. St Mary's Parish, therefore, lay entirely within Caroline County when this county was formed in 1728 from the uppermost portions of Essex, King William, and King and Queen Counties (although three other parishes lay partly or entirely within Caroline County at the time). One of the most interesting survivals from the interiors of our colonial churches belonged to the second parish church (1748) of St Mary's Parish, which was known as the Mount Church (from a nearby creek of that name) and which from 1810 to 1835 housed the Rappahannock Academy. The site of the Mount Church and the academy lies five miles west of Port Royal on route 17.

The interesting remnant of the Mount Church is an early pipe organ, which was sold first by 1810 to Christ Church at Alexandria, next to the Episcopal Church at Shepherdstown in West Virginia, and then about 1863 to St Thomas's Church at Hancock, Maryland. This last church gave it to the Smithsonian Institution in Washington around 1905.

A sign (concerning this organ) that may be seen at St Peter's Church in Port Royal is a bit confusing, for, although the organ is, indeed, a very old instrument, it is not the oldest example of an organ imported from England into Virginia or the other colonies. Also, it was never used at St Peter's Church, which was not built until 1836. It is now on display along the rotunda on the second floor of the Museum of Natural History at the Smithsonian.

95

St George's Parish was first organized in 1714 out of the western-most portion of St Mary's Parish and comprised a circular area (five miles in diameter) around the settlement of German Reformed miners at Germanna on the Rapidan River. St George's Parish was much enlarged in 1721, when the coterminous county of Spotsylvania was created out of the uppermost portions of Essex, King William, and King and Queen Counties.

Two vestry books (1726-45 and 1746-1817) of St George's Parish have survived and are on loan at the University of Virginia.

12. Upper Church, Stratton Major, King and Queen

The third Upper Church of Stratton Major Parish in King and Queen County stands on the southwest side of route 14, about 5 miles northwest of Centerville, and 8.6 miles south of King and Queen Courthouse. It seems to have been built, between 1724 and 1729, just south of its immediate predecessor. Footings of this earlier church (possibly around 1675) were uncovered by a bulldozer several years ago. The site of the first Upper Church (possibly around 1665) is either identical with or lies very close to that of the present Mattaponi Church in the northern part of the county.

Stratton Major Parish was formed from Blisland Parish in 1655 and King and Queen County was created out of New Kent County in 1691. The origin of the parish's name is obscure, although one authority has attributed it to a Major family in the county in early times who may possibly have come from one of the many Stratton parishes in England (there are to-day as many as ten). It is also possible that Major (meaning "Greater") may have been part of an English parish's title.

The existing Upper Church's brickwork of Flemish bond with glazed headers is of the highest calibre. Below the bevelled water table is English bond. The church measures 64' x 33'-9" on the outside and its walls (2' thick) are now strengthened by eight tie-rods. The walls are largely intact, although cracks are to be noted: 1) on the east wall, above all three windows; 2) on the south wall, towards the western end; 3) on the west wall, above the circular window; and 4) on the north wall, in two spots in the upper portion. Holes for stove pipes have been filled in on the side walls, but a hole still exists on the chancel wall. Repairs occur on the west wall immediately above and below the water table.

The rowlock courses under the wood sills of the large windows are new, as is the row of stretchers under the sill of the south window on the chancel wall. Rubbed brick exists at the corners, in the arches and jambs of the large windows (four each in the north and south and two in the east), and around the rims of the smaller, circular windows (one high in each of the lofty gables); and rubbed and gauged brickwork adorns the elaborate doorways on the west and south.

On the south side the doorway separates the easternmost window from the other three. On the north side the wall has no opening opposite the south doorway. The semi-circular arches of the ten principal windows consist of full bricks alternating with pairs of halves, as do the surrounds of the smaller windows. In 1898 the principal windows had brick lunettes, as the west doorway still does, although these lunettes are un-doubtedly post-colonial.

Eight bricks have been crudely replaced in the surround of the circular window on the west and five bricks are falling in the other small window. Six bricks are crumbling in the arch of the south window of the chancel wall and three are in bad shape in the arch of the easternmost window of the south wall. At the bottom of each of several jambs there is a new brick.

Queen closers are to be seen on the jambs of all the large windows save three: they mark only the lower two-thirds of the left jamb of the south window on the chancel wall and the right jamb of the easternmost window on the north wall, and only three closers (irregularly used) occur on the left jamb of the easternmost window on the south wall. Queen closers are also to be seen at the sides of the south doorway and the salient corners (above and below the water table), but their use at the western doorway is quite irregular. Ventilation holes, thirteen in all, occur on all four walls.

Both doorways have classical pediments. The west doorway has a segmental-arched pediment and a semi-circular arch. The raked cornice of this pediment seems to have been composed of four courses. The upper-most course is now gone and the next one seems to have been originally a cyma reversa, but it, too, has been replaced in modern times (except for end pieces only) by a fascia. Another fascia and another cyma reversa complete these mouldings. The horizontal cornice comprises two cyma reversas separated by a fascia. The upper cyma reversa is badly worn and the other two mouldings are repaired in the middle. The pilasters have

97

the usual gauged bricks in three sizes. The arch and jambs of this doorway have full bricks alternating with pairs of halves. Eight voussoirs in the arch have been replaced and new slivers have been inserted in the spandrel immediately above the arch. The pedestals at both entrances have been all but obscured by the concrete steps and cheek walls of modern times. The lamps at the entrances are also inconsistent with these fine walls.

The south doorway has a triangular pediment and a flat arch. The cyma recta in the raked cornice is badly worn, but the cyma reversa, fascia, and cyma reversa below it are intact. The upper cyma reversa of the horizontal cornice is also worn, although the fascia and lower cyma reversa are in good condition. There are no pilasters, but the jambs (of three sizes of brick) and the pedestals are all raised. Glazed headers are used in the tympanum of the pediments in both south and west. There are bad cracks in the tympanum on the west and a new brick in that on the south. The arch is intact, but is beginning to fall.

Shrubs and ferns line the walls of the church, and the large yard is partly shaded. On the northeast of the chancel are remains of seventeenth-century tombstones, the earliest of which is from 1686 (and is at present all but covered by loose fragments of stone). The historical marker on the highway is in error, for it confuses the existing building with the new Stratton Major Parish Church of 1768 that replaced both this building and a Lower Church, and was the largest and most expensive church ever erected in colonial Virginia.

After it was abandoned in 1768, the Upper Church of 1724-29 seems to have been used for worship by Baptists and various other groups until around 1842. After several years' use as a school, its wooden elements were destroyed by fire, but the church was rebuilt in 1850. Both Methodists and Baptists then used the building until the former gained control. Still owned by the Methodists, it is known, somewhat confusingly, by them simply as Old Church.

The walls and openings of Upper Church are remarkably like those at Mattaponi Church.

The vestry book (1729-83) of Stratton Major Parish has been published and the original manuscript is on deposit at the State Library in Richmond.

13. Elizabeth City Parish Church (St John's)

The fourth Elizabeth City Parish Church occupies the northwest corner of West Queen and Court Streets in the city of Hampton. The first church, which was known as Kecoughtan Church, was possibly built as early as 1613-16. Such an early date is thoroughly in keeping with the rate of construction of churches at Jamestown and on the Eastern Shore in the earliest times. The second and third churches were erected in 1624 and 1667, respectively. The present walls date from 1728. The actual settlement of Kecoughtan took place in 1610, although Cape Henry where the colonists first landed and planted a cross lay within the original bounds of Elizabeth City County. Kecoughtan, which is named for the Indians of the area, was one of the four original cities or boroughs of 1618. The name of Kecoughtan, however, gave way to Elizabeth City the next year. The parish and the county were named for the Princess Elizabeth, eldest daughter of James I and the grandmother of George I. Both the parish and the town of Hampton have been in continuous existence since the early plantation of 1610. The name of St John's for the present church is first known only from 1827.

The fourth church has suffered much from wars and the ravages of time. It is laid in brick of Flemish bond with glazed headers (except for the English bond below the bevelled water table) and is shaped like a Latin cross. On the outside it measures a bit over 75' east to west and 60'-8" north to south. Its walls are 2' thick. The transepts and the chancel have the same length: each projects a little over 15'. The nave is around 29'-3" long. Both the body of the church and the transepts are 30'-4" wide on the outside.

Of the original window-locations, there are now two in the east end of the chancel, one in the south side of the chancel, one on each side of the south transept, one on the west side of the north transept, and two on each side of the nave. There were formerly similar windows on the east side of the north transept and on the north side of the chancel, but these are now enlarged masonry arches filled with wooden grills (behind which are organ pipes). Also in their original locations are three circular windows (4' in diameter), one each in the south, east, and north. These three windows and the ten remaining large windows (with semi-circular arches) have arches that alternate full bricks with pairs of half-bricks (or full bricks incised in that manner). Two windows also light the gallery in the west and a very small window marks the north wall of the nave, hardly more than a foot east of the easternmost window on that wall. This small window probably illumined the pulpit, which was then at the northwest corner of the crossing. This singular window, furthermore, has a strongly sloping sill (on the interior), does not have rubbed brick at the head or the jambs, and has a rowlock course for its (semi-circular) arch.

Rubbed brick marks the three aforementioned circular windows, the two circular windows in the west gable, and the salient corners as well as the arches and jambs of the ten remaining, large semi-circular windows. However, the rubbed brick of the arches is of an orange cast, whereas that of the jambs is of a darker red. Also, the left jamb of the left window of the chancel wall may possibly be of ordinary rather than rubbed brick, although it is difficult to be positive about this.

As at a number of other colonial churches in Virginia, the use of queen closers at the jambs of the windows of the church at Hampton is somewhat capricious. They are to be found only: 1) on the left jamb of the right window and the right jamb of the left window of the chancel wall; 2) on the right jamb of the window on the south wall of the chancel; 3) on the right jamb of the window on the east wall and both jambs of the window on the west wall of the south transept; 4) on the lower two-thirds of the right jamb and the lower half of the left jamb of the left window of the south wall of the nave; and 5) on the right jamb (with two closers on the left jamb) of the westernmost window on the north wall of the nave. Slivers of brick are to be seen on the jambs of the small window and a single closer marks the left jamb of the window on the west wall of the north transept. Closers are also used at all the salient corners, even below the water table, and they are likewise still to be seen on both jambs of the west portal and the right jamb of the north portal.

All three doorways—south, west, and north—once seem to have had brick pediments, but these have been removed and the doorways enclosed by modern brick vestibules. The north vestibule was built in 1870 and the other two at some later date. A brick tower with a wooden belfry was built in the west in 1762. The brick pediment on the west was, therefore, probably removed in 1762. The pediments on the side portals were probably removed around 1870 or later, for a triangular pediment still adorned the south doorway in a representation of the church in *Leslie's Illustrated* of August 17, 1861. The colonial church also possessed the usual tablets and a churchyard wall, first of wood and then of brick. The present wall, however, is more recent. The colonial edifice seems probably to have had three galleries, but only those in the north and west have been replaced. Records exist for the erection of only these latter two, but, inasmuch as one seldom if ever hears of a north gallery without a south gallery in our colonial cruciform churches and inasmuch as it would seem more logical to build a south gallery facing the pulpit rather than a north gallery behind it (despite the usual colonial indifference to sight-lines from a liturgical point of view), it seems probable that a gallery was also built in the south.

Only slight damage was incurred by the church during the bombardment of Hampton by the British in 1775, but the building was desecrated by British troops through use as a barracks in the War of 1812, when the churchyard also became an abattoir. After this war, the church and yard went to such ruin that nothing was left but the walls and "a leaky roof". It was, however, restored to service in 1826-27. The building was burned along with the rest of the town on August 7, 1861, by Confederate forces. Therefore, the entire woodwork of the structure had to be replaced a second time in the nineteenth century. This second renewal took place in 1870. The upper portion of the west wall of the nave and the tower had also fallen in the fire of 1861. The remains of this tower were removed in 1870 and the present tower (which has been nicely executed to match insofar as possible the original masonry on the church) was erected in the northeast only in 1901.

The present east wall of the chancel has been increased in width by a foot on the inside in order to conceal a modern chimney. Although the chimney seems no longer to be used (and is, indeed, scheduled for early demolition), it can still be seen above the apex of the east gable. The crosses on the roof represent modern additions.

The numerous repairs to the window arches include: 1) six or seven new bricks in the right arch and at least half of the left arch on the chancel wall; 2) repointing or a few new bricks in the arches on the south wall of the chancel and the east wall of the south transept; 3) six new bricks in the arch on the west wall of the south transept; 4) repointing in the left arch on the south wall of the nave; and 5) two new bricks in the westernmost arch on the north wall of the nave. The arch on the west wall of the north transept needs retouching. Repointing marks the surrounds of the circular windows in the north and east gables. Four or five new bricks have also been inserted in the surround of the circular window of the north transept. The lower portions of the two circular windows in the west gable are either original or have been skilfully constructed of old bricks. These lower portions are marked by whole bricks alternating with pairs of halves, whereas the upper portions include only whole bricks. The small window by the former pulpit has been widened since colonial times, so that its jambs and arch are probably replacements. All the large, semi-circular windows have been lengthened and as a result two or three bricks have been repaired at the bottom of every jamb.

Repairs to the church's walls consist more in cracks than in replacements. On the chancel wall there is a long crack above each of the three windows as well as shorter cracks above, below, and to the left

101

of the left window and a crack below the circular window. Repairs have also been made below the right window. New bricks may be seen above and below the window on the south wall of the chancel. The east wall of the south transept is marred only by a slight crack below the window. The south gable includes repairs above the former doorway, a large crack above the window, and two cracks below the cornice to the right. The west wall of the south wing shows cracks above and below the window and repairs at the lower right corner. On the long south wall of the nave there are cracks above and below both windows. The upper portion of the west gable is entirely restored. Down each side of this gable a crack has been mended and a small crack exists under each window. The opening of the former west doorway has been bricked in on each side of the modern vestibule. Tie-rods are also in evidence.

On the north wall of the nave there are repairs above the little window and below the westernmost window, cracks below the middle window, and above the westernmost window, and two other small cracks. The west wall of the north transept shows repairs below and a crack above the window; a long, mended rent (with new bricks) can be seen down the left side and a large patch of repairs exists below the water table on the right. The north gable is marked by a bad crack next to the tower wall, by a long, repaired crack that reaches from the apex to the circular window, and by repairs above the vestibule.

Scaffolding or putlock holes have been filled in everywhere except on the north gable (where sparrows delight to nest), although even on this façade one such hole has been filled in. The ventilation holes have been widened in post-colonial times.

Several sets of initials with serifs are to be seen on the east gable, notably "H.H.C." on both jambs of the left window and "NG" on the left jamb.

Outstanding in the present interior is the modern stained glass in the westernmost window in each side of the nave, the two windows in the west gallery, and the window in the south wall of the chancel. The glass in the small window on the north wall was dedicated in 1903 by the Association for the Preservation of Virginia Antiquities to the colonial clergy of the parish.

Despite its ravages, the old church through its walls alone has managed to retain much of its colonial appeal, which is enhanced by the large graveyard that also serves as the churchyard. Although two stones of colonial date (1701 and 1754 or 1758) lie among this yard's multitudinous graves, four very interesting tombstones (ranging from 1697 to 1719) lie near the foundations of the parish's third church by the Chesapeake and Ohio Railway tracks. This site may be reached from the present church by going west on Queen Street, turning right on South

Armistead Avenue, turning left on West Pembroke Avenue, and continuing on that street for about .5 mile. The old site is on one's right.

To the best of the parish's knowledge, the 1701 stone in the present yard has not been moved there from anywhere else and, therefore, how it came to be there so long before the site was used for a church remains a puzzle. It has been surmised that, perhaps, the town used the spot for a burying ground before the fourth church was erected.

Remarkable Silver

Elizabeth City Parish owns some of the most interesting silver in all America. Indeed, it owns the English communion silver in longest use in the United States. This set, which is marked as of London in 1618-19, consists of a chalice and two patens and was originally given to St Mary's Church at Smith's Hundred in Charles City County, apparently in 1619. After the Indian Massacre of 1622, the silver went to Sir George Yeardley (at that time the captain of the hundred and thrice the governor of the colony), then to his widow, and from her to the court at Jamestown. Owing apparently to the fact that Elizabeth City Parish Church was located on the Southampton River and to the further fact that Smith's Hundred had become Southampton Hundred, this set was bestowed upon the Elizabeth City Parish. Traces of gilding are still to be seen on the silver. The parish also owns a third paten (marked London 1698-99) that seems to have been originally given to Martin's Hundred Parish in James City County. Why the paten did not descend to York-Hampton Parish when Martin's Hundred Parish was absorbed by that parish in 1712 is not altogether clear.

The Elizabeth City Parish vestry book (1751-1883) is owned and kept by the parish.

14. UPPER CHURCH, ST PAUL'S (SLASH)

The present Slash Church is located on route 656—between Peaks and Ashland in Hanover County—a fraction of a mile north of the junction of that route with route 657. In colonial times it was the Upper Church of St Paul's Parish, although there is a tradition that it was known once—whether before or after the Revolution is uncertain—as Merryoaks Church. Its current name would seem to derive from its proximity to slashes or swampy woodlands. The existing structure, which was originally erected in 1729, was the second Upper Church. The first Upper Church (1702) is believed to have stood about 1½ miles north and was originally known as Mechumps Chapel of St Peter's Parish. St Paul's Parish was created from St Peter's Parish in New Kent County in 1704. Hanover County was not formed until 1720.

The 1729 frame building was ordered to measure 60' x 20', but it now measures approximately 60'-7" x 26'-6". The church, constructed by Thomas Pinchbeck and Edward Chambers, was finished in 1730. Possibly original or colonial are: 1) some of the clapboards on the east, south, and west walls; 2) the modillion cornice; 3) the double doors and door trim on the west; 4) the sills of the lower two windows in the east; 5) the wooden sills of the foundations (which have now been raised and set on brick foundations); 6) the horizontal board wainscoting; and 7) the hand rail (though not the balusters) and flooring of the west gallery. The trim of the western doorway is of the most rudimentary nature. The raised panels of the doors themselves include a small horizontal panel over a vertical panel, which in turn lies over another, slightly longer vertical panel.

Perhaps, the most interesting feature of the church's construction can be seen only by standing on a bench in the gallery and peering through a trap door with a flashlight. There one will see the undoubtedly original purlins and beams (with wooden pegs), but even more interesting is the fact that the main beams run diagonally rather than straight across the breadth of the church. Also, the vertical supports of the church are arranged in a curious, triangular form, and there is, as is often true with these old buildings, no ridge beam.

The floor of the nave under the west gallery was once a step lower than the rest of the church. When it was raised to a uniform level, the west doors had to be shortened. Beneath the present floor are said to lie the remains of the original brick floor. The gallery stairs (and closet beneath) also appear to be of olden times. There are three windows in the east, two in the west, and four each on the south and north. Except for the aforementioned two lower sills on the east, all of the rest of the windows—sash, glass, and trim—are of more modern origin, as are the north door, the roof, the chimneys, all the present furnishings of the interior, and the additions on the north. The stoops, steps, and walks as well as the little roof on the south are also of recent construction, although the south doors and trim are believed to have been installed around 1900.

In colonial times, Dolley Madison and Patrick Henry are said to have attended Divine Service at the church. The latter's uncle (of the same name) was rector for four decades. Henry Clay ("The Mill Boy of the Slashes") was another who frequented this fane.

Sometime after the Revolution and the Disestablishment, the Episcopalians abandoned the building in favor of St Paul's at Hanover Courthouse. It then became a union Church shared by Methodists and Disciples of Christ and has been owned by the latter since 1842. It is said to have been used once as a school, and also to have been a hospital in the War between the States. It gave its name to a battle in that war. The third Lower Church (1774-77) of St Paul's Parish gave its name to the village still known as Old Church.

The vestry book (1705-85) of St Paul's Parish has been published and the original manuscript is on loan at the State Library in Richmond.

15. THE CHAPEL OF THE COLLEGE OF WILLIAM AND MARY

It is sometimes forgotten that Williamsburg possesses two colonial ecclesiastical structures: Bruton Parish Church (1711-15) and the Chapel of the Wren (or Main) Building of the College of William and Mary. It is also usually forgotten that an Anglican divinity school was a part of the College of William and Mary until it was abolished in 1779, when the College was re-organized under Governor Thomas Jefferson. Eight presidents of the College have been rectors of Bruton Parish Church and two presidents have been bishops of the Episcopal Church.

The Wren Building has known four forms: 1695 (probably finished by 1700), 1709 (finished by 1716), 1859, and 1867-69. The causes of the three rebuildings were all fires: 1705, 1859, and 1862, the last of these "having been designedly effected by drunken" Federal soldiers. The walls remained standing in each instance and were re-used in each new form, including the restoration to the second form that was accomplished by Colonial Williamsburg in 1928-31. The seventeenth-century plan called for a quadrangle enclosing a courtyard but the first and second forms were built only in the shape of an L: the main range (138' x 46' on the outside) running north to south and the north hall (64' x 32') running east to west.

The first form of the main range seems to have had a basement, three full storeys, and a half-storey, and was probably 46′ high to the cornice. It also had a cupola, an arched opening on the east (between the basement windows and those of the first storey) with balustraded steps leading up to it, and balconies, The second form enclosed the third storey in dormers on the east, but retained the west wall at its full height. Governor Spotswood also added pavilions (with a balcony on the second storey) on the east and west as well as a new cupola. Two Italian towers marked the 1859 form on the east, and the west was left plain, the whole structure having a low-pitched slate roof in place of the former half-storey and hipped roof. The 1867-69 shape also had a pavilion on the east, but with a loggia of three arches on the first-storey level.

Whether Sir Christopher Wren actually supplied the design for the first form of the Main Building is uncertain; it is, indeed, possible as yet neither to prove nor disprove the point. However, it is probably too late to attempt to change the name of this celebrated building, as some have suggested; this is partly owing to the fact that almost any institution may have a Main Building, but where else in America can one even hint of a Wren Building?

The hall in the north range of the first and second forms seems to have served for purposes of both entertainment and worship until the present Chapel wing was added in 1729-32 on the south to match the north hall, at which time the Wren Building assumed its present U-shape. The Chapel was built by Henry Cary jr, who also completed the fourth Elizabeth City Parish Church at Hampton in 1728. A dating brick exists in the west wall of the Chapel just to the right of the doorway at about eye-level from the platform. On it are the initials "RK" and the year "1729", upside down. The initials are believed to stand for Richard Kennon (†1736), who was possibly the rector of the College's board of visitors in 1729.

The dimensions of the Chapel are the same as those of the north hall. Its height from the ground to the eaves is about 32′. The Chapel and north hall's form of a double cube offers another instance of the early Williamsburg builders' predilection for geometrical proportions, which is also evidenced in the main range of the Wren Building (a triple cube), in the last Bruton Parish Church, and elsewhere in the old capital. The chief distinctions between the south and north wings of the Wren Building are the Flemish bond of the Chapel in opposition to the English bond of the older hall (although English bond is used below the water table of the Chapel) and in the Chapel's lack of a basement. The north hall's basement is provided with windows. It will be noted that the Chapel is liturgically oriented like all other colonial Anglican places of worship.

A plate in the Bodleian Library of Oxford University, which has been dated as around 1740, shows the Chapel with a hipped roof, five dormers on each side, and a single dormer at the west end; and a child's drawing of 1856 also has a roof with dormers. Both representations clearly show the three end windows and the five side ones and the large western doorway (which likewise extends to the ground in both instances). The Chapel in the "3rd" form (1859-62) had neither dormers nor hipped roof. The exterior of the Chapel in the "4th" form (1869-1928) was quite different from the original (or restored) manner: the western doorway and three oval windows were all bricked up and the only outside entrance throughout this form was a doorway in the north wall, where the second window from the east now exists.

On the south and north walls of the restored form of the Chapel, the entire area above the spring-line of the window arches and the areas below the windows themselves are new. The window arches are also new, and the windows and the eaves were at one stage at least 5′ lower. These walls also possess a number of ventilation holes, although vines on the north and west undoubtedly cover still others. On the upper portion of the west wall, new portions of brick have been added in order to restore the roof to its original height and to accommodate the new horizontal cornice in place of the gable-end of the previous form. Repointing is much in evidence on all three walls. The top of the great window on the west wall also seems repaired.

Rubbed brick is in evidence on all jambs and arches of the openings and at the two outer corners. Rubbed brick also marks both ends of the piers of the western doorway. The Chapel's walls are nearly 3′ thick. Queen closers mark the jambs of all five of the windows in the south wall except the right jamb of the easternmost window. On the north wall, such closers are to be seen on: 1) the right jambs only of the two easternmost windows and the second from the westernmost window; and 2) both jambs of the westernmost window. Only a few queen closers at the upper left mark the middle window. However, they are to be seen on both ends of the piers of the doorway and, interestingly enough, at the inner corners where the Chapel was added to the main range.

The western doorway, which is original, has a heavy, vaulted, slightly flattened semi-circular arch that alternates stretcher over header with header over stretcher and is cemented on the top. The masonry opening is 9′-2″ wide. The jambs are quasi-pilasters or piers that project 20″ and are 2′ wide. Two courses project at the spring-line of the arch at the top of the piers. Glazed headers are used in the piers, even on the sides. Three bricks in the arch form a projecting keystone (a feature that does not exist on the north hall). The steps and sills have been reconstructed.

The semi-circular arches of the five windows on the second-storey level of each of the Chapel's side walls alternate full bricks with pairs of half-bricks, and the brick window sills are bevelled, The easternmost window on the south wall may once have been made into a doorway. A large wheel window exists above the western doorway, and on each side of this doorway there is a smaller, elliptical window. The arches of all three windows are rowlock courses.

The details of the enormous, heavily panelled doors and the wheel window on the west are similar in style to the inner doors on the west and the wheel window on the east at Bruton Parish Church. Four dormers exist on each side of the Chapel and a single example at the west (although the early representations have five on each side, as we have noted). The roof is now hipped and the cornice has modillions. None of the woodwork of the Chapel is old, needless to say.

In the restoration of the Wren Building, all of the partition walls were removed and a steel frame, resting on concrete footings, was erected within the outer walls, with the outermost columns concealed in slots chased in the masonry. It has been pointed out that, as a result of all this, these oldest walls in the town now constitute the old capital's first use of the modern principle of the curtain wall. The weight of all the roofs and floors is today carried by these modern supplements.

Interior of the Chapel

There is very little known about the Chapel's eighteenth-century interior, although we do know that the central aisle (10' wide) was paved with stone imported from England (probably Purbeck or Shrewsbury) and that the Chapel was wainscoted from a point 12½' below the ceiling down to the floor (a measurement of 11½'). It has been inferred from documentary references that the Chapel probably possessed one or more box-pews, and may also have had stalls facing each other (choirwise), or it may have had "forms" (backless benches), or possibly some of each of these types of seats. The Chapel also had a pulpit (which was not always to be found in collegiate chapels), and it seems to have stood in front of the Communion Table (somewhat as Christ Church (1714) in Middlesex County may possibly have been arranged). The William and Mary Chapel also may have had an ante-chapel (or perhaps a gallery) in the west end. The ceiling of the Chapel seems to have been vaulted. The floor was 3' lower than that of the main range of the building.

The 1859-62 form seems to have had a rostrum rather than an altar in the east and no gallery, and is said to have seated approximately 400 persons (although so large a number was probably accommodated only by means of the folding doors that allowed the Chapel and the library to form but a single hall). After the War between the States, the "platform" was moved to the west end (with a superimposed arch and vaulted ceiling above it), against the wall with its bricked-up openings. A single doorway connected the Chapel with the rest of the Wren Building.

The present interior is a handsome albeit, perforce, somewhat conjectural restoration: royal arms (of George I and George II) on the west gallery; high and heavily panelled wainscoting of pine and walnut; choirwise pews (three rows on each side of the aisle) as well as six slip-pews at the rear (four on the Gospel-side and two on the Epistle-side); a slate aisle (which also extends under the first of the choirwise pews on each side); chancel and altar rails of turned balusters; two handsome bronze chandeliers; and memorial tablets. Two doors, one on each side of the altar, now lead into the main (east) range.

The wooden reredos has a segmental-arched pediment and Corinthian pilasters; and four columns and two pilasters, also of the Corinthian order, support the gallery. Despite the arms and plaques, the Chapel seems somewhat unnecessarily unadorned. Flags might help in this respect. A coved plaster cornice like that at Bruton Church is used. The restored side windows have 22 over 16 lights. The ceiling is now flat.

The Wren Building served as a hospital for French troops in the Revolution in 1781, and in 1861 it was used as quarters and later as a hospital for Confederate troops. After the Battle of Williamsburg (May 5, 1862), the old capital was occupied by Federal troops, who needlessly burned the College the following September and also damaged still other buildings in the town during their occupation.

In 1772 Thomas Jefferson drew up plans for completing the Wren Building according to the original design of a closed quadrangle, but as a rectangle instead of the original square. This would certainly have affected the Chapel in some way, but nothing came of the plan (although a beginning was actually made on the proposed west range). Around the same period, Jefferson also drew up a plan for an octagonal chapel in the Tuscan order with a peristyle, which he inscribed as being modelled upon the circular and Corinthian temple of Vesta near the Tiber in Rome. It is assumed that this was planned for the College of William and Mary, but this plan was never executed either.

In 1775 the Chapel was bequeathed by Lady Gooch, the widow of a royal governor, a silver-gilt sacrament or caudle cup and cover, which may originally have been used as a secular vessel, but is in any case a truly rare piece. It was made in London in 1686-87 by Pierre Harache. Also in long use at the Chapel was a silver-gilt paten, which is likewise believed to have derived from Lady Gooch, for it bears the same arms as the cup. The paten was made in 1751-52 by Richard Gurney and Company of London. Bruton Parish Church became the custodian of the William and Mary silver when the College was transferred in 1906 from the Episcopal Church to the Commonwealth of Virginia.

There seems to be some uncertainty as to the exact number of persons who lie buried in vaults beneath the Chapel as well as some disagreement about the exact whereabouts of certain persons who are definitely known to be interred there. There appear to be three vaults in the east and the same number near the second window from the west on the Gospel-side. The former vaults are occupied by members of the Randolph famly: Sir John Randolph (†1739) in one, John Randolph (†1784) in another, and Peyton Randolph (†1776) and possibly his wife (†1783) in the third. In the first of these eastern vaults lies a second body, which some have taken to be that of Lady Randolph, whereas others have taken it to be the body of Governor Lord Botetourt (†1770). In one of the northwestern vaults lies the body of the Rt Rev'd James Madison (†1812), the first bishop of Virginia. Some persons think that the body of Chancellor Robert Nelson (†1813) or Mrs Madison (†1815) lies in the second vault and that Chancellor Nelson or Gregory Page (†1812) lies in a third grave. Mr Page was drowned while a student at the College. Bishop Madison and Chancellor Nelson are known definitely to have been buried in the Chapel and Mrs Madison and young Mr Page are believed also to lie there. Therefore, there do not seem to be enough graves to go around. To make matters a bit more complicated, some authorities (whose opinions are apparently the more highly favored at present) maintain that Lord Botetourt, Bishop Madison, and Chancellor Nelson occupy the northwestern vaults, thus leaving Mrs Madison's and Mr Page's graves unestablished. The most recent interment occurred in 1939 when the ashes of Thomas Roderick Dew (†1846), a president of the College who had died and been buried in Paris, were translated to the Wren Chapel.

The elegant silver escutcheon and fittings from Lord Botetourt's coffin as well as the name-plate from Bishop Madison's coffin are preserved in the College Library.

The Chapel is now officially used only for a "nondenominational" service held in the middle of the week (whenever the College is in session) under the auspices of the Student Religious Union. Presbyterian hymnals seem to be used for these services. However, a Lutheran congregation that is presently without a building also uses the Chapel on Sunday mornings; the clergy of Bruton Parish Church celebrates the Holy Communion in the Chapel once a week and upon special occasions; and many alumni are married there. The Chapel's lofty walls also still stand as a beautiful reminder of the link that bound Church, College, and State in colonial times and continued to bind Church and College until the present century.

16. MANGOHICK CHURCH

Mangohick Church is at the end of route 638, .1 mile south of the village of Mangohick on route 30 in King William County. Mangohick itself is about 10 miles west of Central Garage and 6 miles east of Dawn. The name, Mangohick, is Indian and is also applied to a nearby creek.

The brick church measures approximately 61' x 28' on the outside. It was probably built around 1730 as a chapel of ease for St Margaret's Parish, but became the Upper Church of St David's Parish in 1744. St Margaret's Parish was created out of the upper portion of St John's Parish in 1720 and St David's Parish was formed in 1744 out of lower St Margaret's Parish and the (remaining) upper part of St John's Parish.

A flat brick inset above the (repaired) arch of the south doorway seems to say "1731" with either "WV" or "WY" (or something similar) indistinctly carved between the "17" and the "31". Another flat brick inset to the right of the western entrance seems to read "T A Brown" (with two other initials apparently superimposed on this), and a bit below this brick there is another with what appears to be "T E Moony" incised on it.

The bond of Mangohick Church is beautifully laid Flemish, with glazed headers throughout, except for the English bond below the bevelled water table. The recent additions in the east now leave only the upper portion of the east gable exposed to view. The windows on the north (four) and the south (three) have flat arches, whereas the two windows in the west above the gallery have segmental arches. All nine windows have arches that alternate full bricks with pairs of halves. The two windows originally in the east are now merely doors leading from the church to vesting rooms. The second window from the east on the north side is smaller than the rest and this fact suggests the possibility that it may have provided light for a pew between pulpit and chancel.

On the north wall, the arch of the easternmost window has been repaired and repointed, and the westernmost window has also been repointed. On the west wall, a bad patch exists in the brick lunette of the northern window and a crack in that of the southern window, although these lunettes seem to be themselves replacements. In each of these small windows there are two new bricks on the upper right as well as lower right jambs. Two new bricks also mark the upper right jambs of the two eastern windows on the north wall. Lintels have been inserted at the heads of the south and north windows, and split bricks have been placed at their extremities. Two new bricks likewise occur at the lower right jambs of these windows. The windows on the side walls are all marked by sloping brick sills.

Three ventilation holes exist on each of the side walls, although none mark the west wall; one can no longer know about the east wall. Queen closers are used at the corners (above the water table), on the right jambs of the westernmost and easternmost windows on the south wall, and on both jambs of both doorways.

Repairs to the walls include: 1) on the west, repointing along the barge board on the left near the apex (where repair is needed) and at the lower left below the water table as well as cement patching at the southwest corner and two rows of new bricks under the sill of the doorway; and 2) on the north, a hole that needs to be filled. The upper portion of the north wall is of a brighter cast than that found elsewhere on this wall and in this upper area are also to be noted two long streaks where the mason has placed header over header and stretcher over stretcher. On the exposed portion of the lofty east gable, a crack exists on each side and there is repointing at the apex.

The west doorway is now possessed of a patched, flat arch (which was probably originally segmental) and the south doorway has a flat arch that is completely replaced except for five voussoirs and a fragment of a sixth. These voussoirs alternate a full brick over a half-brick with the reverse of that scheme. New concrete steps exist on the west and new brick steps on the south.

Rubbed brick is used at the four corners of the building, in the arches of all the windows, at the jambs of all the openings, on the remaining portion of the arch of the south doorway, and along the rake on both sides of each gable.

Of the woodwork, the dentil cornice may be original and some of the floor boards in the west gallery are possibly colonial. Several wrought-iron holders for the shutters may also be old. The floor has been raised, and the present interior bears no resemblance to a colonial or Anglican church.

The church was abandoned after the Disestablishment and was then used as a "free" church. Sometime after the War between the States, the building was deeded to a colored Baptist congregation, which still owns it.

17. LOWER CHURCH, ST STEPHEN'S (MATTAPONI)

The second Lower Church of St Stephen's Parish in King and Queen County has long been known as Mattaponi Church. It may have been known locally as Mattaponi Church even in colonial times. At any rate, this has been its name ever since the Baptists took the building over early in the last century. It may be seen on the west side of route 14, 5.7 miles north of the Courthouse and one-half mile south of Cumnor Post Office.

Like the former Upper Church of Stratton Major Parish in the lower end of the county, Mattaponi Church possesses handsome brick walls, beautifully laid in Flemish bond with glazed headers, and doorways with classical pediments. A resemblance in design to that of Abingdon Church has been noted, but the similarity of Mattaponi Church to the old Upper Church of Stratton Major is just as strong. This similarity affects the assignment of a date for the erection of Mattaponi Church, for its neighbor was probably constructed somewhere between 1724 and 1729, whereas Abingdon is generally assigned the year 1755. In Mattaponi Church is still on display a great Bible on the fly-leaf of which is included the church's colonial title and "Anno 1733, June" and on the spine of which is stamped in gold "Brick Church." This might possibly indicate the erection of a new church around 1733, although the Bible could have been used in an earlier church on the same site. It has been written that St Stephen's Parish was created before 1674, that the first church of the new parish had probably already been in use as the first Upper Church of Stratton Major as much as a decade before the creation of St Stephen's Parish, and that this church was going to ruin by 1682. If these things can be assumed to be true, there seem to be two possibilities: 1) the present building may be the third rather than the second church on this site and a date around 1755 may, therefore, be tentatively assigned; or 2) this is the second church (or possibly a third church) and an earlier date, perhaps 1730-34, considered. In view of the resemblance to the surviving building of Stratton Major in the lower part of the county and in view of the pattern of building that existed in the parishes of King and Queen and King William counties in colonial times, the latter date seems somewhat more likely. The fact that "David ee" (or "David Minetree")
Minetr
is cut into a brick above the west doorway is of no help with the problem, for several builders bore that name in the colonial period.

The church itself is built in the shape of a Latin cross and measures around 84½' (east and west) by 64' (north and south). The nave is about 43'-4" long and 32½' wide. The transepts project about 15'-8" and are 26'-8" wide. The chancel projects 14'-6". Flemish bond with

113

glazed headers is also used below the bevelled water table, and rubbed brick is found at the salient corners of the building and on the arches and jambs of the windows (two in each side of the nave and in the east end of the chancel and one in each side of the transepts and chancel). There are no windows in the lofty gables. Rubbed and gauged brickwork marks the three doorways: south, west, and north.

The walls are three brick-lengths thick. Repairs to the walls include mostly cracks: 1) on the chancel wall, a new small door to a cellar; 2) on the south wall of the chancel, repointing at the lower right and bad cracks above and below the window as well as a hole above the water table; 3) on the east wall of the south transept, cracks above and below the window; 4) on the south façade, a bad crack above the pediment and a hole along the barge board on the left; 5) on the west wall of the south transept, bad cracks above and below the window; 6) on the south wall of the nave, a prominent crack towards the west end; 7) on the west façade, cracks at the upper right and over the pediment as well as some repointing at the lower left; and 8) on the north wall of the nave, cracks towards the western end and above the westernmost window. On the walls of the north transept are to be noted: 1) on the west wall, a crack above the window; 2) on the north wall, a filled-in spot where once a stove pipe was inserted; and 3) on the east wall, repointing above the window and at the lower right. Modern chimneys exist at the junctures of both chancel and nave with the north transept. There is also a crack above the window on the north wall of the chancel. Repointing occurs below the water table on the east and north walls of the chancel, the west wall of the south transept, the south and west walls of the nave, and the west and north walls of the north transept. The salient corners are worn below the water table.

"Thomas [?] Hogg" is incised above the northern window on the chancel wall, and in the right jamb of the same window there is also beautifully incised "W • B+". There are sixteen ventilation holes in all, although none seem to exist on the north wall of the nave or on the west wall of the north wing.

The twelve windows all have semi-circular arches. The jambs are intact, but new bricks in the arches (usually at the apex) include: 1) two each in the right window of the chancel wall and in the westernmost window on the north wall of the nave; 2) one or two in the window of the south wall of the chancel; and 3) four each in the windows of the side walls of the south transept and the west wall of the north transept. Repointing in the arches marks the windows in the side walls of the chancel, the west wall of the south transept, and the east wall of the north transept as well as the eastern window in the north wall of the nave.

114

Queen closers are used with exemplary regularity on every window jamb and salient corner (even below the water table), although none are to be seen at the sides of the doorways save for a few on the lower right side of the western portal. Queen closers are also in evidence at some of the ventilation holes.

The reveals of the windows are now all covered by a skim coat of cement, and the existing concrete sills are replacements. Shutters have been used at one time and, if one can judge from the height of the holders that remain and from the closers, it is possible that the windows have been lowered one or two courses at the sills.

The handsome west doorway has a segmental-arched pediment and a semi-circular arch with pilasters and jambs. Three sizes of brick mark the pilasters, and the arch over the doorway and its jambs alternate a full brick with two halves. The four mouldings of the raked cornice of this pediment include a blank course (that was formerly a cyma recta), a cyma reversa, a fascia, and a cyma reversa, whereas the horizontal cornice is made up of a pair of cyma reversas separated by a fascia. The topmost cyma reversas in the two cornices of the pediment are badly worn and the lower cyma reversa in the horizontal cornice contains loose bricks, as does the spandrel. The arch is now crumbling and cracks exist in the tympanum. The concrete steps, stone sills, and doors of all three entrances are post-colonial and the steps all but obscure the brick pedestals.

The north and south doorways have triangular pediments above flat arches (with voussoirs of three sizes of gauged brick). On the raked cornice of the south pediment, a cavetto at the top seems to be a replacement and below the cavetto are a pair of cyma reversa mouldings separated by a fascia. A pair of cyma reversas with a fascia in the middle constitutes the horizontal cornice, and the upper of these cyma reversas is badly worn. The tympanum on the south has been repointed and twelve voussoirs have been replaced in the arch with excessive crudity. The raked cornice on the north pediment has two blank courses, so that only a cyma reversa and a fascia are left. The cavetto at the top of the horizontal cornice is probably a replacement. A fascia and a cyma reversa (with a brick missing) complete this cornice. The arch on the north is in bad shape (and poorly repaired). On both the south and north doorways, raised jambs serve as quasi-pilasters and, at the water table, as quasi-pedestals. Glazed headers exist in the tympanum of all three pediments.

The church was abandoned immediately after the Disestablishment, for around 1803 the Baptists seem to have taken over. It was repaired in 1817 and "modernized" on the inside in 1834. In the winter of 1922-23 it was completely burnt out, but was promptly rebuilt with its original walls. The present interior has a T-shaped hall; the galleries in the transept are now used as Sunday-school rooms. Almost nothing of its colonial appearance is left.

In addition to the Bible marked 1733, the church still has four tablets (Creed, Lord's Prayer, and Decalogue (on two)). It is, however, somewhat of a shock to see the Apostles' Creed so prominently displayed in a Baptist Church, although the Belief is a bit hidden by doors to the modern baptistry. The four tablets were apparently snatched off the wall in the fire of the 1920's. The colonial font has long been the possession of Fork Church, St Martin's Parish, in Hanover County.

The yard is large and rolling and is dotted by many large trees: indeed, it is almost but a clearing in a forest. A stone from 1708, with an interesting inscription in Latin, lies just outside the north doorway, and two other markers (1736 and 1748) may also be seen, near the southeast corner of the church. Countless unmarked graves are known to lie around the church as well as under its former colonial chancel.

18. WESTOVER PARISH CHURCH

The second Upper Church of Westover Parish (which is now the Westover Parish Church), in Charles City County, lies a fraction of a mile south of route 5 and about four miles east of the junction of routes 5 and 156 (the Hopewell Ferry road). The church is situated high above Herring Creek amidst a fine grove of trees and the churchyard is approached by an attractive lane through open fields.

The parish is one of the oldest in the country, for it derives its existence and name from one of the early plantations on the James River, each of which was a separate parish. Westover Parish was, indeed, recognized by governmental authorities as early as 1625, although no church building is known to have existed in the parish until at least several years after that date. The parish, as formally established sometime before 1652, included, as was the custom in early Virginia, land on both sides of the river (the James in this instance). That on the south side was lost to the parish in 1720, but in the same year the western part of Wallingford Parish and the northern part of Weyanoke

116

Parish were added to Westover Parish and five years later the western part of Wilmington Parish was annexed. The parish and county thus became and have remained coterminous. The parish's name is derived from the West family to whom the West Hundred was originally granted.

The present building of 1731, which seems always to have served as the parish church, is constructed of brick laid in Flemish bond with glazed headers above the bevelled water table and English bond below it. Its dimensions are 60'-6" x 28' on the inside. Rubbed brick with a yellow cast (reminiscent of the windows at Bruton Parish Church) marks the four corners of the building as well as the jambs of the four windows on the north wall and the three westernmost windows on the south wall, although four to six new bricks at the bottoms of these three windows on the south are new. Also replaced are both jambs of the easternmost window on the south wall—this opening was originally the south doorway—and all the semi-circular arches on both the south and the north walls. Each of these arches now unfortunately consists of a pair of rowlock courses. The entire, somewhat smaller gallery window in the west is a more recent (and more skillful) replacement, with its semi-circular arch of rubbed brick in fulls and pairs of halves. Likewise of recent and handsome renewal is the western doorway with segmental-arched pediment, semi-circular-arched opening, tympanum with glazed headers, and shallow pilasters. These pilasters should, however, break out at the water table, as they at present do not. This doorway was covered with cement not long after the War between the States because of its wretched condition; it was restored only in 1956.

Queen closers mark all the original jambs and the four corners of the building and are also used in various replacements. Vents are in evidence below the water table. It is difficult to be sure as to exactly what existed originally in the east façade, but the present three openings and much of their surrounding areas are clearly post-colonial alterations. Two windows, however, probably marked the chancel in the colonial edifice. The side walls are in fine condition. The only obvious spot of repair concerns the former south doorway. Ivy covers much of the north wall. The fact that the apexes of the two gables (12 or more courses above the rowlock course on the west and the same number of courses above a row of headers on the east) are obviously replacements indicates that the original structure possessed clipped gables like the Lower Chapel in Middlesex County, Chuckatuck Church in Nansemond County, and certain other colonial churches. It is to be hoped that they can some day be restored at Westover Church. Glazing is more regular on the lower portions of these walls.

The church was abandoned for nearly thirty years after 1805 and during part of that period was used as a barn.

Flagstones from the original 6'-wide aisle may still be seen at the end of the walk as well as in front of the new rectory and around the present parish house. The existing floor level of the church has been much raised and the water table is correspondingly low. The brick wall that once surrounded the church was destroyed and sold, probably around 1861. The building is said to have been used by Federal troops as a stable, although some persons aver that the absence of marks seems strange if this is true. Of the colonial woodwork, nothing seems to have survived the War between the States except the trusses that support the A-roof and arched ceiling. The gallery in the west and the vestry in the east are among the repairs of 1867, when the church was again restored to service. The roof with the bracketed, overhanging eaves is, of course, relatively modern (perhaps from around 1900).

One of the most appealing features of the present interior is a blue banner that was used at the coronation of Queen Elizabeth II at Westminster Abbey in 1953.

The parish owns a paten and chalice made in London in 1694-95. On the cover of the chalice is inscribed the name of the donor, Sarah Braine. A baptismal bowl in this same set was bought from Westover Parish and presented in 1889 to the Henrico Parish Church (St John's), where it is now used as an alms bason. This bowl is cited in a rector's report of 1724 as "a large Bason instead of a font". Another baptismal bowl from this period is owned by Martin's Brandon Parish in Prince George County. Such bowls came into favor during Cromwell's time in preference to fonts, which were apparently too Anglican for Presbyterians and Independents. Westover Parish also owns a set of silver from London of 1731-32 that originally belonged to the first Lower Westover (Wallingford) Church and presumably came into the custody of the second Upper Westover Church as late as around 1920, when Divine Worship ceased to be held at the fourth Lower Westover (second Mapsico) Church (down below the courthouse). It is possible that George Jones was the maker of this chalice and paten (although one authority has ascribed them to Thomas Tearle). The chalice is inscribed: "The gift of Col. Francis Lightfoot—Anno. 1727".

Of the colonial graves in the yard, a fragment of but a single (albeit richly decorated) stone of 1748 remains. The earliest known tombstone in Virginia, however, exists at the probable site of the first Upper Westover Church. This site is .1 mile west of Westover house, by the banks of the James, and is now a spot of great charm. The bridge over which this site is reached is also of charm, but it is, perhaps, more safely crossed on foot than by motor car. The date of our earliest known tombstone is now obliterated, but was 1637, by which time the first church was completed. In addition to this stone of Captain William Perry, there are eight other colonial tombs here (ranging from 1656 to 1737), several of which are handsome altar-tombs and two of which are strikingly fluted and ribbed. Westover house lies 2.5 miles off route 5. One goes .1 mile on route 640 and .3 mile on route 633, and the private road leading to the house is 2 miles long. The junction of routes 5 and 640 is just over 2 miles east of the junction of route 5 with route 156 (coming from the ferry) and just under 2 miles west of the junction of route 5 with the lane that leads to Westover Parish Church.

The families of such neighboring plantations as "Belle Air", "Shirley", "Berkeley", "Westover", "Mt Sterling", "Sherwood Forest", and "Evelynton" have all been associated with the parish from earliest times, and among those who have worshipped in the parish with some degree of regularity are Presidents William Henry Harrison, Benjamin Harrison, and John Tyler as well as Colonel William Byrd, diarist and builder.

The colonial parish's brick glebe house, which is thought to have been built in the period 1720-30, still stands on route 615 (the road to Ruthville), 2 miles north of the junction of routes 5 and 615 (a mile or so east of Charles City Courthouse). The glebe house was sequestered and sold by the state in 1807 and still remains in secular hands.

First Thanksgiving

Also within the bounds of Westover Parish is the shrine that marks the first recorded American service of Thanksgiving held as a separate office of annual remembrance. The several qualifications given for this Service would seem to be necessary, for services of giving thanks to Almighty God were undoubtedly held at Cape Henry, Jamestown, and elsewhere in Virginia in the earliest years of the colony. The shrine at Harrison's landing by the James (about a quarter of a mile below Berkeley Plantation), however, commemorates the Service that was first held there on December 4, 1619 (or November 25 in the new calendar) by colonists who had set sail from Bristol on the 45-ton ship, "Margaret", in the preceding September. In Captain John Woodliffe's instructions of September the 4th, it was ordained "that the day of our ships arrivall at the place assigned for plantacon in the land of Virginia shall be yearly and perputualy kept holy as a day of Thanksgiving to Almighty God".

This Service was also held on the appointed day in both 1620 and 1621, but the Great Massacre of the settlers by the Indians in the spring of 1622 brought about the temporary abandonment of the village at Berkeley. Such an annual celebration seems, however, to have continued in other parts of the Colony. In recent years, the annual services have been resumed (but on or near the modern date for Thanksgiving),

119

and re-enactments of the original occasion have also taken place. A small brick tower, not unlike that surviving at Jamestown, was unveiled in 1956 by descendants of Captain Woodliffe. It consists of a pair of semi-circular arches with a crenellated parapet above. A mural (protected by a glass case) and a granite plaque adorn the inner walls. The monument lies hard by the shore and may be reached (on foot only) by a delightful lane that leads down from the handsome house. The plantation itself lies 1 mile from the junction of Charles City County's main artery (route 5) with route 640. Route 640 leads into 633 and then into the private road of Berkeley Plantation.

19. Christ Church, Lancaster

Christ Church in Lancaster County lies on route 646 about half a mile west of the junction of routes 646 and 3, which is known as Pitman's Corner. This corner is itself about a mile north of Irvington and about four miles south of Kilmarnock.

Christ Church's remarkable state of preservation is owing principally to two unusual conditions. The first stems from the fact that the church was built largely or, perhaps, entirely through the munificence of Robert Carter, a well-known public figure and landowner of eighteenth-century Virginia. It was this endowment by an individual (or at least by a single family) that seemed to prevent the usual spoliation following the confiscatory law of 1802, although the church was, indeed, abandoned after the Disestablishment until about 1832 and apparently again from 1852 to the early 1880's. It was, amazingly enough, only in 1960 that the parish acquired legal title to the property. The second unusual condition in Christ Church's history lies in the absence of any military action in its somewhat remote area during the War between the States.

The traditional date of Christ Church's completion is 1732, but work on a building of such elaboration must have been in progress for a number of years. Carter's will of 1728, which was probated in 1732, might indicate that the church was largely completed by 1728, for in his testament the church's patron left the parish only 200 pounds and the

120

provision that the bricks were to come from his estate—hardly enough, it would seem, for the erection of such an edifice.

The shape of the building is a Latin cross (rather than a "modified Greek cross", as is sometimes stated) approximately 70' x 70' on the outside. The nave is 24' long and the chancel 16'. The church is constructed of brick laid in Flemish bond with random glazed headers. It is unusually tall even among Virginian churches, which generally give a vertical rather than horizontal impression. At its highest point, the ceiling is no less than 33' above the stone of the aisles and the ridge of the roof is 10' higher still.

A great deal of repair to the masonry of the walls and to the arches, particularly in the south transept, was very skillfully done sometime around 1954. At the same time bricks were used to replace a piece of wood shaped like a brick in the north pediment, although this wooden piece might have itself been a replacement. There is the usual bevelled water table with Flemish bond below as well as above it. The walls are 35" thick.

There are elaborate doorways on the west, south, and north. There are two large windows in the chancel end and two in each side of the nave; there is a single large window in each side of each transept and in each side of the chancel; and there is an ox-eye window over each of the three doorways. Rubbed and gauged brickwork adorns the jambs, arches, pediments, pilasters, and pedestals of all the openings as well as the salient corners of the building (where the rubbed work is particularly broad). Queen closers are also used at the corners. The capitals and bases of the pedestals, the imposts, and the keystone of the western doorway as well as the elliptical steps and the capitals and bases of the pilasters of all three doorways are of Portland stone, as are the sills, keystones, and imposts of the twelve large windows and the four keys of each of the three ox-eye windows.

The circular-headed western doorway (21' high) consists of pilasters supported by pedestals and surmounted by a segmental pediment, all of it heavily moulded. The order here and elsewhere in the building is modified Doric and the entablature throughout the structure consists of an architrave (usually of three fascias), a pulvinated (or cushion) frieze, and a dentil cornice. The arched cornice of the segmental pediment of the western doorway consists of: cyma recta, cyma reversa, fascia (forming a drip), soffit, ovolo, fillet, dentil course, and cyma reversa. The horizontal cornice omits only the initial cyma recta. Below the cushion frieze the architrave includes: fillet, cyma reversa, fascia, cyma reversa, fascia, cyma reversa, fascia, and bead. The semi-circular brick arch of the western doorway consists of: cyma reversa, fascia, and bead; the keystone is divided into three parts (the middle part with three fillets) and is surmounted by a cavetto; and the imposts are made

121

up of: fillet, cyma reversa, fascia, ovolo, upside down cyma reversa (sometimes called ogee), astragal (torus), and cavetto.

The capitals of the pilasters of the western doorway are marked by: abacus (cyma reversa and fascia), ovolo echinus (instead of the usual slant), three fillets (annulets), necking, astragal (torus), and cavetto. The bases of these pilasters have a cavetto at the top and below this are: bead, torus, scotia, torus, and large cavetto. The caps of the pedestals begin with a small cavetto and continue with a deeply undercut drip, cyma recta (also deeply undercut), torus, fillet, and cavetto. The bases of the pedestals are composed of: cavetto, torus, upside down cyma recta, and plinth.

The south and north doorways are 12½' high and have triangular pediments, flat arches, pilasters, and entablatures, but no pedestals. The raked cornice of each pediment is probably lacking its original top course and the existing top course (a fascia) is apparently new. The other mouldings are: cyma reversa, fascia (drip), ovolo, fillet, dentil course, and cyma reversa. The horizontal cornice of these pediments omits only the new course at the top. Below the cushion frieze is the architrave: cyma reversa, fascia, small cyma reversa, fascia, and bead. Over the doors the architrave assumes the form of a flat arch, so that each pair of voussoirs is cut to a different center. In each case, the brick arch seems to have been removed and put back, for a steel lintel has now been inserted. The capitals of the pilasters of the side doorways are identical with those of the main entrance on the west; the bases of these pilasters include: cavetto, torus, scotia, torus, small plinth, and large plinth.

All three sets of double doors and their trim are of walnut and are original except for the west doors below the lunette, which have been replaced. Even these doors, however, retain their H-L hinges. The hardware in the entire church is largely original. There is a lock and a key on the west, but no knob; on the sides there is only a wooden bar on the inside and these bars appear to be late nineteenth-century in origin. All the doors (including the lunette) are marked by panel moulding; and a St Andrew's cross is the feature of the lowest panels in each door. On the west, two pairs of vertical panels above the cross are separated by a pair of smaller, slightly horizontal panels. The panels of the lunette follow the curve of the arch. On the side doors, the order of the panels from the top is: small, slightly vertical; long vertical; long vertical; and small, slightly horizontal. The panel mouldings of the restored west doors are: cyma reversa, splay, bead, and raised field; those of the original side doors are: ovolo, splay, ovolo, and raised field. The wood trim of the west doorway has a cyma reversa above: fascia, small cyma reversa, fascia, and bead. On the wood trim of the south doorway the existing outside mouldings (ovolo and bead) are probably new; the others are: fascia, small cyma reversa, fascia, and bead. The outside mouldings of the wood trim of the north are a fillet and a cyma reversa; then come the fascia, cyma reversa, fascia, and bead.

The dozen large windows have semi-circular arches, the same fluted, cut-stone keys (with cavetto-moulding caps) as the west doorway, stone imposts, and stone sills. From an inspection at ground level, there seem to be several instances in which keystones have been replaced in part or entirely. The windows measure 6' x 14'. The sash are also of walnut and have 22 lights over 16. Some of the original glass panes remain. The windows also contain 2" moulded muntins and wooden pulleys. The stone sills consist of three planes, a torus, a drip, and a deep cyma recta; and they are lug sills in that they extend into the masonry beyond the width of the windows. All the sills, interior as well as exterior, slant; and the exterior sills are in most cases badly deteriorated (with at least one instance of a partial replacement: north window of south side of nave). Around each of the three ox-eye or oval windows is a rim of rubbed brick (a full brick alternating with a pair of halves) and a cyma reversa as well as the four keystones.

Elaborate Interior

The reredos, the panelling on the three sides of the chancel, the altar rail, and most of the three-decker pulpit are of walnut, whereas the south gallery and the high box-pews are of pine.

The reredos has pilasters with pedestals, a segmental pediment, the usual entablature, and raised panels. The segmental-arched cornice of the pediment includes these mouldings: cyma recta, fillet, cyma reversa, fascia (drip), soffit, ovolo, dentil course, and cyma reversa; and the tympanum includes a raised panel. The horizontal cornice omits only the top cyma recta. Below the cushion frieze, the architrave includes: cyma reversa, fascia and bead, fascia and bead, and fascia. The capitals of the fluted pilasters embrace: abacus, ovolo echinus, elongated cyma recta, very small necking, astragal (torus), and cavetto. On the bases of these pilasters are: cavetto, bead, torus, scotia, torus, and deep cavetto. The caps of the pedestals are marked by: fillet, cavetto (drip), deeply undercut cyma recta, small torus, and cavetto. The die is a raised panel. The bases have these mouldings: cavetto, small torus, upside down cyma recta, and the plinth.

At present the Decalogue is inscribed in gold on raised panels between the pilasters of the reredos. This work derives from about 1920 and the panels were made out of walnut from a tree in the yard. Records speak of a black cloth or canvas once mounted there with the usual devotions, and photographs also exist with two tablets superimposed on the panels. The present raised panels have semi-circular heads and below each of them is a long horizontal panel. Rumor has it that the original tablets were cut out in the 1860's with a sword, and used in a private house for instructing the young.

The Table of walnut with Queen Anne legs is believed to be original or at least colonial and undoubtedly American. It was mended, along with the font, around 1904 or a bit later. The chancel chairs are modern. The rectangular rail has curved corners (like the pews at the crossing and at the chancel), torus and cavetto mouldings at the top, fluted and turned balusters, and a "concealed" but raised gate. An extra step has been added on top of the original one for the convenience of communicants who have found the reach too high at the Administration.

Just west of the south and north corners of the chancel are pairs of pilasters surmounted by the usual entablatures and a triangular pediment, all of walnut and all on a somewhat smaller scale than the reredos. The raked cornice of the pediment consists of: cyma recta, cyma reversa, fascia (drip), soffit, ovolo, dentil course, cyma reversa, and bead. The horizontal cornice omits the cyma recta at the top and the bead at the bottom. The capitals of the fluted pilasters on the sides of the chancel embrace: abacus, elongated cyma recta, small torus, small cavetto, necking, astragal (torus), and cavetto. On the bases are: little cavetto, torus, scotia, and torus, which are above a baseboard that itself consists of: cavetto, torus, and fascia. The pediments are distinctly off-center. Between the pilasters is a simple raised panel. On each side of the chancel, the eastern pilaster and its entablature turn the corner and continue on the east to the window.

The four windows in the chancel have (interior) walnut sills, whereas all the other large windows have stone sills with some plaster repairs. All the sills are splayed. The walnut panelling of the chancel is continued on both sides of the reredos (at the height of the side entablatures) from the reredos to the window in each side of the chancel. The panelling turns with both of the east windows, but includes only the east side of the side windows and the portions beneath those windows.

There are three large pews at the crossing (the southwest corner is occupied by the pulpit), each of which may seat as many as twenty persons. Twenty pews seat a dozen persons and two other pews (near the north doors), which have benches only on the north side, probably seat five or six. The pews in the south transept are out of line across the (south) aisle because of the extension of the pulpit on the one side and the stairs on the other. The present candleholders are new. The pews and the raised wood floor beneath them were removed in 1932 and treated for termites, but they have all been put back in their original positions except for the northwest corner pew, which has had to be replaced. The panelling of the pews along the aisles consists of a horizontal panel over a larger vertical panel, whereas the chancel panelling uses a row of slightly vertical panels over an identical row of such panels. The mouldings of the raised panels along the aisles and on the south gallery include: ovolo, splay, ovolo, and raised field. The mouldings of the raised panels in the three corner pews and the chancel omit the second ovolo. The panels of the other pews in the church are not raised, but those on the balcony are raised.

The hexagonal sounding board of the pulpit has an ogee dome with a finial, a complete entablature around its edge, and a sunburst on its soffit. The pulpit itself is bracketed out from a pier fixed at the southwest corner of the crossing. The cornice of the sounding board is made up of: fillet, cyma reversa, fascia, cavetto, small torus, small cavetto, fascia (drip), soffit, ovolo, dentils, and cyma reversa. The decorated cushion frieze projects at the corners and is inlaid or painted. The architrave comprises: fillet, cyma reversa, fascia, cyma reversa, fascia, cyma reversa, fascia, and bead. The sunburst on the soffit of the canopy is of pine and appears once to have been inlaid, for the designs are recessed about ⅛ of an inch. The backboard of the pulpit includes a series of mouldings (cyma reversa, fascia, long cavetto, torus, and cavetto) over three raised panels (a small horizontal over two verticals). The mouldings of these panels are: cyma reversa, ovolo, splay going into a cavetto, ovolo, and raised field. The capitals of the fluted pilasters of the pulpit are moulded thus: cyma reversa, fascia, elongated moulding, torus, cavetto, necking, astragal (torus), and cavetto. The bases include: cavetto, torus, scotia, torus, and plinth. Below the plinth are these: large torus, cavetto, small torus, fillet, fascia, two cavettos, torus, fillet, fascia, and bead.

There is an irregular use of raised panels at the reading desk. The mouldings of these panels are only an ovolo, splay, and raised field. The clerk, however, has no raised panelling, although an extra seat exists in the northwest corner of the pulpit. This may be owing to the fact that the clerk's desk at the bottom of the pulpit is a bit cramped for an active precentor. The balusters of the rails of the pulpit stairs are, like the communion rail, fluted and elaborately (albeit differently) turned. The stairs are also marked by scrolled brackets.

The south gallery is supported by four graceful, fluted columns and its front has a series of horizontal raised panels over a series of vertical ones. This gallery and its supports are very similar to the newer portion of the south gallery at St Mary's Whitechapel in the same county. The balusters of the gallery stairs at Christ Church are less elaborately turned than are those of the altar and pulpit. They are also not fluted. The scrolls on the gallery stair stringer are a bit crude. The gallery pews are not original.

The little walnut moulding that follows the spring-line of the ceiling (and turns into the window-openings) is probably original. The walls and barrel vault are plastered. A recent inspection of the area above the ceiling revealed that the lath side was as smooth as the exposed side. The aisles are laid with blocks of Purbeck stone of random sizes. The marble font from England has acanthus leaves and heads of cherubim on the bowl. It was damaged by youthful vandals in the early part of this century, but has been repaired.

At the eaves on the exterior is another full, wooden entablature. The cornice of the roof includes: crown mould, fillet, cyma reversa, and fascia (drip); and below the soffit of the fascia are these: fillet, ovolo, fillet, dentil course, and cyma reversa. Below the usual cushion frieze is the architrave, which consists of three fascias with a bead under each plane. The roof is steep and hipped, and turns up at the eaves, thereby reminding some persons of a pagoda and others of Merchant's Hope and similar churches. The present slate roof, a gift from the Association for the Preservation of Virginia Antiquities, is a replacement for a shingle roof installed in the early 1880's.

At the crossing is a marker of 1674 that ends with the pointed reminder: *Hodie mihi cras tibi.* On the north of the altar is another seventeenth-century marker taken from the chancel of the earlier church (around 1670) on the same site. In addition to unmarked colonial graves in the yard, the handsome tombs of the church's benefactor and his wives as well as a fourth colonial marker lie east of the chancel.

A brick wall around the churchyard, with moulded brick cap and serpentine gates, was still visible in the latter part of the last century and apparently lay just inside the present fence. Its foundations have recently (1959) been uncovered and its restoration has now been undertaken. At the present writing, there is in the church neither heat nor electricity (except for the usual, unfortunate electronic organ), although plans to heat, illuminate, and possibly air-condition the old building are in the air (and, to some authorities, seem hazardous, whether necessary or not).

The parish owns several fine pieces of communion silver: 1) a chalice and paten-cover made by an unidentified London goldsmith who is known to have been working in 1681-82; 2) a flagon from London of 1720-21 (probably by Thomas Folkingham); and 3) a bason from London of 1695-96 by an unidentified maker who is known to have been working in 1694-95. The chalice and paten-cover have the same heart-shaped mark engraved four times on each of them.

Although the fabric of Christ Church has been repaired more

than is readily apparent, it is still more largely intact than any other colonial church. It is likewise second to none in Virginia—indeed, in all America—in scale and grandeur. The excellence of its elaborate details evidences craftmanship of the highest standards of its times, English or American, and is an unceasing object of admiration.

20. St John's Church, King William

The colonial church in, perhaps, the most lamentable condition of all those in Virginia is the handsome building now known as Old St John's in King William County. This edifice may be seen about eight miles southeast of King William Courthouse, sixteen miles southeast of Central Garage, and eight miles northeast of West Point. It lies at a turn in a wooded lane (route 627), only .1 mile south of route 30.

St John's Parish was created in 1680 out of St Stephen's and Stratton Major Parishes (in King and Queen County), and in 1691 that part of St Peter's Parish (in New Kent County) that lay north of the Pamunkey River was added to St John's Parish. St John's Parish became as a result coterminous with King William County when the latter was created out of King and Queen County in 1701. The parish is one of the relatively few in colonial times to be dedicated to a saint (to the Evangelist in this instance rather than to the Baptist).

The original portion of the present building was constructed in 1734. The date of the addition of the north wing is uncertain, but it has been suggested that it was probably erected between 1755 and 1765, as was the wing at its sister church near Acquinton Creek, for that particular decade seems to have witnessed an increase both in population and in attendance upon Divine Worship. Old St John's Church is believed to be the second (or possibly the third) Lower Church of St John's Parish. The first church in this area was called the Pamunkey Neck Chapel and it is thought to have stood at West Point, probably on the site of the present Baptist Church, where a small cemetery still includes a stone of 1728. This chapel, which may have been built as early as 1665, or a possible successor built (probably of brick) on the same site, thus became the first Lower Church of St John's Parish and remained so

127

until it was replaced in 1734 by the existing second (or third) Lower Church—Old St John's.

This 1734 church is about 50'-3" long and 30'-2" wide. The wing is 24' from north to south and 28'-9" from east to west. Inasmuch as the wing is off center five feet to the east, the western portion of the north wall of the original church is 15'-8" long and the eastern portion only 5'-10" long. Therefore, the church is almost as much L-shaped as it is T-shaped; and such a shape seems admirably suited for any liturgically oriented church, for all worshippers enjoy a relatively unobstructed view of both altar and pulpit.

The bond of the handsome brickwork is Flemish (with glazed headers) above the water table and English bond below it. Owing to the present wretched condition of the fane, one is able to see the English bond that is used throughout the inner walls. The glazing of the headers is in a remarkably good state of preservation. Rubbed brick is used at the salient corners, the arches and jambs of all windows (large and small) as well as of the west and north doorways, and, interestingly enough, along the rake of all three gables. Just inside each of these rows of rubbed brick along the rake of the gables, there is also a row of glazed headers.

The use of queen closers varies. They are to be found: 1) at the salient corners (even below the water table); 2) on both sides of the western doorway; 3) on the right side of the north doorway (with a few also on the left side); 4) on the left jamb of the easternmost window and the right jamb of the westernmost window on the south wall; 5) on both jambs of the west window and the two gallery windows of the wing; and 6) on the right jamb of the east window of the wing.

The bevelled water table alternates full bricks with pairs of halves. Ventilation holes seem to have been inserted somewhat irregularly. Tie-rods of recent installation are in evidence (both inside and outside) and account for the present "dished" appearance of the north gable.

The walls of Old St John's (which are 20" thick in both parts of the building) are in superb condition. This is remarkable when it is considered that they have not sheltered, it seems, an active parish since the Disestablishment. Repointing marks the areas on each side of the western doorway. The most striking alteration on the south wall concerns the colonial south doorway (just west of the easternmost window). This doorway was undoubtedly pedimented and has been bricked in with considerable slovenliness. Various spots of repointing and repair as well as a stove pipe also mark this long south wall. Several large cracks may be seen on the east (or old chancel) wall. The small, eastern portion of the original north wall is in good shape and the western portion of this same wall has little to mar it except a spot of repair high in the left corner.

On the north wall of the wing, repairs mark the rubbed brick along the rake on the right side as well as a small area above the left side of the doorway; and several single bricks have been replaced. Cracks also exist above both of the gallery windows. There are no obvious repairs on the walls proper of the sides of the wings except for some repointing on the west below the water table.

Of the three colonial doorways, the north and west examples remain in fairly good condition. The segmental cornice of the pediment of the western doorway includes these mouldings: two cyma reversas, fascia, soffit, and cyma reversa; and the horizontal cornice is the same except for only a single cyma reversa at the top. In the tympanum the brickwork is of Flemish bond with glazed headers. The horizontal cornice breaks out and forms capitals for the pilasters, which are straight shafts with three sizes of brick. The bases of the pilasters follow the water table, break out, and possess pedestals. The bevelled water table turns and runs down by the door frame, as at Vawter's Church in Essex County. The arch of the doorway is semi-circular and its voussoirs were originally composed of full bricks and pairs of halves, as were the jambs. In addition to a certain amount of deterioration, this doorway is marked by a considerable degree of renewal. The segmental cornice is now in part covered with a mortar wash; and the entire left pilaster, the left and top portions of the arch, the left jamb, and the left spandrel are all new and incorrectly replaced.

The raked cornice of the triangular pediment of the north doorway formerly was surmounted by a cyma recta, but this course is now wanting. Both cornices are at present possessed of cyma reversa, fascia, and cyma reversa mouldings. Seven bricks have been replaced in the lower cyma reversa of the lower cornice. The tympanum represents new work. There are no pilasters, but the jambs (of three sizes of rubbed brick) project. The bases of these jambs are rudimentary pedestals and the top course of these pedestals (along the water table) consists of a flat top with a bevelled side. The stone steps of this doorway are, like those on the west, probably not original. The brick sill is missing on the north. A brick carved with "1734" and another with "IH" now may be seen in the fascia of the horizontal cornice, but these bricks are said to derive from the original south doorway. The "IH" might possibly represent John Hipkins, who built the Middlesex churches a little earlier in the century. The arch of the north doorway is flat.

The portal in the east is a post-colonial and somewhat crude insertion.

There are eight large windows—three on the south wall, two in the east (old chancel) end, and one each in each side of the wing and the western part of the original north wall. The left jamb of this last window lies right at the juncture of (old) nave and wing. All of these windows have semi-circular arches with rubbed brick voussoirs of full bricks and pairs of halves. All of them also at some time have been extended at the bottom by six courses, as can be told by the queen closers and rubbed brick at the jambs as well as by the piecing of the window frames. The bevelled brick sills of the three windows on the south are clearly replacements. The brick sills of the other windows are entirely gone. New mortar supports eight bricks in the arch of the westernmost window of the south wall and four bricks in the arches of each of the other windows on the same wall. Nine bricks have been repaired in the arch of the southern window of the former chancel wall, and two bricks have likewise been repaired at the top of the arch of the west window of the wing. Repairs also exist in the lower jambs on the original north wall. In addition to the large windows, there are four smaller windows at gallery level—two in the north gable and one each in the east and west gables. That in the west gable has a flat arch of full bricks and pairs of halves (or, perhaps, merely incised in that manner). At least four bricks of this arch are replacements. The same full bricks and pairs of halves mark the circular window high in the east gable, although no repairs are obvious. This aperture, however, is square on the inside. The pair of small windows in the north gallery has segmental arches of stretchers and pairs of headers. One of each pair of headers is glazed, the upper alternating with the lower across the arch.

Some of the church's woodwork is undoubtedly original and much of it is colonial. Of the door frames and doors themselves on the west (which are not unlike those at Vawter's Church), only the uppermost portions (forming the lunette) in each instance are old; the rest (including sill) is renewal. The mouldings of the frames are cyma reversa, two fascias, and bead. The moulding of the two original, raised quarter-circle panels at the top is merely an ovolo. The frames of the north doorway may possibly be colonial, but the rest is all new. The frames of the windows are probably in part colonial or even original and have the same mouldings as the door frames. However, inasmuch as the old windows and doors and their frames are said to have been removed not too long ago and to have been reworked (and also painted red), it is impossible to know exactly how much is old and how much is not old, and no one connected with the church seems to be able to make a categorical statement as to their age. Most of the panes (21 over 9) and all the sills are recent replacements.

Reredos and Galleries

The outstanding feature of the present interior is a striking reredos that is no less than 13'-3" wide. It is hard to see how this could be an original possession of St John's Church. For one thing, the reredos projects into the middle and eastern windows of the south wall (against which it is now located) and it would certainly fit no better between the windows of the original chancel wall. Its origin, like that of the reredos at Abingdon Church in Gloucester County, is, therefore, somewhat of a guess, and guesses have included (in the case of St John's reredos) Acquinton Church (also from 1734) in the same parish as well as the New Church (1768) of Stratton Major Parish in neighboring King and Queen County, the latter of which seems the more likely.

The raked cornice of the triangular pediment of the reredos includes: cyma reversa, fascia, and soffit. The mouldings of the horizontal cornice are: cyma reversa, fascia, soffit, cyma reversa, dentils, and cyma reversa. Below the plain frieze is a two-part architrave. The four pilasters have fluted shafts and their capitals are composed of: abacus, a somewhat curious moulding (a torus turning into a cyma recta), cavetto, necking, astragal, another necking, and another astragal. On the bases of the pilasters are ovolo, scotia, and ovolo. The pedestals include: elongated cavetto, fascia, the aforementioned curious moulding, two little fillets, and a long, vertical raised panel in the field. On the bases of the pedestals are: upside down cyma recta, fascia, and plinth. There are four tablets, which are now in a basement at 1102 Main Street in West Point. They have gold lettering on a black ground, coated with varnish, and are surrounded by gilded wood frames. There is some doubt as to whether they were originally part of the present reredos. The sides of the reredos are dropped, somewhat in the manner of a Palladian window. Below each of the tablets (two in the center under the pediment and one on each side) is a raised horizontal panel and below that a square raised panel. Between these two layers of four panels each are three chair rails (one in the center and one on each side).

The two galleries (west and north) are both colonial. The west gallery front and stair (which is now collapsed) have turned balusters, and the shallow front is marked by a somewhat primitive assemblage of simple mouldings. Both galleries have a pair of slender, fluted Tuscan columns for supports, although the south column under the west gallery is no longer *in situ*. The front and stair of the north gallery have rails of horizontal raised panels. For some reason, the north gallery has a more authentically colonial air than does its western counterpart. The coping of the rail on the north is a renewal, although the floor is old. It is at present not convenient to judge the floor of the west gallery.

The remains of the most recent plastering of the walls are still visible. The walls are thickened by a slight ledge at the inside floor line and this ledge is lower along the old chancel than elsewhere. The large windows are splayed at top and sides. The ceiling is segmental in the original portion and flat in the wing. The roof trusses were replaced around

131

1926, although some original ones may have been left. No remnants of the colonial floor, pews, or pulpit are extant, although a few crude nineteenth-century benches lie in a heap in the old nave. Flagstones from colonial times do, however, survive. Smaller ones extend from the east to the west doorways and larger ones from that alley to the north doorway. Inasmuch as the chancel was in the east in colonial times, these flagstones have been in great part removed. Some of them are believed to lie in the back yard of the house at 1121 Main Street in West Point. Other colonial flagstones in use in St John's Parish to-day are some of those that formerly served the New Church of Stratton Major Parish and were given, towards the end of the last century, to the modern St John's Church at West Point. Seventy-six of these flagstones now form a walk on the north side of the West Point church.

The exterior cornice and slate roof of Old St John's were probably installed around 1926.

After the Disestablishment, the building seems to have been only occasionally used for Divine Worship, and by various groups, including Methodists and Baptists. Shortly after the War between the States, it is said to have been bought by two Episcopalians and deeded back to the Church, partly in order to keep colored congregations from taking it over as they had done with Mangohick and Cattail Churches in the upper part of the county. Old St John's Church is believed never to have suffered either from fire or from military damage.

If Old St John's Church has truly had no active congregation for over sixteen decades, it seems difficult to understand why such an enormous reredos was ever installed, why such a large doorway as that on the south had to be abolished, and why there was need for a doorway on the east—and this last is a paradigm of rural carpentry, with its wood trim, for example, extending only to the water table. Inasmuch as all these changes were clearly accomplished after the Disestablishment (owing to the liturgical orientation required of all colonial churches by law)—and all at the same time—and also inasmuch as it has been written that this was all arranged "in modern times", it is similarly difficult to understand why so much uncertainty exists to-day concerning the date of these enormous alterations of the building's interior.

One of the interesting facts concerning St John's history has to do with the departure in the 1870's of some of its parishioners for a new Reformed Episcopal congregation at King William Courthouse, for this is one of the few remaining evidences in Virginia of this group that broke away from the Episcopal Church out of Evangelical fervor. Another interesting feature of the parish's history is that its eighteenth-century faithful included Carter Braxton, one of the signers of the Declaration of Independence.

Old St John's is used but seldom and is, indeed, nowadays entirely unusable, although sporadic efforts have been made to preserve its fabric. It seems that there is too little support for the church in the county either among Episcopalians or other Christians (despite the fact that the area is not overburdened with other historical or architectural treasures) and that, therefore, the association for the preservation of Old St John's will have to launch an appeal beyond the Pamunkey and Mattaponi Rivers if this particularly fine example of colonial work is to be vouchsafed to later generations of Virginians. It also seems unthinkable that such an appeal should fail.

The ruins of the north wing (possibly 1755-65) of Acquinton Church (the second Upper Church of St John's Parish) may also be seen if one proceeds 1.2 miles northwest of King William Courthouse on route 30, turns left, and continues 1.8 miles on route 629 to the junction of that route with route 618. However, only portions of its now stuccoed walls (which were extended 14½' at the south end about 1875, when the Methodists rebuilt the wing) survive and these are rapidly deteriorating. Some of Acquinton's bricks might possibly prove useful in renewing Old St John's.

21. OLD DONATION CHURCH (LYNNHAVEN PARISH CHURCH)

The third parish church of Lynnhaven Parish in Princess Anne County was built in 1736, as a brick not far to the right of the west doorway attests. The church (on Witch Duck Road) may be reached from route 58 (between Norfolk and Virginia Beach) by going north from Chinese Corner on route 647 for a distance of 2.2 miles. From Bayside on route 60, one goes south on route 166 for .8 mile, turns left on to route 652 for 1.9 miles, left on to route 648 for .6 mile, and left again on to route 647 for .3 mile—a total distance of 3.6 miles. The church lies in a beautiful yard of lawn, trees, and graves. The second church (around 1692) was apparently also built in this yard.

The site of the first church (1639 or earlier) on Church Point, on the western shore of the Western Branch of the Lynnhaven River, is still known, although part (possibly a great part) of the burying ground around the old church (which was probably of frame constuction) has gradually eroded away. The local but venerable tradition of a sudden flooding rather than a gradual erosion of this area seems not to be reliable.

Lynnhaven Parish was one of the three parishes created out of Lower Norfolk County and Parish not long after 1640. Princess Anne County was created out of Lower Norfolk County in 1691, although part of Lynnhaven Parish lay in Norfolk County until four years later, when Lynnhaven Parish and Princess Anne County became coterminous. Lynnhaven Parish derived its name from the river, which Adam Thoroughgood is believed to have named for his early home in England, Lynn in Norfolk County.

The existing church's unique name seems to derive from the gift to the parish of adjoining lands, although the name of Donation can be traced back only to 1822. The brick edifice, laid in Flemish bond with glazed headers (except for the English bond below the bevelled water table) measures about 65' x 30' on the inside and its walls are 18" thick above the water table. The walls were originally at least 13 courses higher than they are at present.

The most interesting feature of the church concerns the windows of the south and north walls, which may best be studied on the former wall, for all the windows on the north wall (save the right jamb of the westernmost window) are restored. On the south wall there are three large windows with semi-circular arches. To the east of the middle window there is a smaller window with a semi-circular arch and to the west of the middle window there is a small, rectangular window (the head of which was formerly higher than at present). These small windows, high up on each of the side walls, were originally inserted to light and ventilate four hanging pews or private galleries that were added along the walls at various times between 1736 and 1769. The rectangular windows are placed higher on the walls than are the small windows with semi-circular arches. There are four rather than three large windows on the north wall; the additional one is at the eastern end of the wall, in the chancel. Two of the three original windows in the chancel wall are still in use. The third window on this wall is bricked up and may have been filled in before the Revolution to allow for an altar-piece. The two windows in the west gable are modern insertions, but some sort of opening (or openings) undoubtedly existed on that wall in the original instance to light the west gallery.

The large, semi-circular arches (six original and four replaced) of the principal windows as well as the semi-circular arches of the two smaller, replaced windows in the west gable consist of full bricks alternating with pairs of headers, with the outermost of each pair glazed. The semi-circular arch of the small window on the south wall consists of a rowlock course. Only a part of the arch of the similar (replaced) window on the north wall is visible. Neither the original nor the replaced small window with flat head has a visible arch.

All three of the arches on the chancel wall terminate at the bottom with projecting bricks. Each of the arches of the six original principal windows has, at the top, a pair of stretchers by way of an embryonic keystone.

The arch of the northernmost window on the chancel wall is heavily repointed. On the middle (bricked-up) opening on this wall, the left projection is missing and a slovenly patch of mortar now marks its position. The arch of the southernmost window of the chancel wall is badly repaired and its left jamb is badly repointed. The middle and westernmost windows of the south wall have arches that have been crudely repointed at the top.

Two new bricks mark the bottom of each jamb of the bricked-up window on the chancel wall. On the south, seven new bricks occur in the lower left jamb of the easternmost window and eight or nine new bricks in the lower left jamb of the middle, large window. In the westernmost window on this wall, repointing occurs at the lower right and left. The right jamb of the small window with the semi-circular arch has been heavily repaired and both jambs of the small window with the flat head have also been repaired.

Rubbed brick marks the arches and jambs of the three openings of the chancel wall and the three large windows on the south wall as well as the single original jamb on the north wall, but it is difficult to tell about the four corners of the building.

Queen closers are to be seen at the four corners (even below the water table) and in the jambs of the three openings in the chancel wall, the three large windows in the south wall, and the original, right jamb of the westernmost window in the north wall. On the left jamb of the easternmost window on the south wall, six of the queen closers are placed at the ends of full bricks and some of these closers are glazed. The repairs of the middle, large window on this wall include no closers. On the westernmost window of the south wall, there are some extra, glazed closers on the left. No closers exist on the jambs of the small windows on the south wall or on those of the replaced windows on the north and west walls.

Renewal of the masonry includes the upper portions of the east and west gables and all of the north wall save the extremities (a larger portion remaining towards the west end than towards the east end), the water table, and two to four courses above the water table along its entire length. The water table on this north wall has been completely repointed. The eastern extremity of the south wall has only about 18″ left at the top, and about 3′ is visible at the bottom. Repairs occur below all three large windows on this wall, and there is heavy repointing below the water table. On the west wall, heavy repointing is also to be seen both on the right and on the left as well as in the water table. On the chancel façade there exist badly mended cracks above the north and south windows as well as heavy repointing in the lower portion of the wall and in the water table.

New brick sills mark all the windows. Small ventilation holes (a half-brick wide) exist only on the south, although two large holes of modern origin are to be seen on the east and a single such opening on the north. Tie-rods are also in evidence.

Since 1916 the west doorway has been enclosed by a brick vestibule and the south doorway has been made into an entry to the vestry. The south doorway seems to have been moved a bit west to its present position in 1767 to make room for a great pew near the chancel. It is probable that the west doorway consisted of a semi-circular arch of rubbed and gauged brick and pilasters of ordinary brick (which was, however, of brighter cast than that on the walls), for this doorway at Old Donation is believed to have been the model for a doorway on that order that adorned the Eastern Shore Chapel until its forced demolition in 1953 by the United States Navy. The Old Donation doorway in turn is believed to have possibly been modelled upon the doorway of the second church (around 1692).

The sides of all the large windows are splayed on the interior. The reredos, altar, pulpit, lectern, and communion rail were given to Old Donation in 1916 by St Paul's Church in Norfolk. It is believed that the flagstones in the central aisle were also given at the same time by St Paul's.

It was the colonial practice at Old Donation as well as elsewhere to segregate the sexes during Divine Worship wherever the seating arrangement allowed it: the men on the north and the women on the south.

The building was neglected after the Disestablishnent, but was completely repaired in 1822-24. After 1843 it lay abandoned for three-quarters of a century and was utterly burnt out by a woods fire in 1882. Then, like Lower Southwark Church in Surry County and Christ Church in Middlesex County, it became a roofless ruin with large trees growing within its walls. The church was restored in 1916 (and again in 1960), but became the parish church again only in 1943 and presumably retained that status until the diocese abolished parochial boundaries in the early 1950's.

The parish owns a set of English communion silver that includes: 1) a paten (1711-12); 2) a chalice (1712-13), which still bears traces

136

of gilding; and 3) a flagon (1716-17). The paten was made by Anthony Nelme and the flagon by Robert Timbrell. These three pieces are on loan at the Norfolk Museum, although they are still used at the church on the great festivals of the year. The parish also owns a red marble font and a pewter alms bason, both of which are believed to have descended from the first parish church.

Another set of colonial silver still in use also derives from Lynnhaven Parish. This set (chalice, paten-cover, and flagon) was made in London in 1759-60 by William Grundy and is the possession of the Eastern Shore Chapel (now located between London Bridge and Virginia Beach). In 1895 the Eastern Shore Chapel became the parish church of East Lynnhaven Parish, but still retains in its title a reminder of the fact that it was for so long the Chapel of Lynnhaven Parish that served those who lived on the eastern shore of the Lynnhaven River.

The vestry book (1723-1892) of Lynnhaven Parish is on loan at the State Library in Richmond. The colonial portion (1723-86) has been published and is available from the Virginia Historical Society in Richmond.

The oldest (1768) stone in the lovely graveyard at Old Donation Church is also the largest. It was moved, along with several others, from neighboring plantations, about 1930. Although it is the only colonial marker in the yard, there are many other unmarked and unidentified colonial graves in the cemetery. One of the most attractive features of the yard has long been a bench in a shaded spot, for benches are almost never seen in any of our lovely churchyards, but this one at Old Donation has recently been removed.

Cape Henry Cross

One of America's great religious and historical shrines also lies in Princess Anne County: the Cape Henry Memorial, which marks the approximate site of the first landing made in Virginia by the Founders of Jamestown. This landing took place on April the 26th in 1607. Further landings were made on each of the next three days and on the last of these (April the 29th) it is recorded that they "set up a Crosse at Chesupioc Bay" and named the cape for Henry, the eldest son of James I. The cross that they planted may possibly have been of English oak that had been previously fashioned for such an occasion. It is assumed that the setting up of the Cross was accompanied by Divine Worship led by Parson Hunt, who may have also held services on the cape on one or more of the preceding days.

The National Society of the Daughters of the American Colonists erected the present granite cross, pedestal, and encircling wall in 1935 and the quarter-acre of ground upon which the memorial stands was transferred from the Fort Story Military Reservation to the Colonial National Historical Park in 1939. Services are held at the Cross each year, usually on the Sunday nearest April the 26th or at sunrise of Easter Day (or upon both occasions), under the patronage of the Bishop of Southern Virginia.

The Cape Henry Cross lies 3 miles north of downtown Virginia Beach, and a more stirring spot cannot be imagined, particularly if one stands on the dune just to the northwest of the cross and beholds the great arc formed by the Chesapeake Bay on the west and north, the 1791 lighthouse (of Aquia stone) on the south, and the Atlantic on the east. The commemoration of the first landing, in the form of a plaque, is still affixed to the old lighthouse.

22. BLANDFORD CHURCH (BRISTOL PARISH CHURCH)

Blandford Church of Bristol Parish is named for the colonial town of Blandford, which long ago became a part of the city of Petersburg. It has also been known as the Brick Church on Wells's Hill and, for a time, as St Paul's Church. It lies on the east side of Crater Road (routes 301 and 460) at the top of the hill.

Prince George County was formed from Charles City County in 1702 and portions of the county formed part of Amelia County in 1734, part of Chesterfield County in 1749, and Dinwiddie County in 1752. Bristol Parish seems to have been organized as early as 1643. Its southwestern portion became part of Raleigh Parish and its territory on the north side of the Appomattox River became part of Dale Parish, all in 1734. In 1742 its western portion became Bath Parish, which was almost coterminous with Dinwiddie County when that county was created ten years later. In 1745 a strip of Bath Parish along its eastern edge was returned to Bristol Parish.

Bristol Parish was named for the seaport on the west coast of England and seems to have been created out of the plantation parish at Bermuda Hundred (in present-day Chesterfield County). The Brick Church on Wells's Hill is the third parish church of Bristol Parish. The first of these parish churches is believed to have been built about

1645 near the colonial settlement of Charles City (on the Appomattox River, about 3 miles west of Hopewell). The second parish church was Jefferson's Church of 1723, which stood not far from the junction of routes 1 (and 301) and 10 in Chesterfield County. When this church was lost to the new Dale Parish in 1734, the existing building at Blandford had already been ordered.

The original portion of Blandford Church, which was modelled upon Merchant's Hope Church, was finished in 1736 or 1737 and is approximately 64' x 29'. The north wing (approximately 30' long and 29' wide) was added sometime between 1752 and 1769. In 1752 an addition was actually ordered for the south side rather than the north side, but this order was reversed in the same year. The final reckoning on the wing occurred only in 1769.

The structure is of brick laid in Flemish bond above the bevelled water table, although half-way up the east gable the bond becomes predominantly English and irregular. Below the water table of the original portion of the church, the bond is English, but below the water table on the wing the bond is Flemish. The water table is now very low in relation to the ground level. The original floor is said to have been 18" above the ground. The walls of the church are 21" thick.

Repairs to the walls include: 1) on the south wall—heavy repointing along the lower portion, four new patches in the upper areas, and a long crack east of the doorway; 2) on the east wall—minor repointing in the lower area and several cracks; 3) on the west wall—a crack or two below the gallery window; and 4) on the north wall of the original nave —heavy repointing in the upper left corner. The central portion of the north wall of the chancel is completely repaired, as are the entire left jamb and arch of the window, the upper part of the right jamb, and the upper right wall (to the juncture with the wing). Repairs on the wing embrace repointing in the lower area and patching above the window arches on the east wall as well as some repointing below both windows and heavy repointing in the upper right corner and the lower right part of the water table on the west wall. Vines presently cover large areas of the walls of the church, including the north walls of both the chancel and the wing and the chancel wall itself. The apexes of all three gables are now marked by louvered openings. Numerous bullet holes are easily detected. Tie-rods are also in evidence. No ventilation holes, however, can be seen, although they may at present be covered up. The existing cornice may be heavier than the original one. The replaced window in the north wall of the chancel has been put back one course higher than in the original instance. All the windows have bevelled brick sills.

The west doorway is marked by a semi-circular arch; the voussoirs are composed of a full brick and a half-brick alternating with the reverse of that pattern. The south doorway (near the chancel) and the north doorway (in the wing) have been entirely replaced and have flat arches, the south one very crudely executed. The doorways are quite wide: 6'-5" on the west and south and 5'-5" on the north. There is repointing in the arch and in the upper right jamb of the western portal; several new bricks also mark this doorway. The upper left jamb of the northern doorway is likewise renewal.

The principal windows of the church—two in the east, two (out of the original four) on the north wall (one in the chancel and one in the nave), three in the south (all of them west of the south doorway), and two in each of the side walls of the wing—all have semi-circular arches. The voussoirs alternate full bricks with pairs of halves. The arches of the two smaller, later windows in the gallery of the north wing consist of rowlock courses and are repaired. The undoubtedly original, small window in the west gallery has a semi-circular arch. Repairs to the windows include: 1) two or three new bricks in each of the east windows and in the northernmost window on the east wall of the wing: and 2) some repointing in the arches of the north wall of the (original) nave and the west wall of the wing.

The church's rubbed brick is not easily summarized. It seems to mark the salient corners of the building and the jambs of the western doorway, the principal windows, and the small western window, but, as to the arches, only those of the western doorway and the windows of the original part of the church. The arches of the principal windows and the jambs of the windows on the south are red; the arches and jambs of both openings on the west are brown; and the jambs of all the openings on the wing are the same orange-brown hue as the remainder of the walls on the wing.

Queen closers mark the salient corners (even in some instances below the water table) and all openings (except for the repaired areas of the west and north doorways and the window on the north wall of the chancel).

The only remaining colonial woodwork inside the church is the large oak beam that now supports the west gallery (which was reconstructed about 1956), although part of the plate on the south side may also be old. The north gallery of colonial times has not been rebuilt.

The original church was built by Mr Thomas Ravenscroft and the wing and churchyard wall were added by Colonel Richard Bland. The segmental-arched ceiling was undoubtedly originally plastered. However, the exposed rafters now to be seen were put in by the present custodians, perhaps around 1922. The present slate roof dates from around 1882. Happily, the upturn at the eaves, which is one of the fea-

140

tures derived from its famous model, has been retained. The exterior sills and possibly some of the exterior trim of the principal windows are marked by wooden pegs and are very old, if not colonial.

The five-foot brick wall (with moulded cap), which encloses one-half of an acre of the churchyard and dates, like the north wing, from 1752-69, is still largely intact (although some repairs of recent date to both wall and cap have been far from skillfully executed). A fragment of a wall that was built at the same time in the southeast corner of the yard around the Poythress family graves is still visible, although it is now covered by ivy. On one of the Poythress stones may be seen scars from a direct hit by a cannonball. A stone ornament from the colonial west gate has recently been set back in place. A number of colonial tombs (including several table-tombs) lie within the walls; one (†1775) lies near the present chancel rail. Figures from the Revolution, the War of 1812, and the War between the States are also buried in Blandford cemetery. Indeed, the beautiful and very large cemetery that completely surrounds the churchyard and extends far to the east and south includes the graves of no fewer than thirty thousand Confederate soldiers.

Although Bristol Parish began to hold its regular worship in Petersburg sometime before 1802 (when the new church was completed), monthly services continued to be held at Blandford Church until around 1803 (and occasional services until at least 1826.) In 1819 Blandford Church was bought by a citizen of Petersburg and given to the town, which unfortunately let it then go to ruin until 1882. In that year a limited degree of repair was authorized by the city council. Mindful of the remarkable and constant care that the Ladies' Memorial Association had given to the graves of Confederate heroes since 1866, the city gave the church into the hands of the Ladies in 1901. Since then it has been restored and made into a Confederate museum or shrine, with its walls marked by numerous memorial tablets. The restoration within the church includes a pulpit modelled upon that formerly used at the old church in Isle of Wight County, doors (1962) modelled upon those at Merchant's Hope Church, and a Table in Queen Anne style. Nineteenth-century chairs flank the Table. On a tablet in the church are the lines of a poem that is said to have been indited upon the walls of the old building around 1841. The authorship of this poem has been ascribed to various persons, including the Irish actor, Tyrone Power.

Although many persons would have preferred to retain the clear glass of our colonial tradition, the Ladies in the first decade of their custodianship arranged for Louis Comfort Tiffany to execute fifteen stained glass memorials (the fifteenth occupies the transom over the west doorway), which were subscribed by the various Confederate and border states. It is these windows that impart to the church its uncolonial darkness. Also in the church now are slip-pews and red quarry tile (covering the entire floor).

The building's long disuse as a church is pointed up vividly by the fact that the Episcopalians in the Blandford area have since the latter part of the last century been worshipping in another building (the Church of the Good Shepherd), only a very short distance north, down Wells's Hill. A memorial service is held, however, in old Blandford Church every June the 9th, and funerals and christenings are also held there from time to time.

The original manuscripts of the vestry book (1720-89) and parish register (1720-92) of Bristol Parish are kept at St Paul's Church in Petersburg.

23. FORK CHURCH

The Fork Church of St Martin's Parish in Hanover County derives its name from its location between the North and South Anna Rivers, close to where they join to form the Pamunkey River. The church lies on route 738 about 4.5 miles west of Gum Tree (on route 1), which in turn is 3 miles south of Doswell and 4.5 miles north of Ashland. The church's date of construction is believed to lie between 1736 and 1740. St Martin's Parish was cut off from St Paul's Parish, also in Hanover County, in 1726. The present building is the second Lower Church of St Martin's Parish. The first Lower Church (around 1722) of the parish was originally erected as the Chapel in the Forks or Fork Chapel of St Paul's Parish.

Fork Church's walls (approximately 34' x 74') are 22" thick and are of fine brickwork laid in Flemish bond with glazed headers of considerable regularity. English bond occurs below the bevelled water table. Rubbed brick marks the jambs and arches of the windows and the four corners. Rubbed brick probably also marks the flat arches and jambs of the south and west doorways, but it is impossible to be positive about this because they are now covered by porches.

Queen closers mark the jambs of the windows on the side walls (three on the south and four on the north) and the four corners (even below the water table). On the east wall, queen closers are used on the left jamb of the western window, but there are none on the left jamb of the other window on this wall. It is not possible now to say anything about the remaining jambs on this chancel wall because of a chimney that was added (along with an appendage on the north) in 1957. The two second-storey windows on the west seem not to be marked by queen closers, but because of the shutters it is difficult to be certain.

Ventilation holes, modern tie-rods, and large vines also are to be noted on these beautiful walls. Repairs on the south wall include an area at the lower left (above and below the water table) and the region near the water table below the western and middle windows. Repointing occurs below the middle window and also variously below the water table. Two cracks are also to be noted towards the eastern end of the south wall. Two cracks likewise mark the chancel wall, and the apex of the gable has been replaced. Inasmuch as the entire west gable is also renewal, it is possible that the church may once have possessed shallow clipped gables. On the west wall repairs are also to be seen below the water table at the left (and also at the right of the doorway) as well as above the water table at the lower right. Only six small cracks above and below the two westernmost windows mar the north wall.

The segmental arches of the eleven windows are composed of full bricks and pairs of halves except for the two western windows, which seem to have incised lines instead of joints. Replacements in these arches of the various windows are few: 1) on the south wall, four or five bricks in the westernmost window, three in the middle window, and five in the easternmost window; 2) on the east, two loose bricks in the right window; 3) on the north, repointed joints in the two westernmost windows; and 4) on the west, two bricks in the left window and a repointed joint in the right window. The windows have bevelled brick sills.

The south doorway corresponds in position to the easternmost window on the north wall. The westernmost window on each of the side walls lies east of the gallery front.

The two porches are of post-colonial construction, probably from the early or middle nineteenth century. Each of them is marked by a wooden, pedimented roof with crude modillions, by brick pilasters applied over the jambs of the doorways, and by square brick columns. These columns possess classical entasis (tapering towards the top) and wooden capitals, and they rest on brick pedestals. On the columns are to be seen staggered series of queen closers. On the west, wooden pilasters have also been applied over the brick pilasters, and the brick steps, brick floor, and concrete sill are recent. On the south, the concrete step, concrete floor, and wood sill are also new; and the pedestals are not so high as those on the west because the ground falls away on the west and the pedestals follow the height of the water table. The south porch is also a bit smaller. It is to be hoped that some day the parish will remove these porches—or at least the western one—and, perhaps, restore the pediments that in all probability marked the original doorways.

The frames and sills of the eleven windows are original or colonial, as are probably the sash (with their muntins) and a great deal of the glass panes themselves. The mouldings of the window frames include: fascia, cyma reversa, fascia, and bead. The trim of the doorways as well as the double doors on both the south and the west are also original. The mouldings of the door frames are: fascia, cyma reversa, fascia, scotia, fillet, torus, fillet, and elongated cavetto. Around the corner are a cyma recta and a fascia. Some authorities have called this assemblage of mouldings a bolection, owing to the fact that the torus moulding projects beyond the others. However, this is a primitive example when compared with the usual, graceful S-shaped profile of the eighteenth-century bolection. Nonetheless, this is one of Fork Church's most interesting features. There are five horizontal raised panels (progressively larger from top to bottom) on each door. The large wooden case of the rim lock and the keeper and other metal accessories on the south doors, the six H-L hinges on each of the pairs of doors, and the wooden cross-bar on the west doors are still other colonial remnants of great interest. The modillion cornice likewise appears to be of eighteenth-century origin.

The colonial pews were cut down in 1830 and the present pew-ends would seem to derive from the original examples. The pew-backs also seem old, but are of lesser antiquity than the ends. On the pulpit the raised panels on the front (four) sides, on the door, and on the inside of the long, back side are probably derived from the colonial pulpit, as probably also are several of the panels of the present lectern. The pulpit was originally placed against the north wall between the first and second windows from the east, and this location as well as the original height of the pews can still be detected by the ridges in the plaster. From 1830 to 1913 the pulpit was located in the center of the chancel. In the latter year it resumed its present location, on the north wall not far from the altar. The long side at the back of the pulpit prevents the pulpit from assuming an octagonal shape.

The wainscoting may be old, but is probably not colonial. The oak floor joists are, however, believed to be original; and part of the floor under the pews and aisles is said to be of colonial construction. This church seems to have been distinctive in that it may never have had flagstones for its aisles. Beneath the floor are believed to be the foundations for the 1722 church. Although this has never been proved, the 1722 church is known to have stood near, if not on, the present site.

The west gallery and stairway certainly formed part of the 1736-40 church and the gallery rail is also possibly old, but the partition and doors below the gallery are of later date. The organ and case that are now in the gallery were moved there from downstairs in 1913. The ultimate origins of this organ are, however, uncertain, although it would seem to be from the middle of the last century in manufacture.

The original mortised timbers of the roof with their wooden pegs were supplemented in 1900 so that the additional weight of the slate roof might be supported. Before that time, a new roof also seems to have been put on in 1870, when the church was repaired after the War between the States.

Fork Church's large marble font came from another colonial church, Mattaponi Church, in King and Queen County. Fork Church's colonial silver was burned in 1936 when the residence of one of its communicants was destroyed by fire. Dolley Madison and Patrick Henry attended services here upon numerous occasions, and the novelist, Thomas Nelson Page, was a regular communicant in his time. Parson S. S. Hepburn, grandfather of the actress, Katharine Hepburn, was the rector of the parish from 1893 to 1903.

The graveyard and walls all seem to be post-colonial. The yard is spacious and well provided with trees. Fork Church may lack the grandeur of some of our elaborate colonial churches, but its fabric is more largely original than many of our more famous examples.

24. FARNHAM CHURCH

The parish church of North Farnham Parish in Richmond County is one of the few churches in Virginia, whether colonial or modern, that dominate a village scene in the appealing way that so many European churches do. The church and village of Farnham are at the junction of routes 692, 602, and 607, about .25 mile north of route 3, and 12 miles east of Warsaw.

North Farnham and South Farnham Parishes were created from Farnham Parish about 1683. The Upper Parish of Lancaster County had been formed into Old Rappahannock County in 1656 and was subdivided in 1661 into Sittingbourne Parish for the upper region (lying on both sides of the river) and Farnham Parish for the lower region (also lying on both sides of the river). In 1732 North Farnham lost its western portion to Lunenburg Parish at the latter's creation. Richmond and Essex Counties were formed in 1692, when Rappahannock County was divided at the Rappahannock River. In 1721 King George County was formed out of the western portion of Richmond County.

The word, Farnham, for parish and creek seems to derive initially from an early settler with that cognomen. Although it was usually spelled with an F (only on the silver is "Pharnam" known), there are instances of its having been spelled "ffarnham" (as one still sees "ffrench" and similar words spelled because of an early shape of capital F).

The present building of 1737 at Farnham succeeded an earlier church (around 1660) that had, perhaps, been built (about three miles west of the village of Farnham) even before the Upper Parish of Lancaster (and later Rappahannock) County was divided into two parishes. This second North Farnham Parish Church of 1737 is built of brick laid in Flemish bond with glazed headers. The water table consists of a cavetto and an ovolo, and the brick below the water table is of English bond. The shape of the structure is a Latin cross, approximately 63'-8" x 58'-2". The nave is 24'-3" long and the chancel 14' long; the transepts project 16'-7". All four arms of the cross are about 25' wide. The walls are around 2' thick.

From the lack of tooled joints, it is apparent that all the walls have been repointed. The gables are post-colonial, for the original roof was probably hipped (like most of the other colonial churches north of the Rappahannock River). All three doorways (west, south, and north) have been replaced, although the pedestals in each instance are original. Only the pedestals of the west doorway possess the moulded brick of the water table. The elaborate replacement of the western doorway includes some stone ornamentation, a projecting segmental brick cornice, and a wooden cross. The two windows in each side of the nave and the single window in each side of the two transepts and in the south side of the chancel all have new arches and new brick sills. The window and most of the wall on the north side of the chancel can no longer be seen because of the recent addition of a vesting room there.

The only original arches that remain are the two in the east end of the chancel, although the two windows have unfortunately been filled in with cement (and are recessed). These circular-headed arches are composed of gauged and rubbed brick, each voussoir containing bricks of three sizes. Rubbed brick also marks the corners of the building, the jambs of the remaining large windows, and the two original arches. Queen closers have been used at the salient corners, at the window jambs, on the western pedestals, and irregularly on the southern pedestals. The jambs of all the principal windows seem to be original. The brick sills of the two original chancel windows seem only slightly repaired, whereas the other sills are replacements. The ventilation holes are original, although at least one of them has been much enlarged.

Following the Disestablishment, the church seems to have been used as a barn as well as a distillery. In 1814 men of the Virginia militia were engaged in a skirmish with raiders from the British fleet at Farnham and, as a result of this encounter, bullet holes are still visible on the south face of the south transept. After this, the church continued to go to ruin until it was recovered in 1834, when only the walls were left. In the War between the States, it served as a stable for Federal troops. It was again restored to service in 1873, but was gutted by fire in 1887. It was then not restored until 1921, when the present walls were entirely repointed; the gables replaced; all the window arches and sills (except those in the east end of the chancel) replaced; the two eastern windows filled in; the three doorways replaced (above the pedestals); two circular windows installed in the west wall (and one in each of the transepts); the sacristy added on the northwest; and the pews, floor, and all other woodwork (except the present reredos and shelves for flowers) installed. In 1959 the reredos and shelves were put in and the interior painted (the plasterwork for the first time). Colonial precedent, however, has not been closely followed in either of the modern restorations.

The colonial parish owned valuable silver that was forcibly sold by law in 1802. This silver was later bought by a local citizen and given in 1816 to a Washington Church, which in 1876 gave it back to the parish. North Farnham Parish now uses a flagon and a paten of this silver, but St John's Church of Lunenburg Parish in Warsaw has at present a chalice and another flagon from the same set. These pieces of silver seem to have been made in London in 1720-21 by Joseph Fainell (although in at least one instance they have been ascribed to Thomas Farren). On the vessels are a sunburst, the IHS, and a cross (with an elongated central arm) as well as the words, "Pharnham Parish", and the 1816 and 1876 donations. The Farnham communion silver is all but identical with that of St Paul's Parish in King George County.

The Register (1672-1800) of North Farnham Parish is kept at the clerk's office in Warsaw. The processioners' records (1739-79) of the vestry of South Farnham Parish are kept at the Diocesan Library in Richmond.

The churchyard has the air of a village green, for it is always well kept and has no boundaries other than the village roads. A tomb from 1767 lies just east of the chancel, but this is not its original location, which is now no longer known.

25. GLEBE CHURCH (BENNETT'S CREEK)

The Glebe Church is situated on route 337 (King's Highway), only .4 mile east of the village of Driver in Nansemond County. In colonial times it was known as Bennett's Creek Church from its proximity to the west fork of that stream and was the parish church of Suffolk Parish (which was created before the city of Suffolk was founded and never included that city within its bounds). It derives its present name from the fact that the parish was one of the rare churches in Virginia that managed to retain its glebe lands. This accomplishment was owing to the provision in the acts of Disestablishment that individual gifts were to be exempt from confiscation. These glebe lands (approximately three hundred acres on the east side of the Nansemond River) are still ecclesiastical property, the income from which is shared jointly by Glebe and Chuckatuck (St John's) Churches.

The present church was originally built in 1737-38. The former year is lightly carved in a brick on the east wall near the present front (east) doorway. The building measures 48'-6" x 25'-4" outside and is, therefore, one of the smallest surviving colonial churches. Its walls are around 20" thick and are beautifully laid in Flemish bond with glazed headers. English bond occurs below the bevelled water table.

In 1759 an addition (24' x 23' inside) was ordered for the north side with the result that the church assumed an L-shape, the juncture occurring at the northeast part of the original structure. The original west gallery was supplemented by a north gallery as well as by a hanging pew or private gallery in the southeast. The north gallery seems to have had a locked stairway and the hanging pew seems to have had an outside covered stairway. Still another private gallery was added in 1777.

After 1787 the church went to ruin until 1856, when the north wing was taken down and its bricks used to complete the north wall and to erect a little vesting room at the west doorway. Among the bricks from the former wing now in the repaired north wall are several dated examples, including one with 1771 carved on it, near the present doorway. The chancel was also moved to the west and a gallery built in the east in 1856. Apparently by then, nothing was left of the colonial edifice but the walls, and they themselves are now heavily patched. Of the original north wall there remain about two brick-lengths at the eastern corner and the area west of the (original) middle window. The topmost portion of the north wall, however, is patched to within 4' of the northwest corner of the building. The west wall seems to be mostly original, although there is repointing on the upper right as well as just above the vestry roof on both sides. On the south, the area above the middle and westernmost windows and below the easternmost window as well as the brick lunettes all seem to be post-colonial. On the east, the rent between the modern door (and a V-shaped section above it) and the handsome, original brickwork on each side is severe.

Queen closers occur at the corners, but irregularly at the jambs of the windows. On the south wall they mark the upper half of the right jamb and the upper two-thirds of the left jamb of the middle window, and the upper two-thirds of both jambs of the westernmost window. On the former south doorway (now the easternmost window on this wall) queen closers exist only on the lower jambs. The (replaced) easternmost window on the north wall also has some closers; and there are two on the upper right jamb and four on the upper left jamb of the westernmost window (although in each instance one of the closers is hardly more than a sliver). A few closers are also used at the modern east doorway.

Rubbed brick characterizes the corners of the building and the arches and jambs of the windows.

The windows and doorways have undergone almost constant alteration. Originally, there were three windows on the north, two on the south, and one each in the east and west as well as doorways in the west and south. Owing to the diminutive size of the building, it is probable that the doorways were of simple nature, but one can only guess at their exact shape. When the L-shape was assumed, only one window remained on the north wall, although the north wing included four large windows. In 1856 the middle window on the north wall was restored (and its right jamb is original), and the eastern window on that wall became a doorway. Around 1900 the north and south doorways became windows, and the chancel window was enlarged into a door. More recently, a door has once again been inserted in the north wall. The windows seem to have been lowered at the sills in both 1759 and 1856.

The arches of all the five existing large windows are now segmental and are composed of full bricks alternating with pairs of half-bricks. The small, rectangular window on the upper west wall has no arch and appears to be original. Of the window arches, that over the former south doorway is the only one that is crudely executed. On the south wall the upper jambs of the former doorway and the lower jambs of the other two openings have been repaired. Two new bricks also exist at the top of each jamb of the latter two windows. As to the three large windows that have remained in service as windows from the earliest instance—the western window in the north and the two westernmost windows in the south—it is difficult to see how their arches could have remained intact in view of the extensive repairs that have been made around them. Furthermore, the arch of the replaced window on the north wall appears to be of the same age as the others. They may all derive from 1900, for

149

the same arch also exists above the east doorway (with its marble lintel and plaque). However, if these five arches were done in 1900, it would seem that the present crude work at the former south doorway (changed into a window in 1900) must derive from a different date. The bricks presently in the arches of the three original windows could, nonetheless, derive from the original arches.

The cornice and roof are recent and the wood pediments that have replaced the old brick gables are completely out of keeping with colonial precedent, as is the entire heavy interior. The church, in its present mutilated condition, bears a remarkable resemblance to Pungoteague Church on the Eastern Shore, for they are of the same age and display the same, superb original masonry.

The predecessor of the present building was erected around 1643 by the Nansemond River (near the modern toll bridge) and served as the parish church of East or Lower Parish until around 1725 when it became the Lower (or parish) Church of Suffolk Parish.

Unmarked colonial graves lie on the west and south sides of the present edifice, and a burying ground for slaves exists in the thick woods north of the church and its new parish house. The original manuscript of the vestry book (1749-1856) of Suffolk Parish is kept at the clerk's office in Suffolk, as is the parish's register (1704-1839).

The vestry book (1743-93) of Upper Parish, Nansemond County, has been published and the original is on deposit at the State Library in Richmond. St Paul's Church in Suffolk is said to own two other remnants of this parish from colonial times. The one is a 1751 Bible and the other is a hanging, traditionally given in Queen Anne's time, that has been variously described as an altar cloth (probably incorrectly), a pulpit fall (probably also incorrectly), and a funeral pall. It is made of "deep red cut silk velvet, bordered by a 2″ silver galoon" and measures approximately 7′ x 5′. This ornament is on loan at the Norfolk Museum of Arts and Sciences, but the whereabouts of the Bible is not known (and at least one authority even doubts that the parish ever owned the Book).

26. PUNGOTEAGUE CHURCH

Pungoteague Church in Accomack County was originally in Accomack Parish, but became part of St George's Parish in 1762. It has served as the parish church in both instances, but not continuously in either parish. It became St George's Church rather than Pungoteague (or Pongoteague) Church only in 1800. The building may be seen on route 178 only .2 mile north of the village of Pungoteague, which itself may be reached by means of: 1) route 180 from U. S. route 13 at Keller (3 miles away); or 2) routes 619 and 180 from Painter, also on U.S. route 13 (and 4 miles away).

The first settlement of the Eastern Shore (or Dale's Gift, as it was then named) occurred as early as 1614. The area constituted one of the original eight shires of Virginia in 1634 and the county was named Accomack after the Indian designation ("the other-side place") for the Eastern Shore. Most of these Eastern Shore names, including Pungoteague, are of Indian origin and their orthography is various and much confused. Pungoteague seems to have meant Sandfly River to the Indians.

The early county's name was changed to Northampton in 1643. Two counties were later formed (probably in 1662): the lower as Northampton and the upper as Accomack. They were, however, reunited as Northampton in 1670, but were separated again only three years later and still remain divided, although their boundaries were somewhat changed in 1677.

The Accomack settlement was probably a plantation parish at least as early as 1623 and was divided into two parishes in 1643. The upper parish soon became known as Nuswattocks Parish and then as Hungars Parish, but the Lower Parish seems to have retained that name throughout its existence. In 1647 the dividing line between the two parishes was located six miles farther north. Northern limits were never given for the northernmost parish on the Eastern Shore in early times, for it was assumed that the parish would extend to the Maryland line. In 1652 a third parish (Occahannock Parish) was created in the upper part of the peninsula and this became Accomack Parish in 1662 at the formation of Accomack County, with which it was coterminous. In 1691 the Lower and Hungars Parishes in Northampton County were reunited as Hungars (and still remain so). St George's Parish was created out of the lower portion of Accomack Parish in 1762, when the upper portion (nearer the Maryland line) retained the name of Accomack Parish. St George's was possibly named for St George's Hundred, an Eastern Shore plantation.

The first Pungoteague Church (probably 1667-77) was also probably the first parish church of Accomack Parish, for two earlier churches in the area seem to have passed away before the creation of the parish.

This church or its successor may have been replaced as the parish church of Accomack Parish by Assawaman Church (probably 1693-94), if we can judge from an inscription on a cup that has survived. The second (existing) Pungoteague Church was succeeded as the parish church of St George's Parish by the New Church that was completed in 1767 and stood (until 1838) about two miles south of the court-house on a road leading to Onley.

It was long held that the remains of the colonial church at Pungo-teague dated from as early as 1652-60, but all authorities seem now agreed that around 1738 is a more likely date and that these remains represent the second church on this site.

In its original shape, the present building was in the form of a Latin cross with a semi-circular apse (like Trinity Church (perhaps 1690) near Church Creek in Maryland) and with a hipped, gambrel roof and was, indeed, quite a handsome and interesting structure. Because of its shape it was called, none too reverently, the Ace of Clubs Church. It was not abandoned after the Disestablishment until the War of 1812 and was restored to service only seven years after that conflict. It was again repaired in 1858, but became a stable for Federal troops in the War between the States. After this desecration, nothing remained except the roof and the walls; and one of the wings had been raided for bricks to build a cook-house for the troops. It was, indeed, in such ruinous condition that, when it was repaired around 1880, the chancel and nave were torn down and their bricks used to close in the openings of the wings. The present church, therefore, consists only of parts of the original transepts. These original parts comprise: 1) in the south, all except the doorway and the area above it; 2) in the west and east, the extremities and portions (chiefly lower) of the second bay from the end; and 3) in the north, the patched middle portion of the gable. The upper portions of the south and north gables are entirely gone and the lower portion of the latter can no longer be seen because of a vesting room that has been added, possibly of old brick. The arch of the north doorway has also been covered up.

Rubbed brick marks the corners of the present building. The church, which is now 57'-3" north to south and 25'-3" east to west, is built of brick laid in Flemish bond (both above and below the bevelled water table), with glazed headers. The original brickwork on the south façade is of the highest precision and beauty.

The present cornice, roof, tower, and frame portions of the gable are, of course, entirely out of keeping with the church's colonial antecedents and remains. The windows (including five on each of the long walls) are also from recent times.

The parish owns a chalice and a paten from London of 1734-35. At

Emmanuel Church, Jenkins Bridge (in the same county, but in Accomack rather than St George's Parish), there is also another fine piece of communion silver, the aforementioned chalice (London, 1749-50), which is remarkable for its stem in the shape of a turned baluster. Emmanuel Church is the successor of old Assawaman Church.

The vestry book (1763-86) of St George's Parish is at present kept in the clerk's office at Accomac Courthouse.

The churchyard at Pungoteague Church contains several fine sycamores, but seems to have no colonial stones.

27. BOROUGH CHURCH, NORFOLK (ST PAUL'S)

The Borough Church of Norfolk, which has been known as St Paul's only since 1832, was informally (though never officially) known as the Borough Church because Norfolk had been created a borough by royal charter in 1736, only three years before the existing edifice was built as the third parish church of Elizabeth River Parish. It lies in a spacious churchyard at the corner of Church Street and City Hall Avenue in downtown Norfolk.

About 1636 New Norfolk County was created out of Elizabeth City County. In the next year, New Norfolk County was subdivided into Lower Norfolk and Upper Norfolk Counties. Upper Norfolk was later renamed Nansemond County. In 1640 Lower Norfolk County became a parish of the same title, but this parish was soon divided into three parishes: Elizabeth River, Lynnhaven, and Southern Shore. Southern Shore Parish was, however, no longer in existence by 1645. When Lower Norfolk County was subdivided in 1691 into Norfolk and Princess Anne Counties, most of Lynnhaven Parish fell into the latter county. In 1695 Lynnhaven Parish and Princess Anne County were made coterminous. At the same time Norfolk County and Elizabeth River Parish were also made coterminous, and this continued to be true until Portsmouth Parish on the west and St Bride's Parish on the south were cut off in 1761.

The old Borough Church's bricks are laid in Flemish bond with glazed headers above the water table. English bond exists below the water table, which has almost disappeared below the ground on the east. The chancel and transept arms of the Latin cross are almost equally long: the former projects 18'-6" and the transepts 15'-3". The church as a whole measures approximately 86'-6" x 63'-6"; the nave is 33' wide and the transepts 26'-3" wide. The nave is approximately 42' long and the walls are almost 30" thick.

There are three large windows in each side of the nave, one in each side of the south transept, one in the west side of the north transept, one in the south side of the chancel, and two in the east wall. All of these windows have semi-circular arches and are original. In the beginning there were two more of these large windows. The one on the north side of the chancel has been enlarged into an opening for the vestry and organ room. The window on the east side of the north transept is, however, still visible behind a stair and retains its brick arch and jambs, but is now filled up partly with cinder block and partly with metal grillwork. Also original are the large circular windows in each of the transepts and the small circular windows high in the south, north, and east gables as well as a small window with a semi-circular arch in the west gable. The present, large circular window in the west does not seem to be colonial, but it also does not seem to be modern, as some authorities have averred. It has been suggested that, because of the new brickwork between the two windows of the west gable, the small window may have been moved up. However, this need not necessarily be true, for many instances of new masonry occur between vertical pairs of original windows on a number of our old churches.

Repairs to the semi-circular arches include repointing in the right arch of the chancel wall, the arches in the south wall of the chancel and in the side walls of the south transept, the westernmost arch on the south wall of the nave, and the arch in the west wall of the north transept. A loose brick is to be noted in the left arch of the chancel wall. The circular windows in the south gable have both been heavily and crudely repaired at their tops. The small circular window in the chancel wall is marked at present by a mortar patch. Both of the circular windows on the north gable are presently covered by ivy.

In view of the rather harsh treatment endured by the church at various times, it is possible that the splendid condition of the semi-circular arches (particularly at their summits) may be owing to some very early mending, but, if this be true, they have certainly been mended with consummate skill!

Rubbed brick is to be found at the salient corners and at the arches and jambs of the windows, although the brick of the jambs and corners is of a darker color, and it is difficult to be positive about the brick around the circular windows. Furthermore, the small, semi-circular window either has no rubbed brick or, through weathering, the rubbed brick has turned quite dark.

The arches of the thirteen semi-circular windows and the three large circular windows consist of whole bricks alternating with pairs of half-bricks, whereas the arches of the three small, circular windows consist of rowlock courses.

Queen closers are to be found at the salient corners and on all the jambs of the remaining, lofty windows with semi-circular arches, although owing to the presence of ivy one cannot be certain about the entire extent of the jambs of the middle and westernmost windows on the north wall of the nave. Queen closers also occur on the right jamb of the small window with the semi-circular arch in the west gable, but the left jamb is covered by ivy.

The water table and the brick sills of the large windows with semi-circular arches are distinctive in that they might better be described as chamfered rather than bevelled. All of these window sills are original save that of the right window on the chancel wall.

The three doorways (on the south, west, and north) probably were surmounted by brick pediments in colonial times, but all nineteenth-century representations seem to indicate the presence of frame vestibules on the order of those presently to be seen. The sills of the large windows with semi-circular arches are splayed on the interior. There seem to have been no fewer than five galleries in the church in colonial times. The small windows now have louvers.

The church has suffered from wars, neglect, and congregational strife. It was burned along with the town by American forces in 1776 and lay in ruins for nine years. Although it was rebuilt in 1786 through a lottery authorized by the General Assembly, it was in wretched condition again within a decade. Two factions developed within the parish and the larger group left in 1798. By 1803 the building was once again deserted by Anglicans, although from then until 1827 it was variously used by Baptists of both races. In the latter year the congregation of Christ Church worshipped in it while it was without its own building. In 1832 the old church received both a new name and a new congregation.

The Federal forces requisitioned the old church as a chapel from 1863 to 1865. The present interior, with its high pews, was restored only in 1913. The vesting room that occupies the northeast corner seems to have replaced, at some unknown time, a belfry that was in existence there by 1853. A belfry was first erected in the west in 1834, but the present, separate tower was constructed to the west of the church only in 1901 (and the present cupola and cross on the church itself at a still later date).

The only original portions of the church, therefore, are the walls, for none of the wooden portions survived the colonial era.

On the chancel wall there are repairs under the right window and heavy repointing at the lower center and right as well as a crack above the right window and repointing above the left window. About one foot of the north wall of the chancel at the northwest corner and about the same length of the east wall of the north transept at the wing's northeast corner are still visible, as are large parts of the upper walls in both cases. The north gable is almost entirely covered by ivy. The west wall of the north wing is heavily repointed in its lower portion (below the sill level) and has a mended crack above the window. A large hole has been bricked in at the bottom. The north wall of the nave is also almost completely covered by ivy, but one can see repointing below the easternmost and westernmost windows. On the west gable there is heavy repointing at the lower right and in the water table, in addition to the aforementioned new masonry. On the south wall of the nave, the lower portion is entirely repointed, and there is also repointing above the easternmost window. Mortar patches occur above the other two windows on this wall. Repointing marks all of the lower portion of the west wall of the south transept (from a line about two feet above the window sill to the ground) as well as a stretch above and along the left side of the window. The lower portion of the south gable is also repointed, and mended cracks exist between the windows and above the small window. On the east wall of the south wing there is some repointing on the upper left and lower right as well as above the window. The south wall of the chancel shows repointing above and below the window and at the lower right corner.

Despite all this, the church's masonry is in remarkably fine shape.

Ornamental Bricks

Among the church's most interesting features are certain projecting bricks and a Revolutionary cannonball. The former, which consist of "1739 S B", may be seen on the south gable, straddling the doorway (and the vestibule). The numerals mark the year of the church's erection and the initials represent Samuel Boush. It is not known whether Colonel Boush, who was the borough's first mayor, memorialized his father or himself. The son is believed to have given the bricks and nails for the building. The ornamental bricks were originally glazed, but are now painted red. The cannonball, which may be seen high in the south wall of the chancel, was fired on New Year's Day in 1776 by Lord Dunmore's fleet—perhaps, from the warship, "Liverpool". It lay in the ground below for three-quarters of a century before it was found and put back where it had struck the building. The projecting courses of brick now attendant upon the cannonball are also to be noted, as is an old fire-company marker of uncertain age and origin.

Near the southwest corner of the church is an interesting marker of 1687-88 (decorated with the customary skull and crossbones) that was brought to Norfolk in 1875 from Weyanoke Church in Charles City County. There is a gravestone from 1673 (which is presently uncomfortably close to a pile of rubble and poison ivy) as well as stones from 1691 and 1694, although the former (1691) does not mark a grave in this yard. There are numerous eighteenth-century graves. The yard has served as a cemetery since 1641, although only four persons have been allowed to be buried in it since 1836. There are also undoubtedly many graves beneath the church itself. The city workmen in recent years have discovered a foundation (about 15′ x 20′) under the church that might derive from the chapel of ease that was built in 1641 and became the second parish church, possibly by 1655. The site of the first parish church (also probably erected in 1641) is not definitely known, but the church is known to have stood at Seawell's Point, within the United States Naval Operating Base and near its main gate.

No church in Virginia, whether old or new, can boast of a more beautiful yard than the old Borough Church with its 1.75 acres. Its delightful fountain, great variety of shrubs and trees, and high walls never cease to offer loveliness, although a recent hurricane did no little damage. The handsome wall around the yard was originally constructed in 1759. Because of this wall one cannot walk in the yard directly from the eastern end of the chancel to its southern end.

The parish museum contains the chair that JohnHancock is believed to have used to sign the Declaration of Independence as well as a piece of armor plate from the "Merrimac" and early photographs of many of Virginia's colonial churches. The parish's colonial silver, which is now on loan in the Norfolk Museum, consists of a silver-gilt chalice (London 1700-01), another silver-gilt chalice with paten-cover (London 1722-23), an alms bason (London 1750-51), and a flagon (1763-64). The chalice and paten-cover were made by Thomas Farrer, the alms bason by John Robinson, and the flagon by Fuller White.

The original manuscript of the vestry book (1749-61) of Elizabeth River Parish is kept at the Seaboard Citizens National Bank in Norfolk.

28. HEBRON CHURCH

Hebron Church in Madison County represents the oldest Lutheran congregation in the South and its building is the oldest church erected and still used by Lutherans in all America. It is one of the four surviving wooden churches of Virginia's colonial heritage. The church lies on route 653, a few yards from the junction of routes 653 and 638. This junction is itself three-quarters of a mile north of the junction of routes 638 and 231 (the road from Madison Courthouse to Sperryville) and two miles from the county seat.

The congregation was established before 1726 by Germans who had migrated from the vicinity of Germanna (on the Rapidan River between Culpeper and Fredricksburg), where from 1717 they had been workers in Governor Spotswood's vineyards and iron mines. The first church was built of unhewn logs in 1726 and occupied the same site as its successor, the present structure, which was originally constructed in 1740. The colonial portion of the existing church is represented by the part that extends from east to west and measures approximately 50' x 26'. The small vestry on the north that was a part of the colonial building has been replaced more than once. The latest (1961) replacement is also an enlargement, for it seems formerly to have measured 9' x 13', whereas it now measures 14'-3" east to west by 12' north to south.

Originally there were three doorways in the principal part of the church—in the south, east, and west—as well as galleries in the east and west and a pulpit on the north side. The timbers of this building were hewn. The east and west doorways are off center (to the south), probably so that the aisle might avoid the central columns supporting the galleries.

Sometime between 1790 and 1802 the present south addition (26'-2" east to west by 24'-6" north to south) was constructed. It is equidistant from the original east and west ends of the church. In this addition was built the organ loft. The timbers of the new transept, which became the nave, were sawn rather than hewn. The present interior cornice probably dates from the time of the addition.

In 1850 the original box-pews were removed and their raised panels used as rails for the fronts of the three galleries and as the wainscoting for the three wings of the main floor. The fragments of panels that are in evidence at various corners would seem to confirm the conversion of these panels from their earlier use. Examination of some of the wainscoting removed during the recent repairs strengthens this view, for the backs were finished. The rail of the south gallery is a replacement and the 1790-1802 rail of this gallery was higher than at present. (The rail in each of the three galleries consisted merely of a curtain suspended from a 2" x 6" piece of wood until 1850.) The stair of the south gallery, however, has probably served as a hazard for choristers ever since its construction. The lower floors in the original pair of galleries may be colonial, but the rest (including the stairs) has been replaced, although the stairs are not of recent origin.

Much of the original wall structure—upright timbers and cross-braces—seems to be intact, but the clapboards have long been replaced, most recently in 1961. Many of the original timbers are still marked by Roman numerals. Handmade nails and wooden pegs abound in the church. The two original galleries are supported by a single pillar each. The western columnar support is original and is marked by chamfering with lamb's tongues and exaggerated entasis. The eastern column is a renewal. The south gallery is supported by two similar but smaller columns (without, however, the entasis).

The disposition of the windows (all square-headed) is interesting. A large window is located on each side of the chancel on the north wall and just beyond each of these large windows is a smaller window. There is also a window in each of the three gables, although those on the east and west are at present false and covered by shutters. The window behind the organ in the south gallery has been retained with glass. In the lower storey of the south addition a pair of large windows exists on the east side, and another pair as well as a third, smaller window (just east of the pair) light the west side. The wood sills and trim as well as the sash and panes are all replacements, although the headers under the windows are original and the sash are not recent. The large window on the east of the pulpit is 3″ shorter at the bottom than its counterpart on the west of the same wall, thus requiring the use of a row of shorter panes above the meeting rail. The original shutters were board-and-batten.

The windows in the gables undoubtedly lit the three galleries as long as the church still retained its original arched ceiling, and an arched ceiling may yet be seen above the organ loft in the post-colonial addition. The greater part of the church, however, now has a flat ceiling, which was first installed in 1850.

Two sets of painted designs adorn the church's interior. The first set was painted by a Mr Francis Staling of Harrisonburg in 1870; the second set (consisting of the six large sections over the chancel and nave, as well as the area behind the (former) pulpit) was executed in 1885 by a Mr Giuseppe Oddenino, who was also responsible for the still more elaborate examples in the Mitchells Presbyterian Church in neighboring Culpeper County. Exactly what decoration Mr Staling executed is uncertain, but it possibly included the designs back of the pulpit and under the galleries. That behind the pulpit was "moved" 10 to 12 inches nearer the center in 1940, but the painter who duplicated it is already forgotten. In the 1961 work it was replaced by panelling. The ceiling over the galleries seems unfinished and the design on the north wall is presently (1961) being removed.

The roof trusses are said to be still largely intact. The modern metal roof yet exhibits a kick at the eaves. The pulpit of goblet shape (with sounding board) was removed around 1850. Its replacement was in turn replaced around 1870 by a pulpit and an altar that continued in use until 1961. The present lectern dates from 1877, according to its markings. Around 1884-85 new sills were put in, the vestry room was rebuilt, the metal roof and modern blinds added, and the walls replastered. In 1934 a furnace (later replaced) was installed. The walls and floors were renovated and many new furnishings given around 1939. The organ was also electrified in the 1930's; the church was wired for electricity in early 1930. The original foundations consisted of stone piers, and complete stone underpinnings were added only in 1870-75. All of this stonework was replaced by concrete block with brick veneer in 1961. The narthex on the south is also from 1961, at which time almost the entire building beyond its skeletal structure was renewed (partly owing to termites) and the chancel completely changed. A feature of the 1961 vestry is the addition of an exterior door on the north where none had been before, as well as two small windows (on east and west) where only one (on the north) had existed before.

The present organ was installed at the construction of the south addition. It was built by David Tannenburg of Lititz, Pennsylvania about 1800. It is a remarkable instrument, with eight stops of great clarity and equal variety. Its keys are reversed: the "white" keys are ebony and the "black" keys are ivory.

Hebron Church is rich in communion vessels that seem to have been received as the result of the two commissions that were sent to Europe (around 1726 and in 1734). In pewter it owns a tray, two patens, two flagons, and a baptismal bowl, all of which were made, given, and inscribed by Thomas Giffin of London. The pair of flagons is dated 1729, the rest 1727. On the tray is engraved the Institution of the Lord's Supper; on the patens is Christ on the Cross. In silver the congregation owns a chalice, originally lined with gold, which according to a long inscription in German was given by a Mr Fürgen Stollen of Lübeck in 1737. Also inscribed on the chalice is I Corinthians XI, 25 and the proclamation that God's Word and Christ's Teaching shall never perish (all in German). A small, decayed wooden container that is still used for the silver may easily be original. Another silver piece is a small plate with an iron cross on the rim, which is taken to be a companion to the chalice. These pieces constitute the oldest Lutheran communion set in the South, but they are seldom if ever used nowadays because the congregation several decades ago adopted the individual cups of other Protestants, owing to hygienic concern.

The silver appears to be one of the results of the second commission. (Other bounty from that trip included putty and cut-glass for the windows as well as books both theological and otherwise.) The pewter would seem to have derived from the first commission, although it is not known whether the vessels came from Anglican or Lutheran charity. All the Church's communion vessels were hidden by courageous women of the congregation when the neighborhood was ransacked by Federal soldiers in the War between the States. It was then that a wafer box (apparently of pewter) was stolen by a Federal soldier.

Also among the Church's valued possessions are the subscription book of the second commission, the deed (1733) to the glebe farm, the Church's constitution (1776), and the deed to the church lot, which was acquired in 1790—fifty years after the present building was constructed. The subscription book of 179 pages (the first three of which are missing) is written partly in Dutch, English, French, and Latin, but principally in German. The constitution is entirely in German. As legal Virginian documents, the others are, of course, written in English. (English was first used in worship at Hebron around 1787, but German was not entirely disused until about 1835.) These various documents are at present being kept by members of the congregation, but are apparently not all available for inspection.

The glebe farm (about a mile west of the Madison-Sperryville road) was not sold until around 1868. The first German school in the South was begun at Hebron Church in 1748 by its pastor. The Church as a body owned slaves for a long time. The Church's first cemetery of 1900 lay on a hillside between the church and the county seat. The present cemetery, hard by the church (and walled with river rock in 1930-31), was first used in 1904, although earlier graves have since been moved there from the first cemetery and from private burying grounds. One of the most attractive features of the churchyard consists of the stiles that mark each of the three gates. Similar stiles are believed to have existed in the earliest times of the church.

The first church was originally known simply as "the German Chapel", but may possibly have also been called "Die Hoffnungsvolle Kirche" (or "The Hopeful Church"). It seems to have been named Hebron sometime after the first church's erection and the congregation's formal organization. Although the congregation has lost much of its Lutheran heritage in both its liturgy and music, it has retained a great deal, including its name.

The Germans who settled on the banks of the Robinson River and the White Oak Run chose a vale of considerable beauty a few miles east of the Blue Ridge. When one of the oaks in the churchyard had to be felled in 1961, its age was reckoned as at least two hundred years. Four other great oaks, however, still help to shelter Hebron Church, a memorial of highest interest not only for Lutheran and German culture, but also for Virginia's colonial history.

29. St Mary's Whitechapel

St Mary's Whitechapel (or, as it is sometimes known, St Mary's White Chapel) and its large, handsome yard occupy the northwest corner of the junction of routes 201 and 354, three miles south of Lively in Lancaster County. The church was named for St Mary's in the Whitechapel district of London whence several of its earliest communicants derived.

A great deal of ambiguity as to names and separate identities marks the parochial history of Lancaster County. When that county was formed out of York and Northumberland Counties in 1651, it lay on both sides of the Rappahannock River and constituted but a single parish, which may possibly have been called Lancaster Parish. In 1656 the upper portion of the county became Rappahannock County and this county was in its turn divided (at the river) in 1692 into Richmond County on the north and Essex County on the south. The remaining portion of Lancaster County that lay south of the river became Middlesex County in 1669.

The single parish of Lancaster County was divided in 1654 into upper and lower parishes, corresponding respectively to Rappahannock and Lancaster Counties of 1656. The lower of these parishes may have been called Lancaster Parish. This lower parish was divided at the river in April of 1657 and in the next month two parishes (Lancaster and Peanckatanck) were formed on the south side of the river. These two southside parishes were re-united into Christ Church Parish in 1666 and their combined boundaries formed Middlesex County in 1669.

By 1661 two parishes (upper and lower) were in existence in the northside part of Lancaster County, but no records of their creation are extant. There are also no records of their separate names, although by

1669 the upper parish was known as St Mary's Whitechapel and the lower as Christ Church. (Early efforts of this Christ Church Parish on the north of the Rappahannock River to distinguish itself from Christ Church Parish on the south of the river by being called "Great Christ Church Parish" failed, probably because the southside parish had the greater area as well as the greater number of churches.) However, records do exist showing that an informal union of these two parishes (St Mary's Whitechapel and Christ Church in Lancaster) into a greater parish existed in both the late seventeenth and the early eighteenth centuries, for they seem to have shared the same rector and glebe farm throughout the colonial period. The greater parish is in some documents called Trinity Parish.

Through an egregious error on the part of the General Assembly, the two parishes were united in 1752 as Christ-Church Parish and a single vestry was elected a few years later, although separate vestry meetings were held for a while and separate vestry books maintained at the two churches much longer.

In 1740-41, transepts were added to a church that had been built for St Mary's Whitechapel as early as 1669, but the original nave and chancel were removed in 1832. The building, which was originally rectangular and then cruciform, thus once again became and has remained rectangular, although its long axis is now north and south. Its present dimensions are approximately 64' x 29' on the outside; the original building (east to west) seems to have been of the same size. The original chancel has recently been outlined with an evergreen hedge.

The brick church is laid in Flemish bond with glazed headers, with English bond below the bevelled water table. Rubbed brick is used in the arches and jambs of the windows and, broadly, at the corners of the structure. Bricks from the early church were used in 1832 to fill in the gaps and these rents are clearly visible in the east and west walls. There are also two sets of patches down the middle of the south and north walls. In the case of the former, a round window (probably to light the gallery) has been filled in with brick, and the present south doorway has replaced the probably larger 1740-41 doorway. On the north wall the central rent in the lower part derives from bricking up the north doorway in 1832 and also—to the south of this—a small door that once led to a small vestry. This frame vestry, like the present west porch, was added after the War between the States (possibly around 1885). The vestry was removed in 1954-55.

The existing south and west doorways derive from 1832, as do the four inner windows of the east and west walls. The four end windows on these walls and the two small windows in the north wall (for lighting a gallery) date from 1740-41. Three of the original large windows have had their semi-circular arches (alternating a stretcher with a pair of headers) repaired, although the southernmost window on the east wall remains in original condition. The principal windows still have splayed sides and sills on the interior. The other sills now have a skim coat of cement put on around 1920. The north windows have flat arches of rubbed brick and their wooden sills are believed to be original.

Of the colonial woodwork on the interior, only the south gallery remains. This gallery was built in 1741 as a side gallery on the east side of the south transept and was to extend from the south doorway to the main wall of the (old) church, with a width of 10'. Six feet was to be allowed for the stairs. These stairs probably began at the southeast corner of the south transept and continued to a landing just east of the aisle, finally arriving at the gallery again at the southeast corner—in short, just the opposite of the present arrangement (which dates from around 1900-03). This gallery has a very interesting, heavily moulded rail with turned balusters and large vertical, raised panels. This original south gallery represents the only side gallery (as opposed to an end gallery) to survive in any of our colonial churches.

There were also west and north galleries in the cruciform church. The north gallery was built in 1740-41, too, and was enlarged in 1773, but removed in 1832 to allow the chancel to be moved to the north from the east. It was probably in 1832 that the south gallery assumed its present L-shape, for the rail of that part of the present south gallery that was added at that time may possibly have come from the west gallery, but more probably from the north gallery. The floor of the addition (on the south, but west of the original south gallery) seems to be more modern. The rail of the original south gallery is still in its original position (with a bench attached to part of it), so that there are in effect two galleries side by side rather than but a single gallery. These galleries are supported by four slender, fluted Tuscan columns. The two rails and pairs of supporting columns of the two galleries are slightly different from each other. Part of the present stairs as well as the additional (western) pair of columns may be colonial, too. The present vesting room beneath the gallery was added in 1954.

The pulpit was put above the Table in 1832, but was removed after the War between the States. It was long stored under the gallery steps. The present chancel rail was installed shortly after the War between the States.

The roof is hipped, and the ends of the cornice on the east and west walls as well as the entire cornice on the other two walls may possibly be colonial. Two brick tiles and fragments of others that once lay in the aisles have been preserved by one of the communicants of the parish.

The parish owns a font (apparently of Portland stone) that was

164

given in 1718, a silver chalice and footed paten-cover that were given in 1669, and two sets of tablets. One set of tablets contains the Decalogue and was presented in 1702 and the other contains the Lord's Prayer and the Apostles' Creed and was given in 1718. The red in the frame of the tablets stems from 1885, when the tablets were sent to Baltimore to be cleaned and repaired. All the donors of the church's treasures were members of the Fox family. The same shield-like mark (GC) is engraved four times upon the chalice and five times upon the paten (including once on the bottom) and derives from an unascribed goldsmith who is known to have been working in London in 1675-76. George Garthorne has been suggested as the maker by one authority.

In the neighboring, venerable parish of Wicomico (which has from the earliest times included parts of both Lancaster and Northumberland Counties within its boundaries), still other colonial silver made in London is in use. The Wicomico Parish silver includes a chalice made in 1711-12 by Francis Garthorne and a flagon made in 1729-30 by William Darkeratt.

The vestry book (1739-88) of St Mary's Whitechapel is on loan at the State Library in Richmond. From 1770 to 1788 it seems to be the vestry book for both Christ Church and St Mary's Whitechapel.

St Mary's Whitechapel was abandoned after the Disestablishment and revived around 1832, when the severe alterations were made.

The graveyard includes a 1696 tomb on the southwest and a series of striking and recently renewed altar-tombs of the Ball family on the southeast. Mary Ball, the mother of the first president, was born in this parish, but is buried in Fredericksburg. The present highway "down Corotoman Neck" (built in 1960-61) goes through what was once part of the graveyard. Indeed, the whole area near the church seems at one time to have served as a burying ground.

30. HENRICO PARISH CHURCH, RICHMOND (ST JOHN's)

The colonial church in Richmond (city) is one of the most famous churches in all America, but it is chiefly as a patriotic shrine rather than as a church that it has acquired its great fame. It was in the original part of this building that the orator, Patrick Henry, ended an address to the second Virginia Convention in March of 1775 with his ever-since famous cry: "Give me liberty or give me death!" The church also served as a barracks for Benedict Arnold's troops in 1781. Needless to say, both church and congregation are the oldest within the capital city.

The original structure (60' x 25') as completed in 1741 consisted only of the present east-west transepts, with, as usual, the altar in the east, the doors in the south (near the chancel) and the west, and the pulpit probably on the north wall just west of the chancel. In 1772 a north wing with galleries was added; it was this T-shaped structure that provided the meeting-place for the noted Convention three years later. It is believed that Mr Henry spoke from the third pew on the Gospel-side. The pulpit was probably then at the junction of transept and chancel. This building would have been demolished in 1820 had financial difficulties not forced work on a new brick church to be abandoned (even though the walls were almost completed).

In 1830-34 the north wing was enlarged to form the present nave and gallery and the pulpit moved to the south wall facing the nave. In the same period the small belfry over the original west gallery was taken down and a tower was erected on the north. This first tower was damaged in 1863 and was replaced in 1866. The second tower, however, was also damaged by a high wind in 1896, after which the conical spire at the top was replaced by a cupola. In 1903 the tower assumed its present form when an extra storey was added and the upper portions (except for the cupola and cross) differently arranged. Although the lower storeys are also differently arranged, it is possible that some of the present framework of the lower portions derives from 1866. It is probable that the 1830-1834 tower was also of the same type, for the intention in 1903 was to return to the 1834 model. However a photograph taken by the United States Army Signal Corps in 1865, when no tower was standing, shows that the first tower (1834-63) was definitely wider (east to west) than the later towers of 1866 and 1903.

The chancel seems to have been moved to the south side, the east doors put in, and the east windows and south door closed around 1857-1860. In 1880 the original west gallery was removed and the then flat ceiling replaced by the existing arched one. An alcove for the pulpit was also added in 1880 and at the same time or somewhat later a vestry was built behind this alcove. The building did not, however, achieve its present cruciform shape until 1905 when the south (chancel) wing was constructed. The pulpit was also moved to its present position (against the south wall of the original nave and just west of the entrance to the new chancel) in 1905.

The church was known for almost a century by a variety of names:

Henrico Parish Church, Richmond (St John's)

The Church, The Old Church, The New Church, Henrico (Parish) Church, Richmond Church, The Town Church, and The Church on Richmond Hill. The hill, which is now known as Church Hill, was called Indian Town Hill in 1737 when the building was ordered to be erected. As a result, the church was also variously known as Indian Hill Church and Indian Town Church. The name of St John's for the present parish church is first recorded only in 1829.

From an architectural point of view, there is very little left in this building of colonial origin. Like the stone (as well as the other wooden and even some of the brick) colonial churches, it is, indeed, a thing of shreds and patches as to original remains. Much of the weatherboarding on the walls of the present transepts, however, is undoubtedly colonial if not original, as one can see by comparing, as to size, these boards with those found elsewhere on the church. Also of colonial origin is the raised-panel wainscoting in the transepts as well as sixty-eight remaining H-hinges and some hand-wrought nails of the pews. Although it is difficult to state an exact number, there are probably between 28 and 34 original pews still in use. However, all the pews were cut down in height as well as otherwise altered in the 1830's. The pulpit and its sounding board (with a sunburst on its soffit) are original, although the former was cut down 18″ and its stairs and railing on the west removed in 1880. The sounding board seems to have been unused from 1880 to 1886 and the back panel that formerly connected the sounding board to the pulpit was removed in, perhaps, 1880.

The original brick foundations (laid in English bond) seem to be largely intact, as are some of the wooden sills and floor joists. Some persons believe that the trim of the two windows that flank the entrance to the present chancel and the trim of the west doorway are colonial or, perhaps, even original. The muntins of the two windows are surely the oldest left in the church. The church's bell that was taken down in 1830-1834 now belongs to the Virginia Historical Society, after a period of service at a school in Martinsville.

Of the hundreds of graves in the beautiful churchyard, the only two demonstrably colonial tombstones lie just east of the present east doorway. Table-tombs also lie under the present chancel, and unmarked graves exist under the old nave and chancel (the present transepts) that are presumably quite old. Indian remains are believed to exist in a corner of the churchyard. Certain bodies are even said to have been uncovered in standing position. Among the well-known persons who lie buried in this cemetery are George Wythe (founder of the law school of the College of William and Mary and the first Virginia signer of the Declaration of Independence), and the mother of the poet and novelist, Edgar Allan Poe. Portions of the 1770 brick wall that replaced a wooden wall may yet be seen on Grace Street and the extreme lower part of Twenty-fifth Street. The churchyard occupies the entire block bounded by Broad, Grace, Twenty-fourth, and Twenty-fifth Streets.

The parish owns a silver paten and chalice from 1718-19 and a baptismal bowl (long used as an alms bason) of 1694-95 that formerly belonged to Westover Parish Church in Charles City County, as well as still another old chalice and paten that were given in 1891. The latter set was originally used in "an old James River Church", bears the London date-letter for 1771-72, and was made by William Grundy. The 1718-19 chalice was made by Ambrose Stevenson and the 1718-19 paten by John Backe. Also in use is a marble baptismal bowl from Curle's Church (about 1720), the building in the lower part of the county that preceded the Richmond church as the parish church. The vestry book (1730-73) of Henrico Parish has been published and the original manuscript is kept at the church. A Bible from the reign of William III was given to the church in 1941 by King George VI. A Communion Table long in use in the parish can also be seen in a pew in the east transept. It is possible that two of the three boards at the top are original, but three legs are from the early nineteenth century and two are replacements of still later date.

Inasmuch as St John's Church continues to have great and deserved appeal for worshippers and visitors alike because of its historic fame, its eminence above the James, its graves, and its trees, it is, perhaps, not too much to hope for the day when both the interior and the exterior can be returned to a style more in keeping with its origins and stature. The T-shape and clear-glass windows of 1772 might even be restored.

The parish of Henrico goes back to 1611 when it was a plantation parish under the celebrated the Rev'd Mr Alexander Whitaker. Henrico County was one of the four boroughs of 1618 and one of the eight shires of 1634. Its large territory was reduced at the formation of Goochland County in 1727 and Chesterfield County in 1749. Henrico Parish was coterminous with the county from the days of the plantation parish until 1643, when Bristol Parish was formed on both sides of the Appomattox River. Twenty years after the formation (1700) of King William Parish for the Huguenots, St James's Parish was created out of the western section of the parish and in 1735 Henrico Parish's remaining area south of the river became part of the new Dale Parish. When Chesterfield County was formed, Henrico Parish and County once again became coterminous and remained so until 1925, when Varina Parish was created on the southeast and Tuckahoe Parish on the west.

First Church on Farrar's Island

The site of the first church of the parish lies on Farrar's Island, down the James River about 10 miles south of Richmond. This spot was actually on a peninsula until the Dutch Gap Canal, which had been begun during the War between the States, was completed in 1872 (although the peninsula had been called an island even in colonial documents). The name of Dutch Gap is thought to derive from the fact that Sir Thomas Dale, the High Marshal of Virginia and the founder of the settlement at Henrico in 1611, drew upon his Dutch experience when he had a ditch dug around the palisaded town of Henrico (which was named for James I's Prince of Wales).

A large granite cross (with the Bible and a superimposed Prayer-Book sculpted on the base) was erected on this site by Churchmen of Virginia upon the 300th anniversary of the founding of the parish and town. The inscription upon the cross, which had been removed by vandals, was replaced in 1961 (the 350th anniversary year). The cross is 4.6 miles east of the hamlet on route 1 that is still known as Dutch Gap, which in turn is about 12 miles south of the James River at Richmond. The only way to reach the spot (except by water) is to take route 616 east from Dutch Gap. After about 1¼ miles, a sharp turn to the right is followed immediately by an equally sharp one to the left. This latter turn leads into a long, wooded lane that marks the beginning of the extensive holdings of the Southern Materials Company, which, indeed, owns all of the land up to the approximately three acres at the eastern tip of the island. Inasmuch as the road to the cross is frequently hazardous and is quite devious in a number of places, the Southern Materials Company requests that advance notice be given of any intended tour of inspection so that visitors may be protected and properly guided by company personnel.

The now wooded site, which has in recent times often been called Henricopolis (without colonial precedent) to distinguish it from the county that shares its name, is an arresting one for several physical reasons. One of them is its location atop the high bluffs created by the Dutch Gap Canal. Another lies in the fact that the northern portion of the old James River that was cut off by this canal is in spots and at certain times hardly more than a marsh and in other instances almost a *wadi*, as archæologists are wont to term a stream bed that is frequently dry.

The ownership and political jurisdiction of these three acres in recent times are also of interest. The city of Richmond seems to have owned part of the site in the early 1870's and used it for a lightkeeper's house, but, when the Federal government took over all lighthouses in 1873, the site was transferred to the nation. In 1899 another parcel was added to the acreage. In 1929 the Federal government, having no further need for the site, turned it over to the care of the Colonial Dames of Virginia, who still own it. In the late 1920's the Virginia legislature passed a law transferring all of Farrar's Island to Chesterfield County except for the three historic acres, which, therefore, have continued to lie in Henrico County and the diocese of Virginia rather than in Chesterfield County and the diocese of Southern Virginia. Other islands cut off on the north and east side of the river by other canals seem, however, to have remained in Chesterfield County.

A second monument on the site in the form of an obelisk (probably 22′ high in contrast to the probable 15′ of the cross) was erected by the Colonial Dames in 1910. However, the University and College of Henrico, the first such institution ever to be built on our soil, was erected through collections taken in 1617 in all the dioceses of the Church of England (under a decree of James I) rather than by a decree from the Virginia Company of London in 1619, as the Dames' inscription has it.

A Service of Commemoration is held on the island by Henrico Parish upon great anniversary years.

The church of the 1611 plantation parish was succeeded as the parish church before 1640 by Varina Church, located a mile or two down the river (to the east). This church (or a possible replacement built on the same site) was in turn succeeded as the parish church by Curle's Church, about four miles still farther down the river. The present building in Richmond is, therefore, the fourth (or possibly the fifth) parish church. Henrico Parish was also known as Varina Parish during part of both the seventeenth and the eighteenth centuries (apparently during the period when Varina Church served as the parish church).

Huguenot Church

Still another monument of religious and political interest that lies in the original bounds of Henrico Parish memorializes the French Huguenot refugees who came to Virginia at the very end of the seventeenth century. This shrine stands by the fourth (1895) and fifth (1954) buildings of Manakin Church of King William Parish. It is situated on the south side of route 711 in Powhatan County, about 7 miles west of Robious (the junction of routes 147 and 711 at the Southern Railway tracks) in Chesterfield County and about 11 miles east of Jefferson (the junction of routes 522 and 711) in Powhatan County. The junction at Robious (no longer marked as a hamlet) is eight miles southwest of the junction of River Road and Huguenot Road (route 147) near the city limits of Richmond.

The Huguenot monument, which is a tall granite slab of three panels surmounted by a cross formée, with fleurs de lys, was erected in 1936 by the Huguenot Society of the Founders of Manakin in the Colony of Virginia. On the cross there is also carved the year 1699. The lands granted by the colony of Virginia to the French Huguenots near this monument were formed into King William Parish in 1700. Worship in

French did not long continue, however, partly because French-speaking clergymen were not always easy to obtain. In 1747 the Service was ordered to be conducted half in French and half in English and in the next year a receipt recorded in the vestry book was in English. Even the French of the vestry's clerk was weak by this time. Therefore, the only worship known to have been held in French by the Manakin congregation in centuries occurred in May of 1962 when the choirs of St Michael's School at Bon Air and St Margaret's School at Tappahannock sang Evensong in that language at Manakin Church. The Huguenots of Virginia were likewise not long in becoming Anglicans, partly because they received much help and consideration from William III, the Bishop of London, and many other Anglicans.

The fourth Manakin Church is said to have been structurally influenced by the reputedly octagonal shape of the first church; the fifth Manakin Church is modelled upon Westover Parish Church in Charles City County. The name of Manakin is derived from the fact that this was formerly a town-site for the Monacan Indians. Visitors to the Huguenot monument by Manakin Church should bear in mind that both the church and the memorial are on the south side of the James River, that the village of Manakin is on the north side of the river, and that, although the church and village lie not far from each other across the river, the nearest bridges span the river at Maidens on the west and at Westham on the east.

31. HUNGARS PARISH CHURCH

The third parish church of Hungars Parish in Northampton County on the Eastern Shore is situated on route 619, about .2 mile north of the hamlet of Bridgetown and just around the corner from the junction of routes 619 and 622. It may be reached by leaving route 13 at any one of three points: 1) Nassawaddox on the north; 2) Machipongo on the south; or 3) Birdsnest in the middle. From the south, one turns left just this side of Machipongo, and Hungars Church is a bit under four miles distant. From Nassawaddox the distance is about six miles and from Birdsnest just over three miles.

The first parish church of Nuswattocks (later Hungars) Parish was erected (probably 1646) on a creek that entered the north side of Hungars Creek about 2 or 3 miles from the latter's mouth. The second church (around 1681) was built just west of the existing building, not far from a colonial highway. The name Hungars is Indian and descended from the river (creek) to the settlement, parish, and church that had all earlier been called Nuswattocks.

The present brick building, close to the head of Hungars Creek, is believed to have been built as early as 1742, but was definitely completed by 1751. As originally built (traditionally by Southy Satchell), it was the longest and next to the largest rectangular church in colonial Virginia. The original length (around 92′ on the outside) is still indicated by a slight depression in the ground on the west. Its width has remained at 44′, but it is now only 74′-8″ long. The Flemish bond of the brickwork is also continued below the bevelled water table. The glazed headers are unusually striking on the north and east walls. Indeed, on the latter wall there are distinct evidences of diapering, particularly in the use of glazed stretchers as well as glazed headers, although the pattern is indistinct. The middle section of this wall seems strangely plain with the diapering above and below. This is, of course, by no means the only example of brick diapering extant on the Eastern Shore. Numerous putlock or scaffolding holes have been retained on the various walls. The ventilation holes near the ground are either recent or have recently been enlarged.

Hungars Parish Church was abandoned after the Disestablishment, but was restored to service in 1819. Various important repairs (such as the removal of the pulpit from the north side to the chancel) were undertaken in 1840, although the building was held to be unsafe only a decade later. It has been said that these repairs of 1840 included the substitution of two aisles for the original central alley and modern pews for the old, large box-pews. However, it has more recently been suggested that Hungars Church seems too wide a building to have had but a single aisle and that the old box-pews were probably cut down and re-arranged rather than removed.

In 1851 Thomas H. Stevenson of Snow Hill in Maryland prevented the loss of the edifice by his superb skill and willingness to lose money. He took down the west gable (which was in bad condition) and the extremities of the north and south walls as far as the first bay from the west. He created a new west gable with the old bricks, completely in the old fashion. Apparently it was also he who replaced the barrel-vault ceiling with a flat one.

The church originally had four windows in each of the side walls, and it still does. This is owing to the fact that the loss of the two westernmost windows was compensated for when Mr Stevenson converted the

172

original north and south doorways into windows. This replacement can easily be seen above and below the second window from the west (on both the south and the north) by the repaired brickwork. It was the extreme length of the building that permitted doors in the middle of these walls, with two windows on each side of each doorway. There was originally only a single door in the west, whereas at present there are two, with a single window above the gallery. All the arches are semi-circular.

Rubbed brick may be seen at the four corners of the building (although the extreme west portions of the side walls, like the west gable, derive only from 1851) as well as at the semi-circular arches and jambs of all the windows (including the two in the east) and at the doors. The window arches are very wide (16"), have keystones of fluted brick tiles, terminate at the bottoms in brick projections, and are marked by buttered joints. The pattern of the arches includes a pair of stretchers alternating with cut brick of varying sizes. The windows are around 14' high and have splayed sides and sloping sills.

The two doors on the west, which were probably originally located on the side walls, measure no less than 10'-2" high and still have their enormous H-L hinges (2' in height). The window trim may be colonial. Although the design and muntins of the upper windows cast some doubt as to their exact age, they, too, may possibly be colonial, as may also be some of the lights. The four fluted columns of solid heart pine and the massive girders (from east to west) that they support as well as certain roof beams and trusses are, however, undoubtedly original.

The original pulpit, which, as we have noted, was moved in 1840, has disappeared, as have (in the opinion of many persons) the old pews. At present there are two modern lecterns, one of which serves as the pulpit. The existing west gallery is a smaller replacement (1851) for the original gallery. The brick pavement of the original chancel is said to be *in situ*. The unusual baldachino seems to derive from the late 1800's and the partition at the rear from 1892, although some authorities feel that the baldachino may be colonial. If this last were ever authenticated, it would certainly confer a unique distinction upon Hungars Church. The cornice, roof, and floor are all probably from 1922. The font may derive from 1819. In 1950 various changes concerning the lighting and heating of the church were instituted. Still other alterations occurred in 1955.

The parish's glebe farm and house are still in existence and may be seen at the end of route 622, about 3 miles southwest of Bridgetown. The house, which was constructed in the eighteenth century (although a part of it may derive from the preceding century), is, unfortunately, not now in the most prepossessing of conditions. The farm seems to have been unfairly lost to the parish in 1853.

Hungars Parish Church owns one of the few complete sets of co-lonial communion silver in existence. It consists of chalice, paten, flagon, and bason, each of which is engraved with "IHS". The set was possibly made by George Smith and bears the London date-letter for 1742-43. Other treasures of Hungars include a cassock of black taffeta and a white surplice from the eighteenth century, an altar cloth of eyelet embroidery with "1749" on it, a Prayer-Book of 1758, and a Bible of 1753, all of which may be seen in the colonial clerk's office at Eastville. The books are labelled with the name of the parish and the year 1763. Still other colonial silver is in use at Christ Church (Eastville), which is also a part of Hungars Parish. The Christ Church silver includes a set (chalice, paten-cover, and flagon) that was made in London in 1736-37 and a rare colonial American alms bason (possibly made by John Cooney between 1705 and 1722). This silver was originally given to the Lower (Magothy Bay) Church of Hungars Parish. The set is particularly distinguished for its finely engraved cipher ornament.

The original manuscript of the vestry book (1758-82) of Hungars Parish is kept at the clerk's office at Eastville.

There seem to be no colonial markers in the large yard of Hungars Parish Church near Bridgetown, but there is an unusual urn (from later times) serving as a memorial; and traces of the kiln used for the present building exist in the eastern portion.

Hungars Parish Church is a striking building and one of the prime glories of Virginia's Eastern Shore.

32. BUCK MOUNTAIN CHURCH

Buck Mountain Church, the parish church of Fredericksville Parish, lies on the eastern outskirts of the village of Earlysville in Albemarle County, on the north side of route 743. From Charlottesville one goes north on route 29 for 7.8 miles, turns left on route 649 for .8 mile, turns left again on route 606 for .9 mile, and turns right for 2.3 miles.

Fredericksville Parish and Louisa County were formed in 1742 from St Martin's Parish and Hanover County. In 1757 a part of St Anne's Parish (lying along the James River) was added to Fredericksville Parish.

The line between St Anne's Parish (which was created in 1744 out of St James's Parish (Goochland County)) and Fredericksville Parish, ran from east to west somewhat like the modern route 250. In 1763 Trinity Parish in Louisa County was separated from Fredericksville Parish, and parts of Fredericksville Parish and St Anne's Parish became Fluvanna Parish in 1777.

Buck Mountain Church is now but one of two churches left in Fredericksville Parish as a result of a number of modern changes. Walker's Parish (around Cismont) was separated in 1839 and Green Springs Parish (in Louisa County) in 1845. In 1925 Monticello Parish was formed from parts of Fredericksville and St Anne's Parishes, Ivy Parish was formed from parts of these two and from Greenwood Parish (created in 1864 out of St Anne's), and a small part of Fredericksville Parish was given to Greenwood Parish. As a result of all this, Christ Church and St Paul's Church in Charlottesville and the church at Ivy Depot were all lost to Fredericksville Parish. In 1933 the extreme northwest portion of Fredericksville Parish was annexed to Neve Parish (Greene County), but in 1957 it was separated from Neve Parish to form Mason Parish.

Albemarle County was formed out of Goochland County in 1744 and was augmented by a portion of Louisa County in 1761.

Buck Mountain Church was one of three frame churches that were erected in the parish shortly after its formation. The Buck Mountain Church was first built in 1747 as a structure 60' x 30'. After the Disestablishment, the building was used at various times in the period 1801-33 by Baptists and members of other non-Episcopal bodies. In 1833 the Episcopalians had to repurchase their own building owing to this use of the church by non-Episcopalians and also owing to the fact that no title to the land was to be found at the courthouse. By the 1830's the old pews had been removed to the west gallery, for benches ("made of the outside slabs from the sawmill, with legs as rude thrust through them and . . . no backs") were preferred by those using the old building. The colonial pulpit, though standing, was ignored in favor of "a few planks" laid "across the backs of two pews".

The building was dismantled and removed to its present location in the 1860's—probably in 1861. The original site, on the "road from Michie's Tavern to Earlysville", is about two miles west of the existing church and Earlysville Post Office. Until recently two gravestones marked the site of the first church, but these can no longer be found.

Although there is nothing indisputably colonial to be seen on the exterior or in the interior of the present building, it is generally believed that the roof trusses and the upright framing members derive from the original church. The floor joists are notched and hand-hewn and are also

175

believed to be original. In support of this belief is the fact that no report of any change since the 1860's has ever been heard or found. Contrariwise, all reports stress the fact that the various trusses and so forth were all carefully numbered at the dismantling. (The fact that the building now measures approximately 50'-2" x 26'-3" does not necessarily have any bearing on the colonial derivation of its framework.) It is also entirely possible that the exterior trim of the west doorway and some of the clapboards are colonial or even original. Some of the wide, floor boards and wainscoting boards are definitely old. The exterior and interior trim of the windows (three on each of the side walls), the pews and chancel, and the panelling on the doors are probably from the late 1800's. The metal roof and wood cornice (with returns at the gable) are more recent. The interior walls and flat ceiling are presently plastered.

The number and disposition of the doorways are distinctive: one each on the west, south (near the west wall), and north (also near the west wall), and one on each side of the chancel leading into a vestry (of more recent construction). The north doorway is now filled in (with clapboards) on the exterior. Hardware (apparently old) to hold locking bars exists at the north and west doors. The chancel doors are single, whereas the other three (in the western portion) are double. Because of the curious arrangement of the doorways at the western end, it has been suggested that, perhaps, the building was reversed at its removal, that the present west doorway may have been a window in the original instance, that the present north doorway may have been the original south doorway, that the present south doorway is new (that is, from the 1860's), and that the original west wall may have had two openings (as the east wall does now). In any case, the building is still oriented.

The stone foundations seem to have been repaired in recent years and the ventilation holes, chimney, and furnace-annex also seem recent. East of the vestry (10'-6" east to west and 14'-8" south to north) is a lofty bell-tower with sides of latticework.

In 1930 the Colonial Dames erected a granite marker memorializing the old building, and their stone may be seen just to the west of the yard. The somewhat rustic nature of the church is still symbolized by a cattle-guard at the gate. Oaks and locusts dominate the large, well-kept yard, which is also in part a cemetery.

The church derives its name from the striking eminence six miles to the west and the mountain itself apparently was named for the many buck deer encountered there. The exact origin of the parish's name seems not to be known.

The original manuscript of the vestry book (1742-87) of Fredericksville Parish is on loan at the State Library in Richmond.

Some persons may question the use of "colonial" to describe the present building, but, if its rafters, joists, and upright members are, indeed, from the 1747 church as they are generally believed to be, then Buck Mountain Church has as much right to be called colonial as at least one other church that is regularly called colonial by all authorities, and almost as much right to the term as another but far better known building not so far from Albemarle County.

33. Providence Church

One of our few frame churches to survive the colonial era stands in Louisa County a short distance from the crossroads formed by routes 250 and 522 at Gum Springs. Now long known as Providence Presbyterian Church, it may be reached by proceeding .1 mile west of this crossroads on 250, turning right on route 634 (the old Three Chopt Road), and continuing for another .1 mile until the church's simple sign points down a wooded lane to the right. Gum Springs is 31 miles west of Richmond and 36 miles east of Charlottesville.

Owing to want of specific documents, no exact year has been assigned for the construction of the building. However, it seems that it was probably erected by the year 1747 as a reading house under the ægis of a prominent early dissenter, Mr Samuel Morris, and shortly thereafter became a Presbyterian meeting house. Just when it was first named Providence is also uncertain, but it was probably so named in colonial times. The change from "meeting house" to "church" was, of course, effected only after the Disestablishment.

The church lies approximately southeast by northwest; its dimensions are 50'-3" x 26'-4". There are three windows in each storey on the north and south walls and two smaller windows at the gallery level on the east and west walls. There are three doorways: on the east (only a foot from the south wall), on the west, and on the south (between the middle and eastern windows). All these openings are replacements except for the sills of the three upper windows on the north and their interior frames, which are probably original. The original native stone foundations are largely still at work, although they have in various spots been supplanted (probably around 1920) by other stonework and brickwork (particularly at the corners). The metal roof derives from 1925 and the siding from 1940, but the cornice is believed to be mostly original.

There has existed a theory that the building was originally erected as a tobacco barn, but the Rev'd Mr Joseph C. Matthews, who served the congregation while a seminarian in Richmond, has discounted this for several reasons. For one thing, the building was too well constructed for an ordinary tobacco barn. Furthermore, the meeting house is situated in the midst of an oak grove that includes trees older than the building and gives no indication of ever having been tilled, as one would ordinarily expect in the case of land adjacent to a tobacco barn. However, the early congregation may easily have used a tobacco barn somewhere in the neighborhood as a temporary shelter.

There is also the feeling that the meeting house was enlarged to the west sometime after its original construction. This seems unlikely, although at present this cannot be proved. However, Providence Church bears a strong resemblance to Slash Church (1729) in Hanover County in its proportions and Slash has had a west gallery from its very beginning. Furthermore, the west gallery at Providence is in all probability considerably older than the side galleries that have been added (and to which access is still to be gained only by stepping over a rail).

The hand-rail of the central portion of the west gallery as well as the board-and-batten front and the huge beam that supports this gallery are probably all original. The hand-rail is hand-hewn and secured to the columns by wooden pegs. The large beam is also marked by these pegs. The pair of columns leading from the balcony to the ceiling and the larger pair that supports this gallery (but is not in line with the upper pair) are also probably original and are all chamfered. The four columns of later insertion that support the side balconies possess both chamfers and lamb's tongues. These side galleries may derive from later colonial times or from nearer 1800. The west gallery is also supported by a narrower, chamfered column on the north end, but its companion on the south has been removed (with only the mortise remaining).

The fact that the gallery front and columns collide with the side windows by no means necessarily indicates that the meeting house was enlarged subsequent to 1747, for this can be owing merely to the primitive craftsmanship of its builders, which is not the least of Providence's many attractions.

The floor of the west gallery is probably colonial if not original. The pews presently in the south gallery seem to be older than those in the north gallery. No pews are in current use in the west gallery, which serves as a Sunday-school room. The roof structure (also with wooden pegs), the small post near the top of the stairway, and the framework of heart pine are also in all probability original. The stair post is marked by chamfered and lamb's tongue mouldings. The stairway, which was formerly steep and began its ascent towards the west, was changed to its present south-and-then-east arrangement about 1945. The wainscoting (on all four sides) and the ceiling are both beaded and are probably colonial, if not original.

Two of the most interesting features of the building are the somewhat crude raised panels that are still to be seen on the back of the first pew on the south side of the church and on the inside of the present pulpit. The former panelling probably was the front for a section of pews rather than part of a pew; and the latter panelling is believed to derive from the old pulpit, which stood against the north wall opposite the south doorway, reputedly with a sounding board.

The various pews (low and with straight but sloping backs) now in the church are marked by two different designs on the lower portions of their ends. Some of these derive from a chapel that was built by the congregation sometime before 1862. This building, at Yanceyville, not far from the South Anna River, was the second chapel established for those members of the Church who lived some distance to the northwest of the old church. It was named for St James because the first chapel had been erected adjacent to a schoolhouse named for that saint. When the second chapel was torn down (in the present century), some of its pews were put to use at Providence. All the pews were entirely reworked in 1952. The walls were last plastered in 1928. Some of the wood laths (filled with mud) are exposed on the stairway wall. The floor was refinished and raised in 1952 and is of a different hue from the rest of the woodwork.

Electricity was installed in 1949, although two wood stoves with a single, curious little chimney still heat the edifice.

According to a will written in 1767 and probated two years later, the congregation received two silver cups that are still in use for Communion Services. Therefore, Providence remains one of the few Presbyterian Churches (and perhaps the only one in Virginia) to retain the common cup in preference to the individual cups of recent decades. Each of the two cups, of quart size, is marked with a leopard's head crowned and a lion passant and initials that seem to be J. N. These markings would seem to indicate that they were made in 1769-70 by John Neville of London. The somewhat rough "G*S" that is to be seen on the bottom of each cup must stand for Gum Springs and may have been chiselled by a nineteenth-century parson, who had more than one congregation in his charge and desired to keep the communion vessels clearly distinguished as to ownership. The will of 1767 is said formerly to have been on loan at the library of the Union Theological Seminary in Richmond, but its present whereabouts is somewhat uncertain.

179

Among those dear to American Presbyterianism who have preached in Providence Church is Samuel Davies (1723-61). The English evangelist, George Whitefield, also spoke from its pulpit, around 1755; and local tradition has it that Presidents Madison and Monroe as schoolboys in all probability attended Divine Worship in this meeting house.

None of our wars seem to have damaged Providence.

The fascinatingly primitive nature of the interior woodwork is reminiscent of Prince George's Chapel and Old Christ Church in Sussex County, Delaware, but is almost unique in Virginia among our surviving colonial structures.

34. Augusta Stone Church

The Augusta Meeting House in Augusta County is also known as Augusta Stone Church. It stands on a hillock on the west side of route 11 (the Valley Pike) at the hamlet of Fort Defiance, which is 7 miles north of Staunton. Immediately to the south of the old church is Augusta Military Academy, which has for a long time used Augusta Church as its chapel.

Many persons have assumed that an earlier Augusta Meeting House existed on the site of the old cemetery, or very near this burying ground (which is still to be seen surrounded by a stone wall) across the pike from the church. This putative first building (perhaps of poles) was possibly erected shortly after 1740, for the congregation was organized in that year. The large cemetery, situated in a cedar grove by the tracks of the Chesapeake and Western Railway, is only a few hundred yards back of the manse and in it lies the real founder of the Church and the builder or supervisor of the original portion of the existing church, John Craig (†1774). Parson Craig became the congregation's first pastor in 1740, so that the congregation is five years older than the formal organization of Augusta County. The old cemetery's rock wall, so characteristic of the Valley, is a restoration made around 1956. The old burying ground seems to have been used from around 1740 to 1900.

The present church, of grey field stone, was built in 1747-49. It was formerly believed that the hamlet of Ft Defiance received its name from the fact that some sort of fortification was erected in the early days of the congregation on account of danger from the Indians. This seems to be but a legend. However, the hamlet's name remains unexplained.

Tradition has it that the women of the congregation at Augusta, as at Timber Ridge Church south of Fairfield in Rockbridge County, brought the sand for the mortar from the nearest stream (in this case from the North River several miles distant) by means of pack horses. The original rough stonework is, however, no longer apparent, for the three walls that are still entirely or partly original were completely repointed in 1921-22, so that a smoothness of appearance now dominates the building wherever ivy does not do so. The original dimensions seem to be approximately 57'-2" from northeast to southwest and 39' from northwest to southeast. The walls are about 20" thick.

The disposition of the openings has varied from time to time. Originally there was a double door on the south side (as there is now once again) and opposite this on the north side a high pulpit with a sounding board above and a reading desk below. Other doors were on the west and east walls, in each instance off center to the north. The two aisles thus ran from the pulpit to the south door and from the east to the west doors, in front of the pulpit, the latter aisle being the longer of the two. There are now three windows on the north and two on the south. However, at some time, probably in the colonial era, a session house was built against the north side of the church, immediately behind the pulpit. A vertical line that can at present be seen just left of the middle window probably indicates the location of the small door that led from the little session house into the meeting house. Therefore, there may originally have been only two windows on the north. It is thought that the little session house may have been built as a lean-to so that it might serve as a kitchen if the meeting house had to become a fort, or so that the minister might have a resting place between the long services and sermons. Flat arches mark all the windows and the south doorway, without any special ornamentation.

In 1855 a number of changes were made. A second double door was added on the southern part of the east wall to match the original door on this side, and both were provided with large transoms above. The original (principal) door on the south became an odd-shaped window. The original opening on the west became but a single door. The pulpit was moved to the west and the square box-pews gave way to "modern" ones facing the west. The south to north aisle was removed and a second east-west aisle was added from the new door on the southern part of the east wall. The little window now in the east gable may also have been added in 1855. No windows seem to have existed in the original east and west walls.

In 1921-22 a stone porch was added on the east and a single large door with an enormous semi-circular arch replaced the two double doors. Remnants of the jambs of these two doors (one of them original) exist in vertical stone joints just outside the present porch piers. At the same time, the south door was restored, complete with transom, cheek walls, and steps.

A shallow (about 3") water table still survives above the modern ventilation holes.

The building's most distinctive feature is its clipped east gable. Presumably the west gable was likewise clipped before the church was first enlarged in 1921-22. The only other surviving church in Virginia with clipped gables is the Lower Chapel in Middlesex County, although other churches once so adorned include Westover and Chuckatuck Churches. The A-roof at Augusta Church now has a noticeable sag and its new slate roof has been installed in an almost decorative pattern. The original roof trusses are completely intact and only one has been repaired. The simple cornice is probably modern.

The present ceiling is segmental-arched, although the original ceiling may have been trapezoidal or barrel-vaulted. A large wooden tie-beam and a wooden cornice were removed in 1922, when the present balcony and narthex were created and the large transepts (for the pulpit and choir as well as additional pews) were added. The segmental arch of the ceiling in the older portion of the building has also been used for the ceiling of the modern section of the church, just as the clipped gable has been retained in the porch, transepts, and the additions to the west. This extensive use of a motif in enlarging or reconstructing a colonial structure is not, however, always æsthetically foolproof, for to present an idea once may be arresting while to do so thrice may easily become tedious.

The present floor, pews, lights, and other furnishings also derive from 1921-22. The existing pulpit was installed at the same time, but slight changes have subsequently been made. The present doors and windows and the wood trim of the openings (including the window sills) were likewise installed in that renewal. The pew and rostrum that are being preserved in the session room (in the newer part of the building) undoubtedly derive from the 1855 alterations rather than from colonial times. The most recent addition (seven classrooms, kitchen, recreation room, and John Craig Hall) occurred in 1956.

Augusta Church is well known, partly because it is the oldest surviving church in the Valley, partly because so many scholars from A. M. A. have been nurtured in it, and partly because it has long enjoyed high rank among Presbyterians in the Valley.

Although it was not always so irenic in later times, the Augusta congregation did not enter into the Old Side-New Side controversy that plagued Timber Ridge and other congregations in the area, probably because Parson Craig was a strong adherent of the Old Side.

One of the most interesting of liturgical documents in Virginian history is provided by the scholarly and wise reply that was made by the pastor and two elders in 1844 concerning complaints about the physical position of the church's clerk during singing and the introduction of new tunes—a reply that is as valid now as then and as valid for Anglicans and other Christians as for Presbyterians (cp. pages 42-44 of J. N. Van Devanter's history of Augusta Church).

The churchyard, adorned with venerable oaks, is both spacious and handsome. The stone session house on the northeast is said to have been moved there in 1847, but it seems more likely that it was built anew, possibly with some of the stones from the colonial session house.

The congregation owns John Craig's Bible (London, 1682), record of baptisms (1740-49), autobiography (1770), and sermon on II Samuel XXIII, 5, but its proudest possession is a large silver communion service that consists of no fewer than three flagons, two plates, and six chalices of colonial origin in addition to six small patens that may be old if not colonial, several modern pieces, and two old spoons of recent donation. Although chalices are no longer in general favor among Presbyterians, other parts of the Augusta service are still in use. From the markings on the flagons, chalices, and two plates, it seems probable that the old silver was made in 1764 by Anthony Calame of London. The case of the patens poses certain questions. One answer is that they may have had to be re-silvered and in that way lost their original marks, but this does not seem likely. It is well known that the congregation secured this silver at considerable pecuniary sacrifice, although why such a small congregation felt that it had to have such a large service is still a matter of conjecture. Indeed, Augusta's service constitutes the largest set of colonial silver owned by any congregation in Virginia.

35. CATTAIL CHURCH

Cattail Church lies in King William County at the end of route 606, a quarter of a mile south of route 611. This junction of 606 and 611 is itself about one-half a mile west of route 360 and three-quarters of a mile east of the junction of routes 30 and 611. The site is about two and one-half miles south of Aylett and one and one-half miles from Central Garage.

There is some doubt as to whether the church was built as the first or the second parish church of St David's Parish when that parish was formed out of lower St Margaret's Parish and upper St John's Parish in 1744. A brick that was found at the last remodelling in 1921 was marked 1751, which agrees with the date generally assigned for its construction. The building is now so altered (with two steeples and a curious pediment—all with green shingles—added at the west end, buttresses added to the south and north walls, and the entire structure stuccoed) that one's imagination is stretched to the utmost to include it among our surviving colonial churches. Indeed, there is nothing visible inside or outside that is at all colonial in fact or style unless four old wooden benches in the gallery should be that old. One can, however, discern the line of the bevelled water table, which at the east end shows that, perhaps, as much as ten feet of that end have been removed and little rooms of frame construction substituted. The remaining portion of the original building now has three windows on both the north and south sides and these openings presumably were marked by flat arches in the initial instance. The easternmost opening on the south side was probably originally a doorway. Its original inside dimensions were probably about 60′ x 30′.

After abandonment and subsequent use as a free church following the Disestablishment, the building was turned over to Mt Sinai Baptist Church, a colored congregation, which still possesses it. Cattail Church is as curious as it is lamentable.

36. AQUIA CHURCH

One of the handsomest buildings in all Virginia is Aquia Church, the parish church of Overwharton Parish in Stafford County. Overwharton Parish and St Paul's Parish (in King George County) were created out of Potomac Parish before 1680. Potomac Parish was the upper part of Appomattox Parish until 1662. Appomattox Parish itself was not created, however, until about 1661, for from 1653 on it was the upper part of Nominy Parish. This represents an almost classic series of upper sections of parishes that were successively formed into separate parishes. The upper parish formed from Potomac Parish was for some time known simply by that designation, and then for a while as Stafford Parish, and finally around 1700 as Overwharton Parish.

The name of Overwharton is said to derive from the fact that an early settler, Colonel Henry Meese (†1682), named his plantation Overwoorten after his native parish (Over Worton) in North Oxfordshire. This plantation, which was also spelled Overwarten and Overwharton, later came into the possession of one of Stafford Parish's rectors, the Rev'd Mr Waugh (1630-1706).

There is considerable uncertainty about the early churches of the parish and county. However, it is believed that Divine Worship according to the Book of Common Prayer has been held in an edifice of some sort on or near the present site ever since shortly after the formation of the county in 1654. There were two places for preaching in the area in 1667, and in 1724 a church and two chapels were reported. No one can say how many frame buildings preceded the first brick structure at Aquia, but the last one was burnt in 1755 along with the new brick church.

Aquia Church did not become the parish church until 1757, for that honor seems to have been held until that time by Potomac Church, which was situated upon the narrows of Potomac Creek, on the right side of route 608 as one goes from Fredericksburg to Brooke. Potomac Church, the date of which (as well as the date of any predecessor) is unknown, was one of Virginia's largest colonial churches. It was apparently abandoned before the War of 1812, but stood until it was completely destroyed by Federal soldiers in the War between the States.

The existing Aquia Church was first built in 1751 with Mourning Richards as undertaker or contractor. This fact is inscribed in the tympanum of the south doorway, where it is also inscribed that William Copein was the mason and that the church was destroyed by fire in 1754 and rebuilt in 1757. From newspaper accounts it appears that the fire must have occurred on March 17, 1754 Old Style and, therefore, 1755 New Style, although the calendar was changed in 1752. As a result of the rebuilding, the present walls of Aquia are believed to derive from 1751-55 and much of the interior from 1757. William Copein also worked on Pohick Church and made the baptismal font still to be seen there as well as the inscription on the reredos and the gallery plaque at Aquia Church, the latter two of which are both signed with the usual "pinxit".

The present church's name is derived from its proximity to Aquia Creek. This stream is famous for its sandstone (or "freestone") that has been used not only on Aquia Church but on other handsome churches and houses along the Potomac River (including the Capitol and White House in Washington) and on the old lighthouse at Cape Henry. The name, Aquia, is Indian and was probably first used of the present church. The Indian word indicated a nut that grew near the creek.

Aquia Church occupies an eminence on the east side of route 1, about thirteen miles north of Fredericksburg, three miles north of Stafford Courthouse, and thirty-six miles south of Alexandria. The site is approached through a steep, wooded slope. Like the other surviving church from colonial Stafford County (St Paul's Church, which is now in King George County), Aquia Church is built in the shape of a Greek cross, and these two are unique for that fact among our surviving colonial churches.

Masonry

Aquia is approximately 64' east to west and south to north. The length of each arm is approximately 16'-2½" and the width around 32'-4". The walls are 24½" thick. The original masonry of Aquia's walls is not of the highest degree of excellence and has in recent decades been heavily repaired, in many instances with considerable slovenliness. The bond of the original brickwork is Flemish with random glazed headers, which are more numerous on the west face and the tower wall than upon the other walls. The water table and walls below it were replaced around the whole church in 1915-16. The new water table itself is in the form of a bevelled brick and the replaced lower walls are marked by common and irregular bonds. On almost every wall, two bricks have been replaced at the bottom of the third or fourth quoin from the base; this probably stems from necessary shoring during the replacements of the stones at the corners of the water table. A coat of yellow paint was removed as late as 1933.

On the west façade, there are repairs below, between, and above the upper and lower windows on the left, and there is repointing above the upper right window and below the lower right window. As on all the other walls, there are also small spots of repairs on this wall. On the south side of the nave, there are repairs above the upper window, and a bad crack has been mended on the upper left portion of the wall. Repointing is to be noticed below the lower window and in the lower right part of this wall. On the west wall of the south transept, there are some repairs near the quoins and above the upper window, and some repointing between the windows.

On the south façade, repairs occur above all three windows in the upper tier (and of course, in the brick portions of the pedestals of the doorway), and repointing exists between all three vertical pairs of openings. On the east wall of the south transept and the south wall of the chancel, there are repairs above both windows. Repairs—some of them unusually unlovely—mar the areas above and below the four corner windows of the east wall of the chancel and both windows in the north wall of the chancel and the east wall of the north transept. There is a large, ugly stretch of renewal on the east façade just above the water table.

On the north façade, replacements include the areas above all six openings and below the lower window on the left. Repointing also occurs between each of the three pairs of vertical openings. On the west wall of the north transept, repairs occur above both windows. Almost the entire north wall of the nave—indeed, all of it save certain stretches along the top and the right side—is new.

The masonry of the tower seems to be relatively intact.

Because of the lay of the land, the water table is deepest on the south side of the building. Tie-rods are variously in evidence. The ventilation holes that probably marked the original water table have not been retained in the replacements. Around the entire church in recent decades has been added a concrete gutter, which also forms a walkway.

Queen closers are used at: 1) the salient corners; 2) the south and west doorways; and 3) the thirty-six windows of the church as well as at the corners and the single window of the tower. Exceptions at the openings include several gaps on the south doorway jambs and no queen closers at all on the left jambs of the southernmost upper window of the chancel façade, the easternmost upper window of the north façade, and the lower right window of the west façade. The upper window on the north wall of the nave has only a few original queen closers (and a few replaced ones) on the left jamb, and only a single example on the right jamb. There are also no queen closers on the repaired jambs of the window below that one. The north doorway has only four staggered closers on its right jamb. An interesting disposition of queen closers may also be seen on the southwest corner of the nave where the closers follow the zigzag pattern of the quoins.

The large number of openings of Aquia Church include great doorways on the west, south, and north and two tiers of windows. In each of the four end walls there are three windows in the upper tier and two in the lower tier, and in each of the eight side walls there is a single window in each storey. In addition, there is also the window in the west wall of the tower.

Rubbed brick marks all the window jambs and arches that have survived from the 1751 church. The arches of the lower tier were originally all flat and the rest semi-circular. Each of the voussoirs of all the window

187

arches originally consisted of full bricks alternating with pairs of halves. Repairs or replacements mark many of the arches. In fact, only eight of the original lower arches remain. The lower window arches of the east wall of the south transept, the three walls of the chancel, the side walls of the north transept, and the north wall of the nave were all replaced in 1915-16. Those in the north wall of the nave and the west wall of the north wing have new soldier courses, but have retained old keystones. Each of the other six arches has a rowlock course without a keystone. The arches of the lower windows in the south and north façades are repointed; the lower right window in the north façade has also been repaired with possibly two or three new bricks. Likewise repaired are the window arches on the left of the west doorway, on the south wall of the nave, and on the west wall of the south transept.

Repairs to the arches of the upper windows are less extensive. One or two bricks have been replaced on the east wall of the north transept; two or three bricks in the middle and south windows of the west façade, the single window on the south wall of the nave, and the south window of the east façade; and five or six bricks in the north window of the west façade and in the west window of the north transept. Repointing includes the arch of the west window of the south façade and that of the west window of the north transept. This latter window also has no keystone. The arch in the north wall of the nave is in great part new, but has an old keystone. Three or four bricks are also new in the single window of the tower, which has no keystone.

Stonework

The chief distinction between the exteriors of Aquia Church and St Paul's Church lies in the former's tower and stone ornamentation in contrast with the latter's great amount of lovely rubbed brick. Aquia stone is used on the former building for the quoins (and originally for their base) and the keystones of all the original windows as well as for the three elaborate doorways. In addition to the quoins and keystones on the tower, stone also forms somewhat of a belt course on the tower's west wall just below the spring line of the window arch, as well as a band at the base of this wall.

The eight original stone bases of the quoins were replaced with concrete in 1915-16. Other renewal of the stonework at that time included: 1) the lowest quoin on the left of the west doorway; 2) the lower stones of both pedestals on the west; 3) the lowest quoin at the southwest corner of the nave; 4) a small portion of the raked cornice and the upper stone of the right pedestal on the south; and 5) almost all of the raked cornice, the center panel of the tympanum, the keystone (and voussoir on each

188

side), probably the top and bottom quoins on the left, and possibly the top portion of the architrave—all on the north.

Deterioration in the stonework includes the pedestals on the north as well as some of the keystones. It has been pointed out as of significance that this deterioration is most severe on the church on the areas that can be reached by a man on horseback.

The elaboration of the doorways of Aquia is second only to those at Pohick Church and Christ Church (Lancaster County). Aquia's doorways are all three marked by triangular pediments. The raked cornice consists of: cyma recta, fascia, soffit, and cyma reversa; and the horizontal cornice (which on the west only is broken by the arch—except at the ends) includes: fillet, fascia, soffit, fillet, and cyma reversa. The tympanum in each instance is also of stone. Around 1945-47, someone (apparently from Richmond) chiselled "Aquia" into the tympanum of the west doorway—a bit unnecessarily, it would seem. On the south there is the aforementioned inscription; the north tympanum is unadorned. Below the cushion frieze of the three doorways, the architrave is marked by these mouldings: cavetto, fascia, cyma reversa, fascia, and bead. The obliteration of all save the extremities of the horizontal cornice, frieze, and architrave on the west doorway is accomplished by three large voussoirs (each of a different shape) on each side of an elaborate, linenfold keystone, which projects both into the tympanum above and into the door frame below. A similar obliteration of the frieze and architrave on the side doorways concerns only two voussoirs on each side of the keystone. The keystones of the three doorways are all different from each other. That on the south is a linenfold keystone. It does not project into the tympanum, but the horizontal cornice of the pediment breaks out over the keystone. The keystone on the north is plain (and may possibly be a replacement), but projects into the tympanum. All three arches are flat.

The architrave is carried down the jambs and is broken in each instance by four quoins on each side. The base of the rusticated architrave consists of a cavetto and an upside down cyma recta; the pedestal consists of two stones resting on brickwork (and a greater number of courses exist on the south than at the other entrances).

On the south doorway, the horizontal cornice continues (and, as noted above, breaks out over the keystone), and there is no base for the architrave. The pedestals on the south consist of sandstone on brick, and at least one of the sandstone blocks is new. The pedestals (and their caps) on the north doorway are the same as on the west. The steps on the west include a marble sill and a marble stoop. These marble pieces seem to derive from tombstones and are believed to have been placed there after the War between the States. The three-sided pair of sandstone steps on the south seems to be considerably older and may be original.

189

The steps on the north also seem to derive from a tombstone and were put there around the time of the War between the States.

The roof of rather low pitch is hipped and covers all four arms of the cross. New shingles were put on in 1915-16. The modillion cornice on both church and tower is old and possibly colonial or even original.

Tower

The tower is a unique feature. It has been called fake, but this is true only because its single solid wall is that on the front. The other three walls consist of sheathing laid upon a wooden framework that in turn rests upon the roof of the church. That the tower is an original part of the structure is best indicated by its stonework, which includes the same (albeit smaller) quoins at the ends of the west wall and the aforementioned belt course, base band, and keystone. The quoins and the intervallic bricks (including some glazed headers) also extend around the southwest and northwest corners of the tower. The roof of the tower is marked by four pedimented gables with modillion cornices. The raked cornice on the west gable is broken and the tympanums of both tower and church are sheathed with copper shingles. The entire tower is surmounted by a strange, little square cupola with a conical roof, and at the apex there is a wooden cross. From a photograph (probably mid-nineteenth century) we know that the apex was then surmounted by a metal finial and ball rather than a cross. The sides of this cupola also appear (in more than one photograph) to have consisted of raised wooden panels and the two eastern corners may have been decorated with wooden quoins. Some artists' sketches have shown a clock in the cupola, but this is believed to have been artistic license. The little cupola is actually perched on the front of the tower.

Interior

So much of the striking interior of Aquia Church has been preserved that it is difficult to say which particular part represents the outstanding feature. Indeed, no other colonial church in Virginia can boast of greater elaboration for its interior, and none presents so elaborate a view from both nave and chancel as does Aquia, for its west gallery front is the equal in ornamentation of its highly carved reredos and pulpit—all of which are believed to be principally of pine and are mostly, at present, painted white.

The triangular pediment of the classical reredos has a low slope. The horizontal cornice includes these mouldings: ovolo, cyma recta, cyma reversa, fascia, bead, modillions, ovolo, dentils, and cyma reversa. The raked cornice has, in addition to all these, the following small mouldings: fascia, cyma reversa, fascia, and bead. In the tympanum there is a raised panel. Below the plain frieze is the architrave, which consists of: fascia, cyma reversa, fascia, cyma reversa, fascia, bead, and fascia. The horizontal cornice and frieze both break over each of the fluted pilasters at the ends. The handsome capitals are of the Ionic order. The flutes of the pilasters are stopped in their lower portions (corresponding to the raised panels). The bases of the pilasters are marked by: ovolo, torus, scotia, torus, fascia, and plinth. Between the pilasters are four Tablets—(from the left) the Law (on two tablets), the Creed, and the Lord's Prayer—on semi-circular, arched panels of poplar (painted black, with the lettering in white). The Law concludes with the response for the Tenth Commandment. The lettering of the tablets has probably been retouched in modern times. Below each tablet is a horizontal and a vertical panel, all of which were replaced in 1933. These new panels were probably modelled upon old ones, for they use the same mouldings as those of the tablets: torus, two fillets, and an upside down cyma recta. The marble slab inscribed somewhat quaintly and pleonastically to the "Race of the House of Moncure" now lies in the chancel floor to the south of the Table, but was until 1933 installed in the reredos beneath the tablets. This slab was originally laid only after the War between the States.

The semi-circular, three-legged Table with marble top and somewhat primitively ornamented legs is believed to be colonial, and the fact that there are no kick marks to be seen adds to the probability of its use for sacramental purposes in colonial times. The chancel chairs derive from before the War between the States, and the communion rail from 1933.

A more ornate pulpit could hardly be desired than that in the southeast angle of Aquia Church's crossing. The ogival top of the enormous hexagonal sounding board terminates in a finial. The mouldings of the cornice, frieze, and architrave are identical with those on the horizontal cornice, frieze, and architrave of the reredos. On the raised panel of the soffit is a raised, six-pointed sunburst (which appears to have been gilded or regilded in recent times). The sounding board is supported by four pilasters. Between the two front pilasters are the following panels: (from the top) small horizontal, long vertical, small horizontal, and short vertical. The capitals of the pilasters are composed of: abacus, echinus, three fillets, necking, and astragal. The two front pilasters have no bases, but instead terminate at the minister's seat. On the base of each of the two side pilasters are these mouldings: ovolo, scotia, ovolo, and plinth. The top rail of the pulpit itself is heavily moulded: cyma recta, fascia, soffit, fillet, ovolo, drip, soffit, large fillet, fascia, and cyma reversa. On each of the five sides of the pulpit, a horizontal raised panel lies above a

191

vertical raised panel. The door to the pulpit has raised panels and H-hinges.

The front of the reading desk is moulded thus: cyma recta, fascia, soffit, ovolo, drip, soffit, fillet, fascia, and cyma reversa. The back of the seat of the reading desk is scrolled, not unlike a curvilinear gable. The reading-desk door is marked by a horizontal raised panel over a vertical one and by H-hinges. The front and southwest sides are adorned with two small horizontal panels over two vertical panels, which are in turn located over two other vertical panels. The clerk's desk itself is triangular and rises towards the front. In fact, all three desks of this superb pulpit give the effect of a ship's prow. Each of the three has both a kneeling board and a shelf. The clerk's desk has scrolled sides and panels. Below the reading desk and behind the clerk's desk is a closet, which may possibly have been used by the precentor to store his music and pitchpipe.

The stair to the pulpit is straight except for a turn at the top to allow for the somewhat singular landing east of the pulpit. A spur leads to the minister's reading desk. The clerk's desk is reached by two steps (on both the southwest and the northeast sides) from the floor and has no door. Several of the steps in the upper portion of the pulpit stair are angled. The rails of the stair are moulded and painted brown, as are the newells, the treads of the stairs, and the floors, shelves, and rails of the three desks. The balusters are turned, the newels are almost blown-up pilasters, and the stringer is scrolled, although quite roughly. Access may be had to the base of the pulpit either from the chancel area (by the present electronic organ) or from the clerk's desk. The base of the wine-glass pulpit is a hexagonal column. Its capital includes: fascia, echinus, fillet, necking, and abacus. The base of this column includes a fillet, a torus, and a fascia.

This magnificent pulpit was almost dismantled and sold by a brother of General Lee and other members of the Aquia vestry in 1869 because the then rector was infirm and could not ascend the steps. Fortunately for the pulpit, Colonel Lee died before the project could be consummated.

The remaining portion of the southeast corner-pew (on the west side by the aisle) that is dominated by this three-decker pulpit comprises a small pew with benches on three sides (and part of the fourth side) and access only from the south aisle. The pulpit-pew was the only pew that was not cut down after the War between the States. The other pews include the three large ones at the other corners of the crossing and seventeen smaller pews, all of which still have benches on three sides. There are five of these smaller pews in the nave and six in each of the transepts. The northwest corner-pew has only one door, but it is divided into two pews just inside the door. All of the panelling of the pews is believed to be original save the east and south sides of the northeast corner-pew.

The dark wood moulding at the top of the pew-sides, pew-backs, and wainscoting is in most instances original, but in some cases it unfortunately betrays the effects of a carpenter's plane. The raised panels of the pulpit-pew along the chancel and south transept aisles have a small horizontal panel over a vertical one. Before they were cut down, the other pews were the same along the aisles, and—along the pew-backs—they either followed this pattern or had a very long, horizontal panel over several lower vertical panels. When the majority of the pews were abbreviated, the top rail was removed and put back in position at the lower height. In most instances most of the upper panel was removed and the pew-side turned over. In several cases the panels were turned upside down. Evidence of just such a procedure lies in the remnants of long horizontal panels that may be seen at the floor in most of the pews of the south transept. Original raised panels are also to be seen below the benches that lie against and parallel with the walls. In most cases the pew-backs have raised panels on the side facing the pulpit. Exceptions are provided in the two pews under the gallery columns of the nave. The panelling along the east side of the pulpit is irregular: on the northern part, these panels are upside down (and one of the smaller panels is now replaced by a hot air register); on the south portion, the panelling is new as a result of the modern addition (subsequently removed) of a small vesting room just east of the pulpit. The present choir stalls (opposite the pulpit) date only from 1933 and replaced a small pew like those at the outside doors. The latches on the pew-doors are post-colonial. The wainscoting in the chancel dates from 1958, whereas that in the nave and the transepts was installed after the War between the States.

The marble floor of the chancel derives from 1933; the marble slabs at the crossing were installed after the War between the States. These latter were moved from the Moncure family cemetery at "Windsor Forest" (about 5½ miles northwest of the church) and, because the marble was smoother on the lower side, these slabs were installed upside down. No graves lie beneath the crossing. Parson John Moncure (†1764) and his wife lie buried, however, under the chancel. As many as six graves are thought to have been moved from other burying places in the county after the War between the States and deposited under the chancel. None of these graves are colonial. There probably was never any stair to this somewhat improvised crypt. In 1915-16 some of the original flagstones were removed to the front walk and new ones put in the aisles (5'-7½" wide). The rest of the flagstones were used to fill in the old road to the church. The pew-floors were replaced with concrete in 1915-16. The three sets of boarding at the northwest, northeast, and southwest corners of the interior were put up when lamps were being used.

West Gallery

No other colonial gallery in Virginia even remotely approaches Aquia's west gallery. The cornice that serves as the rail of the gallery front is rich with mouldings: ovolo, fillet, cyma recta, cyma reversa, fascia, bead, soffit, ovolo, dentils, and cyma reversa. Below these are eight pilasters in all, broken by raised vertical panels. A pilaster surmounts each of the two inner columns supporting the gallery, and a pair of pilasters surmounts each of the two outer columns. The pilasters at the walls project as far as do the outer of the pairs of pilasters; the inner pilasters of each pair are in line with the inner two single pilasters. The cornice breaks out over them all. The frieze is of a single member only, and there is no architrave. The capitals (of modified Doric order) include: abacus, echinus, three fillets, and necking. The shafts are fluted and the bases are marked by: torus, scotia, torus, and plinth. A second cornice breaks out over the four supporting columns and has the same mouldings as the upper cornice except for the fact that the soffit has modillions and below the soffit there are ovolo and cyma reversa mouldings. Below the cushion frieze, the architrave includes: cyma reversa, fascia, cyma reversa, fascia, and bead.

The mouldings of the gallery columns are these: abacus, echinus, three annulets, necking, and astragal. Below the fluted shafts are: torus, scotia, and torus. The names of the first rector and vestry are believed to have been put up on the gallery front in the original construction. There are at present no pews in the gallery, but there are still holes in the floor where pew-rails formerly existed, so that part of the gallery floor is certainly very old if not colonial. The kneeling board along the gallery front is also extant. There are two sets of stairs: one leading from the nave around its northwest corner to the gallery and another leading from the northwest window of the gallery's west wall into the tower. The latter stairway is much the narrower and is covered by a hatch. The rails, balusters, and stringers of the two stairways match those of the pulpit. The hand-turned balusters are similar, but all vary somewhat from each other. The stringers are more regularly scrolled than is that of the pulpit stairway.

Above the church's coved cornice is a wooden ceiling installed soon after the War between the States. The walls, which were last plastered before the War, are painted an off-white color. The church was wired for electricity in 1933; the great chandelier and lights in the ceiling, however, date only from 1954. The original beams of the roof trusses appear to be intact, although new struts have possibly been installed. All of this

194

may conveniently be seen from the tower room, on the walls of which may also be seen many initials and names (including some from the War between the States). The walls of this storeroom appear to date from the nineteenth century.

The sides of the lower windows of the church are splayed. The interior wood sills and aprons of the lower windows and the gallery windows are additions. The lower windows also formerly possessed shutters. The window bolts are likewise additions. The sash and nearly all the panes (9 over 9) of the lower windows are said to be original, but the knife-edge muntins would indicate a date in the early 1800's. The sash and panes (11 over 6) of the upper windows were removed in 1933 (and rumor has it that they were sold to persons engaged in the restoration of other eighteenth-century buildings in the Commonwealth!). The frames and sills of both upper and lower windows appear to be original. The exterior mouldings of the lower window-frames include a brick and shutter moulding (fascia and bead) as well as: fascia, cyma reversa, fascia, and bead. The new brick mould of the upper window-frames is a cavetto; the other mouldings are the same as for the lower windows.

The door frames are old but may not be original. The mouldings are cavetto, fascia, and bead; and replacements mark the lower portions in all three instances. The doors themselves (1958) constitute a second set of replacements and are similar to the south doors (possibly 1731) of Vawter's Church in Essex County.

The parish's communion silver consists of a flagon, a chalice, a paten, and a footed paten-cover, each of which is inscribed: "The gift of the Rev'd Alexander Scott A:M late minister of this Parish. Anno: 1739". The silver was buried in the wars of 1776, 1812, and 1861-65. It was all made in London by Thomas Farren in 1739-40 and is still in use.

No longer in use, however, is a paten made in 1736-37 and given (by Reynard Delafiae) to Quantico Church at Dumfries in Dettingen Parish and Prince William County. (Dettingen Parish was formed in 1745 from Hamilton Parish, which had been created out of Overwharton Parish in 1730.) Ever since Quantico Church burned in 1934, this paten has been in the custody of the diocese and is now kept in a vault at the Virginia Trust Company in Richmond.

The colonial Bible of Overwharton Parish was thrown into the woods during the occupation of the church in the War between the States. It was later found, but was apparently never returned to the parish. The register of Overwharton Parish (1723-58) has been twice published—in 1899 and 1961, in the latter instance with corrections by Mr George H. S. King of Fredericksburg—and is on loan at the State Library in Richmond.

In the extreme southern portion of the churchyard are a number of colonial graves—ranging from 1733 to 1773—that were moved to Aquia around 1941-43 from a nearby family cemetery that was taken into the Marine Base at Quantico. Their tombstones abound in skulls and cross-bones as well as angels, mouldings, and Latin mottoes. The numerous trees in the yard include oaks, cedars, walnuts, and hickories. A small set of foundations discovered just south of the front gate may represent a colonial vestry or perhaps a colonial kiln.

After the Disestablishment, the church lay in a state of collapse for over fifty years. The parish was reorganized in 1856, but the church was again out of use during the War between the States, when it was desecrated by Federal troops as a stable. It was revived shortly after the War. Major repairs have been undertaken before and after the War between the States, in 1915-16, in 1933, and in 1958 (this last owing to termites). The parish house just down the hill was erected in 1959.

A great deal of Aquia's unique appeal stems from its spaciousness and this spaciousness is augmented by the fact that it possesses more openings than any other colonial church in Virginia; this condition is still further augmented both by the generous use of white paint and by the lack of obstruction for the numerous openings. Aquia Church has, however, suffered badly at the hands of many who have cherished it, for a number of changes and repairs have been instituted that can most charitably be termed only as unfortunate. Nonetheless, much of this renewal is not irremediable, and, despite it all, Aquia Church remains one of our outstanding churches, for few persons can remain unmoved by the baroque glories of its exterior stonework or its interior mouldings and panels.

37. LOWER CHURCH, SOUTHWARK

One of the loveliest spots in all Virginia has been created by the ruins of the second Lower church of Southwark Parish in Surry County. These noble ruins stand just south of route 10 about .5 mile west of the village called Bacon's Castle and about 7 miles southeast of Surry Courthouse. A number of markers (concerning our old churches) that have been erected on the highways or upon the buildings themselves are inaccurate (and have remained so for many years), and the marker to be seen near the southeast corner of Lower Southwark's ruins is one of them. This building was constructed around 1754 and never served any other parish than Southwark.

Surry County was created out of James City County in the probable year of 1652 and lost much of its territory to Brunswick County in 1720 and again in 1733. Sussex County was created out of Surry in 1754. Lawne's Creek Parish was created out of James City Parish in 1640. Chippoaks Parish (to the west along the James) seems to have had a brief existence in the 1640's, but was apparently soon absorbed by Lawne's Creek Parish. This latter parish had three parish churches before it was dissolved in 1740: two (1628 and about 1650) near Hog Island on the James River and a third (probably 1696) on the site of the present ruins. This 1696 church became the Lower Church of Southwark Parish when Lawne's Creek Parish was merged in 1740 with Southwark Parish (which had been created in 1647) and was succeeded around 1754 by the existing building.

Surry County was named from the fact that it lay across the river from Jamestown, as the county of Surrey lay on the southern shore of the Thames at London. Southwark Parish was also named for the corresponding parish in London (which in modern times is commemorated by a diocese of that name).

St Andrew's Parish (Brunswick County) was created in 1720 out of the two Surry County parishes, and Albemarle Parish was created in 1740. When Sussex County was formed, Surry County and Southwark Parish were made coterminous.

The existing ruins of Lower Southwark Church measure 74' x 34' on the outside. The walls are 2½ brick-lengths thick. The outer brick-length is laid in Flemish bond and the inner 1½ brick-lengths is of English bond (apparently for purposes of strength). Below the bevelled water table the bond is also English. There are entrances on the west and the south, and there are four windows on the south, five on the north (the easternmost one matching the south doorway), and two on the east. The present state of the ruins prevents our knowing whether windows also existed in the gables, although there is evidence to show that there was a west gallery, a pulpit (in the middle of the north side), and the usual central and cross aisles.

The arches of all the openings are semi-circular and at this writing seven of them still manage to complete the semi-circle. They all seem to have been composed of full bricks alternating with pairs of halves. Rubbed brick marks the openings and the corners of the building. Queen closers are also still in evidence. The windows had sloping sills. There are at present an unusually large number of ventilation holes.

After the Disestablishment, the church was abandoned and its communicants were not allowed to resume worship in it until 1847 because of animosity towards England and the English faith. The building had, however, from a few years before 1847 been used by members of other Churches, and in the 1850's these groups so disputed the use of the building by the Episcopalians that the latter withdrew in 1854 and erected another church nearby. Lower Southwark Church was burned in 1868, and it is generally believed to have been set on fire by colored people who had been using part of the yard for buryings and did not want to be dispossessed of their graveyard. Some of their graves are still to be seen on the northwest of the ruins.

The old ruins now form the majestic center of a cemetery that abounds in tombstones (some of which, notably several near the north wall of the church, are no longer legible) as well as in a considerable variety of trees, shrubs, and vines. Inside the ruins are two cedar trees, a redbud tree, periwinkle, and ivy of several kinds and effects. It is paradoxical that a place of such beauty should have developed from a series of tragedies.

The old glebe house of Southwark Parish, which was built before 1724, may still be seen on the north side of route 10, about 5½ miles west of Surry Courthouse, although the dwelling has been in private hands since the Disestablishment.

In 1741 the Lower Church of Southwark Parish was bequeathed "thirty five pounds sterling to be laid out in communion plate". In the same will a like sum was also bequeathed to Albemarle Parish. What happened to the silver of Lower Southwark Church is unknown, but the Albermarle Parish silver passed by descent to St Andrew's Church near Littleton and, when that church (erected around 1877) was abandoned in this century, it was lent to St Luke's Church, the Nottoway Parish Church at Courtland in Southampton County, where it is still used. This silver represents one of the few remaining complete sets (chalice, paten-cover, flagon, and alms bason) and was made in London in 1746-1747, probably by William Williams.

The vestry book (1742-87) of Albemarle Parish still survives and is on loan at the State Library in Richmond. The register (1721-87) of this parish is likewise extant and is in the custody of the Virginia Historical Society in Richmond.

38. ABINGDON PARISH CHURCH

Abingdon Parish Church in Gloucester County is situated in a grove of hickory and walnut trees on the east side of route 17, about 7.6 miles north of Yorktown and one mile south of White Marsh. The existing building is the parish's second church on the present site, but there are two views current as to the foundations of the first church (c. 1660). The older view is that the foundations that lie partly under the south transept of the existing church represent the first church. Those at the church are inclined to think, however, that these exposed bricks may be part of a large vault, and that the first church's site was in the south central portion of the churchyard, where flagstones may be seen. According to those who have done a bit of probing in this spot, the first church was probably buttressed. Tradition has it that half an acre was given for this first church by Augustine Warner, whose descendants include both President George Washington and Queen Elizabeth II.

The name of the parish has likewise never been satisfactorily explained, but it is believed that it must have been named for Abingdon in Berkshire, England, by parishioners who may have derived from that locality near Oxford.

The date for the completion of the building is believed to be 1755 and in support of this is an inscribed brick ("WB 1755") in the lower southwest corner of the west wall of the nave. Report has it that another inscribed brick ("BR June 30, 1754"), which has been cut so high in the brickwork that it could have been carved only from scaffolding, exists in the west gable, either just above or just below the horizontal cornice, above the door, although this second brick cannot now be located. It may possibly have been misplaced in the repair of 1897. Also cited is an entry of 1751 in the *Virginia Gazette* of Williamsburg about a contract for a new church in the parish of Abingdon.

The church presents the most superb example of brickwork, laid in Flemish bond with glazed headers. Below the bevelled water table the masonry is laid in the same bond. The building is in the shape of a Latin cross: 80½' east to west and 75½' north to south. The chancel and transepts are 20' long and the nave 25'. All four arms have the same width of 35½' on the outside. It is this great width that contributes so much to the church's spaciousness. In fact, the church is so spacious that its cruciform effect is greatly diminished for the worshipper. The side walls are 25' high and the roof has a 19' pitch. The walls are three brick-lengths or around 27" thick.

The walls are still in splendid condition. The course above the horizontal cornices of the building seems to have been repaired on every gable. On the west wall of the nave, a brick or two have been replaced at a corner of the water table. On the south wall of the nave, there are two cracks; there is a patch below the water table; and there is a new ventilation opening as well as the entrance to the modern furnace. On the west wall of the south transept there is repointing on the upper left. Several bricks have been replaced on the south wall of the south transept, and on the east wall of this wing there is a crack. On the south wall of the chancel a crack has been repointed. Close to the east edge of this wall is a curious bit of masonry: above, there is too much glazing, and below, there is too little. A new entrance and four cracks mark the east wall of the chancel. The north wall of the chancel and the east wall of the north transept are currently covered with dead vines. The north wall of the north wing is also partly so covered. These vines have been left to dry, after being cut, so that their removal would not damage the mortar.

The north transept's west wall is marred by only two cracks; several cracks also may be seen on the north wall of the nave. This is masonry in a remarkable state of preservation after over two hundred years!

There are the usual three doorways in the west, south, and north. The west doorway has a segmental brick pediment. Its raked cornice consists of a cyma recta, a cyma reversa, a fascia, and another cyma reversa. The bottom three mouldings may have been repaired. Glazed headers are used in the tympanum. The horizontal cornice consists of only three courses: two cyma reversas separated by a fascia. The lower two courses seem to have been repaired. The pilasters of the west doorway contain three sizes of rubbed brick. The arch and the jambs alternate full bricks with pairs of halves. The voussoirs in the middle of the arch are new. The base of the pilasters is made up of several mouldings (cavetto and fillet, torus, and fascia) above the water table and pedestal. The brick sill is new, as are the concrete sills of the other entrances.

The south and north doorways each have a triangular brick pediment. The cornices of the pediments are the same as on the west, except that the top moulding of the raked cornices is now missing. The jambs are the same as the western pilasters. The arches are flat, with each voussoir consisting of three sizes of brick. A fluted brick forms an embryonic keystone. The north arch is heavily repaired and only part of the fluted brick remains. The base of the jambs of the south and north doorways is the same as that on the west.

The wooden door frames are mostly original. The semi-circular arch on the western entrance consists of a fascia, a cyma reversa, a wide fascia, a small cyma reversa, and a third fascia. The wooden keystone is fluted on the front and bottom. The capitals of the Doric pilasters include a small cyma reversa, a fascia, the echinus, three annulets, a tiny cavetto, the necking, and three very small mouldings: torus, fillet, and cavetto. The pilasters are fluted only on the front and have no base. A new strip

200

has been added down the inside of each of these wooden pilasters. The two panels of the fanlight do not match those (a small panel over two large ones) of the doors. The doors are probably not colonial. The H-hinges of all three entrances are original.

The door frames on the south and north have flat arches, which, with their architraves, consist of a (new) bed mould, a cyma reversa, a fascia, a cyma recta, another fascia, and a bead. The frames are new at the bottom. The double doors themselves are the same as on the west, none of them being original.

There are two windows in each side of the nave and in the east end of the chancel, and a single window in each side of the transepts and the chancel. The semi-circular arches alternate a full brick with two halves. All jambs are rubbed, as are the salient corners of the building and, of course, the various arches. The voussoirs of the window arches are cut to receive the wooden keystones. Minor repairs have been made to several of the window arches. The brick sills are bevelled, but the sides and jambs of the windows are not splayed. Queen closers are regularly used at the jambs of openings and the salient corners of the building.

The semi-circular arches of the window frames are the same as those of the doorways. The capitals, however, are different and include a fascia, a cyma recta, a fillet, a cyma reversa, the necking, and an astragal. The capitals do not turn the corners. The fluting of the wood keystones is on both the front and under sides. The fluting of the wooden jambs is used only on the front. The lunette contains six lights; the rest of the window is 16 over 16. The upper 22 lights with heavy muntins seem original in most instances, although both sashes of 16 lights are new in the side windows of the chancel and both are old in the north window in the east end of the chancel. The sills of all the windows seem to be new, and the jambs of the north window of the chancel have been replaced at the bottom. They were probably all once guillotine windows, and they all at sometime have had shutters, for many holders remain. Forty panes of the original crown glass were broken by a severe explosion at the Naval Mine Depot in Yorktown during the second World War (on November 17, 1943), although most of the panes in the upper sash and many panes in the lower sash are colonial.

Reredos

The most striking feature of the interior is the enormous wooden reredos presently located against a partition in line with the side windows of the chancel. It was long assumed that this reredos was erected in 1841, but more recent opinion has it that it derives from 1755. Although the reredos is undoubtedly colonial in origin, there is a certain difficulty in assuming that it is original with the present building, for the reredos itself extends 15′ and the space between the two east windows is only 14′-2″. However, it could have been built after 1755 and before the church became somewhat inactive after the Disestablishment. It could also possibly have been moved to Abingdon from some nearby church, and this possibility is strengthened by the elaborate tradition of Petsworth Church in the same county and Stratton Major Church in neighboring King and Queen County. At any rate, the reredos is one of the most elaborate evidences of classical architecture in any of our colonial churches.

The raked cornice of its triangular pediment is broken by a pineapple on an urn, which itself rests on a plinth. The raked cornice includes a cyma recta, a fillet, a cyma reversa, a fascia, carved modillions, an egg-and-dart moulding, small dentils, and a talon. The horizontal cornice omits only the top cyma recta. The frieze now has the opening words of the Te Deum lettered in gold. This inscription was added for Christmas of 1861 and was gilded in 1867.

The architrave consists of a fascia, an enriched talon, a bead and reel, another fascia and enriched talon, a third fascia, and another bead and reel.

The capitals of the four fluted columns are pure Corinthian. Below the necking of the columns is the usual astragal. Two of the four tablets (Decalogue, Creed, and Lord's Prayer) are between the two middle columns and the others occupy the remaining spaces. These tablets are said by some to come from a previous church. A raised panel is below each tablet.

The mouldings of the base of the column are: torus, scotia, torus, scotia, fillet, torus, and fascia. Those of the caps of the pedestals are: fillet, cyma reversa, fascia, cyma recta, fillet, and cavetto. On the bases of the pedestals are an upside down cyma recta, a torus, another inverted cyma recta, a small fascia, and a large fascia. The bases of the pedestals are cut and raised with the chancel floor.

The reredos appears to be about 17 feet in height.

The shafts of the balusters in the elliptical communion rail are plain. The age of this rail is indeterminate.

The flagstones of the original eight-foot wide aisles are gone, although some are still to be seen in the west, south, and north vestibules as well as in the sidewalk leading from the west door to the south door. Of the original box-pews, two sections of panelling may be seen at the rear of the church, but they originally came from elsewhere in the building. Their H-hinges may also be colonial. Also original are the pews in the two original galleries of the transepts. These pews include a large pew on each side of a short aisle and a large, high bench (for servants in colonial times) against the rear wall, opposite the stairway in each instance. The large pews have seats on three sides. The high bench and two sides of

202

each large pew have boards for footrests. Benches also exist on both sides of the small gallery aisles. These seats are believed to have been assigned to the colored "mammies" of the four families of the parish who occupied the four large pews. The pew sidings in the galleries slope downward to the balcony rail. The rails and risers of the galleries' stairs are probably original. The doors to the gallery pews are now lost.

Possibly original are the pilasters under each end of the galleries. On the columnar supports, the Doric or Tuscan capitals seem old, but the shafts appear to be mostly new. The horizontal panels of the gallery fronts include a small panel over a larger one and a series of fasciæ. The panels have a bead at the edge of the field.

Of modern addition are the cross above the lofty reredos, most of the pews, and the sconces. There are no chandeliers. The trusses are believed to be original, but they have been taken down, repaired, and reinstalled.

Although Abingdon Church may not have been abandoned, it was apparently inactive in the early 1800's, for there was no rector here (or at Ware Church) for at least a decade and the Methodists seem to have used the building from 1818 to 1833 and maybe longer still. Anglican worship was, however, restored in 1826 and the church was repaired in 1841, but was wrecked by Federal troops and horses in the War between the States. After the War, repairs (around 1868) included new pews, floors for the aisles, a new pulpit, and a vesting room occupying the entire chancel. At this time the altar was moved to the crossing and was not moved back to its present (probably original) location in the southeast until 1897, at which time the present chancel partition was also erected, a new roof installed, the floor raised, the present ceiling substituted for the old, flat one, and a furnace and inconspicuous chimney added. The claim against the Federal government for damages in the War was finally honored almost fifty years after the event. In 1950 some redecoration and repanelling were undertaken. The present cornice of the building, which is also extended horizontally across the gables (and may have done so in colonial times), probably dates from 1897, but is composed of classical mouldings and modillions.

Silver; Tombs

Abingdon owns several plain silver communion pieces of venerable age: 1) a chalice that is probably an American copy of a seventeenth-century English example; 2) a cover for this chalice (serving as a paten); 3) a cylindrical flagon of 1702-03, made by Samuel Wastell and inscribed as the gift of "LB" (probably for Major Lewis Burwell (†1710)); and 4) a large paten of 1710-11 made by Alice Sheene inscribed "Abingdon Parish Plate". Major Burwell is believed to have given three or maybe all four of these pieces. The flagon is in fragments, however, as a result of a fire at "Rosewell" in 1916 where it was being kept for safety.

One of the two extant copies of the lost register (1678-1780) of the parish is owned by the Virginia Historical Society in Richmond.

In the churchyard are a number of Burwell tombs (with coats-of-arms) that were moved in 1911 from "Carter's Creek" and bear dates from 1658 to 1785, although not all of them are still legible. There are also other colonial tombs (and fragments of still others) on the south of the church.

The east and west walls of the churchyard (with their later extensions to the south) and the somewhat later south wall are colonial. Abingdon's wall has a semi-circular coping with a bevelled water table. The gates are new. The churchyard was extended on the north around 1905.

The colonial glebe house of Abingdon Parish still exists, although it was confiscated at the Disestablishment and still remains in private hands. It was probably built in the last part of the seventeenth century. It is located just west of route 17 about 3½ miles north of the church and about the same distance south of Gloucester Courthouse. The glebe house is actually located just inside Ware Parish. This seems to have been brought about because the two parishes jointly administered a school that was situated close to the line, but on the Ware side, and because the rector of Abingdon Parish served as the headmaster of the Peasley School. A certain amount of confusion sometimes resulted from this in colonial times when parish tithes were collected strictly according to parish boundaries.

Although most of Abingdon Church's colonial interior is, like its furnishings, gone and although other churches may be quainter, older, more historic, or even, perhaps, as handsome, it is doubtful that, when all evidence is weighed, any colonial church exterior in America can possibly be considered more beautiful than the ever appealing walls of Abingdon Parish's church as they stand by the side of the now important road that leads from Norfolk to Baltimore and Washington.

YEOCOMICO

ST PETER'S

AQUIA

ABINGDON

39. TIMBER RIDGE CHURCH

The second Timber Ridge Meeting House stands on a hillside above and just east of route 11 (the beautiful Valley Pike) on route 785. It is five miles south of Fairfield in Rockbridge County, thirty miles south of Staunton, and six miles north of Lexington. The first meeting house, which was built of logs and was completed by 1746, stood on the top of the Ridge about two miles north of the present church. The old burying ground, which is only about one hundred and fifty yards west of route 11, stood just north of the meeting house and still has a few markers, although apparently there are no colonial stones among them. Quite a lot of material from the old meeting house was ultimately used in a nearby dwelling that still stands.

The second meeting house was built in 1755-56 and remains as part of the present, much enlarged church. It was erected during the French and Indian War and, therefore, its walls of grey field stone were constructed to serve as a fort if necessary. There is a legend here, as at the other surviving colonial stone church (also in the Valley)—Augusta Church—that the sand for the mortar was brought by the women of the congregation from the nearest stream (in this instance, the South River) by means of bags slung across the backs of horses. The original floor of the building seems to have been of earth and the pews of split logs, although it is reported that the pulpit possessed a sounding board. The windows had heavy shutters of solid planking. The deed to their church was secured by the members of Timber Ridge in 1759.

The original portion of the church is about 43'-10" long (northeast to southwest) and 35' wide (northwest to southeast). In 1871 the present partly enclosed porch on the north was added. At present there are three windows on the east (cemetery) side and four on the west (Valley Pike) side. Of these windows only the northernmost windows on each side are aligned. The arches of all seven windows are at present semi-circular and include large, projecting stones, but these arches and the right jambs of the east windows as well as the left jambs (and a bit of the right jambs) of the west windows were all replaced in 1899-1900. The sills consist in each instance of a single long stone, although these sills were replaced at the same time. Some repairs are also said to have been made as early as 1817, but their exact nature is uncertain. The wings with the pulpit, "amen corners", and choir were likewise added in 1899-1900.

The two doors of the original north wall that now lead to the porch possibly derive from 1871 and have semi-circular arches, although nothing can be told of their jambs or of the rest of this wall owing to the recent stuccowork on the entire porch. There are three openings on the porch, all marked by semi-circular arches, and above them in the gable is a small circular window and—higher still—a smooth, circular stone marked "1756". Anterooms also exist on each side of the 1871 porch.

About 3' of the original west wall at its northern end seems to be a replacement. Much repair work is likewise in evidence on the east wall, particularly at a large patch between the south and middle windows. A modern chimney on this latter wall might easily be removed, now that it is no longer needed.

The most interesting architectural feature of Timber Ridge's walls probably lies in the stone lintel—a flat arch—of the original east door that may now be seen on the east wall between the north and middle windows. This door was closed up in 1871. There is a shallow water table, which is currently almost at ground level. The ventilation holes are modern.

The wood trim of the windows and doors derives from 1900, as do the doors and windows themselves. Each of the pair of double doors has a fanlight. The windowpanes are arranged in diamonds with a circular pane at the top. The roof is now covered with slate. The new wood cornice consists of only the plainest eaves. The trusses (round poles) of the original A-roof are believed to be largely intact. The large educational building attached to the rear of the 1900 transepts was erected in 1953. The wood ceiling was probably originally marked by a segmental arch, but is now divided into several planes (with gilded quasi-bosses). The sills of the windows slope inwards. The present floor of the original part of the building slopes downwards towards the pulpit. The pew-backs are also of a sloping nature. Both the floor and the pews were installed in 1899-1900. The walls are currently plastered.

The most arresting feature of the interior is a somewhat curious piece of furniture that is 3'-9" long, 2'-4" wide, and 2'-7" high, with chamfered corners and lamb's tongues. On three sides there is a plain rail at both top and bottom, and between these rails are woven strips of wood. On the inside, with access from the rear, there is a shelf in the middle and another at the bottom. On the front of this white oak piece is painted "1756". It is not certain that this represents the age of the table as well as of the meeting house, for, if the table is, indeed, that old, it seems likely that it has been re-assembled or remade at a later date (despite the use of cut nails). It now rests below and in front of the pulpit.

In the congregation's second cemetery (just east of the church's east wall), there is, in addition to various illegible stones, one from 1773 that is of singular interest. It is in the shape of a sarcophagus, has the familiar admonition concerning death for all who read it, and possesses a hue distinct from all the other markers. The maples in the yard derive from 1871.

The fact that Timber Ridge as a congregation or a building has survived for over two hundred years is in itself remarkable, for during its entire history there have been various factions at work among the many Presbyterians on the Ridge. Although the congregation was organized under the auspices of the New Lights (who espoused revivals and other aspects of the Evangelical movement of the eighteenth century), Old Lights were by no means unknown among the members of the early flock. Timber Ridge in the nineteenth century seems almost to have been Scotland in minuscule, for no fewer than three separate branches of Presbyterians were active in the small community for thirty to forty years. From 1814 to 1856, the Seceders (who later became adherents of the Associate Reformed Presbyterian Church) worshipped in the colonial building every other Sunday. After 1856 they erected their own meeting house just across the way. Rivalry between the communities of Timber Ridge and Fairfield was also not always in the former's favor. Among the points that have divided the Calvinists of Timber Ridge (as well as elsewhere) at one time or another (and that have at the same time only confused many other Christians) has been the singing of any praise except metrical translations of David's Psalms. Although the Associate Reformed Presbyterians finally consented to sing other hymns in worship (in addition to the metrical Psalms) in 1946, the A. R. P. church still stands but a stone's throw from colonial Timber Ridge Church.

Despite all these various dissensions, the "jerks" (or "spasmodic downward motions" of the forearms) and other physical contortions that seem to have affected many pious Presbyterians at Timber Ridge and elsewhere in Virginia, Tennessee, and Kentucky around 1800, apparently divided only the clergy rather than the laity. Likewise, the small tokens of hammered lead that entitled "members in good and regular standing" to communicate at the four-day services (at which there were always throngs), remarkably enough, seem not to have caused any friction at Timber Ridge or in its sister congregations.

Among the Timber Ridge congregation's distinguished members was the father of Sam Houston. President Houston of Texas was himself born close by. Many eminent professors, clergymen, and political figures also derive from old Timber Ridge. One of the congregation's proudest associations is, however, its ties with Washington and Lee University at nearby Lexington. In 1773 Augusta Academy was established by the Hanover Presbytery "at a place called Mount Pleasant", near Fairfield, where a classical school seems already to have been in existence. Augusta Academy was moved in 1776 to a site near Timber Ridge Meeting House and renamed Liberty Hall in honor of the Revolution. Timber Ridge's congregation strongly and perhaps singlehandedly supported the academy, but it was not long before the school was of "necessity" moved to the farm of the rector of the academy (who was also the pastor of the church). The farm lay west of Lexington. In 1798 the academy was named in honor of Washington because of a gift made by our first president. In 1822 the institution was moved to its present location and in 1871 its name was once again changed—from Washington College to Washington and Lee University in honor of General Lee, who was its president from 1865 to 1870.

The old buildings of the academy near Timber Ridge seem to have stood until around 1838. Their exact site is, however, no longer known, although it has been surmised that they lay across the Valley Pike from the present church.

Despite the fact that only two walls (both greatly repaired) and, probably, most of a third wall remain of Timber Ridge's colonial meeting house, a strong and honorable appeal yet emanates from the rough and irregular stones of these walls, built in the middle of the eighteenth century on Virginia's frontier.

40. CHUCKATUCK CHURCH (ST JOHN'S)

The third Chuckatuck Church was ordered to be built in 1752 and was completed in 1756 as a part of Suffolk Parish in Nansemond County. Its setting on route 630 (5.3 miles west of Driver and 1.3 miles east of Chuckatuck) is lovely and pastoral, surrounded as it is by large sycamores, cedars, box, and a pond formed by Cedar Creek. The church has been dedicated to St John only since 1828. It is distinct among our colonial churches in that it is not oriented, but instead has its chancel in the northeast and its principal entrance in the southwest.

New Norfolk County, which was created about 1636, was subdivided a year later into Upper Norfolk and Lower Norfolk Counties. Coterminous parishes were set up in 1640. In 1643 the parish of Upper Norfolk was subdivided into three parishes. Of these three, the East Parish soon became known as Lower Parish, the West Parish as Chuckatuck Parish, and the South Parish as Upper Parish. In 1646 Upper Norfolk County was renamed Nansimum, which seems to be an Indian word signifying a "fishing point or angle" and had previously been used for an Indian town and tribe as well as for the river. The county's name was ultimately spelled Nansemond.

It is believed that the word, Chuckatuck, meant "Crooked Creek" to the Indians (and Chuckatuck Creek is indeed, crooked). There is also a legend that it derives from the names of two Indian chieftains named "Chuck" and "Tuck" who, by way of settling a dispute over a name, compromised by combining their own names into "Chuckatuck".

Around 1725 Lower and Chuckatuck Parishes were united to become Suffolk Parish and in 1744 Suffolk Parish's upper (southern) boundaries were extended in order to make the county's two parishes more evenly divided.

The building measures 60'-10" x 30'-6" on the outside and is constructed of brick laid in Flemish bond both above and below the bevelled water table. The walls are 23½" thick. The glazing of the headers is more regular on the west wall than on the south and east walls. High up in the south wall (west of the easternmost window) is scratched "AH†17" and "EH†53". The initials seem to represent Anthony and Esther Holladay, who gave the parish the deed for the land; the numbers are taken to signify the year of the completion of the walls. A host of other initials are also to be seen on these walls. Just whom "AG" and "CH" (which are also to be seen on the upper south wall) represent seems not to be known in the parish.

Originally there were four windows on the north wall (as there still are) and three on the south, but the original south doorway (the second opening from the chancel wall) was converted into a window around the turn of the present century. Also sometime around 1900, the two original chancel windows were bricked in and replaced by a smaller window in the middle of the east wall. The small circular window in the west gable is also original and is at present stuccoed. The classical pediment that must have adorned the west doorway is gone, but the brick pilasters remain in place. From the outside edge of one pilaster to the outside edge of the other is 9'-8". Inasmuch as the south doorway seems to have been 9'-6" wide, there is no reason to believe that there was not also a pediment of some sort at this entrance, too.

The semi-circular arches of the nine principal windows and the small circular window consist of full bricks alternating with pairs of half-bricks, whereas the semi-circular arches of the smaller, modern window in the middle of the chancel wall and of the window that has replaced the original south doorway are composed only of stretchers, as is the semi-circular arch of the western doorway. Repairs to the arches include nine or ten new bricks in the right arch and four or five new bricks in the left arch of the chancel wall. The modern window is marked by a crude arch. On the south wall, the arch of the easternmost window has six new

209

bricks and the arches of the two westernmost windows have three or four new bricks each. The lower right jamb of the easternmost window has two new bricks and the left jamb of the next to westernmost window needs attention. The arches of the windows on the north wall are, like the jambs, covered by ivy. The arch of the western doorway is marked by six new bricks, and the left pilaster has also been repaired.

The use of queen closers except at the corners is irregular. They are to be found on both jambs of the easternmost window on the chancel wall. On the south wall they occur on the right jamb of the easternmost window, on both jambs of the former south doorway (but not at the new window), on the left jamb (with two lacking at the bottom) of the next to westernmost window, and on two-thirds of the upper right jamb of the westernmost window. One or two closers are also visible on the left jamb of this last window, but the rest of that jamb is covered by ivy, as are all the jambs on the north wall. Queen closers also mark the right side of the western doorway pilasters, and six occur on the left side.

Rubbed brick is used at the corners and all the original jambs and arches, and the pilasters on the west include rubbed and gauged brick of three sizes.

Repairs to the church include: 1) on the chancel wall—cracks above and below the two original windows and new masonry between the modern window and the water table; 2) on the south wall—patching at the former doorway (and above it) as well as cracks above and below the easternmost window and a cement patch on each side of the modern window; and 3) on the west wall—a patch between the doorway and the window and an enormous crack along the left side, down to the ground. Despite the ivy, it can be seen that the north wall has been patched along its upper portion and that one or two new bricks have been inserted in the arch of the next to westernmost window. There are also patches of mortar at the southwest corner of the building above and below the water table, and the upper portion of the south wall is in need of repointing.

The fact that the church originally was marked by clipped gables is evidenced by the patched brickwork at both apexes as well as by a change in the thickness of the wall above the gallery line in the interior. Ventilation holes are to be detected only on the south wall. Tie-rods are also in evdence.

The roof, cornice, and chimney (which is on the south wall between the two western windows) are, of course, modern, as is all the interior woodwork. When part of the roof was reshingled in 1952, a shingle was found nailed to one of the rafters bearing the dates and workmen's names for three nineteenth-century shinglings. The roof trusses are believed to be in excellent condition.

The woodwork in the chancel was installed around 1888 and is quite similar to that now in Glebe Church at Driver. The aisle at Chuckatuck Church is still paved with the original flagstones of pinkish-brown sandstone, each of which is 18″ square. They are presently arranged in four rows. Ten of the flagstones were used as steps for the entrance when the aisle was raised (probably around 1900). These ten have apparently been rehoned and are now 16″ x 18″.

There are no colonial gravestones, but brick remains in the southeast part of the yard may represent the second church (possibly 1700). The first church (possibly 1643), likewise of brick, occupied the site of the present building and is believed to have had a brick tower.

The existing, third church was abandoned after the Disestablishment, but was restored for worshipping use in 1826. Federal forces used the church in the War between the States (as a stable, according to tradition), but the edifice was restored again after that desecration. The present west gallery derives from that restoration (around 1870), although the rest of the church's present arrangement derives from the years immediately before and after 1900.

41. St Paul's Parish Church, King George

King George County was formed in 1721 from the western section of Richmond County and lay along the north side of the Rappahannock River. Stafford County, which lay along the south shore of the Potomac River, had been created from the western section of Westmoreland County much earlier—in 1664. Because both of these counties were uncommonly long and narrow, a swap of land was arranged in 1778 so that upper King George became a part of Stafford and lower Stafford became a part of King George. In 1779 King George surrendered its southeasternmost portion (including Leedstown) to Westmoreland County in exchange for Westmoreland's northwesternmost portion (the area between Dahlgren and Potomac Beach). It is because of these exchanges that certain parishes existed in one county in colonial times, but have been in a different county ever since. Such a case is St Paul's Parish, which was in Stafford County until 1778, but has been in King George ever since.

Nominy Parish and Westmoreland County (formerly upper Northumberland County) were created in 1653; Appomattox Parish was created from upper Nominy Parish about 1661; and Potomac Parish, which became Stafford County in 1664, was formed from upper Appomattox Parish in 1662. Within the next decade, there were two parishes in Stafford County, an upper and a lower. The lower parish soon came to be known as Choatanck and finally by 1702 as St Paul's. This last name seems to be derived from St Paul's Parish in Bedford, England.

The first St Paul's Parish Church was probably erected sometime around 1669-70 and is believed to have lain near Choatanck Creek about three miles east of the present building. The second church (soon after 1725) occupied the same site as the present (third) church, which lies just south of the junction of routes 206 and 218. This junction is 6.9 miles northeast of Arnold's Corner (the junction of routes 3 and 206), approximately the same distance from King George Courthouse, and 2.8 miles west of the junction of routes 206 and 301 (near Owens and Dahlgren). The church is, therefore, about 22 or 23 miles from Fredericksburg via route 218 or via routes 3 and 206.

The existing edifice of 1766-67 is a true Greek cross, one of the very few among our colonial churches. The building is approximately 61'-10" x 61'-10" on the outside. The width of each of the arms is approximately 29'-10" and the length 16'. The brick walls (21" thick) are laid in Flemish bond above and below the bevelled water table, and the use of glazed headers is sparse. When the old building was taken over by the county for an academy in 1813 as a result of the Disestablishment, severe alterations were made both inside and outside. These alterations included a number of changes in regard to the openings. Originally, there were three doorways—south, west, and north. In the upper of the two tiers of windows, there were originally three windows each in the south, west, and north façades, two in the chancel façade, and one in each side of each of the four arms. In the lower tier of windows there were originally two in the chancel end, a single window on each side of the three doorways, and a single window in each side of the four arms.

In 1813 the north and west doorways were bricked up and the south windows in the lower storey of the chancel and the nave made into doorways, so that three doorways still exist facing south. The middle windows of the upper tier were also bricked up on the west and north façades. At some other time, the lower window on the east wall of the north transept was made into a door, and at the same time (or at yet another time) the opening on the north wall of the eastern arm was also bricked up. It is assumed that this latter opening was a window, but it seems at one time or another to have been a doorway, for the repairs now extend down to the water table. The four existing doorways all have post-colonial flat arches, but that leading to the vestry is deeper and possessed of a lighter hue.

The arches of the upper tier of windows are semi-circular, whereas those of the lower tier are segmental. All the arches of the windows are composed of full bricks alternating with pairs of halves. Rubbed brick marks the salient corners, the jambs and arches of the windows, and the jambs of the remaining portions of the south doorway. The jambs and arches of the north and west doorways are no longer visible.

The repairs on the walls are in large part owing to the 1813 changes in the openings and also to the replacement of the original window frames. Two bricks at each side of the sills of all the windows are replacements, and replacements are also to be noted in many instances just below the spring-line of the arches. On the south façade there is a large crack below the lower left window, and four new bricks exist in the arch of the upper left window. In addition to some repointing, the entire area between the upper middle window and the new arch of the doorway is one of repair. There was undoubtedly a classical pediment over the original opening, and the present flat arch (of unappealing red brick) is considerably lower than that of the original opening.

Both sides of the upper window on the east wall of the south transept have probably been repointed. On the south wall of the original chancel, the joint at the top of the arch of the original window and the rubbed brick of both jambs are still visible. The east façade seems to be in fine shape. On the north wall of the chancel, six courses of rubbed brick are still *in situ* in the bricked-up portion, as is the rubbed brick of both jambs of the former (lower) window on the east wall of the north transept. The upper middle windows on the north and west façades likewise still have their rubbed brick jambs and arches. The rubbed brick of the jambs of the former (lower) window on the south wall of the nave is also extant.

Queen closers mark the salient corners as well as the ventilation holes of the south and east façades, although their presence at the windows and doorways is irregular, as at Ware and Bruton Churches. There are no queen closers: 1) on the south façade—on the right jamb of the upper left window, the left jambs of the upper middle and right windows, the right jamb of the lower left window, the left jamb of the lower right window, or the upper two-thirds of the original height of the doorway jambs; 2) on the east walls of the north and south transepts; 3) on the south wall of the chancel; 4) on the outside jambs of the east façade; 5) on the side walls of the nave; 6) on the west façade—on the inside jambs of the four corner windows, the right jamb of the upper middle window, or the upper parts of the jambs of the former doorway; 7) on the north façade—on the inside jambs of the lower windows and the upper left and middle windows, or the upper two-thirds of the left jamb of the former doorway; or 8) on the right jambs of the west wall of the south transept. There are only a few queen closers on the left jamb in the upper storey of the north wall of the chancel or on the left jamb of the lower storey of the west wall of the north transept.

The only remaining evidence of the three elaborate, pedimented doorways lies in the surviving portions of the pilasters and the pedestals on the south. These pilasters are composed of rubbed brick (1½ bricks in each course), although the pedestals are not rubbed. The areas between the bottoms of the segmental arches and the flat window-heads are now wooden, whereas the semi-circles of the upper tier are stuccoed on the north arm and provided with wood louvers elsewhere. Several new crawl-space openings have been added below the water table.

The roof is hipped at each of the four gables. The asbestos shingles of the roof were put on around 1930. The roof trusses are believed to be original. The modillion cornice is possibly from the nineteenth century.

The church seems to have been abandoned after 1783. When the county turned the building into an academy in 1813, all the woodwork that had not already gone to ruin was removed, a second floor was installed, and the four wings were partitioned so that eight classrooms and an auditorium (in the crossing) were made available for the young scholars. The academy failed, however, and, although Methodists and Baptists had also used the building since the Disestablishment, the legislature gave it back to St Paul's Parish in 1830. The parish had been revived in 1816 and was also using the old building.

In 1830-31 the schoolroom partitions were removed, except on the north where the rooms in the second storey were assigned to the rector. These rooms and the north partition (with chimney) still exist. The interior of the church, therefore, became a T when the chancel was put on the north of the crossing (just south of the partition). Above the chancel was placed a high pulpit with a canopy over it and a long straight stair at its side. The pulpit remains, although a new canopy was installed in 1959. A similar arrangement of the pulpit over the Table at Christ Church in Alexandria and at Vawter's Church in Essex County also derives from the influence of Bishops Hobart and Meade. Galleries were built in the south, east, and west arms, with columns in both storeys. From 1830-31 probably also come the pews. The details of the pulpit and its column are duplicated on the raised panelling of the pews and gallery-fronts and on the gallery columns.

The window frames of the three upper windows in the north transept are certainly the oldest of the church's present woodwork. They are marked by wooden pegs and the usual architrave mouldings: cyma reversa, fascia, cyma reversa, fascia, and bead. They may very well be colonial. The other woodwork—windows, doors, and door and window trim—and glass seem to be from 1830-31 or from later on in the middle of the nineteenth century. Neither the sides nor the sills of the windows are splayed. The floor dates from 1940, when termites had done so much damage. The floors of the north transept are, however, much older. H-L hinges on closet doors in this (former) transept may be colonial. The dentil cornice of the interior ceiling is probably older than the reeding at the lower part of the gallery fronts. The organ grill over the entrance to the vestry at the foot of the pulpit stairs was inserted in 1959.

One of St Paul's rectors is considered by many persons to have been the first of our missionaries to Africa: the Rev'd Mr Andrus went there in 1820 when American Negroes were being repatriated. Another of its rectors is the distinguished ecclesiastical historian, the Rev'd Dr George MacLaren Brydon.

There are no colonial gravestones in St Paul's expansive yard, but large cedars, elms, and maples dot it and the cemetery, and on the south the 1841 rectory forms the eastern annex to the new parish hall. The brick steps and walks for the entrances to the church were laid only a few years ago. The parish owns a paten, a chalice, and a flagon made by the silversmith, Joseph Fainell, of London in 1720-21. On the flagon is inscribed: "Given by Henry Fitzhugh of Stafford Co., St Paul's Parish, Gent., for the use of the church". Also on the silver are a sunburst, "IHS", and a cross (with an elongated central arm). This plate of St Paul's is identical with the silver of old North Farnham Parish in Richmond County, and one authority has ascribed all this silver to Thomas Farren rather than Joseph Fainell. St Paul's Parish Register (1716-93) is kept at the clerk's office at King George Courthouse.

Many of our old churches have almost twin relationships with other buildings and St Paul's twin is Aquia Church, the other surviving colonial church of colonial Stafford County. Aquia's stone trim is the counterpart of St Paul's rubbed brick; and it is this considerable amount of rubbed brick preserved on its numerous openings that gives St Paul's Parish Church its principal architectural distinction.

42. THE FALLS CHURCH

The Falls Church, which occupies a large yard of four and one-half acres at South Washington and East Fairfax Streets in the community that has adopted the Church's name for its own, in turn received its designation from the Little Falls of the Potomac River a few miles away.

The predecessor of the existing church was a frame structure (1733) and occupied a site in the present churchyard just south of the existing building. The Anglicans in the area seem to have conducted Divine Worship in a private dwelling before 1732-33. This wooden church was a part of Truro Parish (established in 1732) until 1765, when Fairfax Parish was created. In both cases the Falls Church appears to have served as the Upper Church of the Parish. Inasmuch as it was probably the stronger of the two churches that existed in Fairfax Parish when the parish was created, in all probability it served as the parish church until after the Disestablishment and its subsequent abandonment, at which time Christ Church in Alexandria would seem to have assumed this rank. A vestry house was built at the Falls Church in 1766.

George Washington and George Mason were among Truro Parish's distinguished vestrymen. One author has suggested that the Anglican hymnodist and author of the National Anthem, Francis Scott Key, also served the Falls Church upon occasion as a lay reader, but this has not been authenticated. Key, however, was a public orator.

The existing brick building was originally constructed in 1767-1769 to plans that Colonel James Wren, who lived only four or five miles from the Falls Church, submitted for both Christ Church in Alexandria and the Falls Church. Colonel Wren is reputed to have been a relation of Sir Christopher Wren. The Falls Church is built of dark red brick laid in Flemish bond with glazed headers. The kiln for the bricks is said to have been about 300 yards west of the present church. The building's original exterior measurements are 60′ x 40′ and its walls are about 23″ thick. The water table is of two courses: a cavetto over an ovolo. The bond below the water table is English. Like the beautiful ruins of Lower Southwark Church in Surry County, the interior walls of the Falls Church are also of English Bond

Repairs are quite obvious beneath several of the windows of the lower tier: both windows on the west façade (down to the ground); the two westernmost windows on the north wall; the westernmost window on the south wall (to the ground); and the second from the westernmost window on the same wall, to the water table. Other repairs include repointing below the water table on the north wall and replacements in the arches of the westernmost and easternmost windows of the lower tier on the south façade as well as a spot over the south doorway. Repointing likewise includes a stretch on the north wall that indicates

216

the addition of a chimney at some time, and another stretch between the two tiers of windows on the same wall that extends from the middle of the north wall halfway to its western end.

The openings include two tiers of windows: in the lower storey are two on the west, four on the south and north, and originally two on the east; in the upper storey are three on the west, five on the south, four on the north, and originally three on the east. The sides of the windows are not splayed. The two doorways are on the west and south, but, as perhaps at Pohick Church (which is still in Truro Parish), the south doorway seems to be the principal entrance of colonial times.

The arches of the lower windows are flat and alternate a half-brick over a full brick with the reverse of that; the arches of the upper windows are semi-circular and alternate full bricks with pairs of halves. Queen closers are to be seen at all the window jambs, the four corners of the building, the western doorway, and, interestingly enough, at the ventilation holes on the three extant walls. Rubbed brick marks the arches and jambs of all windows, the corners, and the western doorway.

The brick doorway on the west has a triangular pediment with a raked cornice consisting of: cyma recta, fillet, fascia, soffit, ovolo, and cavetto. The horizontal cornice omits only the initial cyma recta. The brick tympanum contains no glazed headers. A narrow frieze has a two-plane architrave beneath it. The capitals of the Tuscan pilasters include: fillet, elongated cavetto, echinus, necking, and astragal. The shaft alternates two bricks with three smaller ones. There are no bases, for the lower two-thirds of the right pilaster and the lower one-half of the left pilaster have been replaced, as have a number of the voussoirs of the flat arch over the doors as well as bricks in the jambs of the doorway. The steps have been replaced in 1906-10 and again in 1958.

The present south doorway (with a full Doric entablature) is a wooden replacement that has been made since the War between the States, for a photograph made by Brady in that War shows a stone doorway after the manner of the western doorway at Pohick Church (and also shutters on the lower windows). The bricks at the very bottom of the brick pedestals of the current doorway, however, appear to be original.

When the church was enlarged in 1959, all of the east wall except the two corners and about two feet at the very top was removed to allow the entire building to serve as the nave, and a new chancel and ambulatory to be added on the east.

All of the roof trusses save one are said to be original, and the modillion cornice seems old and may possibly be original also. The shingles have long ago, of course, given way to a series of slate roofs. The shape of the original hipped roof, however, has been retained.

In the Revolution the church was a recruiting station for the Colonies and before that time the yard had been used by a regiment of Braddock's Army in the French and Indian War. In the War of 1812 the British are said to have searched the church for our fleeing President. However, the great damage in the church's history was accomplished by Federal troops, who first used the building as a hospital and then as a stable. Their destruction is still memorialized by the enormous rents that have already been cited at many of the openings. At the recent alterations, the names of various Northern soldiers were uncovered, scrawled in pencil on the whitewashed brick and plaster near the south doorway. Initials are still to be seen carved on the exterior south wall.

Because no galleries are known to have been built (though they were specified), the sash and trim of the upper windows seem to have escaped damage and are, therefore, believed to be colonial, as are many of the lights (12 over 6) in the upper tier. These windows still have no weights. The trim of these upper openings includes: cyma reversa, fascia, cyma reversa, fascia, and bead. The exterior wood sills on the upper windows are also probably original.

All the other woodwork in the church except a large wooden lintel over the west doorway is renewal, although one of the original upper windows in the chancel now adorns the ambulatory. Some remnants of the woodwork and masonry of the former east wall have been retained in the church's storehouse. The only other remains of the original interior are the eight flagstones that now lie embedded in the chancel pavement beneath the Table. The present font may be somewhat old, but does not appear to be colonial. The interior cornice, cove, and flat ceiling, however, undoubtedly adhere to the original model. The pulpit was originally on the north wall opposite the south doorway.

In addition to the new chancel (with Palladian window, pulpit, and lectern and—immediately below and in front of them—a walnut Table and other furniture in the style of Queen Anne), the new features of the 1959 work include a narthex, U-shaped galleries, and pewter chandeliers and wall sconces. The wooden walls of the chancel are panelled and painted white, as is also the walnut trim of the pews. The 1959 changes represent the fourth large-scale renewal of the fabric of the Falls Church. The first occurred in 1839 when the church was returned to service after long abandonment. After the War between the States, the Federal government is said to have given $1,300 in reparations. The work of 1905 was conducted under the ægis of the National Society of the Daughters of Founders and Patriots of America.

The glebe farm of Fairfax Parish is principally recalled to-day through the Glebe Road. The site of the farm was north of Glebe Road, between Lee Highway and North Washington Boulevard.

A small silver-plated cup that has "Falls Church" engraved on it was

218

stolen by a Northern officer in the 1860's, but was returned to the parish in 1952 by his granddaughter. However, this little vessel hardly seems likely to be colonial or even eighteenth-century in manufacture.

In the large shady yard there appear to be no colonial markers, although unmarked colonial graves must surely exist. There are, however, enormous trees, including a gigantic albeit failing tulip poplar and a white oak believed to be at least 200 years old.

Although the original plans concerned the Falls Church and the other church in Fairfax Parish (the Lower Church at Alexandria), the completed Falls Church bears a greater resemblance to Pohick Church. The most striking difference between the two lies in the substitution of rubbed brick at the Falls Church for the west doorway and the corners in place of the stonework at Pohick.

Some of our colonial churches may seem to be overpraised and over-cited in relation to their sister colonial churches. It is the other way round with the Falls Church.

43. Christ Church, Alexandria

Few churches or cathedrals in America have more visitors than does Christ Church at North Washington & Cameron Streets in Alexandria, although, like several other urban churches in Virginia and elsewhere, it has greater appeal as a patriotic shrine than as a church of the Anglican faith.

In 1765 Fairfax Parish was formed from Truro Parish and included an Upper Church (The Falls Church) and a Lower Church, which was presumably in or nigh Alexandria. The existing Christ Church was begun in 1767 and completed in 1773. James Wren, who may have been a relation of the famous architect of the same cognomen, presented plans in 1767 for the replacement of both of the churches in the new parish; James Parsons agreed to build the church at Alexandria on land given by the founder of the town, John Alexander; and John Carlyle finished the work.

The colonial portion of the edifice measures 60' east to west by 50' north to south, like the Meeting House of a few years later and a

219

few blocks southeast. Also like the Meeting House, Christ Church is of brick, but, unlike the Meeting House, Christ Church still has a hipped roof. The masonry of the church is laid in Flemish bond above and below the water table. There are random glazed headers and even some glazed stretchers. The glazing seems to be curiously concentrated in various patches about two-thirds of the way up the walls (between the windows of the upper tier). The water table is composed of two courses: an ovolo over a cavetto. Queen closers are used at the corners of the building as well as on the window jambs (though not at the great chancel window).

The walls show relatively little repair, although there has been re-pointing below every window on the north wall and above the two upper windows on the east. On the south there is a prominent streak in the middle, from the cornice to the ground, that indicates a change of some sort having been made or, perhaps, derives from a faulty downspout. The ventilation holes are original. The walls are 23″ thick.

Although galleries were not added until 1785, the two tiers of windows are original. On the south and north walls there are five windows in each storey; on the east there is a great Palladian window as well as a window in each storey on each side of the Palladian window; and on the west there is a window in the second storey on each side of the tower. The only doorways in the church are two on the west, one on each side of the tower.

The semi-circular arches of the upper tier of windows are composed of full and half-bricks, with buttered joints, and have stone keystones. The flat arches of the lower tier comprise two courses of brick, for, above the usual voussoirs in each instance, there is a rowlock course, in which there are in many cases glazed headers. As is usual in such treatment, the stone keystones of the flat arches are less splayed than are those in the semi-circular arches. The lower keystones project almost to the top of the rowlock course. The voussoirs of the lower course terminate on each side in stone ornaments. The dark red voussoirs of the lower arches may possibly be only gauged rather than both gauged and rubbed, as the yellow-orange voussoirs of the upper arches are.

Owing to the fact that the east wall immediately above the Palladian window (from the one end of the pediment to the other) is distinct as to masonry from the rest of the wall and also owing to the fact that no queen closers are used here, it seems possible that this great adornment was an afterthought, although it could easily have been installed before the acceptance of the church in 1773. The original eastern arrangement probably had three windows in the upper storey and two in the lower storey (as at the Falls Church until the 1959 alterations). The Palladian window is composed of stone and includes the usual, large, tall window between two smaller windows. The raked cornice of the triangular pediment includes: cyma recta, fascia, ovolo, and fillet, although only the cyma recta is carried entirely through, for the semi-circular arch of the large window all but bisects the pediment. This arch has a keystone and a two-plane architrave. Below the plain frieze is another two-plane architrave. The capitals of the four Renaissance Doric pilasters include the usual abacus, echinus, pair of annulets, necking, and astragal. Two toruses and a plinth mark the base. This base (without a scotia) is a primitive variation of the Attic base. Below the whole window is a long stone sill.

The most striking feature of the Church at Alexandria is the great amount of trimmings of stone taken from the Aquia Creek quarries in Stafford County. Not only are all the windows ornamented with this stone, but so are the corners of the building and its doorways. The stone door stops and horse blocks that were also ordered are, however, no longer to be seen. The stone ornamentation has recently received a coat of cement paint or mortar, partly in order to eradicate a host of initials that have been carved—probably by thoughtless visitors or vandals more frequently than by troops of occupation.

The pair of fine stone doorways has triangular pediments with a series of mouldings almost identical with that used on the Palladian window. Below the plain frieze is an architrave (with a wide fillet and two fascias) that is rusticated by large quoins. The large, three-part keystone of the arch extends through the frieze as well as the architrave. Large stone plinths and sills complete the doorways.

A tower, steeple, and bell were initially added in 1818, but the present tower undoubtedly represents a number of additions made at various times. The brick portion consists of three lower storeys and an upper octagonal storey. The wooden lantern consists of repeated octagons, surmounted by a dome and a weather vane. In point of age, the lower walls seem to be the oldest and the brick octagon and the lantern the most recent. The outside dimensions of the tower at ground level are 17' east to west by 16' south to north. The west wall of the nave of the church and the east wall of the tower are contiguous. The water table consists simply of two projecting courses of brick. Running bond has been used on the brick octagon. The south and north walls of the tower are laid in Flemish bond. On the west wall five rows of stretchers are used for every row of headers up to the top of the second-storey window-arches. From that point up, only three rows of stretchers are laid for a single row of headers. The bonding of this wall is, therefore, the reverse of the west gable of the Meeting House. There are evidences of repointing, particularly on the north wall. Very few glazed headers are to be seen anywhere on the tower.

The openings of the various parts of the tower display considerable variety as to disposition. The opening of each face of each storey of the lantern has a semi-circular arch and wooden louvers. The four principal faces of the brick octagon have in each case a small bull's-eye window above a window with a semi-circular arch (all with louvers). The other faces (on the corners) are the same except for the fact that a small circular window replaces the small oval window. The arches of the brick octagon's windows are in two courses. The extrados (consisting of headers) projects and, on the principal faces, extends on both sides to a pair of pilasters. The intrados of these sixteen windows is a rowlock course.

On the south and north walls of the tower there is an elliptical window (its surround consisting of a soldier course) in the third storey. These windows may have been inserted after the completion of the walls. The side walls also have a small window and a doorway on the first storey in each instance. The brick openings of the first storey all have flat arches. The doorway on the north has been much altered. The doorway on the south is larger and its wooden trim (of late origin) is similar to that of the pulpit arch of the Meeting House. There is a window in each storey of the west wall: a flat arch with the usual voussoirs on the bottom, a semi-circular arch (with full bricks and pairs of halves) in the middle, and a flat arch of a rowlock course at the top. On this wall, queen closers are used, but only on the right jambs. These closers are also to be seen on the right jamb of the former north doorway as well as on the same jamb of the south doorway. There are also evidences of re-pointing between windows on the west wall. A doorway leads into the church on the east of the tower in both of the lower storeys.

The resemblance of the Church at Alexandria to Pohick Church and the Falls Church has often been cited. The strong resemblance of the tower of Christ Church to both the tower and the principal fabric of the nearby Meeting House seems to go unmentioned. Yet it is the Christ Church tower, with its many changes and repairs and, particularly, its ungainly porch (which is more in the nature of a shed than a porch) on the south, that dominates one's usual view of Christ Church. It is from the west that one generally sees the fane and the effect of its stone doorways and quoins is much marred—one is almost tempted to say ob-literated—by the combination of tower and porch. The present tower must in considerable part derive from the 1840's or even later. The south porch is believed by some persons to have been added shortly after 1818, but a later date is entirely possible.

The original juniper shingles of the church's hipped roof have been replaced by slate. The roof trusses are said to be original and in good condition. The modillion cornice may be original. The interior cornice may also be original, at least in great part, and the flat ceiling (with coved edges) is likewise thought to be original.

The wood trim of the two doorways is probably original. The doors themselves likewise seem to be original, although they have been repaired and cut off at the sills. There are four slightly vertical panels on each door. The mouldings of the panels include: ovolo, splay, cyma reversa, and field. The hardware is not old. The wood trim of the windows also seems to be colonial and comprises a cyma reversa and fascia, another cyma reversa and fascia, and a bead. Wooden pegs abound. The lights are 9 over 9 in the lower windows and 11 over 6 in the upper tier. The sides of the windows are splayed.

Palladian Window

Perhaps, the most arresting feature of the present interior is the Palladian window, which has six fluted pilasters instead of the four plain ones on the stone exterior. The extra width embraces the two tablets, for the gilding of which James Wren was paid extra. In addition to the usual Decalogue, Lord's Prayer, and Creed, there is inscribed at the bottom of the left tablet this admonition: "Whatsoever ye would that men should do unto you, even so do unto them: for this is the law and the prophets." The great window has no pediment, but the cornice is elaborately moulded: gold fillet, cyma recta, cyma reversa, fascia, soffit, gold fillet, ovolo, Greek key, and cyma reversa. Below the pulvinated frieze is the architrave: cavetto, fascia, small cyma reversa, and fascia. The primitive Ionic capitals include the abacus, an egg-and-dart series carved into the echinus, and an astragal (but no necking). The base includes torus, scotia, torus, and plinth.

The original position of the pulpit presents a considerable difficulty. It seems hard to believe that a large pulpit and sounding board would have been allowed in the original plan to obscure the Palladian window as it does now. It seems more likely that the pulpit was located on the north wall until the galleries were added. However, it may not have been moved to the center until the rectorship (1811-13) of the future Bishop Meade, who caused so many of our pulpits to be placed in the center above the Holy Table. It is, of course, also possible that the pulpit was originally in the center and that the Palladian window was added shortly afterwards. The present pulpit (without desks but with sounding board) is believed to be old, but it is not original, as is also true of the communion rail (with its wooden urns at the corners). The present lectern is believed possibly to have been the original pulpit or part of it. The top part of the original Table is said to have been incorporated into the modern Table. The font probably derives from around 1818.

It is reported that the pews have been cut down, but this seems difficult to believe because of the level of the window sills. What may have happened is that the former box-pews were converted into slip-pews and supplemented by other slip-pews. President Washington's box-pew is the only one still left in the church. The floor of the aisles has been raised from 4 to 6 inches (almost to the level of the pew-floors) and this accounts for the shortening of the doors. The floors within the pews are believed to be original. The brass and crystal chandelier under the rear gallery is from 1818. The church's organ of 1810 is now in the Smithsonian Institution in Washington.

The church bore only geographical designations until 1814, when it was consecrated as Christ Church. The church was a part of the District of Columbia from 1789 to 1846 (though the Congress seems not to have taken active control until shortly before the War of 1812), but always remained in the diocese of Virginia. President Washington was a member of the parish both before and after the Revolution. Many other presidents have assisted at worship from Washington's pew, particularly on Sundays nearest his birthday. Among recent holders of the office to have done so are Presidents Wilson, F. D. Roosevelt, Truman, and Eisenhower as well as such dignitaries as Marshal Foch and Prime Ministers Lloyd George and Churchill.

General Lee attended the Church both as child and as adult and was confirmed there. His pew (#46) is marked with his autograph in silver like General Washington's (#60). During the War between the States, Christ Church was used by Federal troops and chaplains and was thus the only church in the town to be able to hold services. The name plate on Washington's pew and the Parish Register (1765-1860) were both stolen during the occupation. The vestry book (1765-1842) is, however, still preserved and is kept at the First & Citizens National Bank.

Among the various rectors of the Church have been several who later became bishops, several who became professors at the nearby Virginia Theological Seminary (including the very first professor at that institution), and one who became the eighth Baron Fairfax of Cameron shortly after he was rector (1790-92) of the Church.

The large yard served as a burying ground from 1767 until 1815, although after 1800 only parishioners were allowed to be buried there. Exceptions were made in 1834 and 1879, in the latter year for 37 Confederate soldiers who had died in a local Federal prison during the War. The oldest stone is marked 1771 and another derives from 1773. The present gates and walls of the churchyard are believed to have been erected around 1885-90.

Although much of the fascination of the Church at Alexandria stems from its great use of Aquia stone ornamentation and its patriotic associations, much of it also comes from the building's many unanswered questions.

44. LAMB'S CREEK CHURCH

Lamb's Creek Church in King George County is the second parish church of Brunswick Parish, which was formed in 1732 from the upper part of Hanover Parish. The latter parish was the northern half of St Mary's Parish until 1713 and St Mary's Parish was itself derived from the western portion of Sittingbourne Parish (and Rappahannock County) around 1681. King George County was created from the western portion of Richmond County eleven years before Brunswick Parish was established.

The first Brunswick Parish Church may have been built as early as 1700 and, therefore, was built as a church or chapel of St Mary's Parish, although it became the Upper Church of Hanover Parish in 1713 and the first parish church of Brunswick Parish in 1732. It was always known, however, as Muddy Creek Church owing to its location by that stream. The site of this church has been in Stafford County (just west of the King George-Stafford line near route 3) ever since 1778, when King George exchanged its upper area for Stafford's lower portion. As another result of this exchange, Brunswick Parish lies partly in both counties, although it was in colonial times entirely in King George County.

Lamb's Creek Church is located on route 607, one-half mile northwest of the junction of routes 3 and 607 (which is itself about 12 miles east of Fredericksburg and about 7 miles west of King George Courthouse). The church, which is named for a creek that runs about half a mile east, is believed to have been built in 1769-70 by John Ariss, who is also thought to have built the very similar church at Little Fork (near Rixeyville in Culpeper County) in 1776.

The dimensions of Lamb's Creek are 79'-11" x 33'-11". Its masonry is laid in Flemish bond above and below the bevelled water table. There is a very sparse number of glazed headers, but more exist on the west than elsewhere. The walls are apparently in a fine state of preservation. On the south, a little repointing exists in the water table (as also on the

225

north), the southwestern corner is badly worn, and there are chips on the left side of the doorway. On the east, two bricks have been replaced at the right window. A long area of different character high on the north wall (towards the east) does not seem to represent repairs. Only minor alterations mark the west wall, although here and elsewhere there seem to be a large number of what can only be assumed to be bullet holes. The vents are only a single brick wide, although some are two courses tall.

Rubbed brick marks both doorways (which are located in the middle of the south and west walls), the jambs and arches of all fourteen windows (six each on the south and north and two on the east), and the four corners. Queen closers are also present at all corners and windows. Both doorways have triangular pediments and both of these pediments seem to have been repaired, although the extent of their renewal is not exactly clear. The raked cornice of the south doorway includes a cyma reversa, a cavetto-fascia, and an ovolo, whereas on the west doorway the middle moulding is a simple fascia. The horizontal cornice of the south doorway has a cavetto-fascia and an ovolo, whereas that on the west is marked by a cyma reversa and an ovolo. There is neither architrave, nor frieze, nor capital on either doorway. The arches are flat, each voussoir containing three sizes of rubbed brick. The shallow pilasters (with a half-brick and a full brick in one course and a full brick and a half-brick in the course below) are rubbed, whereas the pedestals are not rubbed. Flemish bond is also used in the tympanum, although the south tympanum has only six courses, whereas the west tympanum has ten. Despite this, it is possible that the south doorway (opposite the location of the original pulpit) was the main doorway, as it probably also was at Little Fork, the Falls Church, and Pohick Church. The "1770" that is incised and painted white in the western arch is a later insertion, as the difference in the brick clearly shows.

The arches of all fourteen windows are semi-circular and alternate full bricks with pairs of halves.

The wood trim of the openings and the doors and windows themselves would appear to be from the early part of this century, except for the sills of the right chancel window and the third from the westernmost window on the north wall, which are demonstrably older than the rest of the present woodwork.

After the Disestablishment the church was partially restored about 1825. It was, however, used as a stable by Federal forces in the War between the States, when most of its interior woodwork and probably most of its furnishings were destroyed (although it is remarkable that the walls seem so little harmed). The building was not restored to service until 1906 and was not repaired until 1908, when the Rev'd Mr

Byrd Thornton Turner, the rector of the parish and a Confederate veteran, managed to obtain $800.00 as indemnity from the Federal government. Among other repairs in the rectorate of Mr Turner (who was the father of Miss Nancy Byrd Turner, the poet) were a new floor and a new roof. The present floor and slate flagstones are, however, from 1954. The modillion cornice (with extra mouldings below) may have been put on in 1908, but the handsome roofing with asbestos shingles is from 1939. The original roof trusses of the hipped roof are believed to be largely intact. The concrete steps are twentieth-century in origin.

The juncture of the interior ceiling and walls forms a cove, and the wooden ceiling is of recent origin, although the somewhat primitive benches (each of which has only a narrow rail for a back) and old lamps have been retained from around 1908. The window heads as well as the jambs are splayed. The last vestige of the church's colonial mural was covered in 1958 by a coat of paint. This remnant showed painted draperies below the chancel cornice. The square pews, pavements of the aisles, pulpit, chancel rail, and tablets from colonial days either were ruined in the War or vanished between 1865 and 1906 when only occasional Baptist services were held in the old church. The Brunswick Parish vestry book is also said to have been taken from the parish by a non-Episcopal minister in this period.

There are no colonial gravestones in the yard, but there are cedar and other trees that are in several instances unfortunately dying. The rough stone marker on the west commemorates the church's descent from Muddy Creek Church, which still has a single colonial gravestone in its yard.

Brunswick Parish owns a Vinegar edition (1716) of the Bible and a 1739 Prayer-Book, but holds only an annual Service—on the last Sunday in August. The Bible and the Prayer-Book are kept in the clerk's office at King George Courthouse. The colonial silver of Hanover Parish is also kept at King George Courthouse, where it is still in use at St John's Church. It consists of a chalice, a flagon, and an alms bason, all of which were made in London in 1750-51 by William Grundy and are adorned with a sunburst, the sacred trigram, and the cross.

227

45. POHICK CHURCH

Pohick Church stands on the south side of route 1, not far from Lorton and Mount Vernon in Fairfax County. It is about twelve miles south of the limits of Alexandria at Hunting Creek and is about 3½ miles northeast of the junction of route 1 and the Shirley Highway. The church is one of the handsomest of Virginia's many handsome buildings.

At least four names are prominently associated with Pohick Church's construction, which lasted from 1769 to 1774, and others were among its examiners. President Washington and the distinguished George Mason were both on the vestry as well as the building committee of Truro Parish at the time of the present church's erection. The south elevation and ground plan are said to have been drawn by the former, and the latter became in effect the builder when he became the executor of the builder's estate. Daniel French was the undertaker and William Copein (who also worked at Aquia Church) was the mason. Colonel James Wren, whose plans were used at the Falls Church in 1767-69 and at the Church in Alexandria in 1767-73, surely must also be reckoned among Pohick's creators, for the same general plan marks all three of these churches.

It has been written that there have been only two Pohick churches, but some authorities are inclined to believe that the present building is the third church. In both views the first church, very probably a frame structure, was erected around 1700 or earlier. If there were three churches, the first is thought possibly to have been erected "somewhere between Cedar Grove and the present Woodlawn" and a second building (possibly around 1725) erected about two miles south of the present church. This latter site near Occoquan Creek is accepted as the location of the first church in the view that allows only two churches. In any event, the church of around 1700 seems to have been erected as a chapel or as the Upper Church of Overwharton Parish and it (or, if there were three churches, the second building) became part of Hamilton Parish in 1730 and of Truro Parish in 1732. The church near Occoquan Creek was known as Occoquan Church until around 1732, when Pohick Church began to be used in its stead. The word, pohick, seems to be related to the Indian word for hickory tree.

The present building measures 66' x 45½' on the exterior and is laid in Flemish bond with random glazed headers. Its walls are approximately 24" thick. Below the water table (a cavetto over an ovolo), the bond is also Flemish. All of the brickwork of the church has been repointed. Replacements include parts of the arches of the end windows on the west, the westernmost windows on each storey of the south façade as well as the second window from the west of the lower group, the four

228

corner windows on the chancel wall, and the upper corner windows of the north wall. The entire water table has been replaced on the north, as have some bricks in the water table on the south.

In the upper tier of windows there are three on the west and east, five on the south, and four on the north; in the lower tier are four on the south and north, two in the east, and only one (between the doorways) on the west. The arches of the lower storey are flat and consist of a whole brick over a half-brick alternating with the reverse of that, whereas the arches in the upper windows are semi-circular, with full bricks alternating with pairs of halves. In these latter arches a number of instances occur in which a full brick has been incised with a line across its center, giving the impression of two half-bricks. The arches and sandstone were ordered to be painted during the original construction, so that these lines (though since repainted) may represent the only remnants of this initial painting.

Rubbed brick marks the jambs and arches of all windows. Queen closers are also used at all the windows, but their use at the corners of the building is irregular. There are none on the east façade, but they are used at both corners of the west façade. Queen closers are also in evidence at a few of the ventilation holes. There are likewise some other very small bricks at the right pilaster of the right doorway on the west. All the stone sills of the windows have been replaced. The sides of the windows are splayed.

Elaborate Stonework

The great glory of Pohick Church lies in its stonework, which includes the large quoins at all four corners and the three doorways. The horse blocks and benches that were originally ordered for the yard are no longer in evidence. The loss of the latter is particularly to be regretted.

The two western doorways are not quite identical with the doorway on the south, which seems to have been the principal entrance, as at the Falls Church. The south doorway has a three-part keystone but only two large stones on each side of the keystone, whereas the western doorways have only a single stone for the keystone with three large stones on each side of the keystone. The raked cornice of the triangular pediment of each doorway includes: cyma recta, cyma reversa, small fascia, soffit, ovolo, and cavetto. The horizontal cornice omits the top cyma recta. The tympanum is also of stone. Below the cushion frieze is the architrave: cyma reversa, fascia, cyma reversa, and fascia. The Ionic capitals include scrolls, egg-and-dart, bead-and-reel, and fillet. There is no fluting on the shafts. The base (two toruses and a scotia) and plinth have been renewed in all instances. Two-thirds of the left pilaster on the south doorway is also renewed. The immediate surround of the doors is rusticated stonework. The large keystones project into the door frames. Each of the arches is flat.

The platform and steps on the south are original; those on the west include only remnants of the original. Flagstones from the original aisles may also be seen on the west. Of the four large cornerstones, only that on the northwest is original. Initials and various symbols have been carved all over the doorways and quoins. Several bricks that were almost perforated by the target practice of Federal troops in the War between the States have recently been replaced.

The stone used in Pohick Church is referred to as freestone and its place of origin seems to be indefinite. It appears to be softer than the Aquia Creek stone of Aquia Church and Christ Church in Alexandria, for the work at Pohick has deteriorated badly. Of the four colonial churches with elaborate stone ornamentation—Christ Church in Lancaster County is the fourth—two (Alexandria and Aquia) are in much better condition than are the other two. The years of abandonment for Pohick Church may easily have something to do with its severe weathering. The Ionic capitals of the doorways are almost gone, but some of the mouldings and planes have been touched up in recent decades.

The modillion cornice of the hipped roof may be original, at least in part. A new roof and ceiling are said to have been put on around 1840; how many roof trusses are original, therefore, is anyone's guess. Of the original woodwork, only the interior cornice and a single baluster from the chancel rail are left, although the wood trim of the small window in the middle of the second tier of the chancel wall may also be original. All of the other window trim, sash, door frames, and doors (with three almost square panels above a vertical panel) are of later insertion. The present frosted glass should certainly be replaced.

The restored interior is not entirely without blemishes, but, with its beige panelling, off-white walls, and scarlet cushions, it is certainly one of the most admirable in Virginia. The communion rail (with four urns) has been rebuilt after the model of the solitary remnant, which was returned to the parish by the family of the Federal officer who had stolen it. The present reredos is in the form of a modified Palladian window, with a broken triangular pediment, and a full Ionic entablature that includes fluted pilasters, dentil courses in the cornices, and three tablets. The cross in the small window that breaks the altar-piece is a piece of walnut recently taken from Mt Vernon. It has been suggested with considerable reason that this window was formerly plastered over on the interior. This may have been done to provide extra wall space for the original Ionic altar-piece of the church. It is also believed that the original reredos was of different arrangement from the present example, and probably of lower height. In support of this has been pointed out the fact that

230

not only is the present pediment broken by the window, but so is, unusually enough, the entire entablature and middle tablet.

The original pulpit was also Ionic, but the present example (which is of mixed order—Ionic on the back board and Doric on the pulpit rail) is purely conjectural. The pulpit has always occupied the center of the north wall, opposite the transverse aisle that leads to the south doorway. The pair of longitudinal aisles and the current arrangement of the box-pews represent the ground plan ascribed to Washington. The early seating rules segregated the congregation as usual by sexes (the men here sitting on the south). The large, sturdy font in the cross aisle probably comes from the first church. The figures on it ("1773") seem to have been carved at a later date. A smaller, marble font, however, does derive from around 1773 and is ascribed to William Copein. The brass chandeliers are said to come from an eighteenth-century French church. The use of gold lettering, fringes, and leaf is according to documentary descriptions of the church's colonial furnishings. Like the Falls Church and Christ Church in Alexandria, no galleries were built in Pohick Church in colonial times, despite the original two tiers of windows. The present gallery was added in the early part of the twentieth century.

After the Disestablishment, services were only occasionally held until 1836. Methodists and members of a debating society are also said to have used the building from time to time. Among those priests who did conduct Divine Worship at Pohick Church during this period was Parson Weems, who set down so much about the Washingtons, including the legend about the hatchet and the cherry tree. Parson Weems was at Pohick Church in 1798, but no one knows the length of his stay. Another priest was in charge in 1812, and in 1836-40 certain improvements were made, but after 1840 another period of inactivity set in. In the War between the States, Federal troops used the handsome structure for a stable and managed to strip the entire interior save for the cornice. In 1874 a partial restoration was undertaken, but the present furnishings and interior derive principally from 1901-16. This last restoration has inspired a number of gifts, including the cross on the Table (from the Bishop of Washington), bronze plaques memorializing those serving in the two World Wars, and pieces of modern silver from military units and others.

Among the church's proud possessions of olden times are: the vestry book (1732-85), which was also used by the overseers of the poor until 1802 and was lost for 75 years (and is now on deposit in the Library of Congress); a folio edition of the Prayer-Book of 1761 that was imported by President Washington and shows Revolutionary emendations; and a Bible of 1796 in two volumes that George Washington Parke Custis said once belonged to Washington. The Bible was given to the parish by Washington's foster-son in 1802, but was later somehow removed from the church, and in 1861 given by a slave to a Federal soldier. It was many years afterward returned anonymously. A silver paten (London, 1711) and cup (London, 1716) with the Lee coat-of-arms are also owned by the parish. The details of their early ownership are unclear.

As is usual in colonial churchyards, many unmarked graves exist at Pohick, some of them probably colonial. In 1925 a monument "To the Unknown Dead of Pohick Church" was erected by the women of a patriotic society. Moved to the old cemetery east of the church in recent decades from Prince William County, from Alexandria, and from elsewhere are markers of 1698, 1749, and 1771 as well as that of "Long Tom", an Indian chief presumably of colonial times. The tomb of 1771 is that of Daniel French, the original contractor. In 1884 the large cemetery on the west was inaugurated. In 1931 the vestry house on the east was erected according to plans of 1772 that had never been executed. Included in the vestry house are a mantel from around 1732 and a fender from the former glebe house of 1753. The parish house on the south dates from 1955; the attractive bellcote is also from recent decades.

Although a church at Fairfax Courthouse has in recent times been designated as Truro Church, Pohick Church was the colonial parish church for both Gunston Hall and Mt Vernon and seems never to have relinquished its status as the principal church in the parish. It would also seem impossible to deny Pohick Church of Truro Parish the claim that President Washington was vestryman for Truro Parish and no other from 1762 to 1784 (except for the four months in 1765 of the first creation of Fairfax Parish, during which the new vestry seems never to have met).

Its association with Washington and Mason and its superb doorways bestow an irresistible appeal upon Pohick Church.

46. Hickory Neck Church (Lower Church, Blisland)

The north transept is all that remains of colonial Hickory Neck Church, and this remnant may be seen on the east side of route 60 about

.7 mile south of the junction of routes 60 and 168Y, and about 1 mile north of Toano, all in James City County. Hickory Neck Church was originally built in 1734 as the Lower Church of Blisland Parish. When this parish was formed (probably in 1653 or earlier) from Hampton Parish, it was a large parish. It was probably coterminous with New Kent County (established in 1654), which then included the entire watershed of the Pamunkey-Mattaponi-York River system.

The origin of the name of the parish is somewhat uncertain. However, the name Blissland (with two s's) is said to have been familiar in English use, and it has recently been learned that one of the settlers of New Kent County in the 1640's came from Bodmin in Cornwall and was the son of the archdeacon of Blisland Parish at Bodmin. It is believed, therefore, that the Virginia parish probably derived its name from the Cornwall parish. Stratton Major Parish (in the present King and Queen and northern King William Counties) was cut off in 1655 and St Peter's Parish (in the present upper New Kent and Hanover Counties and part of King William County) was cut off in 1679. Part of Wilmington Parish (in James City County) was added to Blisland Parish in 1725. In 1767 an exchange in territory between James City and New Kent Counties that did not affect the parochial limits provided Blisland Parish with more territory in James City County. In 1892 the dioceses of Southern Virginia and Virginia were divided at the James City-New Kent line. Because of these alterations, the existing, enlarged north transept near Toano is the only church in the parish in James City County, and Blisland Parish in New Kent County is now dormant.

Hickory Neck was apparently named for an adjoining plantation. The surviving wing was added in 1773-74 and originally extended 25½′ north and was 25′ wide inside. The east wall was 6′ from the east wall of the original building, which was ordered to be 60′ x 26′ inside. The dimensions of the extant structure are 36½′ north to south and 28½′ east to west on the outside, so that the transept has been lengthened about 9 to 10 feet. The walls are about 24″ thick.

The building is of brick, laid originally in Flemish bond. There are many glazed headers on the south and west walls, but few on the other two walls. Below the bevelled water table there is English bond. The entire south wall and the southern portions of the east and west walls (from the present southernmost window in each case) derive from around 1825, when the original chancel and nave were pulled down and their bricks used for this portion of the existing structure. The masonry of the south wall is marked by common bond and a large stretch of repairs. The chimney dates from the nineteenth century; the small porch was added between 1907 and 1918. In addition to its southern end, the east wall is repaired above and below the middle window; and there are

233

ventilation holes in evidence as well as ivy and a large number of initials carved on the various walls.

A vestry has been added on the north, but the gable, despite some slovenly repointing, is in good shape. On the west wall, the flat arches of all three windows are replacements. The tiny inserted slivers help to indicate this, although, on the east wall, the northernmost arch of the three seems possibly to be old, despite the slivers. These flat arches alternate a full brick with a pair of halves. The six windows have splayed sides. The jambs have queen closers (as do the northeast and northwest corners of the building), but no rubbed brick. The windows have all been lengthened about one foot through insertions in the frames. This is also verified by the pattern of queen closers. The windows have had shutters at some time since their lengthening. There is no window on the north or south.

The doorway on the north (now leading to the vestry) seems to have had a flat arch. The south doorway that now opens on the little porch and is also marked by a flat arch probably derives from 1820-30. The frames of the middle and northernmost windows on each side wall are older than those of the southernmost windows of each of these two walls and are probably colonial. Their architraves include a cyma reversa, a fascia, a small cyma reversa, a fascia, and a bead. All the sash are guillotine windows and are of undetermined age, but are probably from the nineteenth century. The wood sills may date from the second decade of the last century, as also may the modillion cornice. The roof is recent.

The interior is not colonial. Two of its most prominent features are five flags (British, French, American, and Confederate, as well as the Continental flag raised by General Washington in 1776) and the coronæ lucis of mediæval design for candles. The coronæ were installed around 1930 by the same craftsman who built the example in the Yorktown Church. No electricity is used except for the organ. The slate tablets of the Law were originally made and installed in Bruton Parish Church at Williamsburg in that Church's first restoration (1905-07) and were secured for Hickory Neck Church by the Rev'd Dr Arthur Pierce Middleton in 1938, when they were replaced at Bruton by the existing tablets.

During the Revolution, British, French, and American troops occupied the yard at various times, and during the War between the States it was occupied alternately by both Confederate and Federal troops. Not long after the Disestablishment, the building was abandoned and the original part ultimately fell into ruin. The present repaired and enlarged wing was occasionally used for Divine Service throughout the period 1825-1907, but it was principally used in those years by the Hickory Neck Academy. In 1907 it was again repaired and used as a church. It was

234

reconsecrated in both 1917 and 1953, in the more recent instance as All Saints' Church (although the old name of Hickory Neck Church fortunately persists in use). The colonial name for the building seems usually to have been simply the Lower Church of Blisland Parish, and the name of Hickory Neck probably first came into use in the late eighteenth century.

Blisland Parish owns the only surviving vestry book (1721-86) of colonial James City County. It is now on loan at the State Library in Richmond.

A tomb of 1748, which now lies on the floor of the porch, was removed from the churchyard between 1907 and 1918. Other but unidentified graves as well as stone fragments and several modern stones exist in the yard, which also has a stone bench on the east for resting, near the foundation of the original chancel.

47. The Meeting House, Alexandria

The Old Presbyterian Meeting House at 317 South Fairfax Street in the charming, old part of Alexandria has undergone many changes since its erection in 1774. The early records of the Presbyterians in the town are not clear, but it seems that, as Dissenters, they held their worship in houses before 1760 and after that in the upper room of the Town House. A congregation was formally organized in 1772. The old Town House is believed to have been demolished and replaced by the present, much larger City Hall, around the middle of the nineteenth century.

The only original parts of this colonial structure on the exterior are the major portions of the side and west walls. On the side walls (which are at present 73'-3" long on the outside), approximately 60' starting from the west is original, the rest having been added in 1853. On the west wall, the two remaining portions on each side of the tower up to a line even with the side cornice seem to be of colonial derivation. The rest of this gable exhibits a different bond of brickwork, for five rows of stretchers are laid for every row of headers, whereas the lower part of this wall and the side walls are marked by three rows of stretchers for every row of headers. This last bond is also to be seen on a number

235

of other eighteenth-century buildings in Old Alexandria. The upper portion of the west wall was undoubtedly laid after the fire of 1835, when the original hipped roof was changed to the present A-roof.

The original (and present) church is 50½′ wide on the outside. Its original size of approximately 60′ x 50′ is, therefore, the same as the somewhat earlier Christ Church, a few blocks to the northwest. The walls of the Meeting House are about 2′ thick. There are random glazed headers and even occasional glazed stretchers. There is some minor repointing here and there on the original walls. The water table consists simply of a projecting brick course and nothing more. Queen closers mark the original northwest and southwest corners and the two later corners on the east, but their use on the window jambs is either irregular (as it also is on the lowest portions of the corners), random, or omitted entirely. When used, they occur only on the courses of headers.

In the original portion of the building, there are four windows in each storey on the side walls and two in each storey of the west wall (one in each storey on each side of the tower). All these windows have flat arches that alternate a full brick over a half-brick with the reverse of that. Some of the arches have been repointed. The windows have stone sills. The colonial church rests in part on stone foundation walls, which may be seen on the south wall and, better still, from the basement of the eastern addition. These stone foundations, which are characteristic of a number of contemporaneous buildings in Alexandria, exist only under the original east wall, under the south wall for but 30′ west of the original southeast corner, and under the north wall 12′ west of the original northeast corner of the building. The other 30′ of the original south wall, the other 48′ of the original north wall, and the west wall have brick foundations. Both the stone and the brick foundations under the original portions are themselves original.

The original doorway is possibly represented by the central doorway that now leads from the vestibule into the principal part of the building, but little can at present be deduced about its original style. On the other hand, it is also possible that the original meeting house may have had two side doors only on the east, or even three doorways (as at present), all in the east.

The existing church is in reality the result of a large number of additions and alterations that have been made throughout the nineteenth century and a number of restorations, renewals, and replacements in the present century. The fire of 1835, the construction of a bell-tower on the west in 1843, and the addition of the eastern end in 1853 have occasioned the most significant of the many structural changes. It was long thought by many authorities that nothing survived the fire and that the church was constructed anew. However, this seems to be an excessive opinion. In addition to the original portions of the aforementioned three walls, we learn from an account indited by the pastor of 1835 that "a part of the windows", "some of the plank broken from the pews", and perhaps a portion of the galleries were among the few parts of the interior that were rescued. Since a tablet that had been placed on the north wall above the grave of one of the congregation's beloved pastors survived the conflagration (and is still to be seen in the same location), it has been assumed that the wooden remnants derived from the north wall.

Whether any of the original wood trim and sash of the windows or the original pews have been incorporated in the present woodwork appears impossible to prove or disprove. Although over three hundred panes of glass had been broken by hail in 1811, it is possible that a few of the present lights may be colonial. Although galleries had been added sometime before the fire, their number and disposition are not known. In view of the later changes that were made, however, it seems unlikely that any original portions of the gallery or galleries remain in the current structure (although the original galleries may also have been U-shaped). Also saved from the flames of 1835 were a clock, books, cushions, stoves, and many organ pipes, but none of these remnants seem still in evidence. The present roof trusses derive from 1837, when the church was restored to service.

The 1843 tower measures 15'-10" north and south and 13-'10" east and west, and consists of four storeys in brick surmounted by a wooden lantern of but a single storey, with a flat roof and no spire. The lantern has a simple cornice, wooden pilasters, somewhat of a Chippendale rail for a captain's walk, and four openings with semi-circular arches and wooden louvers. In the three lower storeys of the tower's west wall there is a window, smaller than those of the church but marked by the same type of arch and sill. The south wall of the tower has a door and a window, whereas the north wall has only a door (off center), all in the first storey only. There is no water table on the tower. Like the church's colonial walls, the lower portion of the tower is laid with a single row of headers for three rows of stretchers, whereas the upper portion has five rows of stretchers for every row of headers.

In 1846 a wooden porch was added on the east, but this was supplanted in 1853 by the present vestibule, pair of gallery stairs, east façade, and granite platform and pair of quarter-circle stairs. The four windows in the upper tier and the two windows and two doorways on the lower storey all possess painted stone keystones that project above the flat arch in every instance, as well as sills of sandstone. The circular window in the pediment has wooden louvers and its arch consists of a soldier course. On the sides, this addition includes a brick recess in

237

each storey with the same shape and size as the principal windows. It seems unlikely that the present wall between the vestibule and the nave of the church could be the original eastern wall, for the present wall is much less than 2' thick. The three crawl-space openings on the sides of the addition and on the west of the tower (with the usual arches) undoubtedly date from 1853 and 1843, respectively. The brick cornice and brick dentils on the side walls are either original or were replaced in 1837. The east façade is laid in Flemish bond above the bevelled water table, but in common bond below it. Above the horizontal cornice is, however, a row of mostly headers. Obvious repairs have been made around the circular window and below the water table.

The present organ and case, with its clear, brilliant tone, probably was installed in 1849. The bell is cast from metal salvaged in the fire. The old manse (called the Flounder House from its resemblance to the succulent fish of that name) was erected in 1787 and is still in use. Its west side is on Royal Street beyond the cemetery from the Meeting House.

Both Southern and Northern forces used the church as a hospital in the War between the States. The Federal troops destroyed the wall around the burying ground. Apparently divisions in the political sympathies of the members of the congregation during the War caused the downfall of the Church as an active body long before its doors were shut in 1889. The building was partially restored by historical associations and various individuals in 1925-28, but it did not house a true Presbyterian Church until as recently as 1949. A new educational building was erected opposite the Flounder House in 1953.

The present interior possesses U-shaped galleries with slightly raised panels on their fronts; a pulpit (in the western end of the building) approached by stairs like those of the entrance on the east and surmounted by a large, semi-circular arch; four columnar supports on each side and two at the rear, in each storey; a coved ceiling in the center; inside shutters and splayed jambs at the windows (two alcoves on each side recalling the long use of stoves); raised-panel pews; and a floor that slopes evenly towards the pulpit (and is probably of mid-nineteenth century installation). The pulpit area of this tastefully renewed interior occupies a great part of the first storey of the tower as well as a portion of the nave. Stanchions allow for the use of candles in the galleries, and elsewhere modern pewter chandeliers and lamps illuminate the building.

One of the Church's proudest associations lies in the fact that memorial services for Presidents Washington and Zachary Taylor were held in its building as well as in the fact that it has long held close ties with the Masonic order, which is believed to have laid the cornerstone of the building.

In the small burying ground between the Meeting House and the Flounder House is the Tomb of the Unknown Soldier of the American Revolution. The old soldier "known but to God" died in 1821, but his grave was made a patriotic shrine in 1929 by several patriotic organizations. Also buried here are many figures of Revolutionary and Masonic distinction. The only colonial marker dates from 1772, the year when the first Presbyterian efforts in Alexandria were officially recognized.

The Meeting House became the town's First Presbyterian Church in 1817 when a second Presbyterian congregation was organized, but in recent years the early building has reverted to its colonial designation.

No one would claim exceptional architectural loveliness for the old structure—and, indeed, in many ways it looks more like a nineteenth-century than an eighteenth-century edifice—but, because of this very difference, because of its many proud associations in the years during and soon after the Revolution, and because of the fewness of surviving Dissenting Churches of colonial times, the Meeting House is of considerable interest to many.

48. LITTLE FORK CHURCH

Little Fork Church in the northern part of Culpeper County received its name from the fact that it does not lie far from the fork of the Hazel and Rappahannock Rivers. Another church in colonial St Mark's Parish was named Great Fork Church because it lay not far from the fork of the Rapidan and Rappahannock Rivers. Of the colonial churches of the Established Church, Little Fork is the only building in this entire area to survive. It was erected in 1774-76 and was never the parish church. St Mark's Parish was formed from St George's Parish in 1730-31. Culpeper was not created as a county (out of Orange County) until 1748. St Thomas's Parish in Orange County was, however, created out of St Mark's Parish in 1740.

Little Fork Church is to be seen at the junction of routes 726 and 624. This junction of unpaved roads is ½ mile from the junction of routes 726 and 229 near the Hazel River and also but a ½ mile from the junction of routes 624 and 229, farther north along this main road

(229). The junction near the Hazel River is slightly over a mile north of Rixeyville and nine miles north of Culpeper Courthouse. The existing handsome brick structure is the second church of that name, for a frame building was standing when the parish was created. This frame building, which was enlarged several times, burned in 1773 and was originally to be replaced by another wooden structure, but plans were altered and brick substituted. It is believed that John Ariss (c. 1725-1799) designed and built both Lamb's Creek Church (1769-70) in King George County and Little Fork Church, and it is certainly true that these churches are as closely alike as any two churches could be. However, it is recorded in 1776 that an Edmund Vass was to be paid five pounds for two sets of plans for Little Fork Church. It is possible only to speculate as to what Mr Vass did in return for this stipend. Perhaps, these plans concerned the frame church that was not built. It is also entirely possible that the original frame building occupied another site, nearer the fork of the two rivers, for it is recorded at the time of the building of the brick church that payment was to be made for 1½ acres of land.

The building measures approximately 83½' x 33½' and is thus a somewhat long church, as colonial churches in Virginia go. The walls are about 22" thick. Its windows measure approximately 8'-8" in height. Of these principal windows, there are six on the south and north (three on each side of the south doorway and the (former) pulpit on the north) and two in the chancel. There are also two somewhat smaller windows high up on the west wall. The arches of the principal windows are semi-circular and consist of full bricks alternating with half-bricks, or, at least, every other brick is divided by an incised line. The western windows possess flat arches of merely a rowlock course. The sides of the windows are not splayed, but the embrasures are now irregularly plastered.

The bond of the brickwork is Flemish with random glazed headers and even a few glazed stretchers. On the north wall, time through mould and moss has created a rainbow of hues sufficient to fascinate any colorist. Rubbed brick marks the four corners of the building, all the jambs of the windows, the arches of the principal windows, and also the jambs of the two original doorways that have been replaced by smaller, narrower doorways. Queen closers also mark all the corners and the jambs of all the openings, including the original doorways. The retention of the rubbed brick and queen closers of the two doorways allows us to know that the two doorways were each originally no less than 6'-7" wide. These openings have been partly bricked in and the new, inserted doorways now have semi-circular arches merely of full bricks. However, the doorways probably in the beginning had classical pediments. Like

240

the Falls Church and Pohick Church, Little Fork Church was probably built with the south doorway as the principal entrance.

The locations for the ventilation holes are probably original. The water table is an ovolo, but this can be told only on the western section of the north wall, for elsewhere on the church the water table and all beneath it (including a gutter) have been covered with cement. The water table is relatively low, for the ground around the church has probably built up through the years. The brickwork below the water table is also Flemish, if one can judge from the small exposed section.

Repairs have been made above every arch, and later repairs have been made in the arches of all the windows except the second and third windows from the west on the north wall and the next to the easternmost window, the westernmost window, and the third window from the west on the south wall. Repointing marks the arch of the easternmost window on the south wall. The rowlock courses of the arches of the windows on the west wall seem to be replacements. The two sets of repairs or replacements are, perhaps, most obvious at the south doorway. The earlier repairs reach in this instance almost to the cornice. Former scaffolding holes on the walls have been somewhat crudely replaced by headers. The northwestern corner of the church is presently in need of attention near the water table and the other three corners have recently been slovenly repaired. Cracks are to be noted on the chancel wall above both windows, on the south wall very near the southeastern corner, on the west wall below the south window, and high up on the north wall. Carvings of dates and names are to be seen near the south doorway and the southeast corner, although they seem to be from either the 1860's or very recent times. The steps of the doorways are replacements.

The roof is hipped and at present is of metal. The wooden, modillion cornice may be original.

The most striking feature of the interior, besides its spaciousness, is the elaborate albeit somewhat crude reredos, which is said to have been executed by the same craftsman who built the mantel at "Salubria", a colonial house in the lower part of the county. The triangular pediment of the reredos is broken by a cross. The raked and horizontal cornices both include: ovolo, fillet, cyma recta, cyma reversa, fascia, bead, soffit (with modillions), ovolo, and dentils. The frieze alternates triglyphs and guttæ with crude rosettes for metopes. Only one-half of a metope is carved at each end; six guttæ exist on the ends and five on the five interior groups. The architrave has but two planes. The primitive Doric pilasters are marked by: abacus, echinus, annulets, necking, and oversized astragal. The shaft is plain and the pedestal is but a cavetto moulding over a plinth-like base. Four applied panels between the pilasters now contain the Decalogue, the Creed, and the Lord's Prayer lettered in gold, but both the gilding and the lettering seem to be recent work. The tablets were at one time dark rather than white as at present, and their borders were probably at one time gilt. Beneath these tablets is a single horizontal panel over two larger horizontal panels. All three panels are applied.

The holes that are to be seen throughout most of the present floor have been said to mark the spots where stanchions stood for tethering horses when the church was used as a stable by Federal troops in the War between the States. However, it is more likely that these holes, because of their regularity, mark the positions of pew-ends. This view would seem to be confirmed by the odd marks just in front of where the old pulpit was located (opposite the south doorway). It is probable, therefore, that two longitudinal aisles marked the original plan. However, the present floor is in all probability not colonial, although it probably antedates the War between the States. The newest part of the floor (in the eastern end) derives only from 1956 as a result of a fire that occurred while Methodists were borrowing the church. The present floor level is possibly somewhat higher than its colonial antecedent. The wainscoting was probably also once higher than the window sills, as evidenced by ridges in the plaster. The present coved cornice probably represents the original shape though not the original material. The wood plank ceiling is new, although the roof trusses are believed to be largely intact.

The sash and trim of the windows are old, but are not likely to be colonial. The panes are modern and are now protected by heavy wire mesh. The doors are replacements, as are the rough pine pews, the plaster, and the entire chancel (except the reredos) and furnishings. The vestry rooms are additions from modern times. It is not possible to prove that a gallery was ever built, despite the height of the western windows. The building is still not wired for electricity.

The church was repaired in 1871. In 1892 the Methodists sued unsuccessfully for possession of the building. Their use of the name "Oak Shade" for Little Fork is unwarranted and should be disallowed as having neither historical precedent nor legal basis. Repairs were again made in 1892-94 and Methodists continued to borrow the church until several years ago when they bought a more modern and smaller Episcopal church at Rixeyville for their use.

The old church is now but a chapel of St Mark's Parish with an annual Service. Although as an architectural monument it is without a superior in Culpeper, Orange, Fauquier, Rappahannock, Madison, and still other nearby counties—a large area, indeed—it is one of the two or three most neglected of our colonial churches. Its yard, for example, is redeemed only by a protecting fence of sorts and a large marble monument erected in 1904 to the memory of the Little Fork Rangers, Co. D of the 4th Virginia Cavalry, which was organized and drilled in the churchyard in 1861 and fought throughout the War. Included on the monument are inscriptions, lists of soldiers, a bas-relief of a soldier's head, and a large statue of a Southern maiden with sword and sheaf. There are no graves, and the yard is not kept up, although several small trees were planted by the Warrenton Garden Club in 1956.

Aside from Little Fork Church, two other tangible remnants of ecclesiastical value still exist within the original area of St Mark's Parish. One of these is the original manuscript of the vestry book (1746-79) of Augusta Parish in Augusta County. The large parishes and coterminous counties of Augusta and Frederick were created in 1738 out of St Mark's Parish and Orange County, although their official organization was ordered to be postponed until such time as the parishes and counties were sufficiently inhabited. This seems probably to have occurred around 1745 (five years after the formation of St Thomas's Parish out of St Mark's Parish). The Augusta Parish manuscript is now kept at the Augusta County clerk's office in Staunton.

The second remnant is a chalice and a paten made in London in 1766-67 and used at St Thomas's Parish Church in Orange ever since. The marks on the chalice are wanting or extremely fragmentary, but those on the paten would seem to include an "FW" (possibly for Fuller White) rather than "WF" as stated by one authority. Both pieces are identically inscribed with "St Thomas's Parish".

APPENDIX 1:
Hours of Divine Service and Access to the Churches' Interiors at Other Times

CHURCH	REGULAR SERVICES	ACCESS AT OTHER TIMES
1. The Tower Church, Jamestown*	Third Sunday after Trinity at 7:30 a.m. (at the Robert Hunt Shrine)	Open 9:00-5:00 daily*
2. Merchant's Hope Church	June & July: 2nd & 4th Sundays at 4:00 August & September: 2nd Sunday at 4:00	Write Mrs Fenner Barnard, Prince George Courthouse, or the Rector, St John's Church, Hopewell.
3. Newport Parish Church (St Luke's)	July & August: Sundays at 11:00	Open 9:00-5:00 daily
4. York-Hampton Parish Church (Grace)	Sundays at 8:00 & 11:00 July & August: Sundays at 10:00 Holy Days: 10:00	Open 9:00-5:00 daily
5. St Peter's Parish Church	Sundays at 11:00	Write the Senior Warden, St Peter's Parish Church, New Kent Courthouse.
6. Yeocomico Church	September-May: Sundays at 11:00 June-August: 1st, 3rd, & 5th Sundays at 11:00	Write the Rector, or Mr Charles M. Sanford, or Mr W. T. Griffith, all of Hague.
7. Ware Parish Church	Sundays at 8:30 & 11:00 Holy Days: 10:00	Write the Rector, Gloucester Courthouse.
8. Bruton Parish Church	Summer: Sundays at 8:30 & 10:00 Sundays at 8:00, 9:30, & 11:00; and 8:00 p.m.	Open 9:00-5:00 week-days & 7:30-5:00 Sundays
9. Christ Church, Middlesex	Summer: Sundays at 8:00 & 10:00 Sundays at 8:00, 9:45, & 11:00	Open 9:00-5:00 week-days & 8:00-5:00 Sundays
10. Lower Chapel, Middlesex (now Methodist)	Summer: Sundays at 8:00 & 10:00 Sundays at 10:00	Write the Pastor at Hartfield P. O.
11. Vawter's Church	Sundays at 10:00	Write the Rector at Port Royal or Mrs J. Sale Shaw at Chance P. O.

244

	Services	Access
12. Upper Church, Stratton Major (now Methodist)	2nd Sundays at 11:15 4th Sundays at 10:00	Write the Pastor of the Middlesex Methodist Charge at Saluda; or Mr C. C. Hall of King & Queen Courthouse; or Mr C. Tazewell Bland of Shanghai P. O.
13. Elizabeth City Parish Church (St John's, Hampton)	Sundays at 8:00, 9:00, & 11:00; and Thursdays at 10:00	Open 8:00-5:00 daily
14. Upper Church, St Paul's Parish (now Slash Christian Church)	Sundays at 11:00	Write the Pastor, Slash Church, Route 2, Ashland.
15. Chapel of the College of William & Mary (now non-denominational)	A mid-week, non-denominational service for the College	Open 7:00-5:00 from mid-June to mid-September & 7:00 a.m. to 11:00 p.m. rest of year.
16. Mangohick Church (now colored Baptist)		Write the Postmaster, Mangohick.
17. Lower Church, St Stephen's Parish (now Mattaponi Baptist Church)	2nd & 4th Sundays at 11:30	Write Mr Walter Harper at Ino P. O.
18. Westover Parish Church	Sundays at 11:00	Write the Rector, Charles City Courthouse.
19. Christ Church, Lancaster	June-August: Sundays at 11:00	Open 9:00-5:00 daily April-November; in other months write the Rector, Grace Church, Kilmarnock; or Miss Laura Virginia Francis, White Stone.
20. St John's Church (King William County)	None at present	Write the Rector, St John's Church, West Point.
21. Lynnhaven Parish Church (Old Donation)	Sundays at 8:00, 9:15, & 11:00 Summer: Sundays at 8:00 & 10:00 Wednesdays at 10:00 (except in summer)	Open 9:00-5:00 week-days & 7:00-5:00 Sundays
22. Bristol Parish Church (Blandford)	Memorial Service June the 9th at 5:00 p.m.	Open from last week in April to All Saints' Day: 10:00-4:15 week-days & 3:00-5:00 Sundays; in other months write Miss L. Gertrude Williams, 311 South Jefferson Street, Petersburg.

23. Fork Church	Sundays at 11:15	Write the Rector, Route 1, Doswell P. O.
24. North Farnham Parish Church	Sundays at 9:30	Write the Rector, St John's Church, Warsaw; or Mr Norman L. Edwards, Farnham P. O.
25. Bennett's Creek Church (Glebe)	Sundays at 9:45	Key is kept on projection over north doorway.
26. Pungoteague Church (St George's)	Sundays at 11:30	Write the Rector, St James's Church, Accomac Courthouse.
27. Borough Church (St Paul's, Norfolk)	Sundays at 8:00 & 11:00 June 14-September 15: Sundays at 8:00 & 10:00	Open 9:00-4:30 week-days & 8:00-4:30 Sundays
28. Hebron Church (Lutheran)	1st, 3rd, & 5th Sundays at 11:00 2nd & 4th Sundays at 9:30	Write the Pastor, Madison Courthouse.
29. St Mary's Whitechapel	1st Sundays at 11:30 Other Sundays at 9:00	Write the Rector, Grace Church, Kilmarnock; or Miss Marjorie Eastwick, Lively P. O.
30. Henrico Parish Church (St John's, Richmond)	Sundays at 11:00	Open 10:00-4:00 week-days & 12:00-4:00 Sundays
31. Hungars Parish Church	Sundays at 11:30	Write the Rector, Hungars Parish, Eastville.
32. Providence Church (Presbyterian)	Sundays at 11:00 (no service on 5th Sundays)	Write Mr R. V. Lancaster jr, Route 3, Box 87, Mineral.
33. Buck Mountain Church	Sundays at 9:30	Write the Rector, The Church of Our Saviour, Rio Road, Charlottesville.
34. Augusta Stone Church (Presbyterian)	Sundays at 11:00	Write the Pastor, Fort Defiance P. O.
35. Cattail Church (now Mt Sinai colored Baptist)		Write Junie Diggs, Aylett P. O.
36. Aquia Church	Sundays at 11:00	Open June 1st-Labor Day: 9:00-4:30 daily; in other months write the Rector or Miss Anne E. Moncure at Stafford Courthouse.

37. Lower Church, Southwark Parish (now in ruins)	None	None required
38. Abingdon Parish Church	Sundays at 9:30 & 11:00	Open 9:00-5:00 daily
39. Timber Ridge Church (Presbyterian)	Sundays at 11:00	Write the Pastor, Route 5, Lexington.
40. Chuckatuck Church (St John's)	Sundays at 11:30 August: Sundays at 8:00	Key is kept on projection over (west) doorway.
41. St Paul's Parish Church (King George County)	Sundays at 10:00	Write the Rector, King George Court-house.
42. The Falls Church	Sundays at 7:30, 9:00, & 11:00; and 6:30 p.m. Wednesdays & Holy Days at 10:00	Open 8:00-4:00 daily
43. Christ Church, Alexandria	Sundays at 8:00, 9:15, & 11:15 Wednesdays at 11:15	Open 9:00-5:00 daily
44. Lamb's Creek Church	Last Sunday in August at 11:00	Write Mr J. W. Cox, Box 107, Route 4, Fredericksburg.
45. Pohick Church	Sundays at 8:00, 9:30, & 11:00	Open 9:00-5:00 week-days & 8:00-5:00 Sundays
46. Lower Church, Blisland Parish (Hickory Neck)	Sundays at 9:00	Open 9:00-5:00 daily
47. The Meeting House (Presbyterian)	September-May: Sundays at 9:30 & 11:00 June-August: Sundays at 11:00	Open 8:00-4:00 week-days; 8:00-2:00 Saturdays; 9:00-12:30 Sundays
48. Little Fork Church	Rogation Sunday at 11:00	Write the Rector, St Stephen's Church, Culpeper.

NOTE: In writing for permission to visit the interior of a church, one should always enclose a stamped, self-addressed post card or envelope.

*Admission to the historic grounds at Jamestown (including the Tower Church and the Robert Hunt Shrine) is 50¢ for each person (except children under twelve, who are admitted free). However, it is customary for admission charges to be waived during the special services and exercises on such days as the Third Sunday after Trinity and Jamestown Day. Admission to the site of the Cape Henry Cross, which is also administered as part of the Colonial National Historical Park, is free, but one must obtain a pass from the sentry on duty at either the west or south gates of Ft Story. One must also drive slowly within the fort, and return the pass to the sentry after visiting the Cross.

APPENDIX II:
COLONIAL VESTRY BOOKS

PARISH	COUNTY	YEARS	LOCATION OF ORIGINAL
Albemarle*	Sussex	1742-87 (2 volumes)	Virginia State Library
Antrim*	Halifax	1752-1817	Virginia State Library
Augusta	Augusta	1746-79	Augusta County Clerk's Office, Staunton
Blisland*	New Kent and James City	1721-86 (2 volumes)	Virginia State Library
Bristol	Prince George	1720-89 (with register)	St Paul's Church, Petersburg
Camden	Pittsylvania	1767-1852	Clerk's Office, Chatham
Christ Church*	Middlesex	1663-1767	Virginia State Library
Cumberland*	Lunenburg	1746-1816	Virginia State Library
Cunningham Chapel	Clarke	1772-1893	Bank of Clarke County, Boyce
Dettingen*	Prince William	1745-1802	Virginia State Library
Elizabeth City	Elizabeth City	1751-1883	St John's Church, Hampton
Elizabeth River	Norfolk	1749-61	Seaboard Citizens National Bank, Norfolk
Fairfax	Alexandria and Fairfax	1765-1842	First & Citizens National Bank, Alexandria
Frederick*	Frederick	1764-1818	Virginia State Library
Fredericksville*	Louisa and Albemarle	1742-87	Virginia State Library
Henrico	Henrico	1730-73	St John's Church, Richmond
Hungars*	Northampton	1758-82	Clerk's Office, Eastville
Kingston*	Mathews	1679-1796	Virginia State Library
King William	Powhatan	1707-50 (in French)	Virginia Historical Society
Lynnhaven	Princess Anne	1723-1892	Virginia State Library
Newport (and Upper)	Isle of Wight	1724-72	Virginia State Library
Petsworth	Gloucester	1677-1793	Clerk's Office, Gloucester Courthouse
St Andrew's	Brunswick	1732-97	Clerk's Office, Lawrenceville
St Anne's	Albemarle	1772-85	Huntington Library, San Marino, California
St George's	Accomack	1763-87	Clerk's Office, Accomac Courthouse

Parish	County	Years	Location
St George's	Spotsylvania	1726-1817 (2 volumes)	University of Virginia
St James-Northam*	Goochland	1744-1860	Virginia State Library
St Mark's*	Culpeper	1730-53	Unknown**
St Mary's Whitechapel*	Lancaster	1739-88	Virginia State Library
St Patrick's*	Prince Edward	1755-74	Virginia State Library
St Paul's*	Hanover	1706-86	Virginia State Library
St Peter's*	New Kent	1684-1758 (with register)	Virginia State Library
Shelburne*	Loudoun	1771-1805	Virginia State Library
Southam	Powhatan	1745-1836	Clerk's Office, Powhatan Courthouse
Stratton Major*	King and Queen	1729-83	Virginia State Library
Suffolk	Nansemond	1749-1856	Clerk's Office, Suffolk
Truro	Fairfax	1732-85	Library of Congress
Upper*	Nansemond	1743-93	Virginia State Library
Wicomico*	Northumberland	1703-95	Virginia State Library

*Those vestry books and registers that are marked with a single asterisk were used by the Rt Rev'd William Meade in the preparation of his book (1861) and deposited at his death (1862) at the Virginia Theological Seminary in Alexandria. They have since 1931 been on loan at the State Library in Richmond.

**In 1931 this book was in the possession of the vestry of St Mark's Parish, but its present whereabouts is not known by the officials of that parish. A photostat copy, however, is on file at the Virginia State Library.

COLONIAL PARISH REGISTERS

Parish	County	Years	Location of Original
Abingdon	Gloucester	1678-1780	**
Albemarle	Sussex (2 volumes)	1739-78	Virginia Historical Society
Bristol	Prince George	1720-92 (with vestry book)	St Paul's Church, Petersburg
Bruton and Marston	York and James City	1662-1797	Bruton Parish Church, Williamsburg
Charles*	York	1648-1789	Virginia State Library
Christ Church*	Middlesex	1653-1814	Virginia State Library

Kingston*	1749-1827	Virginia State Library
King William	1721-54 (in French)	Huntington Library, San Marino, California
North Farnham	1672-1800	Clerk's Office, Warsaw
Overwharton*	1725-74	Virginia State Library
St Paul's*	1716-93	Clerk's Office, King George Courthouse
St Peter's*	1685-1786 (with vestry book)	Virginia State Library
St Stephen's	1661-1810	Virginia State Library
Suffolk	1704-1839	Clerk's Office, Suffolk
Tillotson	1773-74, 1783, and 1785	Virginia State Library

*Those vestry books and registers that are marked with a single asterisk were used by the Rt Rev'd William Meade in the preparation of his book (1861) and deposited at his death (1862) at the Virginia Theological Seminary in Alexandria. They have since 1931 been on loan at the State Library in Richmond.

**The original of the Abingdon Parish register is lost, but one of the two copies extant is owned by the Virginia Historical Society.

PUBLISHED VESTRY BOOKS AND REGISTERS
(Known to the Author)

PARISH	EDITOR	AVAILABLE FROM
Albemarle register	Richards (1958)	The Colonial Dames of Virginia, "Wilton", South Wilton Road, Richmond 26, Virginia. $15.00
Blisland vestry book	Chamberlayne (1935)	Virginia State Library. $5.00
Bristol vestry book and register	Chamberlayne (1898)	
Charles register	Bell (1932)	Virginia State Library. $5.00
Christ Church, Middlesex vestry book	Chamberlayne (1927)	The Rector, Christchurch, Virginia. $15.00
Christ Church, Middlesex register	Colonial Dames (1897)	
Cumberland vestry book	Bell (1930)	Mrs John W. Bell, 1002 Kerns Road, Falls Church, Virginia. $10.00

Henrico vestry book	Brock (1874)	Virginia Historical Society,
Kingston vestry book	Chamberlayne (1929)	428 North Boulevard,
King William vestry book	Fife (trans.) (1913-15) (in	Richmond 20, Virginia.
	"The Va Magazine of History	$2.00 a number whenever available.
	and Biography", XI, 3, 4; XII,	
	1, 3, 4; XIII, 1, 2, 3)	
King William register	Brock (trans.) (1888)	Virginia Historical Society. $5.00
Lynnhaven vestry book	Mason (1949)	Mr George H. S. King,
Overwharton register	King (1961)	1301 Prince Edward Street,
		Fredericksburg, Virginia. $10.00
		Virginia State Library. $5.00
Petsworth vestry book	Chamberlayne (1933)	
St Paul's, Hanover vestry book	Chamberlayne (1940)	Mr George H. S. King,
St Paul's, King George register	King (1960)	1301 Prince Edward Street,
		Fredericksburg, Virginia. $10.00
St Peter's vestry book and register	Chamberlayne (1937)	Virginia State Library. $5.00
Stratton Major vestry book	Chamberlayne (1931)	Virginia State Library. $5.00
Upper, Nansemond vestry book	Hall (1949)	

Those publications listed as no longer for sale may sometimes be secured from the Collector's Old Book Shop, 2 North 7th Street, in Richmond or from another book store in the Commonwealth.

Abacus:	The top (usually square) member of the capital of a column (cp. fig. VII).
Ambulatory:	A passageway for walking around the chancel and behind the altar.
Annulets:	Fillet mouldings, usually in groups of three, between the echinus and the necking of a column (cp. fig. VII).
Apse:	The eastern end of a church when of semi-circular or polyhedral shape; and sometimes, loosely, the entire eastern arm of a church.
Arch (flat, semi-circular, or segmental):	Masonry (above an opening) the bottom line of which is horizontal, semi-circular, or segmental (cp. figures I, IIa, and XI).
Arch, relieving:	An arch (usually a blind arch) that is constructed above a lintel in order to relieve the lintel of the weight above it (cp. fig. IIb).
Architrave:	The lowest portion of a classical entablature, usually composed of one, two, or three fasciæ; also, the trim of a doorway or a window-opening (cp. fig. VII).
Archivolt:	The band of mouldings used to ornament the extrados of an arch (cp. fig. I).
A-roof:	A roof having only two slopes and forming an "A" shape at each gable-end (cp. fig. IXb).
Astragal:	A small, half-round moulding encircling a column below the capital and forming the bottom limit of the necking (cp. fig. VII).
Baldachino (*Italian*):	A canopy or a separate roof over an altar, throne, or tomb, either supported by columns or suspended from above.
Balusters:	Small columns or urns that support the rail of a stair, gallery, or chancel.
Barge board:	A wide board that is located immediately below the edge of a roof at the gable and follows the slope (or rake) of the roof (cp. fig. IXb).
Barrel vault:	An unbroken ceiling of semi-circular shape.
Bason (ecclesiastical spelling of basin):	A dish, plate, or bowl (generally of silver) used for the collection of alms or offerings; or, occasionally, a bowl used for holding the water in the rite of Baptism.
Batten:	A strip of wood laid across a series of boards to fasten them together; also, a narrow strip of wood covering the joint between two boards—hence, board-and-batten.
Battlement:	Cp. *crenellation*.
Bead:	A small, convex moulding of semi-circular section.
Bead and reel:	A moulding of semi-circular section carved into a series of beads alternating with disc forms (cp. fig. VIIIc).

253

Beam:	A horizontal member of a structural frame that supports a weight of wall or roof.
Belt course (or string course):	A band of masonry projecting at least ½″ and, in the case of brick, usually consisting of two or more courses (cp. fig. XIIIa).
Bevelled:	Having the corner cut off at a slant.
Board-and-batten:	Cp. *batten*.
Bolection:	A projecting, generally S-shaped moulding, used to frame a panel or opening.
Bond:	The manner or pattern of laying bricks in order to bind a wall into one compact mass.
Bond, common:	The pattern of bricklaying in which there occurs a single course of headers for every six (or sometimes five or seven) courses of stretchers.
Bond, English:	The pattern of bricklaying in which courses of headers alternate with courses of stretchers (cp. fig. IVb).
Bond, Flemish:	The pattern of bricklaying in which each course consists of alternate stretchers and headers (with every header centered between the (two) stretchers of the courses immediately above and below it). (Cp. fig. IVa.)
Box-pew:	A pew with seats on at least three of the four (usually high) sides.
Bracket:	A slender piece of wood or stone (extending out from a wall and having a flat upper surface) that serves to support a projecting moulding or a shelf.
Brick bat:	A portion of a broken brick.
Bull's-eye window:	A small circular or elliptical window—also known as an ox-eye window.
Bull nose:	Cp. *torus*.
Buttered joint:	A very thin mortar joint in which the mortar is applied to the unit of masonry much in the same manner as butter is spread on a piece of bread.
Buttress:	A thickened wall, or piece of masonry wall at right angle to another wall (usually "stepped" or growing smaller as it rises higher), used to counteract the thrust of an arch, vault, or roof.
Came (or calme):	A small grooved bar of lead used to frame small panes of glass in windows.
Cap (abbreviation of capital):	In general use, the upper part of one of the smaller architectural features of a building, such as a pedestal (in contrast to the capital of a column). (Cp. fig. VII.)
Capital:	The topmost mouldings of a column, pier, or pilaster (cp. fig. VII).
Casement:	A window with its sash (or sashes) hung, like a door, on hinges.

254

Catherine wheel window:	A circular window with radiating spokes (the term being derived from the martyrdom of St Catherine).
Cavetto:	A concave, quarter-round moulding (cp. fig. VII).
Chalice:	The cup or goblet (generally of silver) used for the wine in the celebration of the Holy Communion, usually (in the case of the surviving colonial Virginian examples) in the shape of a bell or a beaker with stem.
Chamfer (v.t.):	To cut away the square edge of an exterior angle, leaving a bevel at forty-five degrees to the two original surfaces.
Chancel:	The eastern portion of a church, including sanctuary and choir and often separated from the nave by a chancel screen or rood beam (cp. fig. V).
Choir (or quire):	That part of the eastern arm of a church assigned to the choristers: or, sometimes, loosely, the entire eastern arm of the church (cp. fig. V).
Clipped gable:	A gable that is cut back near its apex in a hipped form—also known as a jerkin-head (cp. fig. IXc).
Collar beam:	A horizontal timber that forms a triangle with two sloping timbers. In roof construction, it occurs at some point between the plate and the ridge (cp. fig. X).
Coping:	The uppermost courses of a wall or parapet, usually marked by a sloping top for throwing off rain.
Corbel:	The stepping of masonry in which each successively higher course projects slightly beyond the face of the course immediately below it.
Cornice:	The projections that are to be found at the top of a wall; also, the upper portion of a classical entablature (cp. figures VI and VII).
Cornice, raked:	A cornice on a slope—for example, the sloping edges of a triangular pediment (cp. fig. VI).
Coved ceiling:	A ceiling that is joined to each of the side walls by means of a concave curve.
Crenellations:	The uppermost parts of a wall in which solid sections alternate with openings, thus effecting a notched or "toothed" appearance. In mediæval times, defenders of crenellated structures shot their arrows through the openings.
Crossing:	That part of a cruciform church where chancel, nave, and transepts meet; or, in small churches, the juncture of the south-north and east-west aisles (cp. fig. V).
Crow-stepped gable:	A gable-end that resembles steps as it rises from eave to apex (cp. fig. XIIIb).

255

Cruck:

A forked pole or a pair of tree-trunks bent or curved like Gothic arches.

Curvilinear gable:

A gable-end, usually found in Jacobean architecture, that consists of scroll-and-step forms as it rises from eave to apex (cp. fig. XIIIa).

Cyma recta:

An S-shaped moulding (reverse curve) having the convex half nearer the wall (cp. fig. VIIIa).

Cyma reversa:

An S-shaped moulding (reverse curve) having the concave half nearer the wall (cp. fig. VII).

Decalogue:

The Ten Commandments (Exodus XX, 1-17), generally indited on two of the four tablets usual in colonial churches.

Dentil:

One of a series of block-like projections that form a moulding, as in the Ionic order (cp. fig. VII).

Diapering:

A pattern of brickwork usually of glazed headers and most frequently in diamond shapes.

Die (or dado):

The body of a pedestal between the cap and the base (cp. fig. VII).

Dormer:

A projecting vertical window in the sloping roof of a building.

Drip:

A moulding with an undercut edge to prevent water from running back to the wall (cp. fig. VIIIa).

Echinus:

The convex moulding immediately below the square abacus of a Doric capital, usually of slightly elongated, quarter-round shape (cp. fig. VII).

Egg-and-dart:

A decorative design for a moulding that alternates an egg-shape with that of a spear-head (cp. fig. VIIId).

Embrasure:

A bevelling inwards of the sides of an aperture for a door or window.

Entablature:

The horizontal mouldings that are situated immediately above the capitals of the columns of a building and consist of three major parts: cornice (topmost); frieze (central); and architrave (lowest). (Cp. fig. VII.)

Extrados:

The upper or exterior curve of the voussoirs of an arch (cp. fig. I).

Façade:

A face of a building, usually the front.

Fanlight:

A fan-shaped (or, loosely, any) window located immediately above a door.

Fascia:

A wide, vertical, flat band between two horizontal mouldings; or a vertical board fixed to the outer end of rafters at the eaves of a roof (cp. fig. VII).

Fillet:

A narrow, flat band separating two curved mouldings (cp. fig. VII).

Finial:

An ornament placed upon the apex of a roof, pediment, or gable.

256

Flagon:	A vessel like a pitcher (usually of silver or pewter), with handle, narrow spout, lid, and straight, sloping sides, that holds the wine until it is poured into the chalice at the celebration of the Holy Communion. The surviving colonial examples in Virginia do not have spouts, but do have moulded bases.
Flemish bond:	Cp. *bond.*
Flemish gable:	A crow-stepped, Jacobean, or curvilinear gable (q.v.).
Floor sill:	A horizontal timber on which the floor joists rest.
Fluting (or flutes):	Parallel grooves of concave section (usually on the shaft of a column). (Cp. fig. VII).
Footing:	A mass of masonry or concrete that forms the underground base for a wall (cp. fig. XIV).
Frame (of doorway or window):	Cp. *trim.*
Frieze:	The central section (sometimes decorated with triglyphs and metopes) of a classical entablature (cp. fig. VII).
Frieze, pulvinated:	A "cushion" frieze, convex in section.
Gable:	The triangular section of a wall (at the end of a building) that is formed by a sloping roof (cp. figures IX and XIII).
Gauged brick:	Brick that has been cut and rubbed to an exact size for close fitting and is usually laid with buttered or very fine mortar joints.
Glazed header:	A header (brick) that has been fired with a silicon glaze and is, therefore, usually dark in color and slick in texture (cp. fig. IVa).
Greek cross:	A cross with all four arms of equal length.
Greek key:	A decorative design for a moulding made up of interlocking, flat bands.
Guillotine window:	A double-hung window without counterweights.
Gutta (plural: guttæ):	A drop-like, truncated, conical form occurring in groups below triglyphs of the Doric order (cp. fig. VII).
Haunch:	The part of an arch between the spring-line and the crown or keystone.
Header:	A brick that presents its end on the front surface and rests on the greater of its two shorter dimensions (cp. fig. IIIb).
Hinges, H and H-L:	Joints or mechanisms by means of which a door, lid, or gate swings or turns and the leaves of which are arranged (when open) in the shape of an H or an H-L.
Hinges, strap:	A hinge with a pair of long, often tapered leaves or flaps.
Hipped roof:	A roof rising directly from the wall plate on all sides, thus having no gable (cp. fig. IXa).

257

Impost:	The cap of a pier or pilaster supporting the spring of an arch and frequently projecting in the form of an ornamental moulding or capital (cp. fig. I).
In situ (Latin):	In its original or natural location or position.
Intrados:	The inner or lower curve of an arch (cp. fig. I).
Jamb:	One of the two sides of an opening in a wall (cp. fig. XI).
Jerkin-head:	Cp. *clipped gable.*
Joist:	One of a number of horizontal timbers (spaced at regular intervals) that support a floor or ceiling (cp. figures X and XIV).
Kalendar:	Ecclesiastical spelling of calendar.
Keystone:	The central, wedge-shaped stone or voussoir at the crown of an arch, sometimes extending below the intrados and often ornamental (cp. fig. I).
Keystone, linenfold:	A keystone carved in a series of formalized vertical folds.
Kick at the eaves:	A flattening of the slope of a roof as it nears its lower edge or eave, resulting in a curved profile or swag.
Lamb's tongue:	The ogee moulding terminating a bevelled or chamfered cut.
Lancet:	A sharply pointed Gothic arch.
Law, the:	Cp. the *Decalogue.*
Latin cross:	A cross with the lower portion of the upright member longer than the upper portion or either of the arms (cp. fig. V).
Leaded glass:	Panes of glass framed by (leaden) cames.
Lights:	Panes of glass (held in place by muntins). (Cp. fig. XI.)
Lintel:	A horizontal member spanning an opening and carrying a superstructure.
Loggia:	An arcade or gallery with one or more of its sides open to the air.
Louver:	One of a series of horizontal slats or overlapping boards, tilted so as to keep rain and snow out but to let air through.
Lunette:	A semi-circular panel, usually in the shape of a half-moon.
Metope:	The plain or sculpted square spaces between adjacent triglyphs of the Doric order (cp. fig. VII).
Mitre:	The line or joint formed when two members meet each other at an angle, as at the corner of a picture frame.
Modillion:	A form of bracket (sometimes carved, sometimes rather like a large dentil (q.v.)) that is used in a classical cornice.

258

Mortar joint:	The point at which units of masonry are bound together by means of mortar (generally a mixture of sand, water, lime, and cement—in colonial times oyster shell was one of the constituents).
Mortise:	A cut-out slot in one piece of wood into which a projecting tenon of another piece of wood fits.
Moulding:	A deviation from a plane surface (involving curved or rectangular profiles or both) that serves the purposes of transition and ornamentation and is effected by means of carving or application of pieces in relief.
Mullion:	An upright division or post between windows or doors of a close series.
Muntin:	A thin bar that divides and supports panes of glass in a sash or door (cp. fig. XI).
Muntin, knife-edge:	A very thin muntin, with a knife-like edge.
Nailing block:	A small wooden block imbedded in masonry or plaster to which other exposed wooden pieces are nailed.
Nave:	The western arm of a church, sometimes also including the crossing and that part of the eastern arm lying west of the chancel (cp. fig. V).
Necking:	The portion of a column between the echinus and the astragal (cp. fig. VII).
Newel:	A post that terminates the rail of a staircase at the bottom or top, or at a landing.
Ogee:	A profile or moulding with a reverse-curve face (cp. fig. VII).
Ovolo:	A convex moulding of quarter-round shape (cp. fig. VII).
Palladian window:	A semi-circular arched opening with a smaller, square-headed opening on each side and with all three apertures having the same base or sill.
Panel:	A wide piece of thin wood surrounded by a frame or margin, often raised above or sunk below the level of the general surface.
Parapet:	A vertical section of wall that continues above the edge of a roof—usually low, but sometimes high and battlemented.
Paten:	A round plate (generally of silver and sometimes footed) used in the consecration and administration of the bread at the celebration of the Holy Communion.
Paten-cover:	A paten (usually of silver) that also serves as a cover for the chalice in the celebration of the Holy Communion.
Pavilion:	A building (frequently small and ornamental), either part of a larger structure or a separate edifice—often found in parks and gardens and frequently provided with a tent-like roof.

259

Pedestal:	The base of an entire column, pier, or pillar (cp. fig. VII).
Pediment:	The triangular face of the gable of a roof, particularly in its classical form with raked and horizontal cornices (cp. fig. VI).
Pier:	An upright structure of masonry serving as a principal support, either isolated or attached to a wall.
Pilaster:	A shallow pier that is attached to a wall and is treated architecturally like a column.
Plate:	The horizontal timber upon which the rafters of a roof rest and to which they are fastened (cp. figures X and XIV).
Plinth:	The bottom (usually square) member of the base of a column or pedestal; also, the bottom block upon which a door trim terminates (cp. figures I and VII).
Puncheon:	A short, upright timber used in framing; or a split log (or slab) with its face smoothed for flooring.
Purlin:	A horizontal member of a roof structure, running from one truss to another, to which other exposed wooden pieces are nailed (cp. figures X and XIV).
Putlock holes:	In a masonry wall, the holes into which the wooden scaffolding (upon which the bricklayers stood during the construction of the wall) was inserted. When the scaffolding was removed, the various holes were frequently left unfilled, much to the delight of our feathered friends.
Quarrel:	A square- or diamond-shaped pane of glass.
Quarter-round:	A convex moulding having the shape of a quarter-circle in section.
Queen closer:	A portion of a brick, smaller than a half-brick (usually occurring at sides of openings or at corners of buildings erected in Flemish bond), that allows the brickmason to use a full header-brick to turn the corner (cp. fig. XI).
Quire:	Cp. *choir.*
Quoin:	The stone or section of brickwork at the external angle of a building that is emphasized by conspicuous jointing, size, texture, or projection (cp. *rustication* and fig. XII).
Rafter:	A supporting timber that is placed immediately below the roofing material or roof boarding of a structure and follows the slope of the roof (cp. figures X and XIV).
Rail:	A brick or capping (usually of wood) supported by a series of posts, as with a row of balusters.

Raked mortar joint:	A joint in masonry that has been cleaned of mortar for a short distance back of its face.
Reredos:	An ornamental screen of wood or stone behind and above the Holy Table.
Reveal:	The depth of wall thickness between its outer face and the frame of a window or door set in an opening.
Ridge beam or pole:	The top horizontal timber (at the peak or ridge of a roof) against which the upper ends of the sloping rafters are fixed (cp. figures X and XIV).
Rim lock:	A lock that is affixed to the surface of a door (rather than let into the edge of the door itself, as in the case of a mortise lock).
Riser:	A vertical member between treads of a stair.
Rood screen:	Carved grillwork (of metal, stone, or wood) separating the chancel from the nave and surmounted by a rood (crucifix or cross).
Rowlock course:	A course or row of bricks in which the headers are turned up so as to rest on the narrow sides (cp. figures IIIc and XI).
Rubbed brick:	Brick that has been selected for color (usually "salmon") and rubbed to a smooth surface, generally occurring at corners and openings of buildings.
Rustication:	Masonry in which the joints of individual stones (or areas of brickwork) are emphasized by deep grooves in order to impart a feeling of massiveness. In the case of stone, the edges may be bevelled or the surfaces roughened. The term, rustication, is also applicable to door or window trim or quoins that are interrupted by large, plain stones.
Salient corner:	A projecting, exterior corner in which the enclosed space is 90 degrees and the outer space 270 degrees in plan.
Sanctuary:	The easternmost portion of the chancel, including the altar and usually separated from the rest of the chancel by a kneeling rail.
Sash:	Each of the two sliding frames of a double-hung window (cp. fig. XI).
Scaffolding holes:	Cp. *putlock holes.*
Sconce:	A bracket fixture on a side wall for holding a candle (or candles).
Scotia:	A concave moulding with a parabolic shape (sometimes a quarter-circle in section). (Cp. fig. VIIIb.)
Sill:	The lowest horizontal member of a timber-framed wall or partition; or the bottom horizontal member of a door or window frame.
Sleeper:	A timber, laid on the ground or in concrete, to which flooring is nailed.

Slip-pew:	A fixed bench with a back and ends, and with the floor beneath the pew usually raised above the flagstones or other flooring of the aisles.
Soffit:	The underside of a projecting surface, usually flat and overhead (as of a lintel or moulding). (Cp. fig. VIIIa.)
Soldier course:	A course or row of bricks in which the longest dimension is vertical—stretchers turned up on their ends (cp. fig. IIId).
Sounding board:	A reflecting structure made up of resonant material and hung above and behind a pulpit (although the acoustical benefits of sounding boards have in the case of many pulpits been denied).
Spandrel:	The (roughly) triangular space between the extrados of an arch and an enclosing right angle (cp. fig. I).
Splay:	A slanting face or surface (bevelled), usually of the embrasure of a window.
Spring-line:	The lowest point of the intrados of an arch, marking the initial rise of the curve (cp. fig. I).
Stopped flute:	A convex section that "stops" the concave flutes.
Strap hinge:	Cp. *hinges.*
Strapwork:	Ornamentation by means of raised bands, notably in Jacobean architecture (cp. fig. XIIIa).
Stretcher:	A brick that is laid on its longest side and has its narrowest dimension in an upright position (cp. fig. IIIa).
String course:	Cp. *belt course.*
Stringer:	The sloping outside support or decorative end face of a stair.
Strut:	A brace (cp. fig. XIV).
Sunburst:	A design (particularly on silver or on the soffit of a pulpit) imitating the sun and its rays.
Surround (noun):	The wood or masonry frame around a panel or an opening.
Tablets:	Wooden slabs hung in a reredos and inscribed with the Decalogue, Lord's Prayer, and Creed.
Table (cap.):	An altar for the celebration of the Holy Communion.
Talon:	A cyma reversa moulding enriched by carving.
Tie-rod:	A steel rod (generally running from one wall to another) that is used to counteract any tendency of the walls to tilt away from each other.
Tenon:	Cp. *mortise.*
Tooled mortar joint:	A joint in masonry that has been made concave or otherwise indented by means of a tool.
Torchere:	A tall, ornamental candle holder (usually surmounted by a spike).
Torus:	A convex, semi-circular moulding, especially that occurring just above the plinth in the base of a classical column (cp. fig. VII).

262

Tracery:	The decorative pattern in a Gothic window, generally formed by curving, interlacing mullions of brick or stone.
Transept:	One of the two (south and north) wings of a cruciform church (cp. fig. V).
Triglyph:	One of a series of projecting blocks on the architrave of the Doric order, usually decorated with two vertical grooves on the face and a half-groove at each side (cp. fig. VII).
Trim (of a window or door):	The moulded frame around an opening—also known as an architrave (cp. fig. XI).
Truss:	A structural framework that is made up of timbers (usually in a combination of triangular forms) and most often supports a roof (cp. fig. XIV).
Tympanum:	The space that is enclosed by the moulded sides of a pediment (cp. fig. VI).
Vaulted ceiling:	An arched ceiling.
Ventilation hole:	A small opening in a brick wall, near the ground, that allows air to circulate in the area beneath the floor of the building.
Verge board:	Cp. *barge board*.
Voussoir:	A wedge-shaped brick or stone forming part of an arch (cp. figures I and XI).
Wainscoting:	Panelling of the lower parts of the walls of a room.
Water table:	The course that connects the thinner, upper wall of a building with the thicker, lower wall (near the ground) and is generally moulded in order to minimize the effects of weathering (cp. fig. IXc).
Wattle-and-daub:	Interwoven twigs (wattle) coated or daubed with mud or clay.
Wicket door:	A small door (with its own hinges) set within a larger door.

FIG. I

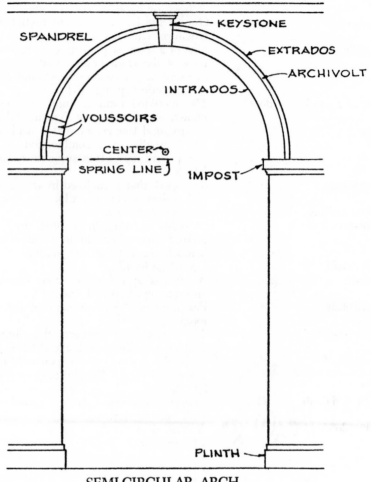

SPANDREL

KEYSTONE

EXTRADOS

ARCHIVOLT

INTRADOS

VOUSSOIRS

CENTER

SPRING LINE

IMPOST

PLINTH

SEMI-CIRCULAR ARCH

FIG. II

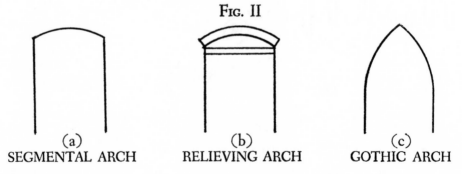

(a)
SEGMENTAL ARCH

(b)
RELIEVING ARCH

(c)
GOTHIC ARCH

264

FIG. III

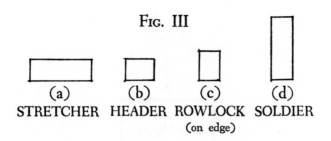

(a)
STRETCHER

(b)
HEADER

(c)
ROWLOCK
(on edge)

(d)
SOLDIER

FIG. IV

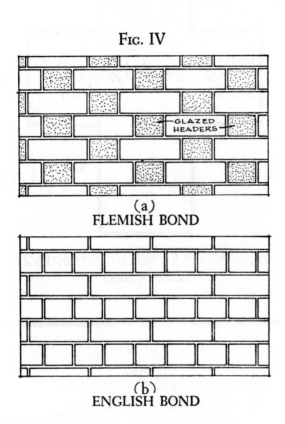

GLAZED
HEADERS

(a)
FLEMISH BOND

(b)
ENGLISH BOND

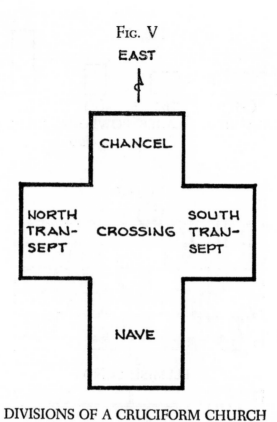

FIG. V

EAST

CHANCEL

NORTH TRAN-SEPT CROSSING SOUTH TRAN-SEPT

NAVE

DIVISIONS OF A CRUCIFORM CHURCH
(Latin Cross)

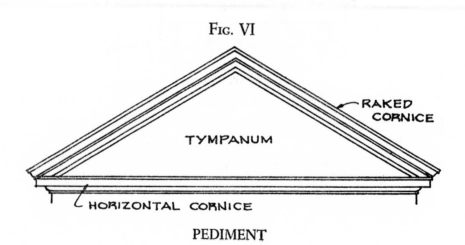

FIG. VI

RAKED CORNICE

TYMPANUM

HORIZONTAL CORNICE

PEDIMENT

Fɪɢ. VII

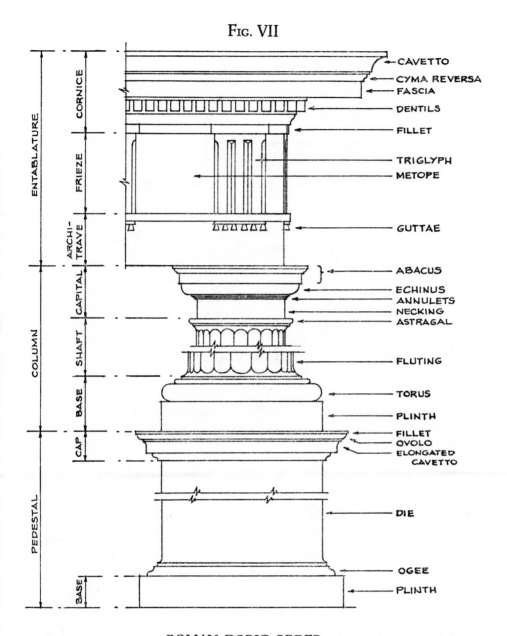

ROMAN DORIC ORDER

FIG. VIII

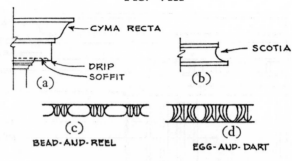

CYMA RECTA

DRIP
SOFFIT

(a)

SCOTIA

(b)

(c)
BEAD-AND-REEL

(d)
EGG-AND-DART

FIG. IX

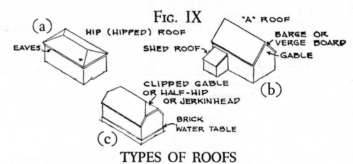

(a)

HIP (HIPPED) ROOF

EAVES

"A" ROOF

BARGE OR
VERGE BOARD

SHED ROOF

GABLE

(b)

CLIPPED GABLE
OR HALF-HIP
OR JERKINHEAD

BRICK
WATER TABLE

(c)

TYPES OF ROOFS

FIG. X

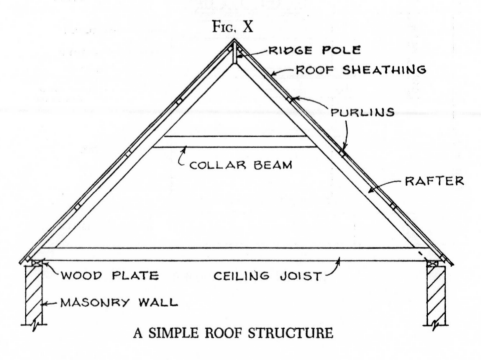

RIDGE POLE

ROOF SHEATHING

PURLINS

COLLAR BEAM

RAFTER

WOOD PLATE

CEILING JOIST

MASONRY WALL

A SIMPLE ROOF STRUCTURE

FIG. XI

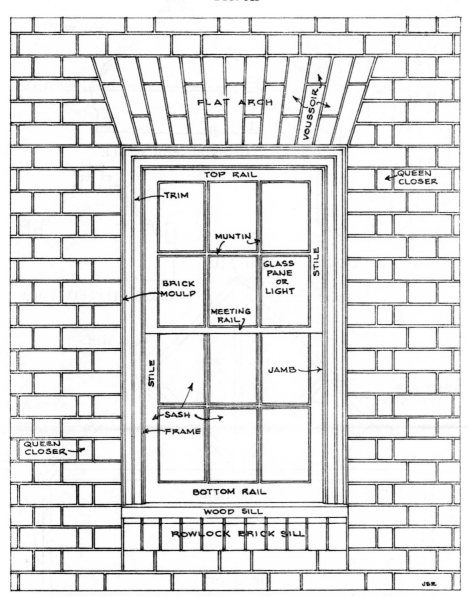

WINDOW WITH FLAT ARCH IN MASONRY WALL

269

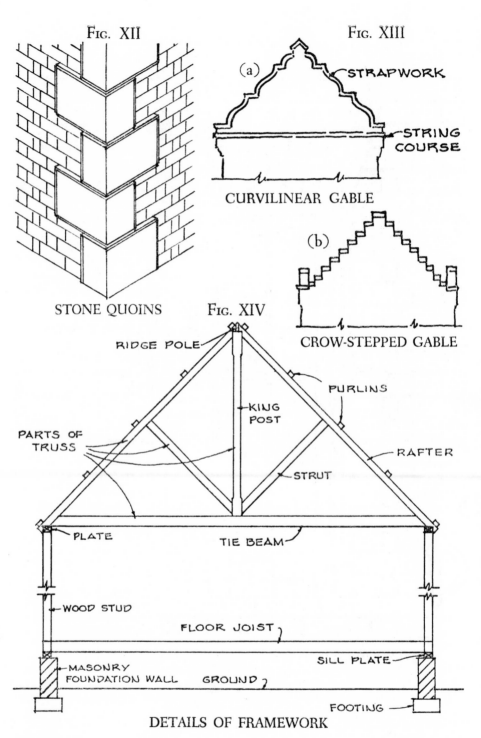

FIG. XII

FIG. XIII

(a)

STRAPWORK

STRING COURSE

CURVILINEAR GABLE

(b)

CROW-STEPPED GABLE

STONE QUOINS

FIG. XIV

RIDGE POLE

PURLINS

KING POST

PARTS OF TRUSS

RAFTER

STRUT

PLATE

TIE BEAM

WOOD STUD

FLOOR JOIST

SILL PLATE

MASONRY FOUNDATION WALL   GROUND

FOOTING

DETAILS OF FRAMEWORK

PARTIAL BIBLIOGRAPHY

*A Brief Sketch of St Peter's Church . . . New Kent County (1957).

*Addleshaw, G. W. O. and Etchells, Frederick, The Architectural Setting of Anglican Worship (1948). London: Faber & Faber Ltd (24 Russell Square, W. C. 1). Around $5.10.

*A History of Abingdon Parish, 1655-1955 (1955), principally by the Rev'd Dr George MacLaren Brydon. White Marsh: Abingdon Parish Church. 50 cents.

Architectural Report on Bruton Parish Church (typescript prepared by Alfred Lawrence Kocher and others). Williamsburg: Colonial Williamsburg, Inc.

*Betjeman, John (ed.), English Parish Churches (1958). New York: McDowell, Obolensky (341 East 62nd Street). $6.50.

Brock, Henry Irving, Colonial Churches in Virginia (1930). Richmond: Dale Press.

*Brydon, George MacLaren, Highlights along the Road of the Anglican Church: The Church of England in England and Her Oldest Daughter, the Protestant Episcopal Church in Virginia (1957). Richmond: The Diocesan Library (110 West Franklin Street). 50 cents.

*Brydon, George MacLaren, Religious Life of Virginia in the Seventeenth Century: The Faith of Our Fathers (1957). Richmond: Garrett & Massie, Inc. (1901 Roane Street). 50 cents.

*Brydon, George MacLaren, Virginia's Mother Church (two volumes, 1947 and 1952). Richmond: The Virginia Historical Society (428 North Boulevard). $17.50.

*Bullock, Helen Duprey, Christ Church Excavations (in Historic Preservation vol. II, no. 4) (1959). Washington: National Trust for Historic Preservation (2000 "K" Street, N.W.). 50 cents.

*Cotter, John L., Archæological Excavations at Jamestown (1958). Washington: National Park Service, Department of the Interior. $2.75.

Dearstyne, Howard, Architectural History of the Wren Building of the College of William and Mary (1950-51) (typescript). Williamsburg: Colonial Williamsburg, Inc.

Dorsey, Stephen P., Early English Churches in America, 1607-1807 (1952). New York: The Oxford University Press.

*Eastman, Reginald W. and Brydon, George MacLaren, an article on the colonial churches in the diocese of Virginia (in The Virginia Churchman, June, 1957). Richmond: The Virginia Churchman (110 West Franklin Street). 25 cents.

Forman, Henry Chandlee, Jamestown and St Mary's (1938). Baltimore: Johns Hopkins Press.

Forman, Henry Chandlee, The Architecture of the Old South: Mediæval Style (1948). Cambridge, Massachusetts: Harvard University Press.

*Forman, Henry Chandlee, Virginia Architecture in the Seventeenth Century (1957). Richmond: Garrett & Massie, Inc. (1901 Roane Street). 50 cents.

*Goodwin, William Archer Rutherfoord, Bruton Parish Church Restored and Its Historic Environment (1907). Williamsburg: Bruton Parish Church. $5.00.

Goodwin, William Archer Rutherfoord and Goodwin, Mary Frances, The Record of Bruton Parish Church (1941). Richmond: The Dietz Press.

*Hatch, Charles E., jr, Jamestown, Virginia (1949). Washington: National Park Service, Department of the Interior. 25 cents.

*Hebron Evangelical Lutheran Church: A Brief History (1953). Madison Courthouse: Hebron Church. 30 cents.

*History of Christ Church, Alexandria (no date).

271

Huddle, W. P., *History of the Hebron Lutheran Church . . . 1717-1907* (1908). New Market: Henkel & Co.

Jones, E. Alfred, *The Old Silver of American Churches* (1913). Privately printed in England for the National Society of the Colonial Dames.

*King, George H. S., *The Register of Overwharton Parish, Stafford County, Virginia 1723-58* (1961). Fredericksburg: The Author (1301 Prince Edward Street). $10.00.

*Kinnear, Duncan Lyle, *Some Events in the History of the Timber Ridge Presbyterian Church and Its Community* (1958). Lexington: Timber Ridge Church (Route #5). 50 cents.

*McGroarty, William Buckner, *The Old Presbyterian Meeting House* (1940). Alexandria: The Meeting House (South Fairfax Street). $2.00.

*Mason, George Carrington, *Colonial Churches of Tidewater Virginia* (1945). Richmond: The Virginia Historical Society (428 North Boulevard). $10.00.

*Mason, George Carrington, various articles on colonial churches in Virginia in *The Virginia Magazine of History and Biography* (volumes LIII, 1 and 4; LIV, 2 and 3; LV, 1 and 2; LVI, 2 and 3; LVII, 3; LVIII, 4; and LXVI, 2). Richmond: The Virginia Historical Society (428 North Boulevard). $2.00 the copy (when available).

Matthews, Joseph C., *Foundations Whose Builder and Maker Is God (A History of Providence Church, Louisa County)* (1959) (typescript). Richmond: Union Theological Seminary.

*Moore, E. W., *History of St John's Church, Richmond* (no date). Richmond: St John's Church. 50 cents.

*Nichols, Janet Bernard, *Sketch of Old Blandford Church* (1957). Petersburg: Old Blandford Church. 50 cents.

*Robinson, Sam, *The Mother-in-Law Tree* (no date). Jamestown: The A. P. V. A. 25 cents.

St Paul's Church 1832, Originally the Borough Church 1739, Elizabeth River Parish, Norfolk, Virginia (1934). Norfolk: St Paul's Church. $2.00.

Saunders, Kirkland Ruffin, *Westover Church and Its Environs* (1937). Richmond: W. M. Brown & Son.

*Scribner, Robert L., *Martin as Merchant, Plus Hope* and *The Old Brick Church* (in *Virginia Cavalcade*, Spring, 1957). Richmond: Virginia State Library. 50 cents.

Slaughter, Philip, *A History of St Mark's Parish, Culpeper County, Virginia* (1877). Baltimore: Innes & Co.

The Church Comes to America (1957). New York: The National Council of the Episcopal Church.

The Historical Church Silver in the Diocese of Southern Virginia (1953). Norfolk: The Museum of Arts and Sciences. $1.00.

*Van Derpool, James Grote and Malone, Dumas, *Historic St Luke's* (no date). Smithfield: St Luke's Church. 35 cents.

Waterman, Thomas Tileston, *The Bruton Church of 1683 and Two Contemporaries* (in *Journal of the American Society of Architectural Historians*, July-October, 1944).

Waterman, Thomas Tileston, *The Mansions of Virginia, 1706-76* (1946). Chapel Hill: The University of North Carolina Press.

*Whiffen, Marcus, *The Public Buildings of Williamsburg* (1958). Williamsburg: Colonial Williamsburg, Inc. $12.50.

*Wyler, Seymour B., *The Book of Old Silver* (1937). New York: Crown Publishers, Inc. $5.00.

*Yonge, Samuel H., *The Site of Old James Towne, 1607-98* (1903). Jamestown: The A.P.V.A. $2.00.

*Presently available for sale

NOTE: Hymns and other poems as well as hymn-tunes have been written in honor of a number of our old churches by George MacLaren Brydon, Vernon Perdue-Davis, Nancy Byrd Turner, George Carrington Mason, Brewster Sherwood Ford, Roberta Newton Taylor, Louisa Venable Kyle, Henry Hallstrom, James Edwin Bethea, James Hail Bennett, John H. Davis, and others. Some of these works are included in the foregoing bibliography; other poems and hymns as well as music are included in the Virginia Music Series (numbers 10, 12, and 14) (at 25 cents the number) of E. C. Schirmer Music Company, 600 Washington Street, Boston 11, Massachusetts.

CORRIGENDA

page 127: Since this report on St John's Church, King William County, was completed, certain repairs have been instituted.

page 150 line 27: The red velvet hanging may possibly be an altar carpet that traditionally covered the Table at all times and frequently hung to the floor on all sides.

page 166 line 13: The pulpit in the 1772 structure stood in all probability on the south wall facing the north wing, as with the other T-shaped churches in colonial Virginia.

page 168 line 15: The gift of King George VI is a Prayer-Book from the reign of William III rather than a Bible.

INDEX

NOTE: Most of our churches are of brick and most of the brick churches are laid principally in Flemish bond; and all of the brick churches have been re-pointed and are characterized by queen closers, glazed headers, and rubbed brick in varying proportions. All our churches have been repaired in some way, great or small, and nearly all of them have been adversely affected by the Disestablishment, the Revolution, and the War Between the States (and, in some instances, also by the War of 1812). Most of the churches were originally and still are Anglican. Owing to these several conditions, it has not been found practicable to itemize in the following index the countless references to Flemish bond, glazed headers, rubbed brick, repairs, repointing, the effects of the Disestablishment and the several wars, or the Anglican (Episcopal) Church. They must rather be sought in the individual articles. The appendices (with information for visitors and lists of vestry-books and registers) are likewise not indexed. For convenience' sake, the various makers of our colonial silver are all listed under silversmiths. In references to certain architectural and liturgical features of the buildings, emphasis has been placed upon the surviving colonial examples.

A

Abingdon Church 1, 59, 113, 131, 199-204
Accomack County and Parish *see* Pungoteague Church
Ace of Clubs Church 152
Acquinton Church 127, 131, 133
Æolian-Skinner organ 76
Africa, missionary to 215
age of colonial churches 1, 4-9, 15-17
aisles *see* flagstones
Albemarle County 1, 174, 175, 177
Albemarle Parish (Sussex County) 197, 198
Alexander, John 219
Alexandria 186, 228, 230, 231, 232 *see also* Christ Church *and the* Meeting House
All Saints' Church *see* Hickory Neck Church
altar *see* chancel
Ambler, John 24
Amelia County 16
American Institute of Architects 76
Andrewes, Bishop 30
Andros, Governor Sir Edmund 77
Andrus, The Rev'd Mr 215
Anglican charity 161, 171
Anglican divinity school 105
Anglican faith 1, 12, 14, 26-27, 37, 198
Appomattox Parish 50, 185, 212
Appomattox River 138, 168
apse 152
Aquia Church 1, 11, **184-196**, 215, 228, 230
Aquia stone 138, 221, 224, 228, 230 *see also* Aquia Church
Archæological Excavations at Jamestown 10, 20-21
arches (masonry) of doorways:
  flat 3, 28-29, 34, 43-44, 54, 60, 91, 98, 112, 115, 122, 129, 140, 142, 189, 200, 213, 217, 226, 230, 234

segmental 3, 43, 52, 82, 87
semi-circular 3, 7, 19, 22, 28, 29, 33, 34, 59, 69, 91, 97, 107, 115, 117, 121, 129, 136, 139-140, 173, 197, 200, 209, 240
arches (masonry) of windows:
  flat 3, 44, 111, 130, 134-135, 181, 184, 187-188, 217, 220, 222, 236, 240
  lancet 3, 22, 33
  Palladian 220-221, 223, 230
  segmental 3, 43-44, 92, 111, 130, 143, 149-150, 213
  semi-circular 3, 19, 28-29, 33, 42, 60, 69, 81-82, 87, 92, 97, 99-100, 107, 114, 117, 123, 129-130, 134-135, 140, 146, 154, 164, 173, 187-188, 197, 201, 209, 213, 217, 220, 222, 223, 226, 229, 240
  surrounds (circular) 39, 55, 60, 69, 97, 99, 108, 130, 154-155, 209, 222
  surrounds (elliptical) 33, 87, 108, 123, 222
  no masonry arches 54, 141
Argall, Governor Samuel 5
Ariss, John 225, 240
Armistead, Mr 86
arms, royal 19, 22, 77, 109
army signal corps 166
Arnold, Benedict 166
Arnold's Corner 212
Ascensiontide 1607 26-27
Ashland 103, 142
Assawaman Church 152, 153
Associate Reformed Presbyterian Church 207
Association for the Preservation of Virginia Antiquities 18, 20, 21, 24, 25, 61, 102, 126
Augusta Academy 207
Augusta County 17, 243 *see also* Augusta Stone Church
Augusta Military Academy 180, 182
Augusta Parish 243

275

Augusta Stone Church 1, 12, 77, 88, 180-183, 205
Aylett 184

B

Bacon, Nathaniel sr 78
Bacon's Castle 196
Bacon's Rebellion 14, 21, 24
baldachino 173
Ball family 165
ballast, legend about bricks for 1
Baltimore 84, 165, 204
balusters 34, 35, 230 *see also* chancels *and* galleries
Bank of Southside Virginia 30
Banqueting Hall (1622) 2
Baptist church 127
Baptists 12, 14, 88, 99, 113, 115, 132, 155, 175, 184, 214
Baptists (colored) 112, 155
bar, wooden 29
barge-board 28, 52, 91
Barradall, Edward 79
Bath Parish 138
battens 9, 53
battlement *see* crenellation
Bayside 133
Bedford, England 212
Belle Air 119
bells 1, 4, 20, 40, 46-47, 67, 155, 167
belt course 3, 19, 51-52, 188
Bennett's Creek Church *see* Glebe Church
Berkeley 119
Berkeley, Lady 23
Berkeley, Sir William 62
Berkshire, England 199
Bermuda Hundred 138
Bethel Church *see* Flat Rock Church
Bibles 25, 30, 36, 77, 94, 113, 116, 150, 168, 174, 183, 227
Birdsnest 171
Blair children 20
Blair, the Rev'd Commissary James 23-24, 63
Bland, Colonel Richard 140
Blandford Church 11, **138-142**
Blisland Parish 41, 96 *see also* Hickory Neck Church
Blue Ridge 162
Bluestone Church 15-16
Bodleian Library, Oxford 106-107
Bodmin, Cornwall 233
Bolles collection 35
Bon Air 171
bonds, common and irregular 51, 139, 221, 235-237 *see also* English bond
books *see* Bibles; documents, ecclesiastical; Prayer-Books; *and* vestry-books and registers
Borough Church 11, 136, **153-157**
boroughs (four) of 1618   25, 168
Botetourt, Governor Lord 110
Boush, Colonel Samuel 156
Boydton 16
Braddock's army 218

Brady photographs 46, 217
Braine, Sarah 118
Brandon Church 30
brass alms basons 36-37
Braxton, Carter 132
Bray, David 79
"Brick Church", confusion over 12, 31, 138
brick churches 1, 6
bricks, dating 7-8, 36, 80, 86, 106, 111, 148, 156, 184, 199, 209
Bridger, Colonel Joseph 8-9, 36
Bridgetown 171, 173, 174
Bristol, England 48, 119, 138
Bristol Parish 15, 28, 168 *see also* Blandford Church
British forces 101, 147, 218
Broken-Back'd Church 41
Brooke 185
Brown, T. A. 111
Brunswick County 16, 31, 197
Brunswick Parish 225
Bruton Parish and Church 1, 9, 11, 13, 24, 25, 60, **62-80**, 106, 108, 109, 110, 117, 213, 234
Brydon, the Rev'd Dr George MacLaren 14, 26-27, 49, 215
Buck, the Rev'd Master 5
Buck Mountain Church 1, **174-177**
bullet holes 147, 226
Burrowsville 30
Burwell family 203, 204
buttress 4, 20-21, 22, 32
Byrd, Colonel William 119

C

calendar 13-14, 185
Calvinistic Churches 14, 207
cames 3, 21, 25, 44
cannonball 156
Cape Henry 26, 99, 119, 137-138
Carlyle, John 219
Caroline County 78, 95
Carter, Robert 120
Carter's Creek 204
Cary, Henry jr 106
casements 3, 44, 48
cathedral 12
Cattail Church 11, 132, **183-184**
Cedar Creek 208
ceilings, beamed 4
cement 34, 43, 107, 115, 164
Centerville 96
Central Garage 111, 127, 184
Chambers, Edward 104
Chance 95
chancel 4, 5, 13, 21-22, 74-76, 93 *see also* panels, raised; pulpits; *and* reredoses
chancel screen 4, 5, 35, 82-83, 88
Chanco 22
chandeliers 4
Chapel of the College of William and Mary 105-110
chapels 11
chapels of ease 13

Charles City (early settlement) 139
Charles City County 25, 103, 138, 157 *see also* Westover Parish Church
Charles Parish 41
Charles River County *see* York County
Charles II 12
Charlottesville 174, 177
Chase City 15-16
Chesapeake Bay 137-138
Chesapeake and Ohio Railway 102
Chesapeake & Western Railway 180
chest 88-89
Chesterfield County 15, 138, 139, 168, 169-170
Chicacone Parish 50
Chickahominy Parish *see* Wallingford Parish
Chickahominy River 25
child's drawing (1856) 107
chimney 4
Chinese Corner 133
Chippoaks Parish 197
Chiskiack Parish 38, 62
Choatanck Parish 212
choir 5, 13, 74-75
Chowning, Carroll C. 85
Christ Church, Alexandria 62, 95, 214, 216, 219, 219-225, 228, 230, 231, 236
Christ Church, Charlottesville 175
Christ Church, Eastville 174
Christ Church, Lancaster County 1, 11, 59, 73, 120-127, 230 *see also* St Mary's Whitechapel
Christ Church, Middlesex County 11, 12, 15, 80-86, 86, 88, 108, 136, 162-163
Christ Church, Norfolk 155
Christ Church, Smithfield 37
Christ Church, Sussex County, Delaware 180
Christchurch School (and village) 12, 80
Christopher, David 16
Chuckatuck Church (and village) 11, 88, 117, 148, 182, 208-211
Church of the Good Shepherd, Petersburg 142
Churchill, Prime Minister 224
Churchmen of Virginia 169
Cismont 175
Clack, the Rev'd James 58, 61
Claiborne, William 22
clapboards 3
Classical Society of Virginia 22
Classical style *see* styles of architecture
Clay, Henry 105
clerk 13, 28, 73, 171, 183
Clough, Parson John 23
Coast Guard Reserve Training Center 38
Cocke, Dr William 78
Colonial Dames 32, 169-170, 176
Colonial National Historical Park 138
Colonial Williamsburg, Inc. 37, 68, 105
Communion, Holy 5, 26, 110
Confederate Fort 10 *see also* Jamestown Church
Confederate Home Guard 57
Confederate Monument 79, 242-243
Confederate museum 141

confirmation service, first in Virginia 40
Congress, The 224
Copein, William 185, 228, 231
Cople Parish *see* Yeocomico Church
corbels 34, 43, 51
cornices (eaves) 4, 48, 69, 92, 104, 112, 126, 144, 164, 178, 190, 230
cornices (interior) 194, 222-223, 227, 230
Cornwall, England 233
coronae lucis 40, 234
Corotoman Neck 165
coterminous parishes and counties 11-12
Cotter, John L. 10, 21
court records 7
Courtland 198
Craig, Parson John 180, 182, 183
Cram, Ralph Adams 22
cratchets *see* crucks
crenellation 4, 32
Cromwell, Oliver 14, 30, 118
cross 137-138, 169, 170 *see also* shapes of churches
crow-stepped gables *see* gables
cruciform churches *see* shapes of churches
crucks 3, 5
crypt 72, 75, 193
Culpeper County 158, 159, 225, 239, 240, 242
Cumberland Parish, Lunenburg County 16
Cumnor 113
Curle's Church 168, 170
curvilinear gables *see* gables
cushion for sermon 13
Custis, George Washington Parke 231

D

Dahlgren 211
Dale, Sir Thomas 5, 169
Dale Parish 15, 138, 168
Dale's Gift 151
damages to colonial churches 14-15
date of construction *see* age of colonial churches
Daughters of Founders and Patriots of America 218
Daughters of the American Colonists 137
Davies, the Rev'd Samuel 180
Dawn 111
de la Warr, Lord 5
Declaration of Independence 132, 157, 167
Decorated style of architecture *see* styles of architecture
deeds 8
Delafiae, Reynard 195
Delaware 180
Dennis, Thomas 35
Dettingen Parish 195
Dew, Thomas Roderick 110
diamond panes *see* panes
diapering 3, 52, 172
Dinwiddie County 15, 138
Diocesan Library, Richmond 147
Disciples of Christ 12, 105

277

Disestablishment, exemptions from effects of 94, 120, 148
District of Columbia 224
documents, ecclesiastical 161, 183
Donation farm 134
door trim 29, 34, 53-54, 72, 92, 93, 95, 104, 122-123, 130, 144, 176, 195, 200-201, 223
doors 29, 53-54, 92-93, 104, 122, 130, 144, 223
doorways, unadorned 3, 7, 19, 29, 30, 69, 87, 107, 136 *see also* arches (masonry) of doorways
doorways with pediments and pilasters 2, 3, 34, 53-55, 59-60, 91, 97-98, 100, 115, 117, 121-122, 129, 144, 146, 155, 189, 200, 209, 212, 213, 214, 217, 221, 226, 229
Doswell 142
Driver (village) 148, 208
Driver family 8, 9
Dumfries 195
Dunmore, Lord 156
Dutch Gap Canal 169

E

Earlysville 174, 175
East Lynnhaven Parish 15
East (or Lower) Parish, Nansemond County 150, 208
Eastern Shore brickwork 7
Eastern Shore Chapel 11, 15, 136, 137
Eastern Shore churches 9, 99 *see also* Pungoteague *and* Hungars Churches
Eastville 174
eaves, kick at the 7, 30, 56, 88, 126, 140-141, 160
Edward VII 77
Eisenhower, President 224
Elay-Swan tract 10
Elizabeth I 2
Elizabeth II 118
Elizabeth, Princess 99
Elizabeth City County 99, 153
Elizabeth City Parish Church 11, 40, 64, 99-103, 106
Elizabeth River Parish Church *see* Borough Church
Elmwood 94
Emmanuel Church, Jenkins Bridge 153
England 1, 13, 35, 36, 43, 44, 50, 62, 95, 96, 198, 199, 212
English bond 1, 19, 42, 45, 51, 57, 86-87, 139, 167, 197, 216 *see also* bonds
English bond below the water table 28, 69, 90, 96, 99, 106, 111, 117, 128, 134, 142, 146, 148, 153, 163, 233
entrances, three 59, 172-173
Epiphany Chapel 15
Episcopal Church *see* Established Church
Essex County 146 *see also* Vawter's Church
Established Church 1, 14, 76, 132, 170, 239
Evelynton 119
Evensong 13, 76, 171

F

Fairfax County and Parish *see* the Falls Church; Christ Church (Alexandria); Pohick Church; *and the* Meeting House
Fairfax of Cameron, the Rev'd Baron 224
Fairfield 181, 205, 207
Falls Church, the 11, 12, 216-219, 219, 220, 222, 226, 228, 229, 231, 241
Farnham Church (and village) 11, 12, 145-147
Farrar's Island 168-169
Fauquier, Governor Francis 78
Fauquier County 242
Felton 67
fenestration, unusual 54, 134
First & Citizens National Bank, Alexandria 224
Fishersville 16
Fishing Point churches 10
Fitzhugh, Henry 215
flags 109, 234
flagstones 4, 29, 60, 84, 93, 118, 126, 132, 164, 193, 199, 202, 211, 218, 230
Flat Rock Church, Cumberland Parish 16
Flemish bond 1, 2, 3 *see also* Note (above) *and* bonds
Flemish gables *see* gables
Flounder House 239
Fluvanna Parish 175
Foch, Marshal 224
fonts 5, 25, 36, 55, 57, 77, 85, 94, 116, 126, 137, 145, 164, 231
footings *see* foundations
Fork Church 11, 116, 142-145
Fort Defiance *see* Augusta Stone Church
Fort Story 138
foundations 6, 20, 21, 24, 39, 63, 66, 96, 104, 157, 163, 167, 172, 176, 177, 199, 211, 235, 236
fragments of colonial structures 1
frame churches *see* wooden churches
Frederick Parish 243
Fredericksburg 84, 158, 165, 185, 186, 195, 212, 225
Fredericksville Parish *see* Buck Mountain Church
Freeman, Douglas Southall 79
French, Daniel 228, 232
French and Indian War 205, 218
French Huguenots *see* Huguenots
French language 170-171
furniture 35-36, 76, 88-89

G

gables: clipped 88, 117, 182, 210
crow-stepped 2, 22, 32, 52
Flemish (curvilinear) 2, 3, 42-43, 48
galleries 4, 5-6, 13, 19, 29, 66, 94, 104, 125-126, 131, 140, 144-145, 158-159, 164, 178-179, 185, 194, 202-203, 237
Garden Club of Virginia 84
Garden Club of Warrenton 243

Garnett family 94
Garter, Order of the 77
General Assembly of Virginia 5, 9, 14, 63, 155, 163, 169, 214
George I 99
George III 77
George VI 168
Georgian style *see* styles of architecture
German Chapel *see* Hebron Church
German Reformed miners 96, 158
German school, language, people *see* Hebron Church
Germanna 96, 158
glazed headers 3
Glebe Church 11, 12, 148-150, 211
glebe farms and houses 57, 95, 119, 161, 163, 173, 198, 204, 218
Gloucester County 38 *see also* Ware *and* Abingdon Churches
Gloucester Courthouse 58, 69, 204
Golden, John 36
goldsmiths *see* silversmiths
Gooch, Lady 109
Goochland County 168, 175
Goodwin, the Rev'd Dr William Archer Rutherfoord 68, 78
Gothic style *see* styles of architecture
governor's pew 73, 74, 76
Grace Church *see* York-Hampton Parish Church
Graves, Alexander 80
graveyards *see* tombstones and graveyards
Great Fork Church 239
Greek cross *see* shapes of churches
Green, Samuel 75, 76
Green Spring 24
Green Springs Parish 175
Greene County 175
Greenwood Parish 175
Grub Hill Church 16
guillotine windows 3, 29, 44, 60, 201, 218
Gum Springs 177, 179
Gum Tree 142
Gunston Hall 232
gutters (base-of-wall) 65, 187

H

Hacker, Henry 78
Hague 57
Hakluyt, the Rev'd Richard 26
Hamilton Parish 195, 228
Hampton (city) 40 *see also* Elizabeth City Parish Church
Hampton Parish *see* York-Hampton Parish
Hancock, John 157
Hancock, Maryland 95
Handel 67
hanging pews 66, 134, 148, 155, 164
hangings for altar 36, 150, 174
Hanover County 41, 174, 178, 233 *see also* Slash *and* Fork Churches
Hanover Parish 89, 95, 225, 227
hardware 3, 25, 29, 53-54, 60, 72, 92-93, 122, 144, 167, 173, 202, 215

Harrison, Presidents Benjamin and William Henry 119
Harrisonburg 159
Harrison's Landing 119
Harrop Parish 25, 62
Hartfield 86
Hatch, Charles E jr 39
Hazel River 239
Hebron Church 1, 11, 158-162
Henrico, University and College of 170
Henrico Parish Church 1, 11, 118, 165-171
"Henricopolis" 169
Henry, Patrick 104, 145, 166
Henry, Prince 137, 169
Hepburn, Parson S. S. 145
Hepburn, Katharine 145
Hermitage Baptist Church, Church View 15
Herring Creek 116
Hickory Neck Academy *see* Hickory Neck Church
Hickory Neck Church 11, 39, 232-235
hinges *see* hardware
Hipkins, John 80, 129
hipped roofs 107, 126, 146, 152, 164, 190, 214, 217, 222, 227, 230, 236, 241
History of Abingdon Parish, A 14
Hobart, Bishop 94, 214
Hoffnungsvolle Kirche, Die 161
Hog Island 197
Hogg, Thomas 114
Holladay, Anthony and Esther 209
Hopewell 27, 116, 139
House of Burgesses, Williamsburg 63
Houston, President Sam 207
Huguenots 170-171
Hughes, William 42
Hungars Parish Church 11, 13, 59, 171-174
Hunt, Parson Robert 5, 137 *see also* Jamestown Church
Hunt Shrine 10 *see also* Jamestown Church
Hunting Creek 228
hymns 13 *see also* instruments, musical; music; *and* psalms, metrical

I

illumination *see* lights (illumination)
imposts 19, 30, 33, 135, 173
Independents 118
Indian names 11, 31, 50, 86, 99, 111, 151, 172, 186, 208-209, 228
Indian wars 8, 19, 103, 205, 218
initials on brick or stone 7-8, 32, 36, 45, 52, 80, 86, 102, 106, 113, 114, 156, 209, 218, 221, 230, 241
instruments, musical 13, 35, 38, 67, 74, 75, 76, 95, 145, 160, 224, 238 *see also* bells; organs; *and* pitch-pipes
Irvington 120
Isle of Wight County *see* Newport Parish Church
Ivy Depot 175
Ivy Parish 175

J

Jacobean style *see* styles of architecture
James I 76, 99, 137, 169
James City County 38, 40, 41, 62, 103, 197 *see also* Jamestown, Bruton Parish, *and* Hickory Neck Churches
James City Parish 11, 12, 197 *see also* Jamestown Church
James Fort 10 *see also* Jamestown Church
James River 6, 10, 28, 31, 62, 116, 118, 119, 168, 169, 170, 171, 174, 197 *see also* Jamestown Church
"James River Parish" 168
Jamestown Island (or Peninsula) 6, 32, 62, 119, 137 *see also* Jamestown Church
Jamestown (Tower) Church 1, 4-7, 9, 10, 12, 18-27, 30, 32, 63, 77, 87
Jefferson (village) 170
Jefferson, President Thomas 105, 109
Jefferson's Church 139
Jenings, Governor Edmund 78
Jenkins Bridge 153
"jerks" 207
Johnson, W. 80
Johnston, J. Ambler 49
Jones, Inigo 2
Jones, Orlando 78
Jones, the Rev'd Rowland 78
Jordan's Parish 28

K

kalendar *see* calendar
Kecoughtan Church 99
Keller 151
Kenbridge 16
Kennon, Richard 106
Kent, England 43
Kentucky 207
Key, Francis Scott 216
keystones 52, 121, 123, 135, 173, 188, 189, 190, 200, 201, 220, 221, 229, 230
Kilmarnock 120
kilns, brick 1, 49, 50, 196, 216
King, George H. S. 195
King and Queen County 64, 95, 233 *see also* Upper Church, Stratton Major *and* Lower Church, St Stephen's
King George County 89, 146 *see also* St Paul's *and* Lamb's Creek Churches
King William County 95, 113, 233 *see also* St John's, Acquinton, Mangohick, *and* Cattail Churches
King William Parish 170
Kingston Parish 59, 61, 62
Kirk (S.) and Son, Baltimore 84

L

Ladies' Memorial Association 141
Lamb's Creek Church 11, 225-227, 240
Lancaster County and Parish 1, 38, 85, 145, 146 *see also* Christ Church, Lancaster *and* St Mary's Whitechapel

Lancaster Parish (Middlesex County) 80, 85, 86, 162
lancets 22, 33
Latin 48, 116, 126
Latin cross *see* cross *and* shapes of churches
Lawne's Creek Parish 25, 197
lay-reader *see* clerk
lead 44, 80 *see also* cames
Lee, Colonel 192
Lee, General Robert E. 192, 208, 224
Lee, William Ludwell 24
Leedstown 211
legends 1, 18, 181
Leslie's Illustrated 69, 100
Lexington 205, 207, 208
Liberty Hall 207
Lightfoot, Colonel Francis 118
lighthouses 138, 169
lights (glass) *see* panes
lights (illumination) 4, 76, 126
"lining-out" the psalms 13
Lititz, Pennsylvania 160
Little Fork Church 11, 225, 239-243
Little Fork Rangers 242-243
Littleton 198
liturgical colors 76-77
Lively 162
Liverpool 156
Lloyd George, Prime Minister 224
lofts *see* galleries
London 162, 171, 197 *see also* silver
London Bridge 137
Long Tom 232
Loretto 89
Louisa County 1, 174, 175 *see also* Providence Church
Lower Chapel (or Church), Middlesex County 1, 11, 86-89, 117, 182 *see also* Christ Church, Middlesex
Lower Church, St Stephen's Parish 11, 64, 96, 98, 113-116, 145
Lower Norfolk Parish and County 134, 153, 208
lower parish or church (or chapel) 13
Lower Southwark Church 11, 84, 136, 196-198, 216
Lübeck, Germany 160
Ludwell, Thomas 62
Ludwell-Statehouse 23
Lumsden (Charles) and Sons 85
Lunenburg County 15-16
Lunenburg Parish, Richmond County 89, 146, 147
Luray 17
Lutheran Church *see* Hebron Church
Lutheran congregation 110 *see also* Hebron Church
Lyells 50
Lynchburg 17
Lynn, Norfolk, England 134
Lynnhaven Parish 15, 153 *see also* Old Donation Church
Lynnhaven River 11, 133, 137

M

Macclesfield 35
Machipongo 171
Madison, Bishop 110
Madison, Dolley 104, 145
Madison, President 180
Madison County 242 *see also* Hebron Church
Magothy Bay Church 174
Maidens 171
Major family 96
Manakin Church 170-171
Mangohick Church 11, **111-112**, 132
Mapsico Church 118
Margaret 119
Marine Base (Quantico) 196
marl church 1, 9, 39, 40
Marl Hill 46, 47
Marston Parish 62, 77
Martinsville 167
Martin's Brandon Parish 28, 30, 118
Martin's Hundred Parish 38, 40, 103
Maryland 1, 151, 152, 172
Mason, George 216, 228, 232
Mason, George Carrington 6, 49
Mason Parish 175
Masonic order 238
Mathews County 59
Mattaponi Church *see* Lower Church, St Stephen's Parish
Mattaponi River 133, 233
Matthews, the Rev'd Joseph C. 178
Mattins 13
Mauck Meeting House 17
Meade, Bishop 214, 223
Mechumps Chapel 104
Mecklenburg County 15-16
mediæval style *see* styles of architecture
Meese, Colonel Henry 185
Meeting House, Alexandria 12, 219, 220, 221, 222, 235-239
meeting houses *see* Lutheran *and* Presbyterian Churches
Merchant's Hope Church 3, 4, 7, 9, 11, 19, 27-30, 88, 126, 139, 141
Merrimac 157
Merryoaks Church 104
Metamorphoses (Ovid) 22
Methodists 12, 57, 61, 86, 88, 98, 105, 132, 214, 242
Michie's Tavern 175
Middle Plantation Parish 38, 82 *see also* Bruton Parish Church
Middlesex County *see* Christ Church *and* Lower Chapel
Middleton, the Rev'd Dr Arthur Pierce 234
Middletown Parish *see* Bruton Parish Church
millstone 55
Minetree, David 113
Mitchells Presbyterian Church 159
Mobile, Alabama 77
Moncure, Parson John 193
"Moncure, Race of the House of" 191
Monro, Mrs 78
Monroe, President 180

Monticello Parish 175
Monumental Church, Richmond 25
Moony, T. E. 111
Moore, Mrs Charles Beatty 85
Morris, James 63
Morris, Samuel 177
mortar joints 7, 19
mortar wash 34
Moscow 17
Mossom, the Rev'd David 48
Mother-in-law tree 24
mouldings *see* doorways (wooden, pedimented, and unadorned); galleries; pulpits; *and* reredoses
Mount Church 95
Mount Holly 57
Mount Pleasant 207
Mount Prospect 41
Mount Sinai Baptist Church (colored) 184
Mount Sterling 119
Mount Vernon 228, 230, 232
Muddy Creek Church 225, 227
mullions 71
murals 159-160, 227
music 2, 183 *see also* bells; instruments, musical; *and* pitch-pipes

N

names of churches 11-12
Nansemond County 153 *see also* Glebe *and* Chuckatuck Churches
Nansemond River 148, 150
Nassawaddox 171
National Anthem 216
National Park Service 18, 24, 25
Naval Mine Depot 201
Naval Operating Base 157
nave 13
Navy, U. S. 136
Nelson, Chancellor Robert 110
Nelson tombs 40
Neve Parish 175
New Kent County 10, 25, 78, 96, 233 *see also* St Peter's Parish Church
New Norfolk County 153
New Poquoson Parish 41
New Testament 25
New Year's Day 13
Newport, Captain Christopher 5, 31
Newport News 31
Newport Parish Church 3, 4, 6, 7-9, 11, 12, 19, 22, 24, 31-38, 63, 141
Nicholson, Governor Francis 39
Nomini Church 57
Nominy Parish 50, 185, 212
Norfolk (city) 133, 204 *see also* Borough Church
Norfolk County 153
Norfolk Museum of Arts and Sciences 137, 150, 157
North Anna River 142
North Farnham Parish Church *see* Farnham Church

Northampton County 151 *see also* Hungars Parish Church
Northumberland County 38, 50, 162, 165, 212
Nott, Governor Edward 79
Nottoway Parish, Southampton County 31
Nottoway Parish Church, Courtland 198
Nuswattocks Parish *see* Pungoteague *and* Hungars Churches

O

"Oak Shade", erroneous use of 242
Occahannock Parish 151
Occoquan Church 228
Occupacia Creek 89, 95
Oceana 15
Oddenino, Giuseppe 159
Old Church *see* Upper Church, Stratton Major Parish *and* Slash Church
Old Donation Church 65, 133-138
Old St John's Church *see* St John's Church, King William County *and* Henrico Parish Church
Old Side-New Side (Old Lights-New Lights) controversy 182-183, 206
Old-Style calendar *see* calendar
Old Testament names 11
oldest Episcopal Church in continuous use 80
Onley 152
Orange County 239, 243
Orchard Run 10
organs *see* instruments, musical
Oriental rugs 36, 76
orientation of churches by canon law and exceptional instances 13, 158, 177, 181, 205, 208, 238
ornaments, brick 52, 135, 156, 173
Orthodox churches 17
Otter River Church 15-16
Overwarten, Overwoorten, and Over Worton *see* Aquia Church
Overwharton Parish 228 *see also* Aquia Church
Ovid 22
Owens 212
Oxford, England 184-185, 199

P

Page, Gregory 110
Page, John 79
Page, Mrs John 77
Page, Thomas Nelson 145
Painter 151
Palace at Williamsburg 63
palisades 3, 10
Palladian windows *see* arches of windows
Pamunkey Neck Chapel 127
Pamunkey River 41, 127, 133, 142, 233
panels, raised 3, 60 *see also* chancels; doors; galleries; pews; pulpits; *and* reredoses
panes (glass) 3, 25, 29, 60, 71, 93, 123, 144, 173, 195, 201, 218, 223, 237

parish church, the 13, 136, 216
Parke, Daniel 78
Parsons, James 219
patriotic shrines *see* Jamestown, Bruton, Henrico, Christ Church (Alexandria), *and* Pohick Churches, *and the* Meeting House
Peaks 103
Peanckatanck (Piankatank) Parish 80, 86, 162
Peasley School 204
pediments 3 *see also* doorways with pediments and pilasters
Pelham, Peter 67
Pendleton, Edmund 78
Perry, Captain William 118
Petersburg *see* Blandford Church
Petsworth Parish 13, 59, 61, 80, 202
pews 4, 5, 13, 93, 124-125, 144, 158, 167, 172, 179, 192-193, 202-203, 223-224, 237
pewter 137, 160-161 *see also* silver
Pharnham 146, 147
Philadelphia 40
pilasters 3 *see also* doorways with pediments and pilasters
Pinchbeck, Thomas 104
pitch-pipes 13
Pitman's Corner 120
plaster 4, 21, 34
Pocahontas, Princess 5, 22
Poe, Edgar Allan 167
Pohick Church 11, 185, 217, 219, 222, 226, 228-232, 241
porches *see* towers and porches
Port Royal 89, 95
Portland stone 29, 164
Portland Parish Church 15, 153
Potomac Beach 211
Potomac Church 185
Potomac Parish 50, 184, 212
Potomac River 186, 211, 216
Potomac region 2
Pott, John 22
Powell, Benjamin 67
Power, Tyrone 141
Powhatan County 170
Pratt, Harden deVoe 49, 56
Prayer-Books 25, 36, 77, 174, 227
Presbyterian churches 16 *see also* Augusta Stone, Providence, Timber Ridge, *and the* Meeting House
Presbyterian hymnals 110
Presbyterian schoolmaster 47
Presbyterians 1, 12, 13, 14, 49, 118, 182-183, 206-207
Prince George County 118 *see also* Merchant's Hope *and* Blandford Churches
Prince George's Chapel, Delaware 180
Prince William County 195, 232
Princess Anne County 15, 153 *see also* Old Donation Church
projecting bricks *see* ornaments, brick
Providence Church 1, 177-180
Providence Forge 41
proportions, geometrical 64, 106
psalms, metrical 13, 22, 183, 207

Public Buildings of Williamsburg, The 64
pulpits 2, 4, 5, 13, 94, 125, 144, 167, 191-192, 223
pulpits, location of 83
puncheons 3
Pungoteague Church (and village) 9, 11, 150, 151-153
Purbeck stone 108
Puritan rule 14, 30, 118

Q

Quaker meeting house 17
Quakers 12
Quantico Church 195
Quantico Marine Base 196
quarrels *see* panes
queen closers, capricious use of 60, 65, 99
queen closers, irregular use of 65-66, 135
quire *see* choir
quoins, brick 2, 3, 9, 32
quoins, stone *see* stone ornamentation

R

Raleigh Parish 138
Randolph family 110
Rapidan River 96, 158, 239
Rappahannock Academy 95
Rappahannock County (modern) 242
Rappahannock County (old) 89, 145-146, 162, 225
Rappahannock River 80, 89, 146, 162, 163, 211, 239
Ravenscroft, Thomas 140
Rawlings and Wilson, Architects 18
reading-desks *see* pulpits
rectangular churches *see* shapes of churches
Reformed Episcopal congregation 132
registers *see* appendix II
reredoses 122-123, 130-131, 185, 190-191, 201-202, 223, 241
restorations 17, 20-21, 22, 32, 34, 35-36, 37-38, 42-44, 46, 47, 48, 49, 55-56, 64-65, 68-69, 70-76, 79-80, 84, 105, 107-109, 147, 158, 159, 160, 172-173, 217, 218, 230, 231, 234, 236, 238
Richards, Mourning 185
Richardson, Richard C. 47
Richmond (city) 18, 25, 84-85, 88, 147, 179 *see also* Henrico Parish Church
Richmond County 89, 211, 225 *see also* Farnham Church
Rixeyville 225, 240, 242
Robious 170
Robinson, Sam 24
Robinson River 161
Rockbridge County 181 *see also* Timber Ridge Church
Rolfe, John 5, 22
Rome, Italy 109
rood screen *see* chancel screen
roof trusses 30, 34, 48, 56, 60, 69, 88, 92, 104, 118, 126, 140, 145, 160, 173, 175-176, 178, 182, 194, 203, 206, 210, 214,

217, 222, 227, 230, 242
roofs, A- 3
Roosevelt, President Franklin Delano 224
Roosevelt, President Theodore 77
Rosewell 204
rims *see* arches
ruins 5-7, 10, 84, 101, 136, 147, 148, 152, 155, 185 *see also* Jamestown *and* Lower Southwark Churches
rustication 189, 221, 229-230

S

St Andrew's Church, Littleton 198
St Andrew's Parish, Brunswick County 197
St Anne's Parish, Albemarle County 174, 175
St Anne's Parish, Essex County *see* Vawter's Church
St Basil's Cathedral, Moscow 17
St Bride's Parish 153
St David's Church *see* Bruton Parish Church
St David's Parish 111, 184
St George's Church and Parish, Accomack County *see* Pungoteague Church
St George's Parish, Spotsylvania County 96, 239
St James's Parish, Goochland County 168, 175
St James's Parish, Mecklenburg County 16
St John the Evangelist 127
St John's Church, Chase City 16
St John's Church, Chuckatuck *see* Chuckatuck Church
St John's Church, Hampton *see* Elizabeth City Parish Church
St John's Church, Hanover Parish 227
St John's Church, King William County 11, 41, 72, 95, 111, 127-133, 184
St John's Church, Richmond (city) *see* Henrico Parish Church
St John's Church, Warsaw 147
St John's Church, West Point 132
St John's Church, Woodend *see* Flat Rock Church
St Luke's Church, Courtland 198
St Luke's Church, Isle of Wight County *see* Newport Parish Church
St Margaret's Parish 111, 184
St Margaret's School 171
St Mark's Parish 239, 243
St Martin's Parish 174 *see also* Fork Church
St Mary's Church, Smith's Hundred 103
St Mary's Parish 89, 95, 225
St Mary's Whitechapel 11, 75, 125, 162-165
St Michael's School, Bon Air 171
St Paul's Church, Charlottesville 175
St Paul's Church, King George County 11, 147, 184, 186, 211-215
St Paul's Church, Norfolk *see* Borough Church
St Paul's Church, Petersburg 138, 142
St Paul's Church, Richmond 84-85, 88
St Paul's Church, Suffolk 150
St Paul's Parish, Hanover County 42, 142

St Peter's (village), Isle of Thanet, Kent, England 43
St Peter's Church, Port Royal 95
St Peter's Parish Church, New Kent County 1, 10, 11, 41-49, 67, 82, 87, 104, 127
St Stephen's Parish 127 *see also* Lower Church, St Stephen's
St Thomas's Church, Hancock, Maryland 95
St Thomas's Parish 239-243
Sainte Chapelle, Paris 37
Sale's Church 89
Salubria 241
Saluda 80
Sandys, George 22
Saponey Church 15
sash *see* window sash
Satchell, Southey 172
sconces 4, 76
Scotland 13, 207
Scott, the Rev'd Alexander 195
Seaboard Citizens National Bank, Norfolk 157
Seawell's Point 157
segregation by sex 63, 136
shapes of churches: 1, 4, 13
   cruciform churches (Latin cross): *see* Bruton Parish Church; Elizabeth City Parish Church; Lower Church, St Stephen's Parish; Christ Church, Lancaster; North Farnham Parish Church; Pungoteague Church; Borough Church; St Mary's Whitechapel; *and* Abingdon Parish Church
   cruciform churches (Greek cross): *see* Aquia Church *and* St Paul's Parish Church, King George
   T-shaped or L-shaped churches: *see* York Church; Yeocomico Church; St Peter's Church; Vawter's Church; St John's Church, King William; Blandford Church; Glebe Church; Henrico Parish Church; *and* Hebron Church
   see also wings
Shepherdstown, West Virginia 95
Sherwood Forest 119
shingles 3
shires (8) of 1634 25, 31, 38, 151, 168
Shirley 119
Shrewsbury stone 108
shutters 4
Sidnell, M. 49
silver 22, 25, 30, 35, 40, 56, 61, 77, 84-85, 88, 94, 103, 109, 118, 126, 136-137, 145, 147, 152-153, 157, 160, 165, 168, 174, 179, 183, 195, 198, 203, 215, 218-219, 227, 232, 243 *see also* pewter
silversmiths:
   Backe, John 85, 168
   Boelen, Jacob (American) 36
   Calame, Anthony 183
   Cooney, John (American) 174
   Darkeratt, William 165
   Fainell, Joseph 147, 215
   Farren, Thomas 77, 147, 195, 215
   Farrer, Thomas 30, 157

Folkingham, Thomas 126
Garthorne, Francis 165
Garthorne, George 165
Griffin, Thomas (pewterer) 160
Grundy, William 168, 137, 227
Gurney (Richard) and Company 109
Harache, Pierre 109
Heming, Thomas 77
Jones, George 118
Nelme, Anthony 137
Neville, John 179
Pearson, William 94
Pyne, Benjamin 77
Robinson, John 157
Sheene, Alice 203
Smith, George 174
Stevenson, Ambrose 168
Sutton, John 61
Tearle, Thomas 118
Timbrell, Robert 137
Wastell, Samuel 203
White, Fuller 157, 243
Williams, William 198
sites of churches 8, 10, 38, 157, 168-169, 170, 180, 205, 211, 212, 216
Sittingbourne Parish 89, 225
Slash Church 1, 12, 103-105, 178
slate 3
Smith, Captain John 4-5, 22
Smith, Bernard 35
Smith, Philip 57
Smithfield *see* Newport Parish Church
Smithsonian Institution 95, 224
Snow Hill, Maryland 172
Somerset, England 62
sounding board *see* pulpits
South Anna River 142
South Farnham Parish 145, 147
South Hill 16
South Parish, Nansemond County 208
South River 205
South River Meeting House 17
Southampton County 31, 198
Southampton River 103
Southern Materials Company 169
Southern Railway 170
Southern Shore Parish 15
Southern Virginia, bishop and diocese of 26, 41, 138, 170, 233
Southside Bank, Tappahannock 94
Southwark Parish 6, 25 *see also* Lower Southwark Church
Sperryville 158
Spotswood, Lt Governor Alexander 63, 67, 73
Spotsylvania County 96
Spurr, Samuel 67
Stafford County 11, 211, 212, 215, 221, 225
   see also Aquia Church
Staling, Francis 159
Staunton 180, 205, 243
Stevenson, Thomas H. 172
Stollen, Fürgen 160
stone churches 1 *see also* Augusta *and* Timber Ridge Churches

stone ornamentation 121, 122, 123, 124, 188-190, 196, 221, 222, 229-230
storeys (two) of windows 2, 4 *see also* Aquia Church; St Paul's Church, King George; the Falls Church; Christ Church, Alexandria; Pohick Church; *and the* Meeting House
Stratton Major Parish 13, 80, 127, 131, 202, 233 *see also* Upper Church, Stratton Major
string course *see* belt course
stucco 39, 44, 46, 184
styles of architecture 2-4, 5, 8-9, 30, 32, 33, 34, 38, 39, 48, 53, 54, 58, 63, 80
Suffolk (city) 148, 150
Suffolk Parish 13 *see also* Glebe *and* Chuckatuck Churches
sun-dial 56, 79
surrounds *see* arches
Surry County 6, 25 *see also* Lower Southwark Church
Susan Constant 31
Sussex County, Delaware 180
Sussex County, Virginia 197 *see also* Albemarle Parish
swag, Tudor *see* eaves, kick at the

T

Tables 5, 35, 55, 76, 89, 124, 168, 191, 206
tablets 116, 123-124, 131, 165, 191, 202, 223, 241-242
Talleysville 41
Tannenburg, David 160
Tappahannock 56, 94, 171
Tarleton, Colonel 8, 36
Tarpley, Joseph 67
Taylor, President Zachary 238
Te Deum laudamus 202
Tennessee 207
Texas 207
Thames River 197
Thanksgiving in America, first 119-120
thatch 3
Third Ridge 10 *see also* Jamestown Church
Third Sunday after Trinity, 1607 26-27
Thoroughgood, Adam 134
Thomas, Seth 68
Tiber River 109
Tiffany windows 141
timber 3, 5, 25
Timber Ridge Church 1, 12, 181, 183, 205-208
time, lag in 2
Tinkling Springs Church 16
Toano 233
tombstones and graveyards 2, 9, 10, 18, 22-24, 36, 38, 40, 47, 48, 57, 61, 77-79, 85, 88, 94, 98, 102-103, 110, 116, 118-119, 126, 127, 133-134, 137-138, 141, 147, 150, 157, 165, 167, 169, 170, 176, 180, 189-190, 191, 193, 196, 198, 199, 204, 205, 206, 224, 232, 235, 239, 242-243
torcheres 35
towers and porches 1, 2, 4, 6-7, 10, 19-20, 31, 32-33, 42-43, 45-48, 50, 51, 52, 54, 64, 65, 67, 68, 69-71, 72, 77-78, 100, 101, 143-144, 155, 166, 187, 188, 190, 211, 221-222, 236, 237, 238
Town House, Alexandria 235
tracery 2, 3
transepts *see* shapes of churches
Travis graveyard 23
Trinity Church, Church Creek, Maryland 152
Trinity Church, Portsmouth *see* Portsmouth Parish Church
Trinity Parish, Lancaster County 163
Trinity Parish, Louisa County 175
Truman, President 224
Truro Parish *see* the Falls Church; Pohick Church; *and* Christ Church (Alexandria)
T-shaped churches *see* shapes of churches
Tuckahoe Parish 168
Tucker Hill 50
tuning-forks *see* pitch-pipes
Tunstall 41
Turner, Nancy Byrd 227
Turner, the Rev'd Byrd Thornton 227
Tyler, Bishop 55
Tyler, John 63
Tyler, President John 119

U

Union Theological Seminary, Richmond 179
University of Virginia 96
Upper Church, St Paul's Parish, Hanover County *see* Slash Church
Upper Church, Stratton Major Parish 96-98, 113
Upper Norfolk County 153, 208
Upper Parish, Nansemond County 150
upper parish or church (or chapel) 13
Urbanna 15, 80, 85
urns 45, 174

V

Van Derpool, James Grote 34
Van Devanter, J. N. 183
Varina Parish 168, 170
Vass, Edmund 240
Vawter's Church 11, 89-96, 195, 214
verge-board *see* barge-board
Vesta, Temple of 109
vestments 76, 174
vestry-books 9, 83-84 *see also* Appendix II
Virginia, Church of 14
Virginia, Commonwealth of 77, 109, 195
Virginia, diocese of 41, 170, 195, 224, 233
Virginia Beach 133, 137, 138
Virginia Company 170
Virginia Convention 166
Virginia Gazette 199
Virginia Historical Society 137, 167, 198, 204
Virginia militia 147
Virginia's Mother Church 14
Virginia Theological Seminary, Alexandria 224

285

Virginia's Colonial Churches

Virginia Trust Company, Richmond 195
visiting colonial churches 17
Vivaldi 67

W

wadi 169
wainscoting 4, 5, 104, 167, 242 *see also* chancels; galleries; panels, raised; pews; *and* pulpits
Walker, James 86
Walker, William 47
Walker's Parish 175
Wallingford Parish 25, 116, 118
walls of churchyards 24, 49, 57, 61, 66-67, 141, 157, 167-168, 204
Ware Neck and River 58
Ware Parish Church 11, 58-62, 66, 82, 203, 204
Warner, Augustine 199
Warrenton Garden Club 243
Warrosquyoake Parish and County 31
Warsaw 50, 145, 147
Washington (D.C.) 186, 204
Washington (D.C.) church 147
Washington and Lee University 207-208
Washington, bishop of 231
Washington, Martha 48
Washington, Mary Ball 165
Washington, President George 48, 199, 208, 216, 224, 228, 231-232, 238
water tables 3
Waterman, Thomas Tileston 8, 79
wattle-and-daub 3, 18
Waugh, the Rev'd Mr 185
Weems, Parson 231
Wells's Hill 138, 142
West Hundred plantation 116
West Parish, Nansemond County 208
West Point 41, 127, 131, 132
Westham 171
Westminster Abbey 26
Westmoreland County 211-212 *see also* Yeocomico Church
Westover 119
Westover Parish Church 7, 11, 28, 88, 116-120, 168, 171, 182
Weyanoke Parish 116, 157
Whiffen, Marcus 64
Whitaker, the Rev'd Alexander 168
White House, The (New Kent County) 49
White House, The (Washington) 186
White Marsh 199
White Oak Run 161
Whitechapel, London 162
Whitefield, George 180
Whitehall Palace 2
Whitemarsh 36

whitewashing 4, 47
wicket door 3, 34
Wicomico Parish 165
will (1767) 179
William and Mary, College of 24, 63, 66, 77, 167 *see also the* Chapel
William III 62, 168, 171
Williamsburg 1, 24, 25, 44, 199
Williamsburg, battle of 109
Wilmer, the Rev'd Mr 78
Wilmington 57
Wilmington Parish 25, 117, 233
Wilson, President Woodrow 77, 224
window frames 29, 34, 71, 93, 104, 123, 130, 141, 144, 159, 164, 167, 173, 177, 195, 201, 214-215, 218, 223, 226, 230, 234
window sash 3, 29, 60, 71, 93, 123, 130, 144, 173, 195, 201, 218, 223, 237
Windsor Forest 193
Wingfield, Captain Edwin Maria 22
wings (transepts) *see* shapes of churches (cruciform churches)
wings, north *see* York, St Peter's, Yeocomico, St John's (King William), Blandford, Glebe, Henrico, *and* Hickory Neck Churches
wings, south *see* Vawter's *and* Hebron Churches
wooden churches 1, 3-6, 10 *see also* Slash, Hebron, Henrico, Providence, *and* Buck Mountain Churches
Woodlawn 228
Woodliffe, Captain John 119, 120
Wood's Church 15
Wren, Colonel James 216, 219, 228
Wren, Sir Christopher 106, 216, 219
Wren Building *see the* Chapel of the College of William and Mary
Wythe, George 167
Wythe (George) House 79

Y

Yeardley, Sir George 22, 103
Yeardley House 23
Yeocomico Church 1, 11, 34, 46, 48, 50-58, 76, 82, 87
Yeocomico River and Bay *see* Yeocomico Church
York County 25, 59, 162 *see also* York-Hampton *and* Bruton Parish Churches
York River 233 *see also* York-Hampton *and* Bruton Parish Churches
York-Hampton Parish Church 9, 11, 38-41, 103, 234
Yorktown 199, 201 *see also* York-Hampton Parish Church

286

THIS BOOK was designed by the author, who also made all drawings and photographs. All of the manufacture of the book also derives from Richmond: the color plates by Virginia Engraving Company; the printing by Garrett & Massie, Inc., on Permalife Olde White paper of Standard Paper Manufacturing Company; and the binding by L. H. Jenkins, Inc. The edition is limited to two thousand copies.